THE ROAD FROM ARDOYNE

Ray Mac Mánais

THE ROAD
FROM ARDOYNE

The Making of a President

A Brandon Paperback

First published in 2004 by Brandon
This edition published 2005 by Brandon
an imprint of Mount Eagle Publications
Dingle, Co. Kerry, Ireland, and
Unit 3, Olympia Trading Estate, Coburg Road, London N22 6TZ, England

ISBN 0 86322 341 9

2 4 6 8 10 9 7 5 3 1

The author wishes to thank the poets, their representatives and publishers for permission to quote from copyright material: The Trustees of the Estate of the late Katherine B. Kavanagh, through Jonathan Williams Literary Agency, for "Freedom" and "Lough Derg" by Patrick Kavanagh; the Gallery Press for "The Living and the Dead" by John Montague and "Home Thought From Abroad" by W.R. Rodgers; Cló Iar-Chonnachta for "*An Tobar*/The Well" by Cathal Ó Searcaigh, translated by Gabriel Fitzmaurice; Gabriel Fitzmaurice for his translation of *Saoirse*; Bloodaxe Books for "Psalm in the Night" by Mícheál Ó Siadhail; Blackstaff Press for "Breastplate", "The Iron Circle", "Street Name", "Sonnet from Uncollected Poems 1928–86", "An Ulster Landowner's Song", "In This Year of Grace", "Mathematics", and "The Coasters" by John Hewitt; Faber and Faber for "Whatever You Say Say Nothing", "From The Republic of Conscience" and *Preoccupations* by Seamus Heaney, and "Come to the Edge" by Christopher Logue.

Cover design by id communications, Tralee, Co. Kerry
Front cover photograph by Maxwell Photography
Author photograph by Michael Edwards Photography
Typesetting by Red Barn Publishing, Skeagh, Skibbereen
Printed and bound in the United Kingdom by
Bookmarque Ltd, Croydon

Contents

For
Jenny, Aoife and Colm
Lily, Sammy and Eddie

Foreword: A Historical Perspective

> This jewel that houses our hopes and our fears
> Was knocked up from the swamp in the last hundred years;
> But the last shall be first and the first shall be last;
> May the Lord in his mercy be kind to Belfast.
>
> (Maurice James Craig: "Ballad to a Traditional Refrain")

Mary McAleese's people made their way to Belfast from the stony hill country of north County Down and the boggy land beside the Shannon in County Roscommon, with a brief stopover in the fertile lowlands of County Derry, near Lough Neagh. Her near ancestors were farmers, road workers, lay midwives, school cleaners and housewives—country people all, including her grandfather who was an IRA volunteer and his brother who was one of the first members of An Garda Síochána. Mary was born in Ardoyne, in North Belfast, a place where the type of land under their feet is of little consequence to most of the residents. It is the area where she spent the happiest and the saddest times of her youth, the area which suffered the most sectarian killings during the Troubles, and the area which, more than any other place in Ireland, has left its stamp on the woman who would become President of Ireland.

Belfast is one of the youngest cities in Ireland, a place divided and sub-divided according to religion, political affiliation, culture, sport, flags and emblems and historical perspective. The internecine strife, which for so long has been the scourge of the city, is, according to Mary, an ineradicable blot on generation after generation of Belfast people who condoned bloodshed in the name of religious or political beliefs. But that is the story of Belfast from the beginning, from that summer of 1609 when Sir Francis Chichester started the Plantation of Ulster. He drove the rebellious native Irish into the bogs and hills and peopled the good land with loyal British subjects from the Lowlands of Scotland and the North of England, his aim being to ensure that Britain would have no more trouble with the north-east corner of Ireland. Over 350 years later, another Chichester of the same stock, Major James Chichester Clark, Prime Minister of Northern Ireland, was still trying to achieve that objective.

In every generation since that fateful first decade of the seventeenth century, sectarian strife has smeared relationships between the descendants of the Protestant planters and the Catholic native Irish. In 1641 the Irish rose up against the Planters, and in 1649 Cromwell took his revenge. In

1685 the Catholic King James II came to the throne of England and sought to establish Catholics in positions of authority, but after the Jacobite/Williamite Wars of 1688–1691, Protestant ascendancy was reasserted with the victory of King William of Orange. The eighteenth century saw fierce competition for land in Ulster between Catholic and Protestant tenant farmers and the rise of secret agrarian societies. The end of that century saw the establishment of two organisations that were historically very significant, one of greater longevity than the other: the United Irishmen and the Orange Order.

The Great Famine of the nineteenth century left the Catholic population decimated, and the advent of the Industrial Revolution added economic divisions to the already strong cultural and religious differences. The campaign for Home Rule at the end of that century was matched by the growth of Ulster unionism, with its close links to the Orange Order. The partition of Ireland in 1921 gave constitutional affirmation to the rift between the two communities, and relations reached a nadir around this time. Between July 1920 and May 1922, 455 people were killed and over 2,000 injured in the infamous Belfast pogroms, sectarian attacks on the Catholic/nationalist population. Pogroms erupted again in the thirties and forties. The IRA border campaign of the fifties gave rise to more conflict in Belfast, and the most recent and most destructive Troubles had their genesis in Belfast during the 1960s.

Only once, in 1932, did the working-class people from both sides of the religious and political divide stand side by side in Belfast to challenge the government of Northern Ireland. The immediate reason for the solidarity was the low level of relief payments to the poor, lower by far in Belfast than in the cities of Britain. Sixty thousand people came together to march by the light of torches through the streets of the city. The curious mix of orange and green bands that led them in their protest played the same simple tune over and over, a popular song of the day called "Yes, We Have No Bananas", the only piece of music common to all bands, as their normal repertoire consisted of partisan tunes. People power won the day, and the Prime Minister James Craig was forced to increase the Outdoor Relief by 50 per cent.

The name Belfast, or Béal Feirste, means "the Mouth of the Farset", a river that in turn got its name from a sandy, tidal ford. The city straddles the river Lagan where it flows into Belfast Lough, about twenty miles south of the place on the coast of County Antrim where the first settlers came to Ireland. The city has a splendid setting: the deep and expansive U-shaped lough is ringed by rolling hills to the south and the mountainous face of the Antrim plateau to the west. Between the mountains and the hills, the Lagan has cut a broad fertile valley through which run the main roads south and west and the railway line to Dublin.

Belfast is a peculiar place, a place of incongruities: majestic cliffs, beautiful glens, natural woodlands and some of the meanest streets in Ireland. Three Belfast people have won Nobel Peace Prizes, yet the city has suffered the longest-running urban guerrilla campaign in the world.[‡] Once upon a time Belfast was the most radical of Ireland's cities. It hosted the founding of the Society of the United Irishmen on Cave Hill in 1791, a society whose avowed objective was "to unite Catholic, Protestant and Dissenter". Belfast was the home of the first real Irish republicans more than 200 years ago, and most of them were Presbyterians. During the last hundred years, however, for reasons of political power, the authorities actively promoted the traditional divisions between the two communities, resulting in the growth of ghettos.

These ghettos were usually founded on a parish basis, with the church and schools inside the cultural and religious perimeter, the boundaries that have become euphemistically known in recent years as "interfaces". Belfast people have traditionally married within their own religious persuasion and, until recently, within their own areas. This has created a series of webs within the ghetto system, a network of relations and in-laws which insulates, to some degree, the views of the people inside from those of the people outside.

The people of Belfast have difficulty being loyal to their city. Their allegiance extends more readily to districts or groups, or to Ireland, or Britain. It is hard to imagine a Belfast United soccer team. Despite all the differences, most Belfast-born people have a droll kind of affection for the place, a strange love-hate relationship. Maurice James Craig says it well:

> O the bricks they will bleed and the rain it will weep,
> And the damp Lagan fog lull the city to sleep;
> It's to hell with the future and live in the past:
> May the Lord in his mercy be kind to Belfast.[§]

---

‡ Mairéad Corrigan, Betty Williams and David Trimble were all awarded Nobel Peace Prizes.

§ "Ballad to a Traditional Refrain" from *Some Way to Reason*, 1948.

Chapter One

Inauguration

Take me to the top of the high hill
Mount Olympus laughter-roaring unsolemn
Where no-one is angry and satirical
About a mortal creature on a tall column.
(Patrick Kavanagh: "Freedom")

There is not a cloud in the sky. The ancient buildings look freshly scrubbed, the granite towers and ramparts of Dublin Castle sparkling under the winter sun. Since early morning, coaches and buses have been streaming into the Upper Yard, bringing young people from every county in Ireland. Now the 800 schoolchildren stand in a fidgety, quiet ring around the yard. In St Patrick's Hall the great and the good of Irish society are gathered: two former presidents, the taoiseach and six former taoisigh, the leaders of the main political parties North and South, members of government, TDs and senators, ambassadors, representatives of the churches and the judiciary, the chief justice, the commissioner of An Garda Síochána, the secretary of state for Northern Ireland. Members of the Number One Army Band and piper Liam Ó Floinn are ready on the balcony above the table where the new president will sign the oath of office. Liam has composed a new piece of music entitled "An Droichead" specially for the occasion. On both sides of the central passage, the colours of the dresses, robes and tunics clash vibrantly, and shoes, belts and buckles sparkle under the arc lights of the television teams.

Outside, in the Castle Yard, the children, the photographers, and the print, radio and television journalists wait impatiently for their first glimpse of Mary McAleese, the newly inaugurated eighth President of Ireland. Every school in the state is closed in honour of the occasion, and hundreds of thousands of young people are watching this ceremony on television. The invitation to the inauguration is a two-edged sword: unlike the children at home who know exactly what is going on in St Patrick's Hall, those in the yard are restless with their lack of information. The fussing increases as the morning wears on. The teachers are chatting together, the pupils calling to each other in stage

10

whispers. The sign they have all been waiting for comes at last, and a hush falls over the thousand people in the yard.

At twenty-five minutes past noon, the silence is shattered by the crash of artillery: a twenty-one gun salute from the defence forces for their new commander-in-chief. Before the last report rumbles over the city, the children see a new flag being raised. Slowly the soldier draws the thin rope. As the banner clears the rooftop, its folds fall away and it cracks open in the breeze, the gold harp on the deep blue background stark against the cerulean sky. As the presidential flag takes its place on top of the Castle beside the national flag, the waiting crowd now knows that the country has a new president. The gathering is openly noisy now, shouting and cheering replacing the whispers and talk, children pushing and shoving each other with nervous apprehension. The teachers have given up trying to keep them calm.

In the middle of the yard the soldiers of the ceremonial guard of honour stand in haughty solemnity. Behind them are the joint bands of the Curragh Command and the Western Command with their instruments at the ready. The motor cycle cavalcade is in an arrow-straight line. All the military are seemingly oblivious to the cold and the noise and the fuss. They have no control over the delay, but as soon as the president exits the building and enters the yard, the protocol will pass to the defence forces, and the rest of the ceremony will pass off with military precision.

The whispered words "She's coming!" pass around the perimeter of the yard in seconds. Sentences remain unfinished and all heads turn, as in a Mexican wave, and all eyes fasten on the wide open door. Two army officers are the first to be seen, as they slow-march into the yard and turn to either side of the door like sentries. At the first glimpse of the cashmere coat, the crowd erupts and the new president enters Dublin Castle Yard to a tumultuous welcome. Waves of applause envelop her and rebound from the ancient walls of the castle that was for so many centuries a symbol of repression. Almost unnoticed, the president's senior aide-de-camp, Colonel Bernard Howard, precedes the taoiseach Bertie Ahern and the tánaiste Mary Harney. The last of the lead party to leave the building is Dr Martin McAleese, the president's husband. Even the keenest observer would have been forgiven for missing the brief but intense exchange between Martin and his old frined, and Mary's great supporter, the Belfast solicitor Denis Moloney. Their simultaneous, solemn, but miniscule nods, while their eyes remained locked and their faces impassive, said simply: "A job well done."

The members of the group now stand and smile, obviously enjoying the rapturous welcome for the new president. On her way down the grand staircase, moments before, President McAleese's heart had been beating faster than normal, but now she sees a sight which stills her racing pulse and makes her smile even wider. Directly across the yard is her old friend Kathleen Boyle, with her pupils from the St Louis Convent in Kilkeel, County Down. A widening of smiles passes between them, and the president's gaze moves slightly to the left. Here is another sight to gladden her heart: teachers and pupils from Blythe Street Primary School from Sandy Row in Belfast, an area synonymous with Protestantism and loyalism. She had been working with the people of the area and the school during the previous year and had made certain they got an invitation to the inauguration, but she had not been at all certain they would attend. She appreciates the brave journey they have made. Here is the sign she has been waiting for: a positive reply to the invitation in her inaugural address, "Come to the edge". She is happy they have walked out with her on the bridge. All around the yard the children still cheer, wave flags and shout their messages of congratulation. But this is now a military occasion.

"*Ar aire!*" The bellowed command to come to attention is immediately followed by the crash of hundreds of polished military shoes coming together as one. A solemn silence descends on Dublin Castle Yard. In the hush the three footsteps of Captain Mark Hearns are clearly heard as he moves forward and halts directly in front of the president. Slowly, majestically, he raises his sword to a vertical position. He holds it for a moment at the full stretch of his right arm, the thin sunshine of early winter making the polished blade glisten and sparkle. With practised formality he draws the hilt in towards his face. As he completes his salute, a lone drummer begins a roll, and the flag of the brigade is dipped in an act of homage reserved for the commander-in-chief. As the conductor of the joint bands raises his baton, the drum roll continues, adding to the solemnity of the event. A crash of cymbals shatters the tension, and the air is filled with the familiar strains of the "Presidential Salute".

Mary McAleese is standing at attention, her aide-de-camp three paces behind her in the shade of the portico. The lustre in her eyes is one of the few indications that she is fighting hard to hold back the tears. She looks relaxed but Martin can see the telltale signs. With difficulty she controls the shake that threatens to ripple through her body. Her eyes are fastened on the national flag: the green, white and orange. She has just declared publicly and solemnly that she will be the white between the other two colours, that she will use the high office bestowed on her by the people to be a bridge between the unionist and nationalist traditions on the island. As the cameras zoom in on her face, she is the picture of supreme confidence, yet her emotions are in turmoil. She is both sobered and elated by the challenge awaiting her. Her assurance is tempered with apprehension, her normal panache with a certain timidity.

At this moment she is being assailed by the old memories, the old contradictions. Here she stands as President of Ireland, surrounded by all the panoply of state; the most powerful and influential people in Ireland are gathered to pay tribute to her as their new head of state; the flags are flying in her honour; the defence forces are honouring her as their supreme commander; but in her own mind, just now, she is still the slip of a girl from Ardoyne. As the band plays and the flags crack in the breeze, she can't help dwelling on a time and a place where the flying of the Irish flag was seen as seditious, where the playing of the national anthem was considered treasonable. She is thinking of her youth in her native city, just a hundred miles up the road from where she is now standing—nearer than Donegal or Kerry or Galway—a place where all things Irish belonged to the ghetto, to the subculture, to the underclass. She is thinking of the long, eventful, personal pilgrimage she has made to be where she is today.

Chapter Two

A Baptism of Fire

"For Northern Ireland, those five days [12–16 August 1969] were a watershed, not only because the British Government and its Army became inextricably and fatally involved, but because the clock was set back fifty years . . ."

(*The Sunday Times* Insight Team, Ulster, 1972)

Young Mary Leneghan was happy with life in general and delighted with herself in particular that fine summer evening. It was Thursday, 14 August 1969, and she was strolling through the grounds of the Woodbourne House Hotel[‡] on Suffolk Road just outside Belfast in the company of her school friend Eileen Gilmartin and Fr Honorius Kelly, a Passionist priest from the monastery in Ardoyne. The three had just finished a celebratory dinner in the hotel and were now sauntering in the general direction of the priest's car with a view to being back in Ardoyne before nightfall. The reason for the celebration was the results the two friends had obtained in their A level examinations. On the strength of Mary's achievements she had been offered a place in the prestigious School of Law of Queen's University Belfast. What more could a young woman ask for? As her mother never tired of telling her: "You should be down on your knees thanking God, Mary Leneghan." Indeed she was a fortunate girl.

All too soon they reached the car and headed back home. As they skirted the Andersonstown estate on the edge of West Belfast, the priest was smiling indulgently as the girls prattled on about their favourite singer, Roy Orbison, and the pros and cons of *Midnight Cowboy*. When they weren't talking music or films, they were talking college and plans for the future. Neither of them had any intention of marring this perfect summer evening with talk of the increasing sectarian tension in the North of Ireland. None of the three had a word to say about the 112 people hospitalised in Derry two nights previously. The Battle of the

---

‡   Woodbourne House Hotel, later Woodbourne RUC Station.

Bogside might never have happened. There wasn't a whisper about Orange marches or civil rights marches or Apprentice Boys' marches.

Twilight was falling, the streetlights flickering on, as the priest drove up Twadell Avenue towards its junction with the Crumlin Road, the top end of Ardoyne. Ahead of them was a motley group of men, neighbours who would normally be watching television or talking an evening walk but who were now standing in a line with sticks in their hands, blocking the road; and there in the middle of this strange collection was the gentle Jack Gilmartin, hurley in hand.‡

"What's going on?" inquired the priest, as he stuck his head out the car window.

"We're protecting the parish, Father," was the general message from a dozen men talking together. "They're burning us out."

It was then the girls and the priest saw the flames lighting the night sky over the roof of the monastery. Mary heard the screams and what she would later recognise as the crack of rifle fire and the rattle of sub-machine guns. Before she could be stopped, she was running towards the corner, her arms flailing and her long legs leaving the rest behind. In spite of her fitness, she was soaked with sweat and could feel her heartbeat in her throat. As she reached the junction with the Crumlin Road, she stopped and stared in disbelief and horror. The familiar, peaceful road she had left just a few hours earlier was now like a scene from one of the priest's own sermons about the end of the world.

From the chapel gates to the corner of Palmer Street, the road was black with policemen, B-Specials and loyalists from the Shankill area. Some of the houses on the front of the road, opposite the chapel, were in flames. In the light of those flames, Mary could see the array of weapons in the hands of the police and strangers: pistols, rifles, sub-machine guns, clubs and pickaxe handles and petrol bombs. Many of the attacking civilians were wearing crash helmets and white armbands. As she stood and stared, the police were leading charges into Herbert Street and Hooker Street, and the loyalist civilians, streaming in behind them, were throwing petrol bombs into any house they could reach. Already many of the small terraced houses nearest the road were ablaze.

Mary stood awestruck. All her life she had been taught to respect and obey the law and the keepers of the law. But now the eighteen year old could not reconcile that with what she was seeing: the forces of the state

---

‡ Jack Gilmartin from Geevagh, County Sligo, later described by Mary as "one of the gentlest men ever to come out of the West of Ireland".

were attacking the people they were sworn to defend; the forces of law and order were going outside all known boundaries of law and order. Later she would ask herself whose law and whose order the RUC were maintaining that night, but then was not the time for such questions.

Again and again the police led charges into the streets of Ardoyne. Again and again hastily erected barriers of vehicles and furniture blocked their way. As the attackers tried to climb over these makeshift barricades, the defenders showered them with stones and pieces of broken pavement. When the cars and furniture were set on fire, someone got the idea of using buses to block the streets. Groups of young men made their way through the back streets up to the bus depot on the Ardoyne Road, took three double-decker buses, drove them down Chatham Street and parked them across the narrow streets leading in from the Crumlin Road. Within seconds they had set them on fire.

But how long could burned-out buses and stones hold out against rifles and pistols? The people behind the barricades were making petrol bombs from milk bottles, rags and petrol siphoned from cars. But what good were these against machine guns? Where was the famous IRA, the defenders of the people, who had been collecting money for arms in the pubs for years? Where were the arms? There were rumours that the IRA weapons had been sold to the Free Welsh Army earlier that year to disrupt the investiture of Britain's Prince Charles as Prince of Wales. Mary had also heard it whispered that there never were any arms; that the money had long since been spent on drink and gambling. The only thing certain was that there were no IRA weapons, nor was there any IRA leadership, in Ardoyne that night. Within a few days graffiti would appear on burnt-out gables: "IRA—I RAN AWAY".

As the RUC and B-Specials fired into the narrow streets, the situation was becoming desperate. Then, from their vantage point, Mary and her friends could see a man with a catapult taking a kneeling position on the corner of Butler Street; his ammunition—marbles. Each glass marble he fired against the granite wall of the chapel grounds, behind the police, exploded with a crack like a gunshot. There was panic as the RUC and Specials ran to take cover, certain that a sniper was firing at them from behind the barricades.

Some of them found shelter behind the Shorland armoured car which had been brought up to support the police. Now, with its turret-mounted Browning heavy machine gun adding to the cacophony, the Shorland entered Herbert Street and forced its way between the bus and the burnt-out remains of the house on the corner of Chatham Street, number 5A. As the armoured vehicle cleared the barricade, the RUC, Specials and loyalists streamed in behind it. There was no light in any house beyond the barricade, and the streetlights had long since been smashed. A shower of petrol bombs and broken pavement slabs came out of the darkness at the attackers and forced them back. Each time the loyalist mob and the police regrouped on the road, the people forced them back, sometimes at a terrible cost.

On one of those incursions, Sam McLarnon was killed as he sat in the sitting room of his house in Herbert Street. Three police bullets went through his window, and one of them hit him in the head. In the report of the tribunal chaired by the British Lord Justice Leslie Scarman into the events of that night it was stated: "Both sides were spoiling for a fight."‡ Referring to the death of McLarnon, Scarman stated: "Clearly, police shooting in the street was for a time heavy."§ In another incursion police shot dead Michael Lynch as he was sheltering in the doorway of a house in Butler Street, about 150 yards from where Mary was standing. All Lord Scarman had to say about Lynch's death was, "Mr. Lynch was killed by police fire into Butler Street. All else is unclear."† Another thing that is unclear is the number of people wounded that night. No official figures for the numbers of injured were ever published. One woman who gave evidence at the inquest into the death of Michael Lynch said that there were eight men with gunshot wounds in her house in Elmfield Street that night.

But who among Mary's relations and friends was injured? Who was burned out? Who was dead? From where she stood she could look 200 yards up the road to where her own house, on the corner of Hesketh Road, seemed to float above all this madness. Near her house there was no smoke, no flames, no sea of dark green uniforms. But as she turned to look back down the road, she could see her Aunt Nora's shop and home opposite the chapel gates, safe, but perilously close to the action. And what about her Aunt Una's shop a few yards further on? She couldn't see it through the smoke. Surely that couldn't be McBriertys' house blazing? It was. Nurse Eileen McBrierty, the local midwife who had brought two generations of Ardoyne babies into the world, was a friend of Mary's mother. Her daughter Annette, who was due to qualify

---

‡ Scarman Tribunal reported in David McKitterick *et al.*, *Lost Lives* (Edinburgh: Mainstream Publishing, 1990), p. 6.

§ *Ibid.*

† *Ibid.*

as a midwife in September, was with Eileen behind the barricades, helping the injured. The next weekend newspapers carried a photograph of Annette holding a newborn baby, the "Baby of the Barricades", which had come prematurely that night. Neither Annette nor her mother knew that while they were out helping, their house was in flames.

Mary could see the corner of Maureen Totten's street, but it was impossible to see if her friend's house was intact. What about Catherine Kane? Was her house in Hooker Street still safe behind a barricade or had the mob reached it and burned it? From where Mary stood she could see most of what was happening. She could also hear the screams and roars of anger and the shrieks of fear above the crackling of the fires and the gunshots. The sharp smell of cordite mixed with the smells of burning tyre rubber and house timbers to produce a pungent odour that remains with her still. The smells and sounds and terrible sights came between Mary and her sleep for many a night following 14 August 1969.

As she thinks back on it now she says: "Of all the feelings I experienced that night, the one I remember most was a terrible helplessness in the face of injustice. I stood at the corner of the Crumlin Road and shook with fear, with terror, with rage, but most of all with frustration at my inability to do anything for the poor people who were suffering in front of my very eyes."

On 14 August 1969, Mary's youthful innocence was blown away with the smoke of the burning houses of her neighbours and friends. As the veneer of civilisation was ripped away in North Belfast that night, she saw up close the ugliness and pure evil of sectarian hatred which had been lurking for years behind the thin coating of respectability. Mary knew that things had changed, but she could not have imagined how deep the changes would go. Realities were transforming before her very eyes; things had gone too far this time, and neither Mary's life, nor the life of anyone else in Northern Ireland, would ever be the same again. They were being swept along on a road they never dreamt they would follow.

Chapter Three

Seed, Breed and Denigration

> This was my childhood's precinct, and I know
> how such streets look, down to the very shade
> of brick, of paintwork on each door and sill,
> what school or church nearby one might attend,
> if there's a chance to glimpse familiar hill
> between the chimneys where the grey slates end.
>   (John Hewitt: "Street Names")

The river Lagan rises on the slopes of Slieve Croob in County Down and flows into the sea in Belfast. Near the mouth of the river the young Mary Leneghan spent her early years. At its source her mother's people lived for generations. On this mountain, which rises little more than 1,800 feet from the surrounding drumlin country, the mighty river on which the *Titanic* was launched is little more than a tiny stream. As it bubbles from the earth and spills its way down the slope, the first human habitation it reaches on its journey to Belfast Lough is the thatched cottage where Catherine McCullough, the president's great-grandmother, was born.

Catherine was the eldest of eleven children and the only one who did not emigrate to America. One of her brothers, John McCullough, married Lilian Fitzgerald, a member of the Fitzgerald Kennedy clan, and they lived on Cape Cod. One of Catherine's sisters, Maggie McCullough, achieved fame of a different sort in America. This great-grandaunt of Mary's had an uncanny propensity for making money. In a few short years, she rose from domestic service to considerable wealth. Mary's cousin, Fr Albert Cosgrove, describes her as "a rack-renter who was very sweet outside business hours". She did not allow children in any of her tenement buildings. Any female tenant she suspected of being pregnant was summarily evicted. Such was her notoriety that the influential newspaper the *Boston Globe* dubbed her "the Boston Pig". She married Ed Boudreau, a man from the French-speaking area of Novia Scotia. He predeceased her, and when she died in 1944 she left her money to the Archdiocese of Boston. In an ironic twist to the story,

Cardinal Cushing used some of the inheritance to found an orphanage in honour of the woman who disliked children.

Catherine, the only one of the McCulloughs to stay at home, saw little or nothing of the American wealth. She married John Rogan, a local man from the parish of Dromara, and they had three children: Mary Agnes, John junior and Cassie, the grandmother of the future president. When other children of her age were playing with dolls, young Cassie was knitting, darning and sewing, baking bread and scones and preparing dinners. Recycling, that most modern of virtues, was a practical necessity in the house on Slieve Croob. Nothing went to waste. The adults' old garments were taken apart and magically reappeared as children's dresses, coats and even trousers. The Rogan children were often complimented, at Christmas and Easter, on their "new clothes", no stitch of which was less that ten years old.

Cassie passed these domestic skills and values on to her own children and grandchildren, and the young Mary Leneghan was her most ardent disciple. It was a proud day for Cassie when Mary was called to the Northern Ireland Bar, dressed fashionably in a suit made by her own hands. Kitchen lore and housekeeping were not all that Mary learned from her grandmother.

Some of the most important battles of the 1798 Rising took place around Slieve Croob, and Cassie was raised on songs and stories of the rebellion. She learned the names of the heroes of Saintfield and Ballynahinch at an early age. The rebel leaders Betsy Gray and her brother George spent much of their time around Tullyniskey at the foot of Slieve Croob, and General Harry Munro was eventually captured on the slopes of the mountain. Cassie saw nothing strange in the fact that these local heroes, and most of the leaders of the United Irishmen in the counties of Down and Antrim, were Presbyterians or members of the Church of Ireland: William Orr, Henry Joy McCracken, William Steele Dickson, Jemmy Hope, William Warwick, Samuel Boal—there is not a native Irish name among them. Mary Leneghan was still a young girl when it was pointed out to her that a particular political viewpoint is not the prerogative of a particular religious group.

Cassie Rogan was nineteen years old when she married John McManus in 1921. John and his brother Arthur junior were the only children of Arthur McManus and Catherine Murray. When the War of Independence broke out, John defied his father's wishes and joined the IRA. He went south, where he was active around County Meath. After the signing of the Treaty he returned to County Down to marry his childhood sweetheart, but found that Dromara was not a healthy place for a former IRA man. The Belfast pogroms had spread to County Down, and many Catholic men had gone on the run. Shortly after the wedding, his brother Arthur went to Dublin to join the newly formed police force, An Garda Síochána, while John also left home to seek work in Scotland.

For several years John was back and forward before he was offered a job as a bread server with Hughes' Bakery in Maghera, County Derry. He and Cassie, with their first two children, another Arthur and another Catherine, moved to the lowland town on the other side of Lough Neagh in 1927. It was not long before Bridget was born, and then Evelyn and Seán. On the morning of the spring equinox, 21 March 1931, Claire McManus, the mother of the future president, was born. Then came Una, and Bernadette, who died when she was only nine weeks old. Celine was the last of the family to be born in Maghera; Declan and Anne were born after the family moved to Belfast. In 1937 the management of Bernard Hughes' wanted John McManus to move to the city, where the headquarters of the bakery was located on the Springfield Road. With sorrow and trepidation the family said goodbye to Maghera, to Fairhill School, to the Glen Chapel and the cemetery where baby Bernadette was buried, and took the road to Belfast.

As a result of the riots of 1932 and 1935, the ghettos of Belfast were more secure than ever, and working-class people were reluctant to live in "mixed areas". John and Cassie could not get a house to rent in the Falls Road area, near Hughes' Bakery, and eventually they settled in a small house in Duneden Park in the parish of Holy Cross. The Ardoyne saga had begun. The children loved the place and settled very quickly, and John soon became a well-known local character. Mary's earliest recollections of her grandfather describe a man who was at peace with himself and with the world around him:

> I remember my grandfather sauntering around the streets of Ardoyne, always impeccably dressed in a three-piece suit, with a pipe in his mouth and a hat on his head, just like Bing Crosbie. The people called him "the Major" because of his military bearing and his background in the Old IRA. To me he was a gentle giant. He had two hobbies: whist and gardening. He played whist a few nights a week, and he cut the lawns of neighbours for streets around us. He was the only man who ever cut the gardens of Glenard with a scythe.

Mary's paternal grandmother, Brigid McDrury, was born in 1898 in the townland of Ardglass, County Roscommon, halfway between Carrick-on-Shannon and Croghan. She was one of a family of four daughters born to William McDrury and Mary McGreevy, the others being Mary, Nora and Sarah Jane, who was always called Eileen. Mary McGreevy died of cancer of the womb in 1910, while the family was still very young. Their father, who was a railway worker, was killed in 1924 while walking along the track on his way home from a fair in Carrick-on-Shannon. Mary, the eldest, was a monitor in Mistress O'Dowd's School, near their home. Work was scarce in Roscommon at the start of the 1920s, but the mistress was friendly with the Burke family, who owned the Royal Avenue Hotel in Belfast, and she found employment for Mary in Lipton's shop in Lisburn, just outside the city. Eileen soon joined her, but the two sisters were not long reunited when their lodgings were burned down in the pogroms and they moved into Belfast.

Mary McDrury married Patrick Cassidy, a former RIC man from County Tyrone, and was known in the family ever after as "Mrs Cassidy". She bought a small tobacco and confectionery shop on the Antrim Road and then a similar shop on the corner of Butler Street and the Crumlin Road, opposite Holy Cross Church. The Ardoyne connection was strengthening. When Nora left home she went to live with Mary and Patrick Cassidy before starting a hairdressing business, also on the Crumlin Road. Eileen married Willie O'Hara, a local man, and opened an off-licence in Crumlin Street. For three sisters from a poverty-stricken background in Roscommon to start up and run successful businesses, to carve comfortable, secure lives for themselves in the 1930s, was a rare feat. By the time the Second World War came to Belfast, their businesses were well established, and so was the connection with Ardoyne.

Brigid McDrury stayed at home. She loved the countryside, the easy pace of life on the Roscommon-Leitrim border, the music and the house dances. She also had her eye on a man. Frank Leneghan was a son of Patrick Leneghan from Ardglass and Anne Flanagan from Duneen, Balinameen. Like the president's people on her mother's side, many of the Flanagans had emigrated to America in the 1880s. Among them was one Patrick Banahan Flanagan, the first of Mary's forebears to enter the legal profession. He was called to the Chicago Bar in 1895 and was appointed a federal judge just after the turn of the century. His grandson, Joseph Evans, followed Judge Flanagan's footsteps to the federal bench seventy years later.[‡]

---

‡ Source: Balinameen Heritage Group and Consulate General of Ireland, Chicago.

Frank Leneghan had no legal ambitions, nor any desire to travel. He wanted to marry Brigid McDrury. He and Brigid had been friends since their schooldays, and no one was surprised when they eventually married and settled down on Frank's small farm in Ardglass, fourteen acres of poor land overlooking the Shannon. Their little house had the best view for miles around, but good views do not put soup in the pot. As the family grew, Frank had to take on extra work in the quarry, on the roads and at the local lime kiln. Paddy Leneghan, the president's father and the eldest of the Leneghan clan, was born on 5 July 1925. After him came Dan, Mary, Willie and Michael. In the 1930s the family moved to another farm in the townland of Carroward. The piece of land was no better, no bigger, but it had a road frontage and was easier to access. The house, though, was the big attraction: a square cottage with a high pitched roof and a view for miles across the flood plain of the Shannon; a little palace, all 450 square feet of it!

Frank Leneghan was a deeply unhappy man, a complainer, a martyr in his own mind. He bitterly resented his poverty. The fact that his poor holding was so close to the vast lands of the Kirkwood family, the famous estate of Woodbrook about which David Thomson wrote so beautifully in his book of the same name, made his suffering even harder. But even the Kirkwoods were only in the halfpenny place compared to the Pakenham-Mahons, whose nearby lands were more extensive still. The uneven distribution of wealth in the area stuck in Frank Leneghan's craw and contributed to his surly and vexatious temperament. He was a man on whose shoulders the worries of the world found a cosy place to settle. Like many men of his generation, he was reluctant or unable to express any great emotion, and his resentment smouldered within him, affecting all around him.

In stark contrast to Mary's other grandfather, Frank had no hobby other than caring for the kitchen fire. He was a magician with a tongs and a creel of turf. He would patiently work the fire as Brigid cooked the dinner: one end blazing to boil a pot hanging from the crane, the other smooth with hot ashes for baking bread. His evenings were mostly spent poking and banking the fire, muttering at his dog and saying not a word to Brigid. He looked on his wife, and on all wives, as chattels whose views were not worth considering. Mary feels that he realised he was isolating his wife by his lack of communication and that he felt a certain compassion for her in her lonely existence, but that the combined forces of his nature and his circumstances meant he was unable to do anything about it. His own opinions were black and white and he lived by a list of doctrines. Whatever the Catholic Church or Eamon de Valera had to say on a subject was law. Towards the end of his life, when he was staying with his son and daughter-in-law Willie and Cepta Leneghan in Dublin, he was exposed for the first time to an ITV drama. He could not believe that anything so immoral would be allowed on the airwaves, and when he could not discover how to turn the television set off, he covered the screen with a copy of the *Irish Press* to protect himself from the corrupt foreign influence.

Paddy Leneghan describes his father as a devout man. The family rosary was not enough to satisfy his religious hunger every evening. Most Irish families who said the rosary in those days had their "trimmings", favourite extra prayers and supplications for special intentions; but Frank's trimmings extended to the Litany of the Blessed Virgin, which had to be recited from start to finish. Frank was half-deaf, and the young Leneghan family often took advantage of his deaf ear to have a bit of fun during the evening prayers. Mary gives an account of a litany which will not be found in any prayer book:

> "I don't suppose you say the family rosary up there," he once remarked. We defended our home valiantly, lying that of course we said the rosary every night. "Right so," he conceded, "you can give out the litany at the end." Once we had started the litany I could get no further than "Mirror of Justice". My sister, God bless her, came to the rescue. Leaning towards his deaf ear she took up where I left off. "Church of England," she added firmly. "Pray for us," he replied unperturbed. "Church of Ireland . . . Church of Scotland," she continued, and when she ran out of churches she took up bingo calls: "Two little ducks. Legs Eleven. Clickety Click." He prayed happily for them all.[‡]

Mary's memories of her Grandmother Leneghan are bright and happy. Brigid went to great lengths to hide her loneliness and suffering, and it was only in later years that Mary understood what the poor woman was going through. She was a cleaner in Woodbrook School and also served the neighbours as a midwife of sorts. Like many amateur local midwives in those days, her only training came from the woman who preceded her, and her expertise was mostly inherent. When she was newly married, and even when the children were young, she enjoyed having friends and neighbours in for a house dance. Frank didn't have much time for this frivolity, and his disapproval eventually eroded

---

‡   Mary McAleese, *Reconciled Being–Love in Chaos* (Berkhamsted: Arthur James, 1997), p. 95.

Brigid's enthusiasm. However, her love of literature remained vibrant, and Mary can still recite long passages of poetry she learned at her granny's knee.

Mary remembers her grandmother as a genuinely holy person. She was a humble soul who accepted her lot in life with serenity and found solace and strength in her faith. Every morning, in all weathers, she used to walk the two and a half miles to Drumlyon Church. It was her custom to arrive much too early for mass, and the priest used to leave a key for her under the doormat. She would do the Stations of the Cross and then sit and pray in the flickering light of a couple of candles. Those times of solitude in the dimly lit chapel were very special to her. After mass she always stayed on and meditated for a while before setting out on the long journey home.

Mary describes her grandmother as a mystic, a person who was in communion with God at all times in a simple and ascetic way, a person whose contact with her Creator was real and alive and totally intuitive. Her faith brought her great contentment, whether she was praying in the chapel, working at home or in the fields, or simply walking the road. Many years later, when Mary was learning about Christian meditation, a technique said to have been recently introduced into Irish spirituality from the East, she understood that it was nothing new in this country. This was the meditation her grandmother was using half a century previously.

When Mary was fourteen years old she was left with her grandfather for a weekend. Brigid was dead by that time and there was only Frank, Mary and Pup the dog in the house. The weekend stretched into a week and then into a fortnight. Her aunt and uncle, Willie and Cepta Leneghan, had left her there to visit her grandfather on their way to Tullamore. The plan was to collect Mary on their way home, but the plans were changed. Paddy Leneghan was too busy to go and collect his daughter, and she was told to wait there until someone came for her. The days passed slowly, and still no one came. For the first time in her life Mary felt isolated. Her relations and friends from the area, who were mostly a few years older than she, were off working for the summer. She couldn't get a word out of her grandfather except the odd grunt and the prayers in the evening. She spent most of her days standing on the ditch looking down the lane towards the Carrick road, waiting for a car, but no car came. She was getting an idea of the sort of life her grandmother had had with this grim and sullen man.

Frank Leneghan had a particular problem with Paddy's wife and family. It distressed him greatly that his son had married a woman from the Six Counties and that his grandchildren were born in the North. He was wary of Catholics who lived near "that Orange crowd", as he called them. He felt his grandchildren were somehow defiled by proximity to Protestants and that his seed was now contaminated. Mary feels that her grandfather was very much a product of his time and place. He was born at the end of the nineteenth century and belonged to a generation whose parents and grandparents had vivid and bitter memories of the Great Famine. The area around Croghan is littered with famine graves, and stories of suffering and starvation are still vibrant in the folk memory. He was reared among men who saw all English people as their enemies and viewed all non-Catholics with suspicion.

Of all the women who have touched Mary's life, none, other than her mother, have influenced her as much as her two grandmothers, Brigid and Cassie. Like them, she is inclined to keep her deepest thoughts and worries to herself. Like them, she teases out her personal problems and uncertainties, as she says herself, "in the clamorous silence of my own heart".[‡]

Paddy Leneghan was fourteen years old, in 1939, when he took the road to Belfast to join his three aunts and look for a job. "There was nothing for me in Roscommon those days but slavery and poverty. My Aunt Nora had plenty of room in her house and I settled in with her." The Second World War was rumbling to a start when Paddy settled in Ardoyne. The coming of war put an end to many activities in Belfast, but it did not affect the drinking. Paddy had no trouble finding work as a barman in the Alderman Bar on the Crumlin Road. He then worked for a while in Frank McKenna's off-licence in Flax Street. When Frank bought a pub on Sandford Road in Dublin, Paddy moved south with him to work there and in a second pub in Wellington Street in Dún Laoghaire. By this time he was out of his apprenticeship.

When the war ended Paddy returned to his Aunt Nora's home in Belfast to work once more in the Alderman Bar. Belfast was teeming with returning evacuees, mostly young people who had been sent to country areas where they would be safe from the Blitz. Aunt Nora found a new young apprentice hairdresser from among them, a local girl just back from the Slieve Croob area of County Down where she had spent a few years with her Aunt Mary Agnes. Paddy Leneghan says that from the moment he saw her he was captivated: "You could say I fell in love

---

‡   Mary McAleese, Diary.

with her as soon as I saw her, and the more I saw of her the more I fell in love with her. I was caught."

When he asked his Aunt Nora who she was, she told him the girl's name was Claire: "One of the McManus family from Glenard, that family with all the good-looking girls."

Claire was smitten also. "Paddy was very handsome. He had a great sense of humour, but he was also very sensible."

Claire and Paddy were married in Holy Cross Church, Ardoyne, on 5 June 1950, and they lived for a while in a flat in Skegoniel Avenue, off the Antrim Road. The area was strange to both of them and they missed Ardoyne terribly. When Claire became pregnant, her fretting for the closeness of family and friends intensified. Within six months they had found a house to rent in Ladbrook Drive, the next street to Duneden Park, where Claire had been reared and where her mother and father still lived. It was only a small house, a two-up two-down, but it was all they needed. They were happy to be back among their own.

Mary Patricia Leneghan was born on 27 June 1951 in the Royal Victoria Hospital, Belfast—"the Royal" as it is more commonly called. That particular date is important in the West Belfast Catholic calendar as the feast day of the Mother of Perpetual Succour. In the Redemptorist church of Clonard, a couple of hundred yards from where she was born, it marks the culmination of the annual novena, and thousands of people throng the church, the car park and the street for the occasion. So she was called Mary. Her grandaunt, Mary Cassidy, was told the baby was also called after her. From the day Mary was born she was noisy. She and another child, the first son of Fred Daly, the famous golfer, made so much noise that the poor over-stretched nurses consigned them both to the bathroom. Claire, her mother, says, "The nurses told me that Mary and Fred Daly's son were the two noisiest children ever to be born in the hospital. They said it was our bad luck that they both arrived on the same day."

Mary had started as she meant to continue. Her father was told to take the child home the day after the birth. One of the first dates the infant Mary learned was the date of her birth, and she once embarrassed her poor parents by announcing to visitors, "My mammy and daddy got married on the fifth of June and I was born on the twenty-seventh."

Claire says that the day of Mary's birth was one of the most important days of her life: "Nine times I made the journey home from the hospital with a new baby, but there was something special about the first time. I think most mothers would feel the same. I don't love Mary any more than the others, but there was a special satisfaction and pleasure about her birth. I remember every single detail of that first pregnancy and labour and the terrible mix of emotions after the delivery."

Her own mother and father, Cassie and Seán McManus, were on hand when Claire and Paddy arrived home with Mary. Cassie used to admit to friends that from the first time she held Mary in her arms she knew there would always be a special tie between them. Without saying much about it, everyone acknowledged the special relationship between the child and her granny. Even much later, when Mary had sixty first cousins, all vying for Cassie's attention, that unique bond remained.

When Mary was born Paddy was working in Skelly's Bar, on the Grosvenor Road. Two weeks later Paddy announced that Mrs McCormack, the owner of the bar, had offered him the job of manager. Life was looking up for the young family—a new house, a new baby and a new job. Ardoyne was a wonderful place!

Ardoyne is known throughout the world as a nationalist, Catholic enclave, but originally Ardoyne was a Presbyterian locality. Michael Andrews founded a small weaving village there in 1815 when the area was known as Edenderry. Ardoyne, or *Ard Eoin* in Irish (St John's Hill), was the name of the gentle rise where Andrews built his fine house. He liked the name "Ardoyne" so well that he decided to call the village by the same name.

It was a tiny place of whitewashed, thatched cottages set around a small factory which produced royal damask on handlooms. The people had their own Presbyterian church and school and lit a bonfire every year on the night of 11 July to celebrate the victory of the Protestant King Billy, then Prince William of Orange, over the Catholic King James of England at the Battle of the Boyne, on 12 July 1690. With the coming of the industrial age, there was no future for the weaving village.

Jack Allen, one of the last of the weavers, gave a vivid account, in the 1920s, of the death of his native place: "Ardoyne Village was swept away because its crime was a particularly serious one in Ireland: loitering without intent. The handlooms that had woven linen for royal palaces were flung into a lorry and taken away. Belfast marched over our wee place. They drove a clean concrete street through the silent village like a dagger through its heart."[‡]

The "clean concrete street" was the Crumlin Road, the main thoroughfare to Aldergrove International Airport these days and the

---

‡ *Horizon*, June 1999, p. 14.

road on which Mary lived as a teenager. The Rosehead River, which nowadays flows underground, ran through the old village and parallel to the new road. It was the reason that Ardoyne, as it is known today, was built. Along its banks the industrialists built their linen mills and dug their ponds for the rotting of the flax. Then they built the warren of streets packed end to end with small terraced houses for the mill workers. They gave them imaginative names, some of them from exotic place: Havana Street, Jamaica Street. Some were called for the English nobility: Herbert Street, Chatham Street, Disraeli Street. Some had echoes of English country estates: Oakfield Street, Fairfield Street. Only one had a natural affinity with Ardoyne: Flax Street. The houses in these streets were typical Belfast two-up two-downs with no gardens, their doors opening directly across the narrow streets from their neighbours' doors. Even in the 1950s many of the houses had no electricity. In the sixties they still had no inside toilets or hot water.

Despite this, Mary describes life in Ardoyne as being "like a cocoon", one of the positive aspects of living in a ghetto. Her parents are of the opinion that the cocoon was a thin one, but they admit to an amount of truth in what Mary says. Like many others who left Ardoyne for grander places over the years, they all still miss the openness and friendliness of the people.

In 1867 the Bishop of Down and Connor invited the Cross and Passion Order, or the Passionists as they are better known, to build a church and monastery on a sizeable site between the Crumlin Road and the Woodvale Road. Fr Ignatius was the first rector and later became Archbishop of Bucharest. He opened the first chapel in 1869, and the present-day magnificent church, with its twin verdigris spires, was opened in 1902. Cardinal Logue was the principal celebrant of the first mass, and four bishops and fifty priests assisted him. The parish of Ardoyne stretched, as the people used to say, "from the jail to the mountains and from the Shankill to the moon".‡ The priests were given a great welcome by the parishioners, half of whom were farm workers at that time. If there was a farm worker living in Ardoyne fifty years later, when Mary was baptised in that church, nobody knew anything about him, or her.

The urge to proclaim their identity is a central theme in the life of people living in a ghetto, and to the people of Ardoyne the Catholic religion is a major component of their identity. Since those early days at

‡ The jail: Crumlin Road Prison, a mile and a half from the Passionist monastery.

the end of the nineteenth century, the people have been heavily influenced by the priests of the Order of the Cross and Passion. When Mary was living in the parish, there were upwards of twenty-five priests in the monastery. Each priest was responsible for a few streets and got to know the people very well. The stories of their leadership and good counsel in times of trouble and hardship are part of the folklore of the place. As recently as September 2001, when the children of Holy Cross Girls' Primary School were being attacked on their way to school each morning by loyalist men and women, the Passionist rector, Fr Aidan Troy, played a pivotal role in diffusing the sectarian aggression. At an early age Mary came under the influence of these men, who combine a busy pastoral mission with a life of prayer and contemplation. It was the latter element of their life that most impressed the impressionable young Mary Leneghan.

That was the parish of Holy Cross, Ardoyne, when Mary Leneghan was a girl in the 1950s: the linen mills south of Brookfield Street still producing around the clock; the houses of the wealthy on the Upper Crumlin Road to the north; the chapel and the maze of little streets in between. All life was there: the pawnshop, the pub and the bookies', the chapel, the courthouse and the jail—temptation, sin, judgement, punishment and forgiveness, both spiritual and temporal, all in one place.

Chapter Four

The Edge of the Ghetto

"'Tis hard to find a well nowadays,"
says Bridget filling the bowl again.
"They're hidden in rushes and grass,
choked by green scum and ferns,
but, despite the neglect,
they've lost none of their true mettle.
Seek out your own well, my dear,
for the age of want is near:
There will have to be a going back to sources."
(Cathal Ó Searcaigh: "*An Tobar*/The Well")

In matters parental Claire Leneghan was not as strict as her own mother, but the old values and the old child-rearing methods were deeply ingrained in her. She says she was harder on Mary than on any of the other eight children, simply because she was the eldest. Paddy maintains that he treated all his children exactly the same and expected no more or no less from any of them. Both agree that there was good discipline in the home but that happiness and love were more important to them than obedience. There were many ups and downs, fallings in and fallings out, and plenty of fun in between.

P.J. McAllister was married to a sister of Claire and had a farm in Dromara. When the McAllisters decided they needed a holiday in Butlin's, Paddy was asked to look after the farm in their absence. Off the Leneghans went for a couple of weeks in the country. Mary was four years old and was told to stay out of the way at milking time. Claire says she was not worried that some physical harm might befall the child, but rather that her tender ears might never recover from the kind of language Paddy used with the poor recalcitrant cows. But Mary was entranced by the twice-daily ritual in the byre and succeeded in seeing and hearing all that was to be seen and heard. Back in Belfast, Claire was hanging washing on the line one day when the screams and whoops of children led her to open the door to the back lane. There was her darling,

31

angelic daughter standing with a stick in her hand, a group of children ranged around her, and Mary roaring with each swish as the stick split the air, "Hould up to hell o' that, ye auld bitch ye!" Paddy is not prepared to admit that either he or Mary used any word stronger than that.

The Leneghans and the McManuses were a tight family group in Ardoyne. As Claire says, "If you kicked one of us, we would all be limping." Paddy and Claire were neighbourly people and devoted parents, and Mary's early memories of home are fairly happy. She remembers her home as a *"céilí-ing"* house, where neighbours and friends were always made welcome. Because Paddy worked in the bar trade, there was always a drop of whiskey or a couple of bottles of stout in the house. Many a winter's evening a priest could be found sitting up to the fire with a glass of punch in his hand. Paddy says of the priests, who lived under a vow of poverty, "God love them. They would stand in the snow to get a taste of my whiskey or Claire's home-made scones."

The Leneghan children were raised to be forthright in their views. Openness was encouraged, but however fine the line between frankness and impertinence, that line was clearly observed. Her parents maintain that Mary was a model child in many ways: always obedient and respectful, a great help around the house and constantly cheerful. They also say, with a sense of pride, that she could have very fixed views. She was slow and careful in establishing beliefs about important issues, they say, but once she had examined a question from every side, her opinion very soon became a conviction. At times this was a cause of frustration to her parents, whose view might be the polar opposite, but a well-thought-out position was always respected. Freedom of expression was all very well, but Claire and Paddy were not behind the door with their own opinions, and with nine children in the house and as many different views on a topic, their reply often consisted of, 'We respect your opinion but . . . !"

Mary's parents were reasonably devout people. No one in the house would be allowed to miss Sunday mass. They were regulars at the Monday night novena in Holy Cross, Ardoyne, and the annual Redemptorist novena in Clonard, on the Falls Road. The children were herded out to the confraternities and benediction once a week. However, despite their insistence on religious observance, even in the thorny area of religious practice and respect for the clergy, Claire and Paddy were broad-minded. When Mary came home in bad form from the children's mass one Sunday, Claire wanted to know the reason.

"The priest said a woman's place is at home with her children," complained Mary, "and that a woman should always do what her husband tells her."

"Don't mind that sort of auld blather," said Claire. "That man doesn't know what he's talking about."

Reverence for the clergy among the faithful in Ardoyne bordered on awe, but in the Leneghan house the respect did not always extend to what they had to say. Mary soon learned that priests, like everyone else, sometimes spoke on matters that were beyond their remit or their understanding. Her parents' sharp, sometimes cynical, sometimes critical attitude towards all forms of authority settled easily on their daughter. Besides the priests there was always another voice to be listened to, a voice inside the head which insisted that any attitude to be taken on board had to make sense.

The Passionists, like most religious orders, had a healthy system of promotion and demotion. The provincial leadership appointed the rectors and vicars to the monasteries for a fixed number of years, and the leadership team themselves were elected every few years by ballot of the membership of the Province. Mary was reared with a keen awareness of the democratic process in action in her parish and found it hard to imagine that a different system could be considered fair. It therefore came as a surprise and a disappointment to her to be told during school lessons that God had a pyramid of holiness: the higher one's position in the structure of the Church, the nearer to perfection one came. The pope, of course, was at the top and the laity at the bottom. Mary was angry. Her mother, who reared nine children and slaved in the home from dawn to dusk and often longer, who willingly abandoned her personal ambitions in favour of her children, was further from God than . . . ? This was the first of many "religious" views that Mary, as she says herself, "consigned to an early recycle bin".

There were two primary schools in Ardoyne: Holy Cross Girls' School, which was in an old building in Chief Street, and Holy Cross Boys' School, which consisted of a collection of Nissen huts in Butler Street. There was a weekly parish collection to build two new schools, but Claire and Paddy decided to send Mary to the Convent School of the Sisters of Mercy. This was situated further down the Crumlin Road beside the Mater Hospital and near the Crumlin Road Prison. The rest of the girls would follow Mary to the nuns, and the boys would go further down the road to the Christian Brothers in Donegall Street.

Mary's memories of primary school are very mixed. As in most primary schools in those days, some of the teachers used corporal punishment, and there were among them some who used it to excess. It was a cause of much resentment to her that adults were allowed to strike children for any reason. The few years of her primary education when she had teachers who did not use a cane brought the terror of the other years into sharp contrast. She says they were like night and day. During those few years of brightness, she says she understood more clearly the injustice, the indignity and the humiliation of physical punishment and swore she would never lift a hand to her own children or allow others to do it.

Though Mary later excelled in secondary school, Claire says she was an average primary pupil whose reports were no better than any of the other girls, and sometimes worse. She accepts that the use of corporal punishment could have contributed to this. When the time came to sit the eleven-plus examination, Mary left all her worries behind her and passed with no difficulty.

By the time she was of school-going age, the family no longer lived in Ladbrook Drive. They had moved a couple of hundred yards to Balholm Drive, a street which crossed the top of Ladbrook Drive and Duneden Park, where her grandparents lived. Number 22 Balholm Drive was a bigger house, with three bedrooms. It was also a house which could not be rented, so Paddy and Claire had to take out a mortgage for the first time.

The Leneghans had some well-known neighbours in their new street. Mary was friendly with Marion McFarlane, whose brother Brendan, later better-known as "Bic" McFarlane, spent some years as a student for the priesthood before joining the IRA. He was the man who succeeded Bobby Sands as commander of the IRA in the Maze Prison when Sands went on hunger strike. Another neighbour of the Leneghans who later spent time in prison was Billy Bates. Claire has a particular reason to remember Bates as a boy: she says he was the first person to encourage Mary to use bad language. Both Paddy and Claire clearly remember the day they came upon Billy and Mary at the front door of the house, Mary shaking her head in mute defiance and Billy urging her on repeatedly with the words, "Say 'Shite', Mary! Go on! Say 'Shite!'"

Nora Leneghan was born a year after Mary, and then Claire lost a baby. When she was expecting John she contracted rubella, as a result of which John was born profoundly deaf. After John was born Claire lost another baby. Damien was born next, and then Kate and Patrick. After

Patrick's birth the family moved again, this time to the other side of the Crumlin Road, to number 23 Mountainview Gardens. The family was growing but Paddy was working hard. He had left his job with Mrs McCormack and gone as manager to Convery's Bar in Skipper Street. By the time the family moved to Mountainview, he was working as a representative for the drinks company, R.P. Cully, a subsidiary of Bass. Not only had he a better salary, he also had a car: a Ford Prefect, which the Leneghan family made full use of at weekends.

Mountainview was a small, quiet, new development, an oasis, a few streets of semi-detached houses between the Crumlin Road and the fields stretching behind it to the woods of Glencairn. In the spring, when the Leneghans moved in, it was only partly built. This house also had three bedrooms, but they were larger. There was a small garden in front and a much larger one at the back. Mountainview Gardens was on the "Upper West Side" of Ardoyne, both geographically and socially. Mary was very happy here. She looks back on that time as one of the happiest periods of her younger life. Here the days were full of sunshine and the laughter of friends, the evenings warm and cosy with her family round the fire. Her most vivid memories are the smells: the intoxicating perfume of the flowers in the garden and the warm, secure, homely smell of the fresh brown bread coming from the oven.

The Leneghans were the first Catholic family in Mountainview, but their eldest child was still innocently unaware of religious differences, even in Belfast. Hugh Traynor, the scrap metal merchant, and his wife Marjorie were supposed to move in before them, but they decided to stay in Herbert Street until the autumn. It has been said of Mary that she was raised among rabid republicans. Her old neighbours from Mountainview would have a different story to tell. The Leneghans were a novelty to their Protestant neighbours. Now there were Catholic and Protestant children playing together on the street and running wild in the fields. The young Leneghans were blind to the wonder of it all and to the worries of parents. They saw no difference between themselves and their new friends . . . until the month of July and the start of the marching season.

The Dixons lived next door to the Leneghans. Billy, the father, a manager in the Ormo Bakery, was a friendly man and a good neighbour. When Paddy came home from work on the eve of the Twelfth of July, he found a large Union Jack tied to the lamp standard outside his house and red, white and blue bunting draped over the hedge, the railings and all around the windows. He was shocked. He went into the house, came out with a scissors and proceeded to cut the bunting in small pieces, took down the Union Jack, and left the lot in the street.

A grand master of the Orange Order lived in Mountainview Gardens, and early next morning a band led a procession of Orangemen into the street to collect the master and accompany him to the main parade. Most of the neighbours were out to enjoy the music and many of them to welcome the band and the marching men; but if any of them noticed the red, white and blue heap in the gutter outside Leneghans' house, no one said a word to Paddy.

Next day Paddy was cutting the back lawn when Billy Dixon came out to cut his own grass:

"I had nothing to do with that stuff hanging outside your house," he said.

He proceeded to blame a neighbour from further down the street, a man whose daughter was friendly with Mary.

"I hope it won't happen again," said Paddy.

"I'm sure you'll find you won't have any more problems," replied Dixon, and continued with his lawn mowing.

Paddy Leneghan is a republican in the original sense of the word. He believes absolutely in the democratic republic as the most desirable of political systems: government of the people by the people for the people. It grieves him that the term republican in the Ireland of today has a focus that is too narrow to accommodate him and many like him; that too many people think only of guns and bombs instead of the noble, high-minded principles of Rousseau, Washington and Tone. Paddy is also a nationalist. He would love to see the island of Ireland reunited and independent. Like many other republicans, he sees violence as an unacceptable instrument to achieve the ideals of republicanism. He and Claire detest violence and reared their family according to the dogma that violence is wrong. But they also taught them to stand steadfastly for what they believe in, not to foist their opinions on others and not to allow others to intimidate them.

He had made a stand and everyone in Mountainview knew just where he stood. By the end of that summer the Traynors had moved into the street, followed by a third Catholic family, the Gilmartins, whose daughter, Eileen, was to become one of Mary's closest friends. Mary had plenty of Protestant friends as well. When the Dixons moved out, another Protestant family, the Watsons, moved in next door. They were gentle, friendly people and soon became so close to the Leneghans that both families used to go on holidays together. Their son, Robin, was of an age with Mary and the two children played a lot together. In later years it was a source of great amusement to both families, and embarrassment to Robin and Mary, to remind them that they once shared a bed while on holidays in a cottage in Newcastle.

In most Protestant areas of Belfast, bonfires are lit on the night of 11 July to commemorate the victory of King Billy at the Battle of the Boyne. Catholic bonfires were traditionally lit on 15 August, the Feast of the Assumption. For a couple of weeks in advance, adults and children would gather the planks, tyres, old furniture and any combustible material. This would be carefully stored in case of sabotage in the form of a premature blaze. Bonfire nights, whether Catholic or Protestant, were occasions of sport, merriment and tribalism. Mary Leneghan was an exception to the last of these. Many a warm July day she spent around Glencairn with her Protestant friends, collecting branches and hauling logs. Many a Twelfth morning she and her friends raked the special treats from the embers of the bonfire, potatoes that had been left to roast at the edge of the fire the night before. As Mary was enjoying her Twelfth Feast, she was unaware that the fire, the roasting of the potatoes, the singing and the dancing were all to celebrate the assertion of dominance by one group of people over another. She didn't know that on many of those bonfires an effigy of the pope was roasted along with the potatoes. It was all so much fun and sport, and she enjoyed every knee-scratching, finger-burning minute of it. It says something of the broad-mindedness of Paddy and Claire that they allowed their children to participate so freely in what was, to many Catholics, an expression of Protestant triumphalism.

Among the Leneghans' Protestant friends in Mountainview, the Maxwells were very special, and Mary and Florence Maxwell were inseparable for many years. When Mary first came face to face with sectarianism, at the tender age of ten, and was called a "Fenian bastard" for the first time, it was Florence who defended her against her own co-religionists. Mary still refers to her as "my Fenian defender". The Protestant girl was very taken with the the rites and ceremonies of the Catholic Church. At that time, May processions and Corpus Christi processions were very much a part of the liturgical year, and Florence was fascinated with them. Her own Church had neither First Communion nor Confirmation, a source of great disappointment to the child because of the lack of opportunity to dress up so beautifully, and also to collect a few shillings. Florence would often dress up in Mary's First Communion clothes and practise walking in procession. Mary also learned a lot about

Florence's church and got to know the minister, Sidney Callaghan. Neither of them realised that they were the exception in Belfast, rather than the rule. Cross community communication and exploration was the most natural and pleasant of tasks for the two young friends.

When the Leneghans moved from Mountainview, and later out of Ardoyne altogether, Florence was the only one of Mary's childhood Protestant friends who kept in contact and visited her regularly. Years later, when young women on both sides of the political and religious divide were being tarred and feathered for "fraternising" with the British army, Florence married Stuart Taylor, a Scottish soldier. For security reasons the marriage ceremony took place in Thiepval Barracks in Lisburn. Mary and her parents were present, and Nora Leneghan was Florence's bridesmaid.

Eileen, Florence's mother, was a part-time doffer in a linen mill on the Crumlin Road. Her job was to change the bobbins on the machines in the spinning room, a relatively easy job compared to that of the young women who stood all day in their bare feet in six inches of water beside the looms. As well as having severe skin problems on their legs and feet, many of these women contracted mill fever, a disease which ended hundreds of young lives in the Belfast linen mills. Jack Maxwell worked in the Short and Harland Aircraft Factory in those days. There he was friendly with a fitter from north County Antrim, one Charlie McAleese, Mary's future father-in-law. When Jack Maxwell died in the year 2000, the minister said, during the funeral oration, that Jack had told him, shortly before he died, that the proudest day of his life was when he attended the inauguration of his old neighbour and good friend, Mary, as President of Ireland.

As a child in Mountainview, Mary was struck by the different places people would go to worship on a Sunday morning. There was only Holy Cross for the Catholics, but no two Protestant families in the street seemed to go to the same church. Mary and her mother often shopped on the Shankill Road. Here every corner that hadn't a pub had a church or a mission or a meeting hall. There was Church of Ireland, Presbyterian, Methodist, Evangelist, Baptist, Plymouth Brethren, Congregationalist, Moravian, Unitarian . . . They seemed to go on and on. Their church buildings seemed very different from the majestic edifice of Holy Cross, Ardoyne. The Protestant churches were plain and simple, both outside and inside. Mary's young friends were enchanted by the stories of beautifully coloured statues, the smoke from the swinging thurible, the wafting fragrance of the incense, the glittering mosaics, the flickering of candles and the dancing shadows which hid the secret corners and side altars of the ornate Catholic churches. When Mary, as a grown woman, undertook to do a series of programmes entitled *The Protestant Mind,* she had the advantage of an early education in the wealth of diversity within the Protestant tradition and the simple, stripped down, no-nonsense approach to worship and to life in general that is characteristic of the Northern Protestant.

In the world of the Gaelic Athletic Association, Ulster counties, more than those of other provinces, are inclined to support each other against outsiders. The young Mary Leneghan carried this to an extreme degree by supporting a neighbouring county against her own. Although she was born and bred in County Antrim, she has been an avid fan of the Down football team as far back as she can remember. This contradiction caused her some problems during her youth and early adulthood, especially when she started going out with Martin McAleese, who spent a while playing minor football with Antrim. In the early 1960s the footballers of County Down were the toast of Ulster. They were the first team to bring the Sam Maguire Cup across the border, and to show it was no fluke they carried it home again the following year. The members of this team were superstars in Belfast. Their photographs adorned the walls of many bedrooms, including that of Mary Leneghan, and of all the stars on that team none shone brighter than the captain, Paddy Doherty.

In 1962 Mary suffered a bout of scarlet fever and was ordered to stay in bed for a week. Not only did she not mind being confined to her room, but all her friends were envious of her because who else but the famous Paddy Doherty himself was working on the building of the new houses across the road. Mary's week in bed passed quickly as she spent each day trying to catch the eye of her hero.

Mary's early life was extraordinary in many ways, but none of it seemed at all unusual to her. Part of this strangeness had to do with living on the edge of a ghetto. She was an avid fan of Gaelic games, she danced with the McAleer School of Dancing, she played camogie for Ardoyne Kickhams: all of these activities were clear expressions of a nationalist identity. Yet in the part of Ardoyne where she lived, she spent her time playing and socialising with children who understood nothing of these activities and very little of her obvious Irishness. Curiously, Mary was equally at home and equally happy in both worlds.

When the Leneghans moved to the Woodvale Road, the Shaw family lived a few doors away, and as a result of that strange phenomenon that causes opposites to attract, the families soon became firm friends. The

Shaws were Plymouth Brethren and lived according to a strict code of behaviour. They did not drink alcohol, did not use tobacco, did not go to dances or pubs, and generally lived a very quiet, sober and staid life. They were good neighbours: kind, generous and thoughtful. When Anna Shaw was getting married, she asked Kate Leneghan to be her bridesmaid and Paddy and Claire were invited to the wedding.

Because the Shaws were abstemious people, there was not much chance that anything stronger than tea would be available to drink the health of the happy couple. It was going to be a dry wedding in a dry place, a Temperance Hotel on the Shore Road. Paddy Leneghan was not the only guest who was not looking forward to an alcohol-free celebration. Bob Shaw, the grandfather, liked a drop of whiskey also, but the poor man was not allowed to touch a drop. A couple of days before the wedding, Paddy dropped by the hotel and introduced himself to the doorman. He soon discovered, as he had suspected, that a deal could be made. A supply of whiskey was secreted in a storeroom beside the men's toilet at the top of the stairs. The morning of the wedding was bitterly cold, and by the time the guests reached the hotel they were shivering. As soon as the photographs were taken, Paddy sidled over beside Bob Shaw.

"Wouldn't a glass of whiskey be a great comfort on a day like this?" said Paddy to the older man.

"God forgive you for mocking a poor auld sufferer," replied Shaw.

"Oh, I'm not mocking at all," said Paddy as he took the man's arm and guided him across to meet the smiling doorman. The wedding guests were a polite lot and refrained from remarking on the frequency with which the two men visited the toilet during the celebrations.

They were all great friends and neighbours, often in each other's houses, comforting each other in times of trouble, open with each other about their hopes and their worries, but no one in either family suspected that John Shaw, Anna's brother, was a murderer. He was a member of the UVF and was later convicted of five murders: four Catholics and a Protestant whom he thought was a Catholic. He shot this last man outside Holy Cross Church on the Crumlin Road, opposite a shop belonging to Mary's cousin Paddy Cassidy. When Cassidy heard the shot he ran out and gathered the victim in his arms. He comforted him in his dying seconds and, thinking he was a Catholic, whispered an Act of Contrition in his ear. This was a random sectarian murder, as were the other murders Shaw committed. At his trial, before being sentenced to five life terms, John Shaw described himself as a seeker of revenge for the evil deeds of the Provisional IRA.

His family were distraught when his secret life was discovered, when they found out about the five men he had killed in cold blood and the families he had left broken-hearted. The Leneghans were distressed also. Paddy afterwards wondered if the fact that the Leneghans were friends and neighbours and obviously opposed to violence would have saved them from being "legitimate targets" in the eyes of John Shaw. He still wonders. Many years later, when Mary, as president, was asked to speak about one atrocity from the thousands of murders that were committed during the Troubles, she spoke about that Protestant man, shot "by accident" outside her parish church in Ardoyne simply because John Shaw thought he was a Catholic. She went on to speak about Shaw's other victims: people without names for him, without faces, without backgrounds, without reasons to justify the sudden ending of their lives except the fact that they were born into the wrong religion.

The Leneghans moved to number 142 Woodvale Road because the house in Mountainview was no longer large enough for their needs. The new house was bigger and had two bedrooms in the attic. These would soon be needed because Patrick was born shortly after they moved in and Kate arrived the following year. Although the Leneghans now lived closer to Holy Cross than ever before—directly behind the monastery— in fact they lived in a Protestant area. The Church of Holy Cross, referred to locally as "the chapel", is the heart of Ardoyne, even though it is situated on the edge. It is built on a height, and its twin verdigris spires are visible from most parts of the parish. The people are proud of their church and take great comfort from the view. Although the Leneghans now lived only fifty yards from it, the comfort of this view was denied them by the high wall at the back of the monastery. A hundred yards from their new home, the Woodvale and Crumlin roads converged like the confluence of two streams at the corner where Mary stood on the evening of the 14 August 1969.

They had a few Catholic neighbours in Woodvale, amongst them the O'Reillys, who had lived on the road for years and who would, years later, share a day of horrific memories with the Leneghans. If Claire was feeling sorry for herself because of the growing number of children in the family, she felt even more sympathy for Mrs O'Reilly. She had thirteen children. The young O'Reillys were older than the Leneghans. In fact, the oldest of them were of an age with Paddy and Claire. Tony and Myles O'Reilly were between the generations, Myles being fifteen years older than Mary and Tony seventeen, and they treated her like one of their little sisters. Both young men had sparkling personalities, which helped them to span the generation gap and later contributed to their success in business. They ran a popular restaurant, the Golden Pheasant Inn, in Baillies Mills on the Ballynahinch Road, outside Lisburn, a favourite haunt of Mary's when she was in her early twenties and a place that would haunt her dreams in years to come.

Both Mary and her mother say they were never content in the house on the Woodvale Road. It was north facing, constantly in shadow, with a massive wall opposite and a tiny garden behind. The busy main road meant that the children could not play outside their front door as they had done before. It was a spacious house, but old and dark and depressing, and the children had no neighbours of their own age. It was here that Mary began to learn street sense, or as she says herself, "My antennae started to grow, those feelers that twitch to let you know what side of the road to walk on if you want to be safe." Her convent school uniform made her a target. Having been attacked twice on her way to school, she took to carrying a hurley along with her school bag. The attacks soon stopped.

Mary was not the only armed member of the Leneghan clan in those days. One day when he came home from work for his lunch, Paddy came upon Patrick Leneghan going up the stairs with an axe in his hand.

"Where are you going with that axe?" Paddy asked his son.

"I gonna hatchet Mary!" was the terse response.

No one can remember the reason why Paddy's eldest daughter was to be beheaded, but even Mary admits that Patrick's recourse to summary execution would probably have had some basis in Mary's bossiness. The future president was no angel.

The Leneghans' old gas cooker was in such serious need of repair, or replacement, that it had an over-eighteens restriction. The children were repeatedly warned not to touch it. Kate had just been born and Claire was still in the maternity hospital, and Mary, being now the woman of the house, was anxious to display her culinary skills, despite the dire warnings about the dangerous cooker. When Paddy came home to make lunch for the children, he found his eleven-year-old daughter standing proudly behind a kitchen table stacked with scones and fairy cakes. The Riot Act was solemnly read, and Mary was warned of the gravest of dreadful consequences if she ever again endangered the lives of the family by using the faulty cooker.

It was after twelve o'clock when Paddy came home from work that same night. Through the lingering pub odours of tobacco and alcohol, Paddy smelt the chocolate cake as soon as he opened the door. The evidence was everywhere to be seen: crumbs and flakes of chocolate on the table and scattered on the floor. Twice in one day? Despite his warnings? He could hardly believe it of her. Direct action was called for, and he took the stairs two at a time. Mary cried herself back to sleep that night, nursing her wounded pride and a stinging backside, but the desired result was achieved. She refrained from further honing her baking skills until a new and safer cooker was installed.

The Leneghans decided to move once more. Claire was pregnant again, and more space was needed for the growing family. Paddy had by this time bought the Long Bar in Leeson Street, off the Falls Road, and the family was now fairly secure, financially. He and Claire wanted a house that would not only be bigger but more modern; a more airy, brighter home, one with a bigger garden, but still within the parish of Ardoyne. Shortly after they made the decision to move, their dream home came on the market. It was a big semi-detached house on the corner of the Crumlin Road and Hesketh Road, a quarter of a mile up the hill from the chapel. Shortly after the family moved into number 657 Crumlin Road Phelim was born, and Clement, the last of the Leneghan children, arrived four years later.

Up on the hill, beside the site of the original Ardoyne village, the family was happy. They were within a couple of hundred yards of Claire's parents in Duneden Park, within a short walk of all their old friends and neighbours, five minutes from the chapel and the shops; but life in this part of the parish was very different. Up here there was no sign of poverty. They had a different class of neighbour. An RUC man lived opposite them alongside the Revd Llewellyn Wynne, minister of the Presbyterian church on the Ballysillan Road. Next door was Dr McCarthy and his sister, principal of Holy Cross Girls' School. Above them lived the Revd Jimmy Arbuthnott, a Church of Ireland minister whose church was at the bottom of the Grosvenor Road.

Paddy and the Revd Jimmy soon became firm friends. They would often meet on the road late at night, Jimmy walking his dog and Paddy coming home late from work. Both were friendly, chatty men. The initial "Good night; grand weather" soon developed into full-blown conversations. One night Paddy invited Jimmy in for a nightcap, and the two men discovered a mutual interest in a glass of whiskey and each other's company.

Paddy was wakened early one Sunday morning by a frantic banging on the front door. When he went down to investigate, he discovered a distraught Jimmy, who explained that he had just got word that his son, who was on a holiday in France, had suffered a burst appendix. The young Arbuthnott had been staying with a family who took him with them on a pilgrimage to Lourdes, and he had been taken ill at the shrine. Jimmy wanted to be with him but did not have the price of the plane ticket. Paddy did not need to hear any more. Jimmy was off on the next available flight. Some time later, when Jimmy's son was safe and well in Belfast, the two friends were having a drink by the fire.

"Of course, you know," said Paddy, "why that young fella of yours got sick in Lourdes?"

"No," said the minister, "but I suppose you're going to tell me."

"Because he's the only Protestant that ever said a prayer at the Grotto," said Paddy, as he refilled Jimmy's glass.

Paddy and Jimmy were close friends for several years. Jimmy's church was within walking distance of the Long Bar, and when some Catholic youths covered the façade with anti-Protestant graffiti, Paddy organised the clean-up operation. Mary was always fond of the quiet, kind, fun-loving minister. He used to drive to Dublin on a regular basis to visit his son, who was attending Trinity College. Mary and Eileen Gilmartin asked him to bring them with him one day, as they wanted to visit a former teacher who had moved to the Dominican Convent in Eccles Street. Jimmy had just bought a new Renault 12 and was anxious to see how well it could perform. They were on the outskirts of Castlebellingham when a garda stopped them for travelling at 70 miles per hour in a 40 mph zone.

"Have you any idea what speed you were doing?" enquired the garda.

"I'm afraid I have no idea, Guard," said Jimmy, who was in his clerical garb. "I have to get these girls as far as the Dominican Convent in Eccles Street in Dublin, and I have to be on the altar myself for twelve o'clock mass in the Pro-Cathedral."

"Go on now, Father, and for God's sake be careful," said the garda. The three friends laughed all the way to Dublin.

Chapter Five

The Religious Rebel

I have no time to worship. I must live:
The days in which we move are marred with wrong.
(John Hewitt: "Sonnet" from *Uncollected Poems 1928–86*)

Mary sometimes refers to the frugality of her early life in Ardoyne, but although the family had very few of life's luxuries, there were many people in the area much poorer than the Leneghans. Mary had wise parents who worked hard, who understood the value of money, who used every penny sensibly and were never in debt. Claire, like her mother and grandmother before her, was an accomplished housekeeper and domestic economist. Nothing was wasted. She could make a wholesome meal from the most meagre of ingredients and proudly asserts that none of her children ever knew what it was to be hungry. The family had a holiday every summer. Even if it was only a visit to Slieve Croob or the farm in Roscommon, the children always got a break from the ubiquitous red brick and the polluted air of the industrial city.

Mary was always impeccably dressed, neat and clean, her hair shining and her shoes polished. Dolours Price, the hunger-striker who spent many years in prison after being convicted of bombing in England in 1971, was in Mary's class in secondary school. "My own school uniform was so shiny you could have used it as a mirror to brush your hair. I was always jealous of the way Mary Leneghan was dressed. She was always immaculate. Her mother must have bought her a couple of new uniforms every year," she says.[‡]

"Not true!" say Mary and her mother. Both agree that she was always well turned out, but she had the same uniform from the day she started secondary school until she left, seven years later.

Claire says: "I bought the uniform much too big for her and turned it up and tucked it in. I let it out a bit every summer. Every day, when Mary came home from school, she had to take it off, sponge it and iron

---

‡ Interview with author.

it, and hang it up carefully. That made a lot more sense than spending money on a new uniform every year."

Being the eldest of nine children has certain advantages in terms of being first in the pecking order, but Mary has cause to remember many of the disadvantages. As she was growing up there always seemed to be a new baby in the house, with all the attendant extra workload on the eldest child. All the Leneghans agree that Mary was the willing workhorse who was always there to help her mother. But she was no Cinderella. She enjoyed life to the full, creating her own space and making sure she had her own time to have fun with her friends.

She always had a keen interest in sport and got a lot of satisfaction from team games. As a teenager she became interested in badminton, a game not usually associated with a place like Ardoyne. During the long winter evenings, young people came from all over the area to the Ovada Badminton Club in Holyrood Hall, or Toby's Hall as it was known, at the bottom of Butler Street. It was a strange choice of game, but it cost very little to play; racquets and shuttlecocks could be borrowed, Toby's Hall had a good high ceiling, membership was open to all, and the hall was heated during the winter.

Paddy and Claire Leneghan had very definite priorities in their family life and in the rearing of their children, and Mary seemingly absorbed them with the very air she breathed: faith, family and education. These were the three cardinal virtues, the three aspects of life to which all other ideals gave precedence in the Leneghan household, and this was the order in which they came.

An abiding interest in education was part of Mary's heritage from both sides of the family. Cassie and John McManus, and Paddy and Claire after them, swore that none of their children would ever stand on a mill floor in Belfast, and none of them ever did. It was not that mill work was beneath them, but they knew that, at that time, Catholics found it twice as hard as Protestants to make their way off that floor and into a better job. Without having studied any statistics, they knew that a good education was more important and more necessary for a Catholic in Northern Ireland than for a Protestant. They also understood that promotional prospects for a Catholic woman were fewer again; that gender discrimination was every bit as extensive as its religious counterpart. It is not surprising, in view of this background, that on the day Mary was appointed the first woman pro-vice-chancellor of Queen's University, and only the second Catholic, Paddy proclaimed it to be the proudest day of his life.

When Mary passed her eleven plus examination, her parents decided to send her to St Dominic's High School, a famous grammar school run by the Dominican nuns on the Falls Road. Places in the school were much coveted, and the girls wore their maroon uniforms, with the emblazoned "*Veritas*" motto, with pride. The fine red brick institution, founded in 1870, sits amid extensive grounds directly opposite the hospital where Mary was born. The Dominicans' College of Education, St Mary's, is adjacent to the school on the same grounds. St Mary's, like St Dominic's, was a female-only institution at the time.

Mary was a diligent student. The motto of the Dominicans is *Veritas* or Truth, and the ethos of searching for truth through study suited her inquisitive nature. Her natural competitiveness and ambition would not have let her rest on her oars, no matter how well she was performing. There was always another goal, another academic hill to climb, another mystery to unravel. But she was also a bit rebellious by nature and found it hard to reconcile the search for truth with an interdict on certain areas of learning.

The Dominican sisters were well known for their promotion of discussion and academic disputation. But even the most broad-minded of the gentle nuns had a problem with the promulgation of Leninism in the school. When leaflets promoting the teachings of Tariq Ali, the Leninist writer, were discovered on the desks of many of the students, Mary Leneghan was summoned to the principal's office. The logic behind the subpoena was simple: "If Mary Leneghan didn't do it, she certainly knows who did." Mary's parents were informed that such knowledge, and the refusal to divulge it, was a capital crime, punishable by expulsion. Not only Mary but most of the student body knew who was responsible, and pressure was brought to bear on the culprits. They, in common with all the students, had often been told that the truth would set them free; and, on this occasion, it did. They admitted their guilt and were duly set free—to pursue their education in some other establishment. No Catholic grammar school would enrol two self-confessed disciples of Tariq Ali, but they eventually found educational asylum in Methodist College.

Mary claims to have had no part in the Tariq Ali episode, and several of her school friends agree with her. There were, however, other incidents in which she was the main protagonist. Her respect for the Dominican nuns as educators is tempered somewhat by her attitude to their teaching of life skills. She feels that their reticence prevented them from preparing their charges properly for life and even for love. There were lively debates in St Dominic's about the controversial encyclical *Humanae Vitae* of Pope Paul VI, the letter in which he clearly set down the Church's opposition to certain forms of contraception. The nuns, however, were not party to such arguments. The discussions were organised by Fr Patrick Walsh, later Bishop Walsh, who was chaplain to the nearby hospital at the time. The Dominican sisters' search for *veritas* stopped short of any truth pertaining to things sexual.

Mother Laurentia had been president of St Mary's College of Education, next door, and after her retirement she taught religion in St Dominic's. One day she was reading to the class from the New Testament: "When the eighth day came and the child was to be circumcised . . ."

Mary's hand shot up.

"Excuse me, Mother Laurentia, what does 'circumcised' mean?" asked the student, her face full of innocent curiosity, her head tilted to the perfect angelic degree of wonderment and her eyes shining with naiveté. Mother Laurentia suspected that Mary, and every other girl in the class, knew the meaning of "circumcision", but she was unwilling, or unable, to bring herself to confront them or to explain the word. To do so would have meant referring to the private parts of the male anatomy, and that would have been a taboo subject for a nun of her years and background. She could have referred the students to the dictionary, but she decided to take refuge in dissembling.

"Well, girls," said the distraught nun, "as I understand it, and I may well be mistaken, 'circumcision' is a distinctive circular mark that is cut on the arm of a male Jew, as a symbol of his Jewishness."

The girls barely managed to control their urge to laugh out loud. They shifted uncomfortably in their seats and nodded to one another. Their faces were unreadable as the nun continued to read from the Gospel of St Luke. That evening Mary read a full definition of "circumcision" in a medical textbook in the library, and the following morning in religion class she had the temerity to raise her hand again.

"Excuse me, Mother Laurentia. I happened to be looking through a medical textbook yesterday evening in the library, and I came across this definition of the word we were discussing yesterday." She proceeded to read from the notes she had taken.

"Well, girls," said the nun, "don't doctors have strange words for certain things."

Most nuns in the 1960s were prudish to a degree about such matters and would avoid any references to sexuality, certainly in classroom situations, but Mary feels that their demureness prevented the girls from getting a proper preparation for life after school. The only "love" that was ever mentioned was love of God or the chaste love due to parents. She says that the inhibitions of the nuns extended to the lay teaching staff also, most of whom were middle-aged women.

But she has very fond memories of one lay teacher in particular. May O'Friel was that rarity among good teachers: a person who could cover a curriculum without any apparent effort on the part of pupil or teacher and, at the same time, nurture in her charges a thirst to learn more for the satisfaction of learning. She took a particular interest in Mary during her last year in the school, in 1969. She noticed her pupil was often wan and tired looking. She did not question her about her pallor and the rings under her eyes, but she made it her business to find out about her home circumstances. She discovered that Clement, the ninth and last of the young Leneghans, had been born on 20 April, the day Mary started her mock A level exams. She learned that Mary's mother was quite ill after the birth and that Mary was, effectively, a substitute mother for the child. Although she could do nothing about her situation at home, she decided she could lighten her burden of travel to school, and she started to give her a lift each morning from her house.

This kind and sensitive soul had a niece who was in school with Mary in St Dominic's, Anna Carraher, who later became head of broadcasting in BBC Northern Ireland. Mary had other reasons to remember Miss O'Friel apart from her benevolence. She introduced the pupils to a whole world of cultural interest outside the confines of the A level curriculum. She encouraged them to go to films, dramas and art exhibitions. She opened up for them the world of travel and the beauty and mystery of other cultures. Twenty years before Mary was born, May O'Friel was promoting the importance of other influences in the cultural life of Ireland, as this newspaper account of a debate in Queen's University shows: "Miss M. O'Friel pointed out the absurdity of imagining that Ireland could work out its own salvation by ignoring other countries. 'Thomas Davis was an apostle of nationality,' said Miss O'Friel, 'yet Davis said: "Every great European race has sent its stream to the river of the Irish mind.""[‡]

In primary and post-primary education in the Northern Ireland of the 1950s and 1960s, there was very little significance attached to Irish culture, history or even geography. Mary learned, by rote, the mountain

‡   *Irish News*, 26 January 1930

ranges and rivers of Britain, the succession of English monarchs and the history of Europe and the world. Some Catholic schools strayed outside the strict confines of the state curriculum in order to give the pupils some taste of their own heritage, but even in these schools, the pressure of examinations meant that such wanderings were not very far ranging. The Irish language could be an examination subject in any school that wished to teach it, but in the system in general the mine of Irish cultural wealth remained unopened.

Paddy and Claire recognised this deficit, and outside the formal educational process, they ensured that their family would take advantage of every opportunity to reinforce their Irishness. Mary was sent to Irish dancing classes, she played camogie, she spent three summers in the Donegal Gaeltacht. Her parents maintain that she and the rest of the family were reared with an all-Ireland view of the country. No border, whether political or cultural, existed in the Leneghan mindset. Mary felt as much at home in Roscommon as she did in County Down. All the family holidays were spent in the Republic, and by the time she was a teenager, she had been in every one of the thirty-two counties. Paddy Leneghan had an abiding interest in Irish history and archaeology, a love he was determined to pass on to his children. "Historical picnics", as he called them, were a regular weekend feature, and the family headed off for places as far afield as Queen Maeve's Grave, the Giant's Causeway, the Grianán of Aileach and Brú na Bóinne, the megalithic tombs in the loop of the river Boyne. The children were not always appreciative of Paddy's cultural efforts on their behalf. They were often tired and peevish on their way home in the car, and Paddy would sometimes pick up a hitch-hiker to distract them. On one occasion they were returning from a day spent in the Glens of Antrim when they picked up an English student who was thumbing a lift. After a while the Englishman, who did not understand the placatory effect he was having on the Leneghan children, commented: "I had been standing there thumbing for an hour, and most of the cars that passed had one or two people in them. Yours is the only car that stopped—a car that has no room for me—a car which is packed to the roof with kids! I'll never understand the Irish!"

In 1963 Mary attended, for the first time, that most Irish of rite-of-passage institutions, the *coláiste samhraidh*, or summer college in the Gaeltacht: a residential course in the Irish language in an Irish-speaking district. She and her friend Eileen Kelly set off for a college that had just opened in Baile na Finne, Fintown, in the mountainous Gaeltacht Láir area of Donegal. The manager of the college was Dominic Mag Fhloinn, a nephew of the parish priest, Fr Seán Mag Fhloinn. The two friends found they were staying in a house that was six miles from the village and the college. Each day they walked the twelve miles back and forth in the unrelenting Donegal rain. After a week, Mary's complaints, and even a letter to her parents, remained unanswered. On their way home on the Friday evening, Mary informed Eileen that they had had enough. The next day they were both going to escape. Saturday morning broke bright and clear, but even the sight of a blue sky did not temper her mood. After breakfast, the two friends set out on the road to Kingarrow and the relative civilisation of Letterkenny.

They were soon overtaken by a man driving a little red sports car. He stopped and asked them where they were going.

"Anywhere far away from Fintown," answered Mary.

"Hop in and I'll give you a lift," said the young man, who made no mention of the fact that he was another nephew of the parish priest. He drove around for a while as the girls complained about the distance they had to walk each day. Before they realised it they were back in Fintown, outside the parochial house. When Fr Mag Fhloinn saw the girls sitting in the car he burst out laughing. As Mary and Eileen were explaining their attempted escape, another car pulled up outside the house. Paddy and Claire had arrived to investigate the girls' complaint about the twelve-mile walk. They had confirmed the distance from the house to the college in the car and were threatening to bring the girls home. The matter was eventually settled when Mary and Eileen were moved to a house much closer to the college, the home of Peadar Mac Gaoithín, his wife and young family.

The Mac Gaoithíns had recently returned from America to take over the running of the post office and shop. Mary and Eileen enjoyed their company and the opportunity to work in the shop, but English was the language of the house, and Mary learned very little Irish during her time in the Gaeltacht. But she enjoyed it so much after moving to her new lodgings that she returned twice more.

More than thirty years later, when Mary was President of Ireland, she was opening a new college in Machaire Uí Robhartaigh in Donegal. During her speech, safe in the erroneous belief that Fr Mag Fhloinn had long since gone to his eternal reward, she told the story of her own experience in Fintown. As the story progressed the audience seemed to be dissolving with laughter. Mary could not understand the exaggerated reaction to her story, until she finished and a priest walked forward to shake her hand and said: "That was a great story, President. I enjoyed it very much. I don't think you recognise me. I'm Fr Seán Mag Fhloinn."

In the days when the Leneghans lived on the Woodvale Road, they had their own key to the back gate of the Passionist monastery, and the children took great advantage of the privilege. The priests' garden was a wonderland, ideal for games of hide-and-seek. Claire says that one of her favourite pieces of music is Albert W. Ketelby's famous sound painting "In a Monastery Garden" because it reminds her of those days when her older children were raised in a monastery garden. The family often used the same garden, and even the monastery kitchen, as a short cut to the Crumlin Road. The children were known by name to every one of the priests and brothers. The liturgical calendar ruled the Leneghan household, and Church feast days and novenas took precedence over all plans and occasions.

It was later in Mary's youth that Fr Justin Coyne became her great *anamchara*, her soul-friend and spiritual director. He had an enormous influence on her ideas and her spirituality. Justin was from Mullingar. He was a tall, thin young man, whose grey hair and pallid skin were the only indications that he was fighting a painful form of cancer. When Mary first met him, he had just returned to the parish of Holy Cross after spending several years teaching history in the order's seminary in Crossgar, County Down. She says he came into her life just in time, as she was on the point of rejecting God.

When she was thirteen years old, one of the nuns told her she would end up as a nun herself . . . or as an atheist. Not long after that the youngster became so fed up with the hypocrisy she saw all around her, both political and religious, that, in a paroxysm of teenage righteous outrage, she wrote to the headquarters of the Communist Party and asked for an application form. Her mother was appalled. Claire was convinced that her wonderful eldest daughter, on whom they had lavished love and affection and all the benefits of a Catholic upbringing and education, was hell-bound in a hurry, her immortal soul handed over to the enemies of God and Church. Her father was more sanguine about the whole matter: "She's a teenager and has a good head on her shoulders—a dangerous mixture. She'll get over this in a couple of weeks."

When Claire looked around to see who could possibly be responsible for this catastrophe, her suspicious eye fell on a man who was an employee and friend of Paddy's. Pat McAllister worked in the Long Bar and was a lifelong socialist. He had fought in the Spanish Civil War as a member of the International Brigade against the forces of General Francisco Franco; he had been wounded and returned to Belfast on Christmas Eve 1938. Nearly sixty years later Pat's life was celebrated in a play, *Tomorrow's People,* written by Martin Lynch and performed in the Lyric Theatre in Belfast.

Mary often walked from St Dominic's High School to her father's pub in Leeson Street to have her lunch, and, more often than not, she spent her lunchtime listening to Pat McAllister's stories. As well as instilling in her a love for Spain and the Spanish language, he opened her mind to the politics of socialism. Pat had served two strike-related prison terms in Canada in the 1920s. He was a scholarly man whose interests included history and literature, especially poetry. Republicanism, socialism, Spanish and poetry added up to a heady cocktail for an impressionable teenage girl. His talk was full of romance, sacrifice, chivalry and mystery, and Mary was a keen and receptive listener, a perfect candidate for Communist Party membership.

One evening Mary was on her way home past the monastery when she met a priest she didn't recognise.

"Are you one of the McManus family?" Fr Justin asked her.

"That's my mother's name," replied Mary. "She was Claire McManus before she was married."

"I'd recognise you from your mother," said the priest. "Where do you live?"

He said he would call to the house soon. He did, and soon he was calling once or twice a week. Sunday evenings were special to the Leneghan children. After the religious programmes ended on television, they could look forward to the Sunday night film. More often than not, just as the film was starting, the doorbell would ring to announce the arrival of Fr Justin. Claire was sure the collective sigh could be heard out in the street. Amid grumbles and groans the television would be turned off, and Claire would ensure that each of her children had a welcoming smile for the visitor.

Mary was the only one of the children who always looked forward to his visits. She and Justin would fall into conversation about matters spiritual and religious. As soon as they were engrossed, the television could be switched back on, and the compromise of murmuring discussion and low volume entertainment was acceptable to all. Mary was enthralled by the words, the manner and the wisdom of the gentle and unassuming priest.

Father Myles Kavanagh, a friend and confrere of his, says that Justin knew every young person in the parish by name. He was the children's priest and had a wonderful communicative skill with them. He adds:

> Justin was useless as a homilist. He was too shy to speak effectively in public. He had to be taken off the children's mass because he tried to talk to four hundred kids just as he used to talk to young Mary. The result was chaos in the chapel. His great strength was one-to-one, or speaking to small groups, and they loved him. He was also a very innocent man. One evening he came to me with a question that was bothering him a lot. A pupil in the girls' school had asked him what a "sex symbol" was and he didn't know how to answer her. I told him that the Blessed Virgin was a great sex symbol because she was the symbol of all that was wonderful and beautiful about a woman. The poor man went off delighted with himself. He was an absolute saint.

Over the years that they knew each other, Justin and Mary discussed philosophy, theology and faith—weighty subjects for a teenager. They reflected on life and death, love of God and love of neighbour. Justin's pet subject was the Church's obligation to love everyone without condition and its duty of loyalty to all "God's people", a subject not much discussed in Ireland of the 1960s. He often spoke of hope and courage. Mary describes him as a man who was saturated in the love of God and humanity, a person who was forthright about the message of the Gospel and who lived his life according to that message.

Mary says that Justin Coyne was the single most important influence in her life. She was thirteen when she met him, and he died five days before her eighteenth birthday, but during those five years he had an effect on her that has lasted to this day. She always has his photograph on her desk and she called her son after him. Over the years since his death she has prayed to him every day and has often felt close to her old soul-friend, her *anamchara*.

During the years they knew each other, Justin was dying from cancer of the spine. It was said, after his death, that he must have suffered terribly for years, but there was never a word of complaint from him. Because of Mary's youthfulness, she thought of him as an old man when she knew him, but he was only in his forties when he died. He had just finished saying mass on 22 June 1969 when he fell in the sanctuary of the high altar. He was dead by the time the doctor arrived. When Mary met his family at the funeral, she discovered that they knew a lot about her from Justin.

Mary was a teenager, and by definition impressionable to some degree, when she knew Fr Justin. It is to be expected that her memories of the man would be gilded somewhat by the passing of time, his qualities exaggerated and his sanctity overstated. If that is the case, then Justin's fellow priests and parishioners are guilty of the same embellishment. All agree that he was a very special person: a wise, innocent, humble and saintly man. When he died Mary lost more than a friend; she lost a guiding light.

Not every priest who visited the Leneghan household was treated with the same veneration. Fr Honorius Kelly was a good friend of the family. Like Justin, he was also a frequent visitor. Unlike Justin, he spent most of his time in conversation with Paddy over a glass of whiskey. Honorius was a learned and clever man, his talk terse and incisive and sometimes irascible. He was a relation of Charles E. Kelly, one of the founders of the famous satirical magazine *Dublin Opinion*, and an uncle of Frank Kelly, the actor. One of his priest friends said of him that "he spoke in cartoons, his thoughts taking form in succinct word-pictures, which were sometimes quite venomous". Another says, less charitably, that he sometimes forgot to engage his brain before he opened his mouth. On being introduced one day to a Derryman, he said, "I was in Derry once. It's a jumped-up Ardoyne." He often referred to himself as "a backstreet priest in a backstreet place". But the people in the backstreet place liked and respected the backstreet priest. He was a kindly and straight-talking man, both of which attributes were respected in the Leneghan house.

Mary's A levels were fast approaching, and she had decided that law was her chosen field of study and that she would like to pursue it in Trinity College Dublin. Claire and Paddy knew that Trinity was seen by many people as a bastion of post-colonial Protestant influence and that attendance by Catholics there was frowned upon by the Catholic Church—or rather by John Charles McQuaid, the Catholic Archbishop of Dublin. Special permission had to be sought, and Fr Honorius was approached to provide the official forms to seek this permission. He arrived with the documents and sat at the fire with Paddy as Mary and Claire filled in the required information. The priest and Paddy spoke of many things that evening, but the priest said not a word about Trinity College. Two weeks after the forms were posted, Honorius arrived again at the Leneghan door.

"I'm here on official Church business," he told Paddy and Claire. "Those forms have arrived back from Archbishop McQuaid's office in Dublin. They weren't happy with some of Mary's answers, and she has to do them all over again."

"Well, sit up to the fire there and warm yourself," said Paddy. "There shouldn't be any problem with the answers, as long as we understand the questions."

As he moved to his usual chair beside the fire he muttered, "I shouldn't have to be doing this anyway."

"Why's that?" asked Paddy.

"Mary should never have put Trinity College on the form in the first place," replied the priest.

"It's a pity you feel that way," said Paddy. "When you came here with the forms in the first place, you didn't mention that you had any problem with Trinity. But now that you have given us your opinion, I'm afraid I've no option but to give you mine."

"And what is your opinion?" asked Honorius.

"It's as simple as this," said Paddy. "If Mary wants to attend Trinity College in Dublin, she'll go there whether it suits you or Archbishop McQuaid or not. It's all the same to us."

The priest's jaw dropped and his face went through several shades of red.

"Anyway," he replied, "Mary shouldn't be applying for law in the first place. She should be going for teaching or nursing. None of your people were ever lawyers. Law has to be in the blood. And anyway, it's not a job for a woman . . ."

Claire had been sitting patiently, quietly listening. She had held her tongue at the priest's interference in a family matter, but at the final remark she could contain herself no longer:

"You!" she said, pointing her finger at the shocked priest. "You! Out!"

"And you!" she turned to her daughter. "Ignore the auld eejit!"

As it happened, Mary went to Queen's University Belfast rather than Trinity College Dublin, for reasons other than the preference of Fr Honorius—finance being the most important motive. The priest, who had never before experienced the sharp edge of an Ardoyne parishioner's tongue, gave the Leneghan house a wide berth for some time. In the month of June he was the celebrant at the wedding of Irish historian Jim O'Hara, a relation of Paddy's, and the Leneghans were present. When all the guests had gone on to the reception, Paddy discovered that Honorius had been left without a lift. He offered to bring him in his own car and the priest readily accepted. By the end of the evening the status quo had been re-established, and two months later Honorius invited Mary and her friend for a meal to celebrate the offer of a place in Queen's School of Law.

Chapter Six

A Spark Is Lit

They stirred up an unwelcome noise,
it set my nerves on edge,
the day they beat those boys and girls
across Burntollet Bridge,

with journalists and cameras there
to send in their reports.
The world no longer seems to care
for healthy country sports.

(John Hewitt: "An Ulster Landowner's Song")

Life was changing at an amazing pace for young people in Ireland in the 1960s. Like many young Catholics, Mary found she had to come to terms with new ways of viewing the world. Old certainties had to be questioned and opinions re-examined. Attitudes towards the role of women, the authority of the Church, authority in general, sexuality, personal responsibility—all had to be re-assessed. Mary says that, unlike many of her contemporaries, the changing times and attitudes were not in the least traumatic for her, as the values of flexibility and openness to change had been instilled in her from an early age.

One area of life in Northern Ireland was changing out of all recognition in the 1960s, particularly towards the end of the decade. It was an aspect that had its roots in the inequality that was of the very essence of the Northern state. After the War of Independence and the signing of the Anglo-Irish Treaty in December 1921, a boundary commission was set up. Their brief was to draw a border separating the new Irish Free State from the part of Ireland that would remain in the United Kingdom. The state of Northern Ireland was established to put a Protestant/unionist government in power and to ensure that it would stay in power. Ironically, the Northern Irish unionists wanted, and were about to be granted, Home Rule—the very form of government they had long opposed. Professor Paul Bew of Queen's University, in a review of Alvin Jackson's book on Home Rule, remarks: "The defects of Home

Rule in Ulster mirrored precisely the critique that unionists had traditionally offered of the nationalist project. Who would protect the interests of minorities, unionists asked in the 19th century? Who, indeed, echoed northern nationalists, fed up with Stormont in the 20th?"[‡]

The founding of the state was a demographic compromise: unionists wanted the largest area of land that could be comfortably controlled by a Protestant majority, and this was deemed to be the six counties in the north-eastern corner of Ireland. The parliament of Northern Ireland was given control over all its own affairs, with three exceptions: minting money, conducting foreign affairs and raising an army. The new Northern government had a set of useful implements to ensure the efficient running of the state and to maintain control over the nationalist population: emergency legislation on a permanent basis,[§] an armed constabulary which was 90 per cent Protestant, and the auxiliary paramilitary Ulster Special Constabulary which was 100 per cent Protestant.[†]

Mary says that when she wrote to seek membership of the Communist Party she did so because of her frustration at the hypocrisy surrounding her: that the political status quo in the North was doing nothing to redress inequities which were blatantly obvious. It is clear that as a teenager she was very politically aware, but she was no exception. Politics, or lack of political action, impinged seriously on the lives of most young nationalists in those days.

They knew that they were unlikely to have a vote in local elections when they reached voting age, if they still lived in the family home. The government allowed only two votes per household, but special extra votes were granted to owners of businesses that had a rateable value of £10 per annum or more: a vote per £10. Catholics traditionally had the larger families and, consequently, many more Catholics than Protestants were disenfranchised. At the same time, Protestants owned 90 per cent of Northern Ireland businesses, some of which allowed their owners up to forty votes. John Hume researched the voting power of Sir Basil McFarland, who was Mayor of Derry in the 1960s and who owned seven companies, each of which was worth six votes. Including his own vote

---

[‡] *The Sunday Times*, 15 June 2003.

[§] The infamous Special Powers Act was the cornerstone of this legislation.

[†] Three units of Special Constabulary—A, B and C—were set up in 1920 by the British administration in Ireland. A and C were disbanded in 1925, but the B-Specials continued until the Hunt Report recommended their disbandment in 1970.

as a householder, he controlled forty-three votes—a potent reason for the nationalist rallying cry of "One Man, One Vote" in the sixties.

Under the Flags and Emblems Act, the police had the authority to enter any place, public or private, to remove a flag or emblem that they considered offensive or prejudicial to good order. These powers were only ever used to remove the Irish flag or nationalist symbols—a constant source of grievance to the nationalist population. Under the same act it was an offence to interfere with the British flag. The implementation of the act was the cause of considerable unrest on the Falls Road in Belfast in 1966, during celebrations to mark the fiftieth anniversary of the Easter Rising.

In the area of public housing allocation, there was blatant discrimination in favour of Protestants. In an attempt to focus attention on this inequity, Austin Currie, a member of the Stormont parliament at the time, led a group of civil rights supporters in the occupation of a house in Caledon, County Tyrone, in June 1968. The local council had allocated the house to Emily Beatty, a nineteen-year-old single Protestant woman with no children. Currie revealed that she was the secretary to a local unionist politician and had been given the house while many Catholic families with small children, who had been on the housing list for years, remained unhoused. To Mary, who was seventeen at the time, Austin Currie was a hero. While others talked he led the occupation of a house and drew the attention of the world press to the injustices of the system. At last there was action.

Gerrymandering was widespread in Northern Ireland.‡ The wards, or electoral areas, were set up in such a way that unionists always had a majority on town and city councils. In Derry, for example, even though two thirds of the population were nationalists, most of them lived in one electoral area, the South Ward, with eight councillors on Derry Corporation. The remaining one third of the population, who were unionists, were divided between the North Ward and the Waterside Ward, each with six councillors. Thus there was always a unionist majority of four on Derry Corporation. The electoral divisions in all towns in the North where there was a nationalist majority were arranged in such a way as to afford a council majority to a unionist minority.

---

‡ Gerrymandering gets its name from Elbridge Gerry who, when governor of Massachusetts in 1812, rearranged the boundaries of a congressional district for political purposes. A map of the redesigned district was said to resemble a salamander, hence Gerry + mander.

Northern Ireland was not the only place to have blatant injustices. Mary and her friends empathised with the civil rights movement in the United States. They were moved by the protest songs of the era sung by Joan Baez and Bob Dylan. The young people read with horror about "Birmingham Sunday" in Alabama and with pride about the marches of Martin Luther King. The civil rights movement seemed to be unstoppable in the States, and people began to question why a similar movement was not active in Northern Ireland. This questioning of the lack of civil liberties and equality really began around the time of President John F. Kennedy's famous visit to Ireland in 1963. JFK was a hero to most Catholic people in Ireland: the first Catholic American president and a man of Irish ancestry. For these reasons, and because of his work for civil rights, the Leneghans, in common with most Irish Catholic families, had a tremendous respect and admiration for him. The fondness was also extended to the pope of the day, and many families had pictures of JFK and Pope John XXIII on their sitting room walls and treated both men as uncanonised saints.

In the last years of the 1960s the world outside Northern Ireland seemed to be changing out of all recognition. The assassination of JFK was followed a few years later by the murder of his brother Robert. Martin Luther King, the champion of civil rights activists all over the world, was gunned down on a hotel balcony in Memphis, Tennessee. Mary saw the tide turning in Vietnam, firstly with the reports of the massacre at My Lai and then with the increasing amount of America-bound body bags signalling that all was not well with the military campaign of the world's great super power. She and her friends saw France teetering on the brink of another revolution, learned to pronounce the name Chappaquiddick, heard the fallout after the f*** word was spoken for the first time on BBC and cheered when Dr Christian Barnard of South Africa transplanted the first human heart. People were entranced by *MASH* and appalled by *Rosemary's Baby*. Fassbinder declared that *Love Is Colder Than Death*, and Mary and her friends and the world and its mother were singing "Hey, Jude".

In Northern Ireland, described by P.J. O'Rourke as "that piece of Ireland that passeth all understanding", nothing much had changed.[†] Mary's chosen field of study, the law, was biased strongly against Catholics and had very few women. In 1966 there were seventy-four positions in the judicial system, of which only six were occupied by

---

† P.J. O'Rourke, *Holidays in Hell* (London: Picador, 1989).

Catholics. Even though several women had qualified as barristers over the years, none of them was practising by the time Mary qualified. She had a long and difficult furrow to plough if she were to achieve her ambition to qualify as a barrister-at-law.

After the economic bleakness and widespread unemployment of the 1950s, the economy in Northern Ireland had improved considerably during the "Swinging Sixties".‡ In the areas of health and education, extra money was allocated by the British government to train more doctors, health workers and teachers. The pupil-teacher ratio and the standards required of teachers were improved in Catholic schools.

One of the results of these changes was a new generation of young nationalists who were well educated, who understood and resented their lack of civil rights and equal opportunity and who recognised the corrupt political system under which they lived for what it was. Mary Leneghan was one of these people: one member of a generation filled with righteous indignation and the educational advantages and energy to do something about it. All over the North the educated nationalists were on the move. Dr Con McCluskey and his wife Patricia had founded the Campaign for Civil Liberties in Dungannon in January 1964 "to collect data on all injustices done against all creeds and political opinions". As a direct result of that campaign, the Northern Ireland Civil Rights Association (NICRA) was founded on 1 February 1967, and Noel Harris was elected as its first chairman. That same year the Derry Housing Action Committee was born, and a young man called John Hume became its first chairman.

Gerry Fitt, at that time a member of parliament in Westminster for the Republican Labour Party, spent a lot of time and energy bringing the plight of nationalists in Northern Ireland to the attention of Labour Party MPs in England. There was a group of like-minded people on the ground in the North, people who recognised that whingeing and complaining were getting them nowhere and who wanted to take their protests on to the streets. There were university people like Bernadette Devlin, Rory McShane, Ronnie Bunting, Eamonn McCann, Michael Farrell and Kevin Boyle. Among the local politicians who were ready to take up the banners were John Hume, Austin Currie, Ivan Cooper,

---

‡ Between the middle of the 1950s and the middle of the 1960s, 230 new companies were set up and 200 more experienced economic expansion. Many more jobs were created when American, English and Continental European firms were attracted to Northern Ireland. There was a significant increase in the number of multinational corporations: from seven in 1958 to twenty-seven in 1968.

Paddy O'Hanlon and Paddy Devlin. When nationalists of the calibre of these people decided it was time to stand together to address their grievances, the spark was well and truly lit in the powder keg.

Some historians say that the "Troubles" in Northern Ireland started properly on the 5 October 1968 when Eamonn McCann organised a Northern Ireland Civil Rights Association march in Derry in support of the Derry Housing Action Campaign. The demonstration went ahead despite being banned by William Craig, minister of home affairs in the Stormont government. The RUC attacked the marchers, among whom were Gerry Fitt and three Labour Party MPs from England. RTÉ filmed the violence, and it was shown all over the world. Apart from the riots that lasted for two days and two nights, there was another significant consequence of the march. Four days later, two thousand students came together to march from the Queen's University Belfast to the City Hall to protest against the behaviour of the RUC in Derry. A counter-demonstration under the leadership of Ian Paisley blocked the march, and the students sat on the road for three hours before returning to Queen's. That evening the People's Democracy was founded. Although Mary was still in secondary school she joined the PD. It was a significant force in the struggle for civil rights. As a party well to the left of centre, it fielded candidates in Northern elections until 1982, and Bernadette Devlin and Michael Farrell were two of its best-known leaders.

Within three months of its founding, all the world knew about the People's Democracy as it was the PD who organised the famous march from Belfast to Derry which started on New Year's Day 1969 and climaxed at Burntollet Bridge. It lasted four days and was modelled on Martin Luther King's March on Washington, the one made famous by his "I Have a Dream" speech. Forty people started out on the first stage of the march from Belfast to Antrim. On the second day they walked to Maghera and were joined by many more people. By the third day, as they approached Claudy, there were more than three hundred people marching.

On the fourth day, just as they reached the bridge at Burntollet, seven miles from Derry, the marchers were attacked by a crowd of 200 loyalists and several off-duty B-Specials. Each time the students tried to escape into the fields or into the river, the RUC beat them back with batons on to the road and into the hail of rocks and bottles coming from the loyalists on the high ground by the roadside.

Mary sat at home frustratedly watching the attack on the television news that evening, nursing a sprained ankle. Her mother says she was lucky to be unable to walk as it saved her banning her daughter from joining the marchers. It was one of the few marches she missed. As a member of PD and NICRA she carried placards on many occasions, often when demonstrations were attacked. Although she never had a leading role in either of these organisations, she was vocal enough as a member. On one memorable occasion she spoke strongly against a PD motion to stage a demonstration in Dublin in protest at what was seen as lack of southern support for the civil rights movement. She felt there was more important and more urgent work to be done in the Six Counties. Those early days of the civil rights movement were momentous days for everyone, not least for the future President of Ireland. It was hard for her to accept how blatantly partisan the forces of law and order were, and how little they cared who knew it.

She says of the marches, "It was a frightening thing for a young person who was brought up to respect law and order to find out that, where I lived, the only law was unionist law and the only order was unionist order."

Chapter Seven

The Crucible

> The night-sky red, crackle and roar of flame,
> the barricades across the ruined street,
> the thump of stones, the shots, the thudding feet;
> as mob greets mob with claim and counterclaim,
> each blames the other, none accepts the blame,
> for fears entrenched will not permit retreat,
> when creed and creed inhospitably meet,
> and each child's fate's foreshadowed in its name.
>
> (John Hewitt: "In This Year of Grace")

Mary's first real understanding of the one-sidedness of the forces of law and order was on that horrific evening, 14 August 1969, when she stood at the top of Ardoyne watching the genesis of thirty years of Troubles. When she reached home that night, both she and her family were distraught from the horror of the events they had witnessed. Her frustration was mirrored in the faces of her mother and father. In all of them there was also a fear left unspoken: how long before their own house came under threat?

In the morning Mary went down the road. Smoke still rose from the remains of the burnt houses and the makeshift barricades. The people she met were stunned, traumatised, unable to come to terms with the terror of it all. Where would all this end? Coming towards her on the road was Fr Honorius, his arms outspread in a typically dramatic gesture.

"We were fiddling while Ardoyne burned, Mary," said the priest, who had not slept, but had spent the night on the streets tending the wounded and the dying. All the talk was of Hooker Street, of the houses that were destroyed there and the injuries inflicted on the residents.

Mary's friend Catherine Kane lived in Hooker Street. She began to run. As she reached the corner of the street she saw that the Kane house was one of the few left standing. She spent that Friday morning in Catherine's house, making cups of tea and plans for a family that were going about the business of packing as if they were sleepwalking. Early in the afternoon, the Kanes joined many other families leaving the area and making their way up the Falls Road where the charitable organisation Shelter had brought in some caravans as emergency housing for those who were dispossessed or afraid to go back to their own areas. Those who had no relations in safe areas, or who were unable to find temporary accommodation, found refuge in school halls, parish halls and classrooms, where lines of mattresses were laid out on floors. The scene on the Falls Road that day was reminiscent of film footage of the Jews entering the Warsaw ghetto. Mary accompanied the Kanes up the road, passing groups of people pushing prams and handcarts loaded down with bits of furniture and salvaged possessions. The survivors of Bombay Street and Clonard joined those from Ardoyne and the Lower Falls, all making for the biggest, and by definition the safest, ghetto of them all—Andersonstown. All over West and North Belfast people were helping people they did not know. Blankets, sheets, pillows and clothes were handed out to total strangers in the knowledge that they would never be seen again. It didn't matter. The nationalist population of Belfast was terrified, particularly those who lived in fringe areas.

The Leneghan house was on the fringe of Ardoyne. Mary and her family were as happy as anyone else when it was announced that British troops were being deployed on the streets of Belfast and Derry. James Callaghan, the British minister for home affairs, was travelling in a Royal Air Force plane when he was handed a radio message requesting the deployment of British troops. He wrote himself into the history of Ireland by scribbling the words "permission granted" on the back of the scrap of paper. Within hours, thousands of British soldiers were on their way to the towns and cities of Northern Ireland. They were under the command of Lieutenant General Ian Freeland, who had taken up duties as GOCNI just a month previously. The troops were arriving just in time. Many more houses were burnt that night, two more people were killed and hundreds injured.

As the politicians were planning to put British troops on the streets of Belfast, Paddy Leneghan was planning to move his family out of the city. Anyone who had lived on "the wrong side" of the Crumlin Road was now gone. The road itself, from Flax Street to the chapel, was like a no-man's-land, littered with broken glass and stones, the result of intermittent forays by both sides into "enemy territory". Any shop or pub that had not been burnt was boarded up, the stock long since removed for fear of looting. Day and night the people's nerves were stretched to breaking point by the sounds of gunshots, breaking glass and petrol bombs. In Ardoyne, disorder had surrendered to anarchy. The report of the British Law Lord Leslie Scarman into the occurrences of those few days later stated, "The police, plagued by fatigue, casualties and rumour, had by the morning of August 15 abandoned the effort to maintain or re-establish law and order in the area of the Crumlin Road."[‡]

The panic affected everyone. On one occasion, after a group of loyalists had forced their way into the area, Mary ran up the road, past her father and into her house. She made straight for the kitchen where she collected an armful of milk bottles. She had seen petrol bombs being made and knew what was needed to make an effective weapon: a milk bottle, some petrol and a piece of cloth as a stopper and fuse. As she was carrying the bottles out of the house her father stopped her.

"Where are you going with those milk bottles?" asked Paddy.

"I'm going down the road to make petrol bombs," said his daughter.

"Put those bottles back where you got them," said Paddy, in a voice that could cut stone. "I did not raise a rabble!"

Mary says she was stopped in her tracks by the statement and by the passion in her father's voice. She says she was rooted to the floor as she fought down her anger and frustration and considered the implications of what he had just said. As she walked to the kitchen to return the bottles, she was turning her back on more than the front door. She never made a petrol bomb and never threw one, although there was many a quiet, good-living, peace-loving family within two hundred yards of the Leneghans who thought of the petrol bombs that sat each night inside their front door as the only protection they had.

The Leneghans, like most of the families around them, were sure that the trouble would not last very long. No one was prepared for the new reality: explosions and gunfire, arson and destruction, gas and rubber bullets, injury and murder. During those days in mid-August, more than 1,500 Catholics homes and 300 Protestant homes were burned or deserted in Belfast. Ten people were killed and 745 seriously injured, 154 of them with gunshot wounds. Most of the shooting happened in the Ardoyne area. If this was to be the new reality, then Paddy Leneghan was not prepared to let his family live with it. Mary's episode with the milk bottles only strengthened his determination. He packed the family and as many personal belongings as they could fit, into the car and set

---

‡   McKittrick *et al.*, *Lost Lives*, p. 40.

off for Dublin. Nora was the only Leneghan who stayed behind. She was working on a production with the Young Lyric Players and insisted that she wanted to remain in Belfast.

A couple of days after the Leneghans left Belfast, Paddy's pub was chosen as headquarters for the first of the many local defence committees which would soon spring up throughout the city. Paddy Devlin spoke of it in his autobiography, *Straight Left:* "The Long Bar in Leeson Street, run by a very friendly man called Paddy Leneghan, had been taken over as an unofficial headquarters by this new leadership. I felt it was important to get these citizens' defence committees under some sort of organised control. The committees had been set up by local priests like Canon Pádraig Murphy as well as local businessmen like Tom Conaty."‡

Before August was very much older, the Leneghans left it all behind them. As they left Belfast to drive to Dublin, they didn't know if they would ever see their home again. Mary, without Nora, was the inter-generational buffer, sharing the concerns and fears of her parents and trying to make the whole traumatic leave-taking seem like a great adventure to the children. After a couple of phone calls, Paddy found a suitable house to rent on Kilmacud Road in the south of the city. He and Claire had some money saved for "a rainy day", and now that the deluge had started in earnest, they were prepared to spend whatever was necessary. If the money ran out, they would to go to Roscommon and stay with Paddy's people for the duration. As it happened, they stayed in Dublin for a month, astounded at first and then offended by the lack of interest all around them in what was happening just up the road. Mary was more than offended by this strange North-South fissure, the elective deafness at the mention of Belfast. The arm's length attitude left her livid.

As a member of the National Committee of the Society of St Vincent de Paul, Mary knew the senior members in Dublin. She went to see the president of the organisation to bring him up to date, face to face, on conditions in the North. She says she did not get much of a hearing, so she contacted two of her friends on the National Committee, Bob and Bill Cashman. When she still had no success in persuading the committee to view the situation north of the border as a humanitarian crisis, she wrote a critical letter, reproving them strongly for doing too little, too late. Although she remained friendly with Bill and Bob

---

‡ Paddy Devlin, *Straight Left* (Belfast: Blackstaff, 1993), p. 110.

Cashman, she lost some heart in the organisation over what she saw as its slowness to get fully involved.

When the Leneghans moved back home in the middle of September, Ardoyne was a much quieter place. A mile and a half of "Peace Lines" had been built in Belfast by British army engineers to keep citizens from either side of the political fence away from each other. Nationalist hunger for justice was assuaged somewhat when RUC Inspector-General Anthony Peacocke announced that disciplinary action was to be taken against sixteen constables as a result of an inquiry into events at Burntollet and Derry on 4 and 5 January. To add to the sense of optimism, the report of the Cameron Commission, on 16 September, placed much of the blame for the August disturbances on the Stormont government and the RUC. On 22 September all barricades in Belfast were taken down. Normality looked as it if might be given a chance— and for a few short weeks a new routine of British army patrols did give peace a chance; but it was short-lived.

As the months passed, and the body count rose steadily, and the people of the North became more and more polarised, the area around the Leneghan house became one of the most dangerous and exposed places in Ardoyne—what came to be euphemistically termed an "interface area". Number 657 Crumlin Road is on the corner of Hesketh Road, which runs into the Protestant Glenbryn estate. In the year 2001 the world saw how people from that estate treated the children of Holy Cross Girls' Primary School as their parents tried to bring them to school each morning. Thirty years earlier, people from the same estate treated the Leneghans in a similar fashion.

One evening as Mary was driving home, she was within a couple of hundred yards of her house when she saw a girl being attacked by a group of young women. As she got closer she saw that the victim was her sister Kate, now lying on the ground being kicked by five residents of the Glenbryn estate. Knowing that her own intervention would make little difference, she drove on to her own house, got her sister Nora, and having rushed back down the road, managed to drive off the attackers. Kate was quite badly injured, but by far the greater damage was done to her confidence and her nerves. Paddy and Claire decided it was time to send her and two of her brothers to boarding school. Kate went to the St Louis Convent in Kilkeel, County Down, and Damien and Patrick went to St Colman's College in Newry. Mary, Nora and the younger children stayed at home.

Shortly before Kate left home, an incident happened which further damaged her already shattered nerves. It was a Saturday evening, and the wisps of CS gas from the rioting down the road were catching in Mary's throat as she stood in the garden of her home. Above the noise of the riot, Mary heard a scream of pain from her own house. When she ran inside she found Kate doubled up in agony on the floor, holding the lower part of her tummy. Groans and moans were punctuated with more screams as Mary tried to examine her sister. Appendicitis! Mary was certain of it. Neither of her parents was at home. She ran to the phone to call for an ambulance, but the phone was dead. The Mater Hospital was over a mile away, down the Crumlin Road. Mary carried her sister a lot of the way, keeping to the back streets where the main road was impassable, ducking into doorways as bottles broke around them and stones flew overhead, dropping flat on the ground each time a shot was fired. On Chatham Street, there were bowls of vinegar on some of the windowsills. The sisters plunged their handkerchiefs into the liquid and covered their mouths and noses as a protection against the gas. Kate was perfectly content with the tranquillity of the St Louis Convent in Kilkeel after these events.

Mary's brother John was profoundly deaf and needed special education. He had attended a pre-school for the deaf in Jordanstown, outside Belfast, before going to Mary Immaculate School in Stillorgan, in Dublin. He then returned to Belfast where he attended a special secondary school for the deaf, also in Jordanstown. In his teens he used to spend one or two evenings a week at a youth club in the National Institute for the Deaf in College Square, in the centre of Belfast, and was usually left home to his door by a kind Protestant minister. On this particular night, the minister was not there and John took a bus up the Crumlin Road. The bus stop was almost opposite the Leneghan house, on the other side of the road. John had only to cross the road and he was home.

He was sixteen years old and innocent of the ways of the world. Alone in his silence, he heard nothing as the three men followed him. He heard nothing of their hurried planning, nor the scrape of their boots on the concrete as they rushed up behind him. He could never have dreamed that men would want to hurt him. There was a smile on his face as he approached the hall door, reliving the fun of the evening and looking forward to telling his family all about it. He saw only the shadow cast by the street lamp and three figures looming out of the darkness behind him, a bottle held high in the air. He turned, but it was too late. The bottle smashed across his head and split his skull. The men moved in on the defenceless boy, punching and kicking. The broken bottle was shoved into his face, cutting off a piece of his nose and some of his face.

Inside, Mary and the rest of the family were frozen with fear as they heard the screaming, the breaking of glass and the dull thuds as the blows rained down. They heard the thumping of the boots as the attackers ran away and the barely perceptible moaning from their doorstep. Mary ran to the door and pulled it open. At first she didn't recognise the pitiful figure that fell into the hallway, whose blood was now soaking into the carpet at her feet. She bent down to wipe the blood from the victim's face and only then recognised her own little brother.

He was rushed to hospital in an ambulance. John almost died that night. The doctors said he was very lucky to come through the ordeal. Mary was beside herself with anger and frustration. Although the RUC investigated the case and although John was able to name his attackers, no one was ever charged with the assault. The story has a tragic tag: one of the attackers named by John was convicted of the murder of a Catholic a few years after the assault.

Still seething because of the inadequacy of the system, Mary wrote an angry letter to the *Irish News*, demanding the return of corporal punishment for crimes of serious assault. She wanted the attackers whipped. Time soon healed her visceral need for such retribution, and it wasn't long before she recognised the letter writing for what it was and regretted seeking a form of punishment that went against much of what she later stood for.

John's nerves were never the same after that assault, and it was a long time before he was prepared to go outside his front door again. Paddy and Claire were unsure of what to do. They considered sending him to England, where he could continue his training as a hairdresser and where life would surely be safer. Some time afterwards, when they were living in the west of the city, two other incidents made them absolutely certain that Belfast was no place for a young man who was both deaf and justifiably exceptionally nervous.

One evening he was walking past a squad of British soldiers who had just erected a temporary traffic roadblock near his home. When they called on him to stop, he, of course, didn't hear them and continued walking past. Eyewitnesses later said that the soldiers ran after him, knocked him down with their rifle butts and proceeded to beat him while he was on the ground. Eventually, when they discovered the reason why he had not stopped, they allowed him to continue, but he was quite badly hurt. Paddy and Claire complained to the commanding officer in the local barracks. The following day a major arrived at the Leneghan house to apologise to John and to issue him with a special pass, signed by himself, which he was to show at roadblocks in future.

The following Saturday, as he was making his way home, another roadblock was erected in the same spot. This time he knew what to do: he watched the face of the nearest soldier very carefully, waiting for him to speak. John was an expert lip-reader, but the soldier's heavy Scottish accent defeated him. He walked towards the soldier and put his hand in his jacket pocket for his pass, but no sooner had his hand gone inside his coat than the soldier hit him with his rifle. A few other soldiers came to the assistance of their comrade, and John was once more battered to the ground. Eventually the pass was discovered, but the soldiers claimed they thought he was putting his hand inside his coat to pull out a pistol.

The year 1972 was a bad one for the Leneghan family and for many families in Ireland. It started with Bloody Sunday. On the 30 January, soldiers from the British army's First Parachute Regiment shot dead thirteen civil rights marchers in Derry. Another died a short time later from wounds received on the day. Just as Lord Justice Scarman, having listened to 440 witnesses over 168 days, painted an unrecognisable picture of the events of August 1969, so Lord Justice Widgery gave a totally erroneous account of the tragic events in Derry on Bloody Sunday. He was helped in his conclusion that many of the people who were killed on that day had handled arms, or had been beside people who had fired guns, by the testimony of one Dr John Martin. When the same Dr Martin was being cross-questioned by Christopher Clark in 2002, at Lord Saville's inquiry into the same events, he admitted that he had been mistaken.[‡]

It was a terrible start to the bloodiest year of the Troubles. By Christmas 496 people had been killed: 258 civilians, 134 soldiers, seventeen members of the RUC and two RUC reservists, seventy-four Republican paramilitaries and eleven loyalists paramilitaries. They were killed in all parts of Ireland and abroad. Two people were murdered in Dublin and seven in Aldershot, in England. Bombs exploded north, south, east and west. No place in the North was safe, and no place in Ireland suffered more than Ardoyne. That year, as in every year of the Troubles, Mary's home parish was at the top of every list of murders and tragedies. In the year 1999, when accounts of all murders in Northern Ireland since 1969 were gathered, it was discovered that 20 per cent of them were committed in that one little area.

---

‡   *The Irish Times*, 4 September 2002.

The worst of all those years was undoubtedly 1972: Bloody Sunday, Claudy, the Newry Customs Office, the Abercorn, Bloody Friday . . . It was the year the first person was killed by a rubber bullet, the year the one hundredth British soldier was killed, the year the IRA exploded twenty-three bombs in one day. It was the year of "Operation Motorman", when the British army went into the "no go areas", as they were called. By the start of the year the security situation was so bad that Brian Faulkner, then prime minister of Northern Ireland, declared a ban on all parades and marches of any kind. On 18 March, William Craig, former minister for home affairs in the Stormont government, made his famous speech at a Vanguard rally in Belfast's Ormeau Park, a speech which included the words "We must build up the dossiers on the men and women who are a menace to this country, because one day, ladies and gentlemen, if the politicians fail, it will be our duty to liquidate the enemy."[‡]

It was the year that a British Tory government under Edward Heath prorogued Stormont. The Northern Ireland (Temporary Provisions) Act dismissed the Northern government and brought Northern Ireland under the direct rule of Westminster. The elected representatives in the North, being left with very few powers beyond the administration of waste disposal, graveyards and public toilets, were quickly dubbed "the ministers for bins, bogs and burials". William Whitelaw was appointed the first secretary of state for Northern Ireland. Vanguard organised strikes throughout the North in protest against the prorogation of Stormont. Some unionist politicians began to talk seriously about the possibility of a unilateral declaration of independence à la Ian Smith in Rhodesia.[§] By the month of July the North was in a shambles. Over one hundred people were killed that month, the majority of them in North Belfast, and most of those in Ardoyne.

Halloween fell on a Tuesday that year. On the Saturday before Halloween, all the Leneghans except Paddy, who was working in the Long Bar, were having a cosy night at home. Those at boarding school were at home for the mid-term break. Patrick had got special permission to stay up late to watch *Match of the Day*. When the match was over he

---

[‡] The Ulster Vanguard movement was essentially a political pressure group within unionism. Among its leaders were the Revd Martin Smyth and Captain Austin Ardill. Other members included David Trimble and Reg Empey. Ulster Vanguard had its own paramilitary group: the Vanguard Service Corps.

[§] Seven years earlier, on 11 November 1965, Ian Smith, then Prime Minister of Rhodesia, declared UDI after talks between himself and Harold Wilson broke down.

wished everyone good night and off he went up the stairs to bed. He was halfway up when everyone heard the loud cracks. Claire thought he had fallen down the stairs and was out of her seat and heading for the hallway when she heard him shout, "There's a crowd outside our house and they're breaking the pavement!"

Before he had finished the sentence, one of the pieces of pavement came through the front window, showering those on the sofa with broken glass. The whole family went down on the floor, some crawling behind chairs and others under the table. Nora jumped up and went through the hallway into the dining room. As she passed the front door, the glass from its windows exploded into the hallway. Young Claire crept over the broken glass on her hands and knees into the dining room to make sure Nora was all right. Now that both of them were together, they decided to open the venetian blinds a little and look out. They saw what Patrick had seen from the landing window: an enraged mob of men and women breaking pieces of paving slabs and throwing them at the windows, shouting and screaming at the top of their voices, "Fenian bastards! We'll burn you out!"

Kate stood up and screamed and screamed and screamed. Nora left her there screaming, and she and John tore the shelves out of the press in the hallway and nailed them across the broken panes in the front door. Damien had both the common sense and the composure to go to the fuse box and plunge the house into darkness. During all this Mary was frozen with terror, the only time in her life, she says, that she was mentally paralysed. She sat on the floor, amazed at the courage, the improvisation and the unruffled leadership around her. Damien, at fourteen years of age, was giving the orders. Nora, imperturbable in the midst of chaos, had taken the phone off the wall in the hall and stretched the cable around the corner so that the RUC could be called from the relative safety of the dining room floor. In her semi-comatose state, Mary saw Patrick and Damien making for the door with two hurleys, with the obvious intention of scattering the mob. This was enough to rouse her from her stupor. She jumped up, stretched out her foot and tripped them. She grabbed them, pulled them back into the sitting room and held them until her mother had the opportunity to talk sense into them.

Nora called Mary into the dining room, shoved the phone into her hand and told her to ring 999 again. Eventually Mary got through to the RUC but was told she would have to wait. Again and again she called them, through what seemed like an eternity. Each time she got the same answer: "We'll have a patrol there as soon as we can. We're very busy tonight."

By this time every window in the house was broken and the family was scared witless. Gradually a hush fell in the house, and they realised there was no more noise coming from the road: no stones, no broken glass, not so much as a malevolent shriek. Mary chanced a peep through the blinds and saw that the crowd had disappeared. She also saw a strange white car on the far side of the Crumlin Road. After a few minutes the car moved away, but came back several times during the night.

The phone rang. Claire grabbed it, certain it would be the RUC on the line, but it was Paddy calling from the Long Bar.

"Is everything all right there?" he asked his wife.

"Yes. Of course. Why wouldn't it be?" she replied, trying not to worry Paddy. With the mob now gone there was no need for him to know until he came home.

"I know everything's not all right. Now, tell me what's wrong!"

"How do you know whether everything's all right or not?" she replied, trying to keep the emotional catch in her voice from betraying her.

"A man came into the bar just a minute ago to tell me there was an attack on 657 Crumlin Road," said Paddy. "He heard it on the RUC frequency on one of those radios. Now, will you for God's sake tell me what's happening!"

Mary understood that members of the IRA were regular listeners to the radio frequency used by RUC patrols. She was told afterwards that the white car that parked opposite their house contained an armed IRA unit. In the light of the arrival of an RUC patrol three hours after the attack, with the words "We believe you have a complaint," Mary says she has no option but to admit, however reluctantly, that the only protection her family had that night was from the IRA.

The fact that he had to leave his family every evening to go to work preyed on Paddy's mind. He usually came home very late, and often he did not reach home at all. His efforts to reach the Crumlin Road in the early hours of the morning were often thwarted by roadblocks, barricades, riots and shooting. On nights such as these, he usually stayed with his first cousin May Fitzpatrick, a daughter of Mrs Cassidy, who had a house in Beechmount, just a mile up the Falls Road from the Long Bar. She had given him a key to her door and told him to let himself in any night he couldn't get home. However, after the attack, he could not imagine himself living with the worry of being unable to get home to his family at night. He and Claire made up their minds. They would not stay another night in that house on the Crumlin Road until the security situation around Ardoyne improved dramatically.

Claire's sister Una McManus had a house in Whiteabbey, near Glengormley. It was arranged that Claire and the children would stay with Una and that Paddy would stay with his cousin May in Beechmount. Each morning Paddy would drive across the city, have breakfast in Una's with the family and bring the boys to the Christian Brothers' School. Claire would bring the girls to the Mercy Convent School and then drive on to the house in Ardoyne. The children would go home from school to 657 Crumlin Road, where they would have their dinner, do their homework and then, as darkness fell, they would all go to Una's house for the night. Mary had moved into a flat in 100 Wellesley Avenue with her friends Margaret and Pat Campbell from Tandragee, County Armagh, during this period.

The constant to-ing and fro-ing through the heavy traffic and the bad weather of late autumn and early winter was very wearing, and on many occasions the Leneghans were tempted to stay overnight in Ardoyne. The appeal of their own house was never stronger than on the evening of 7 December, nearly six weeks after the attack. There was a rainstorm that day and darkness had fallen early. Everyone in the house had a cold and the children were all irritable. Claire thought of lighting a big fire in the sitting room, putting hot water bottles in the beds, baking something nice for the children's supper and letting them spend a night in their own cosy home. The next day was the Feast of the Immaculate Conception, a free day from school, and the whole family would be back in Ardoyne for ten o'clock mass anyway. The thought of having to wrap up the children, go out in the torrential rain, fight her was through the traffic across the city and try to get them warm and settled again in their aunt's house was almost too much to bear. Claire was between two minds. Her resolve was slipping. At last the allure of her own home became too strong, and she rang her sister Una and told her not to expect them that night.

No sooner had she put down the phone than Mary rang. She was going to a party in Queen's University that night and wanted Nora to go with her. When she heard her mother's plan to stay in the house, she implored her to change her mind. Party or no party, if the family was staying in the house Mary would come home. Nora arrived in just then, and when she heard her mother's decision, she lent her voice to Mary's.

She was adamant that she wouldn't go a party and leave her mother and the children in the house overnight. When Paddy came home for his dinner he listened patiently to all opinions, and then, very quietly, but very firmly, he laid down the law: no one would stay in the house. Nora would take Claire's car and join Mary at the party in Queen's, and he would drive Claire and the children to Aunt Una's. He would take no chances.

Nora went off in Claire's little Mini to join Mary. Claire went around making sure that lights were left on here and there so that people would think the house was still occupied. Everyone then piled into Paddy's green Renault 16. As Paddy was getting into the car, he noticed another green Renault 16, exactly like his own, parked directly behind him.

"Who owns that car like our one?" he asked Claire. She told him it belonged to a friend of the girl next door.

"Well, he shouldn't be parking it at our gate," said Paddy. "There's plenty of space for him down the street."

Next morning, after ten o'clock mass, the family went back to 657 for breakfast. As he parked the car outside the house, Paddy noticed several shiny metal objects on the road and the footpath, glistening in the winter sunshine. Then he looked up at the house itself. All looked normal; all the downstairs windows were in one piece. He raised his eyes. Every upstairs window was smashed and the ragged remains of the curtains were flapping through the jagged holes. His mind was slow to take it all in. As he bent to retrieve one of the metal objects, he realised that they were spent bullet cases. Still in shock he picked up twenty-three of them as he made his way into the house to phone the police.

Mary and Nora arrived soon afterwards. It was immediately clear to both of them what had happened. Paddy and Claire recall Mary shouting, "We're leaving this place now and we're never coming back!"

This time the RUC and the British army were not long coming. As they accompanied the adults through the upstairs rooms, they saw bullet holes in every wall and ceiling, every door and wardrobe. But the thing that frightened the family more than anything else was the fact that the bedclothes and mattresses on every bed had been shredded. Nora's bed in particular was "like a colander", as Mary described it. How did the attackers manage to put bullets through the beds if they were shooting from the road outside?

A British officer explained: one machine-gunner had fired from the road and another from the upstairs of an empty house across the road, the one in which the Revd Wynne had lived and which was situated higher than their own house. It was clear to everyone that this was an attempted mass murder; that the attackers had thought the green Renault 16 at the gate was Paddy's. Because the lights were lit on the landing and in the bathroom, the attackers thought the Leneghans were at home and asleep in their beds. The relief at their narrow escape was counterbalanced by the horror of it all. The whole family was in a state of shock, holding on to each other for support, the children crying and the adults trying to comfort them. Standing together in the bullet-riddled main bedroom, they had to keep reminding themselves, and each other, that at least they were all safe. But Mary knew this was the end of an era. The people who had planned and executed the attack had not succeeded in killing any of them, but they had driven them out of Ardoyne, out of a home where they had known happiness and contentment, and they had killed something special in the Leneghan family.

In the middle of it all Paddy needed a cigarette. There were soldiers and police personnel all over the house, in every room and in the front and back gardens. Paddy pushed his way through them, out to his car where he had left the cigarettes. Three RUC men were standing beside the car, and as Paddy closed the car door to go back into the house, one of them spoke to him:

"Excuse me, Mr Leneghan. Do you realise that the tax on your car is out of date since the first of December?"

"What did you just say to me?" stuttered Paddy. He could not believe what he was hearing. "What did you say?"

"I said the tax disc on this car is out of date," replied the policeman.

Paddy turned and shouted to a British army officer who was standing in the garden taking notes: "Hey! Come her a minute till you hear this!"

Then he turned again to the RUC man: "Would you mind repeating to this soldier what you just said to me?"

"All I said," replied the policeman, "was that your tax disc has expired since the first of the month."

Paddy turned again to the British officer.

"Maybe this will give you some idea why you fellas have been sent over here from England. With the likes of this bastard of an RUC man supposed to be protecting us, what chance do we have? He's here to investigate an attempt to murder us in our beds, and all that's worrying that bastard is the fact that my car tax is a few days overdue. Do you see now what we have to put up with?"

Paddy admits that he came very close to hitting that policeman.

Gradually the extent of the horror was coming home to him. He says he spent the morning thanking God for the good sense everyone showed when making the decision the night before. But what were they to do now? An emergency meeting was called, and he and Claire, Nora and Mary gathered together in the sitting room. One thing was certain: they could not come back to 657 Crumlin Road. Christmas was coming and they had no house. Until another house could be found in a suitable location, the current lodging arrangements were to continue, with one exception: no one would be coming back to 657 after school. They were finished with it.

They needed a house, one that would be big enough for a family of eleven and in a safe location, and that ruled out Ardoyne. Paddy heard that the Bon Secours sisters had bought a large house in Fruithill Park, in Andersonstown, with a view to demolishing it and building a nursing home on the site. They had bought the house from the Benner family, the fruit importers, and it had been unoccupied for some time. Now the nuns were having difficulties with planning permission and the house was still vacant. The Leneghans could rent it until the planning difficulties were resolved.

Fruithill Park runs between the Andersonstown Road, which is an extension of the Falls Road, to the Glen Road. It is like a hilly corridor of old upper-middle-class respectability between the Andersonstown estate on one side and Kennedy Way on the other. It is a beautiful road with lovely old detached and semi-detached houses set in large mature gardens. Two hundred yards from the bottom of the road is Casement Park, the GAA stadium, with Fruithill Tennis Club and Fruithill Bowling Club in between.

Number 20, the property offered to the Leneghans, had a huge jungle of a back garden, more than an acre which, as well as plenty of trees and shrubs, also contained an old World War II bomb shelter and a tunnel running between it and the house. The garden, which backed on to the Andersonstown estate, had long been used as a playground by the children of the estate and as a short cut to the Falls Road. However it also had more sinister uses. On the day after the Leneghans escaped the attempt to murder them, a patrol of the King's Own Scottish Borderers Regiment came through this garden and decided to search the old bomb shelter. They discovered the tail of a rocket, complete with fins, and rather than calling in the bomb squad to defuse it on the spot, they decided to bring it with them to their base in Fort Monagh, near the top of Fruithill Park. The next morning, as some soldiers were examining the device and holding it as they posed for photographs, it exploded. Colour Sergeant Henry Stewart Middlemass was killed and two others were seriously injured, one of them losing the sight of both eyes. It was thought at the time that the weapon was booby-trapped, but it was later revealed to be part of a faulty old rocket of English manufacture, one that the IRA had dumped in the Blitz shelter, despite the fact that the place was a known playground.

In an ironic twist to this story, the first the family heard of this incident was when Mary was practising as a barrister in Belfast. One of the first cases she was given was the civil suit taken by the families of the two soldiers who were injured. Only then did she realise that the rocket part had been found in their own garden. She was incensed. She still speaks angrily of the people who left a lethal weapon in a place where children played. She is convinced that if the British army patrol had not found the device it would have killed or maimed one or more of her own brothers or sisters.

On Sunday, 17 December 1972, the Leneghans were ready to move into their new temporary accommodation. Paddy went back to Ardoyne to collect the post from the old house. He paid a brief visit to his aunt Nora McDrury for a cup of tea after mass and told her he was going up to the old house.

"Do you think that's wise?" asked Nora.

"It's lunchtime on Sunday," replied Paddy. "Nothing ever happens at lunchtime on Sunday."

When he reached the house he made some phone calls and was riffling through the post when someone knocked on the door. Paddy, being cautious enough not to open it without knowing who was there, went up to the landing window and looked out. When he discovered that the caller was his old friend and neighbour Charlie O'Hanlon, he invited him in and offered him a drink to toast their last time together in the house. As the two old friends drank and talked, they heard a few shots fired.

"They're at it again, Charlie!" said Paddy.

"Sure they never stop around here," replied his friend.

As they continued their conversation, they paid no heed to the next burst of gunfire, nor the one after that. After half an hour Charlie left and Paddy was finishing off the few jobs he had to do when the door was knocked on again, this time with a lot of force. Before he had a chance to go to the landing window, he heard the English accents and the squawk of static from the radio and knew that his new visitors were British soldiers. He opened the door.

"Are you Patrick Leneghan?" asked the officer.

"I am."

"How long have you been in the house today?"

"I've been here a couple of hours."

"Do you realise this house has come under fire three times in the last hour?" Paddy's mouth suddenly went dry.

"We'll wait here until you're ready to leave, Sir," said the soldier.

"Well, you won't have long to wait," said Paddy, "for I'll be out that door before you." And he was.

Mary has this to say of the move to Fruithill: "Apart from the events of 1972, I have very happy memories of the time we spent in that house on the Crumlin Road. In stark contrast, I was never at peace in Fruithill Park. Every day I lived in that ghetto was like a nightmare. It was an awful mistake to move there in the first place, but it was well into December, and my father was very anxious to have the whole family together, under one roof, for Christmas."

Claire speaks of it in similar terms: "We left one nightmare and moved straight into another one."

When Paddy went to see the house it was derelict. Nineteen windows were broken and many of the doors were hanging off their hinges. Someone had made an attempt to burn the house down, and the interior was full of scorch marks and worse. Glaziers, carpenters, painters and decorators were brought in to try to make the house habitable for Christmas. Then came their own beds and furniture. Fires were lit to dry out the place and give it a semblance of cosiness, and their own familiar pictures were hung on the freshly painted walls. Mary and Claire worked hard on the curtains and drapes. It was coming together.

The excitement of homemaking was short-lived. They soon discovered that the children were not the only people to use the garden as a shortcut. Many of the local adults, and even the British army, passed by their windows. It seemed to Mary that every youth in the area felt he had a proprietary right to use the garden as a loitering area, as a place for lighting fires and even as a toilet. Claire was constantly tormented by them looking in the windows, shouting insults, writing obscenities on the walls and even sometimes coming into the house. Several times the garden hose was turned on and put through the letterbox or an open window.

John had a beautiful Afghan hound which had survived several attacks in Ardoyne. It did not last a month in Fruithill and had to be given away. The dog was not the only one to be stoned. Claire was hit several times as she was hanging washing on the clothesline. Mary soon learned that life in the middle of this ghetto was worse than life on the edge of another ghetto. The Leneghans were seen as outsiders, as people who were different, who were living in a big house. The discrimination here was not religious, not political, but it was no less painful because of that.

After a couple of months Paddy Leneghan had had enough. He wrote a letter to the *Andersonstown News*, explaining that his family had been driven out of Ardoyne after an attempt to murder them in their beds. He said he understood that those who tried to kill them looked on them as enemies; that although the attack was completely immoral and monstrous, the attackers could probably justify their actions on the basis of culture, religion, history or whatever. He explained that he had moved his family to the Andersonstown area to be safe among his own people.

He finished: "We came here after being tortured by the other side to find we are now being tortured by our own side. Can any reader explain to me why we have once again become victims, in the middle of West Belfast, in the heart of the biggest and so-called safest nationalist stronghold of them all?"

Paddy knew the answer to his own question better than anyone else, but he wanted to give his pedigree. It worked.

The following Sunday evening two strangers came to the Leneghans' door. They didn't introduce themselves. They said they were there to make sure the family would have no more trouble. The strangers sat in a car outside the house for several hours and, for the first night since they moved in, the Leneghans had no trouble. Before they left, the two men gave Paddy a guarantee that his family would have no more interference from the youth of the area. He believed them.

"The bush telegraph was very effective in the place. The word went round very quickly that the Leneghans were to be left alone. I give them ten out of ten for cuteness."

Chapter Eight

Love in a Curfew

Mo ghrá go daingean thú
Lá dá bhfaca thú.
(I loved you completely
From the first day I saw you.)
(Eibhlín Dhubh Ní Chonaill: *"Caoineadh Airt Uí Laoghaire"*)

The 1960s are sometimes evoked as a time of free thinking, free expression and even free love, but the Belfast of those years bore little resemblance to that perception. The opportunities for Catholic teenage boys to socialise with Catholic teenage girls were few. Most clubs and sporting associations for young people were single sex organisations, but, ironically, the Catholic Church was one of the few establishments that provided mixed social outlets.

Mary Leneghan, as well as attending regular meetings of the Society of St Vincent de Paul, was a regular speaker at meetings of the Patrician Society. The meetings gave young people, under the supervision of a spiritual director, an opportunity to discuss a wide range of social issues. In many ways they resembled an unstructured debating society.

Mary has many friends from those days of the Patrician meetings. She first met Alban Maginness, the former SDLP Lord Mayor of Belfast, at these teenage arguing contests. He and his friend Denis Murray were pupils in St Malachy's College, a boarding and day school where permission for evening absences for boarders was very infrequently granted. But Patrician meetings were regarded by many of the clergy as character forming and conducive to solid thinking. When Mary wrote to Canon Larkin, the principal, to ask if the boys might attend, he consented wholeheartedly. It is entirely possible that the priests knew something that Mary and her friends did not, for many of those Patrician pals later did very well in their chosen fields. From among them, Martin Montgomery later lectured in Strathclyde University, in Scotland, and the brothers Seán and Martin Donnelly became doctors and practised in Belfast. It could be that the meetings attracted young people with ambition and an intellectual spark. It is certain that those who participated regularly found their thinking and speaking skills being well honed.

Despite Mary's boast that one of the attractions of such meetings was the opportunity to mix with young men, many of her friends say that she was shy in male company. When it came time, in St Dominic's, for her first formal dance, she could think no further than her own family for a partner. Her first cousin P.J. McAllister was her choice for the occasion. The following year she ventured further afield, and it was Dominic Burke, a colleague from the Society of St Vincent de Paul, who accompanied her. Dominic later married Sally Magee, a school-friend of Mary's, and became director of chirdcare services for the North-Western Health Board, in Derry. Years later, as an expert in the field of childcare, he supported Mary's stance in a threatened conflict with the hierarchy of the Catholic Church on the subject of mandatory reporting of child sexual abuse.

Having had a strict upbringing, the ordinary pleasures of many of her friends were forbidden to her: the weekly hop in the parish hall, the chatting for an hour over a plate of chips in Freddie Fusco's, the gathering at night around the street lamp on the corner, the short skirts, the long boots, the high heels, the low necklines. She was more interested in topical documentaries than *Top of the Pops*, more inclined to the public library than the public house. She did not smoke, and when she eventually decided to discover the charms of alcohol, she drank only the odd glass of Dubonnet. Although she was naturally convivial and loquacious, she was reticent in the company of "the opposite sex", as they were called in those days. That was how she was reared.

She became friendly with Ralph MacDarby, a Dubliner whom she met at St Vincent de Paul meetings. They liked each other a lot, but both were completely unschooled in the art of romance. Ralph invited Mary to Dublin, "to meet his mother". Off she went for the weekend and spent most of her time talking to Ralph's mother. Mary invited Ralph to Belfast to meet her mother, and by the Sunday afternoon he knew Claire better than he knew Mary. Mary and Ralph are still friends. There was never more than friendship between them, thanks perhaps to the time they spent getting to know each other's mothers.

Mary says she never realised that men might be interested in her. She wasn't one of the "beautiful people" of the sixties, but several of her male friends from those days admit to being among her many admirers. One young man who admired her more than most was a certain Martin

McAleese from the Albertbridge Road in Protestant East Belfast. He was a footballer, a scholar, a member of St Mary's CBS debating team—a regular pin-up boy. He says that from the day he first saw Mary Leneghan, the only female company he ever wanted was hers. His memory of that day is still clear. Eamonn Agnew was the teacher in charge of the St Mary's CBS debating team. Although Martin was in the science stream and the debaters were normally chosen from the literature stream, Eamonn had decided that Martin would be worth having on the team. In the spring of 1967 he was grooming young McAleese, Peter O'Keeffe and Martin Donnelly for the following year's team. As part of their training they attended a debate between St Mary's and St Dominic's, in the assembly hall of the girls' school. Martin and Peter O'Keeffe were from the same area and had been good friends for a couple of years, since the evening after mass in St Matthew's Church when they recognised each other as fellow pupils of St Mary's and introduced themselves. Martin was compact, athletic and candid. Peter was big, broad and guarded. One played Gaelic football, the other rugby. The opposites attracted and they became firm friends.

The big assembly hall was packed for the important debate. The students from both schools were nervous in the mixed company, the girls pretending not to notice the boys and the boys raising their voices and thumping each other on the shoulder for no reason other than to mask their bashfulness. Eamonn Agnew had told the three debaters-in-waiting to pay particular attention to a girl called Mary Leneghan who, like themselves, was still in her sixth year of the seven-year secondary cycle, but was already captain of the school team. Martin says he does not remember a word Mary said that night.

"He told us that she had a great command of the English language and a propensity for lucid argument. All I remember is the face. She was a vision and she stole my heart as soon as I saw her. I fell in love with Mary that evening. I was sure she was the girl I wanted to spend my life with, and I was never more sure of anything in my life."

When they left St Dominic's that night, Martin and Peter got a bus into the centre of the city and walked the rest of the way home. Martin talked non-stop about the debate, about the relative strengths and weaknesses of the teams, about anything at all except Mary. His natural canniness would not let him take the chance of awakening Peter's interest in her. That autumn the two friends saw Mary several times at debates, but Martin could not pluck up the courage to speak to her. Neither did he mention his abiding interest to his best friend. His lovesickness did not deter him from getting on with other aspects of his life, including meeting other girls. He was playing football with the O'Donovan Rossa GAA Club, and that year he was again selected to play with the County Antrim minor footballers. But, he says, he was tormented by mental images of Mary.

Having heard that she was a good dancer, he haunted every *céilí* in West and North Belfast in an attempt to meet her, but she was obviously revolving in different orbits. The senior students from the city's four Catholic grammar schools—St Dominic's, St Mary's, St Malachy's and Dominican College, Fortwilliam—traditionally used the Belfast Central Library in which to study and do research, especially on Saturday mornings. Martin decided to follow grammar school tradition and was rewarded by intermittent sightings of Mary. Unfortunately, she always seemed to be in the company of friends, and he never found the courage to approach her.

It was left to Mary to make the initial personal approach, and when it happened, Martin was left almost speechless. It was a Saturday morning at the beginning of June, and Martin was on his way out of the library, disappointed that he had not seen Mary. He was so preoccupied with his own frustration that he failed to recognise the voice that had come between him and his sleep on many nights during the previous year.

"Martin! Martin McAleese!"

She was walking towards him, looking him in the eye. For the first time there was nobody else around to distract her; nothing was going to spoil this longed-for, marvellous moment between the urbane, the poised, the articulate Mary Leneghan and the studious, the sporting, the beguiling Martin McAleese.

"Martin, I'll be eighteen on the twenty-seventh of this month, and we're having a party in our house that night. Would you like to come?"

"Mmm . . . Aaa . . . OK."

"Will you bring your friend Peter O'Keeffe from the debating team?"

"Mmm . . . Aaa . . . Ok."

"Do you know where I live?"

"Mmm . . . Aaa . . . No."

"657 Crumlin Road. Try to be there about nine o'clock."

"Mmm . . . Aaa . . . OK."

"Very good. I'll look forward to seeing both of you.'

"Mmm . . . Aaa . . . OK . . . Aaa . . . Cheerio."

The pain of love that Martin suffered was unrequited, according to Mary. She says there was another young man in St Mary's who looked very like Martin, and any time she saw her lovesick admirer in the library she thought it was the other lad. She first remembers Martin as a seventh year member of the debating team. Her recollection of that first night is very clear, not because of any impression Martin made on her, but because her own team beat St Mary's that night and went on to win the overall competition. She admits that any interest she had in the boys' debating team was not directed at Martin, but at the young man beside him, Peter O'Keeffe. She invited both of them to her party because she knew Peter would not come without Martin.

Fr Justin died on 22 June, just five days before Mary's birthday, and she lost all interest in the party. She wanted to cancel it, but her mother insisted it would do her good and persuaded her to go ahead with it.

Martin and Peter jumped off the Ligoniel bus opposite 657 Crumlin Road and stood staring at the Leneghan house in disbelief. "It was like an oasis of light and music, a complete culture shock to two lads from the grim streets of East Belfast," says Martin. Their upbringing, their families and their neighbourhood were very different from Mary's. Neither of them could imagine a party like this on the Albertbridge Road. Light streamed out on the gardens from every window, and the music and laughter were perfectly audible, even from where they stood on the far side of the road. Mary and Claire were at the door to greet them and guide them through the noisy throng of friends and family to the kitchen. Even more impressive than the beautiful smells emanating from the heart of the home was the sight of Paddy Leneghan unloading several crates of beer and stout on to an already groaning table. They could not believe their luck when he greeted them with the words "Help yourselves, lads, and don't be shy." The two friends thought they had died and gone to heaven.

For whatever reason, be it the welcoming atmosphere or the boisterous fun-loving attitude of the party-goers, Martin McAleese left his shyness at the bus stop that night. The poor diffident creature that stumbled his way through the acceptance of the invitation in the library was now but a pale memory. The old confident Martin was back. As soon as the dancing started he asked Mary on to the floor. As each dance finished his footballing skills became very apparent. He seemed to sense where every one of her would-be dancing partners was coming from and successfully manoeuvred her away each time. Between dances he spoke so passionately and so ceaselessly to her about whatever topic came into his head that no one dared to interrupt him. At the start of each new dance, he just happened to have Mary in position on the floor. Martin was following his plot to perfection. He was so focused on dancing with Mary and keeping her away from everyone else that he was oblivious to all the subplots being acted out around him. On one level, Mary was happy enough to be dancing with Martin because she thought that it would make Peter jealous. On another level, she was annoyed with Peter for not asking her to dance. Peter spent the evening dancing with Mary's friend Catherine Kane hoping to make Mary envious. As the evening wore on Mary realised that, thanks to Peter's timidity and Martin's self-assurance, all her plans were falling apart. In her scheme she was to be with Peter and Martin with Catherine, a contrivance that took no account of one enormous but, until then, unknown factor: her future husband's congenital *chutzpah*. Before they left for home, Martin and Peter had asked Mary and Catherine for a date the following evening and both young women had accepted. Mary's world was rapidly turning upside down.

She says jokingly of that evening that her *anamchara*, Fr Justin, must have had a hand in proceedings. She imagined him sitting in heaven, like an old Greek god on Mount Olympus, playing chess with people: moving Martin in and Peter out, emboldening one, paralysing the other with shyness, arranging destinies despite the best laid plans of mere humans. She did not understand how deeply Martin McAleese felt about her, and she explained his preoccupation with her to Claire as a one-night wonder. Claire had different ideas.

Martin was due to spend the summer working in London where he and his friend Vincent Brennan had lodgings arranged in Notting Hill Gate. Martin had one week left in Belfast, seven days in which to convince Mary that he was the man for her, to secure in her an affection for him that would remain unwavering until he came back from England. He spent every spare minute with her. They went to see Peter Fonda in *Easy Rider* in the Forum and Maggie Smith in *The Prime of Miss Jean Brodie* in the Savoy. They walked the hills and took the bus to the beach. Martin says that by the end of the week Mary was enraptured. As evidence of her fascination with him he alludes to a certain haircut: "It was a very intimate thing she did when she cut my hair. A woman doesn't do something like that for a man unless there is something very special between them."

Mary maintains she was not as taken with him as he suggests. Regarding the haircut, she adds, "He didn't see the back of his head."

Mary and Peter accompanied Martin to the airport, and when they had said goodbye to him, they travelled back to Belfast together on the bus. She was still annoyed with Peter to some extent and their conversation was slightly awkward, covering anything and everything other than personal matters. His A level results had secured him a place on the same course as Mary in Queen's School of Law, but he had decided to defer for a year and was due to travel to Botswana as a volunteer with VSO, Voluntary Service Overseas.

As part of his preparation for the work in Botswana, Peter had to do a course in London and he wrote to Martin, arranging to meet him there. When they met, the two old friends were a little too demonstrative, too friendly. They circled each other like boxers who were wary of one another, avoiding doing or saying anything that might be construed as contentious. Mary Leneghan was the only acquaintance they had in common who did not get a mention all evening. It was with a troubled conscience that Martin said goodbye to Peter that night. His assertions of sadness at the imminent departure of his friend for Africa masked a strong feeling of relief that Peter was going to be out of Mary's orbit for a year. His guilt persisted almost until he reached the tube station.

Paddy Leneghan's brother Mick and his wife Carol managed a pub near Covent Garden, and at the end of July Mary arrived to spend a weekend with them. Martin, who was working as a deliveryman for Walls Ice Cream, arranged to meet her and her aunt and uncle for a couple of drinks. Mick and Carol were very impressed with Mary's "boyfriend", as they insisted on calling him, and Mary did not disabuse them. As they parted that evening, Martin became even more assured of his standing with Mary as she expressed her concern: "Are you eating properly? That's not a great area you're staying in. Are they treating you well in work? Is the landlady nice to you? You know I get worried about you sometimes."

Martin made some suitably non-committal noises but said nothing about the perks of his job: that he delivered ice cream to all the famous hotels in London; that he was on first name terms with the chefs in the Ritz, the Dorchester and the Savoy, and that he was the best-fed Paddy in London that summer.

At the start of August, Peter O'Keeffe was ready to leave for his volunteer year working for the poor people of Botswana. He and Mary promised they would write to each other, and so they did, for a while. A year later, when Peter came home to take up his legal studies, the old Belfast life he had left behind was a dim memory, thanks to the Troubles. There were British soldiers and armoured cars on the roads, and barricades and barbed wire on many of the familiar street corners. There was also a significant change in relations between Peter and Mary. They had written to each other, as promised, for several months, but not a word had passed between them since Christmas. Martin was delighted. It was definitely a one-horse-race . . . or so he thought.

In his assumption that he was the sole competitor for Mary's affections he was correct. The only problem was that Mary did not see herself as a prize. Martin was completely enthralled by her, but for several reasons she was not so sure of her own feelings for him. The first was her unresolved relationship with Peter O'Keeffe, who was now a year behind her in the School of Law, following the same course. They had met a few times since he came back from Africa, but nothing more than a few polite words had been exchanged, a lack of communication which Mary found unsettling. She knew that Peter and Martin had renewed their old friendship, and she felt that perhaps Peter was avoiding her in order not to upset Martin. It was time for her to find answers to a few questions.

Another reason for her hesitancy was Martin's eagerness to marry. The thing he wanted most in the world, he constantly told her, was to be settled down with her, but she was not yet ready for the roses around the door and the slippers by the fire. She was also disconcerted by what she saw as his proprietorial attitude. He would have been happy for them to spend their free time exclusively together. Mary enjoyed the times she and Martin had on their own, but she loved being part of a bunch. She revelled in the wisecracks and the quipping that were part of the group scene, the arguments and disputes that flared and fizzled out again before anyone was seriously offended. She had a large circle of friends, both male and female, some of them very close to her, and their company was very important to her. More than anything else she needed to maintain her separateness. As one of nine children her space was very important to her. Her mother had married at nineteen and had spent all her young adult life rearing children. Since Claire was a child she had wanted to be a nurse, but eleven pregnancies later that ambition was consigned to the world of "what might have been". Mary did not want her own aspirations to go the road of her mother's and did not want any close ties—not just yet.

Martin, speaking as a man who had been in the science stream in school, describes the relationship between himself and Mary as undulating like a sine graph. He says he enjoyed the fiery, tumultuous, up and down nature of their courtship. When the graph line of their relationship neared the nadir, the couple sometimes fell apart for days or even weeks on end, but when it soared above the baseline life was beautiful. Such a time was the holiday in Salou.

In the summer of 1970, Mary and a group of friends rented an apartment in this popular resort on the east coast of Spain. Kathleen Boyle and Mary had organised the holiday and they had not invited Martin. It was to be a group break, not a "couples" holiday. Anyway Martin had a summer job in a pub in East Belfast and would not be able to get the time off. Once again his tenacity was underestimated. As soon as he heard about the holiday, he bought a ticket on the same flight and announced that he would be joining them in Salou. If Mary's parents had known Martin was going to Spain, she would have spent the three weeks trying to get a suntan in Belfast, so Martin had to make his own way to Aldergrove Airport and stay out of sight while Paddy and Claire fussed around the check-in desk. The travellers eventually persuaded Mary's parents to go on home and Martin appeared from behind a pillar just in time to get his bag checked through. Mary was uncomfortable about the deception, particularly as she didn't want Martin to be with the group in the first place.

After the first evening in Salou all discomfort was forgotten. The group dynamics were perfect and everyone was soon at ease. Martin was sharing a room with Ciarán Diamond, a friend of Mary's, and the two lads soon became good pals. The sunshine and the *mañana* atmosphere helped them all to relax. After three weeks of unbroken beautiful weather, of stimulating conversation and long comfortable silences, of sunbathing, walking and swimming, of eating, drinking and dancing together, Mary felt she was falling in love with Martin.

He says, "They were, without a shadow of a doubt, the three most romantic weeks of my life."

One day the group of friends visited Tarragona, and Martin and Mary bought rings for each other—not engagement rings, but tokens of love and affection. All was well with the world . . . until they came back to Ireland. They were home just in time to share another milestone in the troubled history of Belfast.

Mary was a volunteer worker in the offices of the Central Citizens' Defence Committee on the Falls Road. Her work there consisted of advising people of their rights and entitlements in such diverse areas as rehousing, unemployment assistance and compensation for damage caused by British army or RUC searches. After lunch on Friday, 3 July, Martin left her to the CCDC building and walked on down the Falls Road towards the city centre. As he approached North Howard Street, he heard the rumble of heavy engines and the squeal of tyres. He looked up and saw a convoy of Saracen armoured cars and heavy British army lorries swinging out and turning up the Falls Road. The last few lorries stopped in the middle of the road, disgorging swarms of soldiers who hastily erected barbed wire barriers across the side streets, effectively blocking off the area. At the same time, other lorries and armoured cars were throwing up obstructions and erecting roadblocks in a ring around the whole district. Martin turned to go back, but it would be some time before he would be able to join Mary in the CCDC offices.

She was alone there when she heard the roaring of the heavy engines, the clattering of the low flying helicopters, the shouted orders of soldiers and the defiant roars and frightened screams of civilians. When she looked out the window, the Falls Road seemed to have been transformed into a battle scene from a film. Everywhere she looked there were heavily armed soldiers, armoured cars and personnel carriers. An amplified disembodied voice from a Saracen armoured car was ordering people into their houses until further notice. Some minutes later, the same voice announced that the area was now under military curfew and that anyone who ventured on to the streets was liable to be shot. The Falls curfew had begun, a curfew that would last thirty-four hours and leave hundreds of houses ransacked, scores of people injured and five men dead.

The British army found weapons and explosives in a number of houses, but the manner in which they treated the civilian population in general destroyed whatever goodwill was left between them and the Catholics of West Belfast. The soldiers went from house to house, leaving behind a trail of devastation and wrecked homes. According to complaints received by the British army after the curfew, most of the damage was caused by the Devon and Dorset Regiment and the Black Watch, a mostly Protestant regiment from Scotland. The searching did not go unopposed. The British army came under fire on many occasions from both wings of the IRA, and most of this shooting took place around the offices of the CCDC.

Mary spent a long time lying on the floor with the telephone in her hand, trying to contact Paddy Devlin. When she could not get through to Devlin, she tried to ring her father in the Long Bar. The pub in Leeson Street was about two hundred yards from where she lay, but it might as well have been miles away. When the phone in the pub was not answered, she rang home and was relieved to hear that her father was there having his lunch when martial law was declared in the Falls area.

The coming of darkness only intensified the terror. Up and down the road, outside the CCDC, tracer bullets lit the night, and the screams and the rattle of gunfire were unrelenting. She saw a man shot dead that night. He was on top of a building across the road from her when he was hit by several bullets and fell backwards off the roof into the street. The pure horror of watching a man shot to death had such an effect on her that she decided to take a chance on breaking the curfew. All she wanted was to get home. She and Martin left the backdoor open behind them and made their way to the high wall at the end of the backyard. Once they were over that wall they could make their way through Clonard to the Springfield Road. She was on top of the wall and ready to drop down the other side when the shot rang out. She and Martin froze. They were not going to risk their lives to get home when they could remain in relative safety in the CCDC offices. There was no need for discussion—both of them turned and ran back inside.

A much-relieved Mary bolted the back door behind her and resumed her station on the floor under the front window. Shortly after that Paddy Devlin arrived, having braved the patrols on the Falls Road itself.

He gives his own account of that night:

> The shooting increased as darkness fell. The high-pitched whine of the armoured cars as they manoeuvred round the narrow streets and the occasional burst of heavy calibre fire filled me with dread. The shooting only stopped at dawn. The CCDC Headquarters was on the main Falls Road, at the boundary of the curfew area, and we spent the night listening to the battle, fortified by tea, coffee and soup laid in for just such an emergency. During the thirty-four hour curfew the phone rang constantly, giving us first-hand accounts of what was going on. The military no doubt had the line bugged in the hope that some IRA chief would use it to talk to his men.[‡]

They were also fortified by the only kind of sandwich Mary could rustle up—pickled beetroot, which was not very well received. The curfew ended on Sunday morning at nine o'clock. As Mary was leaving with Martin and Paddy Devlin, they passed the reporters and television cameras, the milk lorries and bread vans, the relations and friends of the residents and many of the residents themselves who were caught outside the cordon, all flooding into the Falls Road.

On Monday morning Paddy had to go to the CCDC offices with a message. Not being familiar with the building, he stuck his head into the wrong room. Two local men were helping a third man to fit a priest's

---

‡   Devlin, *Straight Left*, p. 129.

collar round his neck. Paddy excused himself and backed out, but not before he had recognised the man in clerical garb. The would-be priest was none other than Patrick Hillery, the Irish minister for foreign affairs, later to become sixth President of Ireland. He was on a secret fact-finding mission in the area, a secret that was not very well kept as he was perfectly recognisable, with or without the collar, to many people on the Falls Road. The visit was later condemned by the British government and by James Chichester Clark, Prime Minister of Northern Ireland. The senior British civil servant, Sir Edmund Peck, remarked to Donal O'Sullivan, then Irish ambassador to Britain, "Hillery's unsolicited crossing of the border had 'made life hellishly difficult for Stormont and London.'"‡

Two days after the Falls curfew something happened that was, for Martin at least, almost as traumatic. Paddy and Claire found out he had been in Spain with Mary. He was barred from the Leneghan house, and Mary was warned not to have any more contact with him. She, of course, complied with her parents' interdiction, but Martin could not understand why they could not meet in secret. No matter how often she explained that she was not prepared to disobey, Martin's attitude remained the same. Shortly before Christmas, Mary was confined to bed with the flu, and Martin did not have even the opportunity of an "accidental" meeting in college. He decided he had had enough of this prohibition. Off he went to 657 Crumlin Road. He was opening the gate as Paddy was coming out of the house. As the two men approached each other, Paddy reached out to shake Martin's hand. Martin accepted the gesture gratefully and said, "I hear Mary has the flu. How is she?"

"She's getting better," said Paddy, "but she's still in bed. Go on up and have a chat. She'll be glad to see you."

And that was that. The statute of limitations had expired. Once again all was well between Mary and Martin.

The harmony was not to be long-lived. When they broke up at the start of spring, Martin threw the ring Mary had bought for him in Tarragona in the fire. By the end of spring he was bitterly regretting his rashness, as they were back together again and Mary wanted to know where the ring was. That summer Martin was back in London working once again for the Walls Ice Cream Company. This time he managed to get jobs for Peter O'Keeffe and another friend, Thomas King. Mary was also working in England that summer, in a hotel in Blackpool. Martin

‡   Extract from State Papers 1970, reported in *Sunday Business Post*, 7 January 2001.

found the idea of them both abroad in the same country at the same time, yet separated, too frustrating to bear. He left his job and his two friends and took the train for Blackpool, where he got lodgings near Mary's hotel and a job making warning stripes for heavy goods vehicles. It did not bother him that the lodgings were much worse than the place he had left in London, nor that the job was noisy and dirty and badly paid. He was near Mary, was able to go out with her every evening enjoying the wonders of Blackpool without the constant vigilance of Paddy and Claire. All was well between Mary and Martin . . . for another while.

It was Monday, 9 August 1971, and they both listened with more care than usual to the seven o'clock news that morning; Mary while she was preparing breakfast in the hotel and Martin as he was shaving before going to work. The BBC newscaster announced that the British government had introduced internment without trial in Northern Ireland during the early hours of that morning. There were widespread riots following incursions by British army and RUC personnel into nationalist areas, and hundreds of people had so far been arrested.

It was only when they arrived home that they heard the full story: that seventeen people had been killed that morning, that thousands of Catholics had fled across the border into the Republic, that hundreds of Catholic families had been forced out of their homes and that the McAleese family were among the latter. Charlie and Emma and the children were given five minutes' notice by their Protestant neighbours to pack two bags and leave their home. The house was then ransacked and fouled by people who had lived beside them for years. Charlie McAleese later said they were lucky that the only things thrown at them, as they fled through a gauntlet of hate up the Albertbridge Road, were insults and curses.

There was only one other Catholic family living on that part of the road at the time, the Smyths. A member of that family, Philip, now a priest in England, gives an account of what happened that day:

> There was only one other Catholic family in the road with us and they were the McAleese family. My mother was on very friendly terms with Mrs McAleese. One of my vivid childhood memories— I was no more than a boy of eight years—was the very sad day when Mr and Mrs McAleese and their family were put out of their home. My mother brought up tea and comfort to the family and I remember walking through the wrecked house. I was particularly shocked when Mrs McAleese told my mother of how the family picture of the Sacred Heart had been smashed and trampled

94

underfoot by the attacking mob. This is an image that has stayed with me. Some weeks later it was our turn and we were put out of our home at gunpoint by a mob.[†]

When Martin returned to Belfast a couple of days later, the family had been put into emergency accommodation in Rathcoole, an area where Catholics were in a very small minority and which was as dangerous as East Belfast. In the early sixties Rathcoole had been a small Catholic enclave, but by 1971 it had become the biggest housing estate in Northern Ireland, its population swollen by hundreds of Protestant families who were rehoused there because of the redevelopment of the lower Shankill area. As more and more Protestants moved into the estate, the Catholics moved out in droves. The McAleeses were swimming against the demographic tide. Among those leaving was the family of Bobby Sands, the first of the ten men to die on hunger strike in the Maze Prison ten years later.

Kevin McAleese, Martin's young brother, was attacked and badly injured on his way home from his first day at his new school, and the letters UVF were carved on his arm with a broken bottle.[§] Martin was furious, angrier and more frustrated than he had ever been in his life. His family had just been forced out of their home, compelled to move to a dangerous area, and now his brother was lucky to be alive. His parents seemed to be accepting their lot with stoicism, but he would have none of it. He would never accept the label of second class citizen.

A week after the attack on Kevin, Steve Biko, the South African anti-apartheid activist, made his famous statement: "The most potent weapon in the hands of the aggressor is the mind of the oppressed." The statement resonated strongly with Martin. He fully understood the sense and the wisdom in what Biko said and took strength from the African.

Just as he described his early relationship with Mary as being "like a sine graph", so Mary had her own fitting description of their stormy friendship. Being an avid student of Irish dancing, she compared their relationship to a popular *céilí* dance: "We were sometimes up and sometimes down, like 'The Waves of Tory'." It is, of course, in the nature of waves to undulate, but they also inevitably break. When Mary and Martin broke up in the autumn of 1971, it seemed they would never get back together again. Several friends of Mary's in the Law School asked her out, but she did not spend time with anyone in particular. She

---

†   Letter from Philip Smyth to Mary McAleese, 20 February 2001.

§   UVF: Ulster Volunteer Force, an illegal loyalist paramilitary organisation.

had been telling Martin for some time that she needed her own space. Now that she had it she wanted to enjoy it. She loved going for a cup of tea or a meal with different people, enjoying good company and being able to walk away with no ties or complications. She also enjoyed doing this without Martin's making her feel guilty.

Just before Christmas something happened that changed her attitude and made her reconsider the decision she had made. She was at a meeting one night in a room that had a faulty gas heater. One person came half an hour late and found the others almost asleep from the effects of the gas. The incident left Mary shaken, but also impelled her to take a stark look at her life, to reassess her priorities, the opportunities she had taken and those she had missed. She decided to contact Peter O'Keeffe.

She was going back to work in the hotel in Blackpool during the Christmas holidays, but she would be home before New Year's Eve. She called him to arrange a meeting.

"I haven't seen you for a while. Somebody was telling me you might have picked up one of those tropical diseases. You haven't? Good!"

It was a strange Christmas. Although there were great difficulties between Martin and Mary, there were absolutely none between Martin and Mary's family. He had often spent the night in Mary's house, sharing a bedroom with the boys, when it was too dangerous to go home. All the Leneghan children were very fond of him, particularly the boys. As far as Paddy and Claire were concerned, their daughter would find no better man. During that Christmas period, Martin spent several evenings in their house, having a drink with Paddy, watching television and amusing the younger children. Mary rang home every night, and every night she got the same sermon:

"Do you know poor Martin is here again tonight? It's an awful shame you two aren't going out together any more. I suppose you know the poor fellow's broken-hearted, not that you would care very much. Sure you know in your heart and soul you'll never find better than poor Martin."

"Poor Martin! Poor Martin!" All she seemed to hear from her family and friends was "Poor Martin!" But she stood firm. In fact, the more they complained the more determined she became that she would have nothing more to do with "poor Martin". She came home after Christmas and turned a deaf ear to all that was being said. She collected Peter in Claire's little red Mini, and the pair went off to a party in Andersonstown, in the house of Anne and Pat Trainor, relatives of

Mary's. The house was thronged with people and alive with music, candles and happiness. The magic of Christmas and renewed friendship was very strong that night.

For a few days it seemed the two friends were getting to know each other all over again. They filled in the gaps from the time the letters stopped: stories from Africa and Ardoyne, their hopes and successes and failures. There was lively intellectual engagement and a strong spiritual understanding between the two. Mary says she felt a magnetism that was cerebral and, although purely platonic, was in some ways even stronger than physical attraction.

Peter's brother Denis and his Finnish wife Sylvi invited them to see in the New Year, 1972, in their house in Bangor, County Down. The four young people gelled, and the evening was full of easy conversation and gentle fun. At midnight Sylvi taught Peter and Mary an old Finnish custom: to take an ember from the fire and make a wish on it for the year that was just beginning. Whether the wish worked or not, it was the last time Mary and Peter were ever out together.

Why did the enchantment of that Christmas suddenly evaporate with the New Year? Was the shade of Martin McAleese, best friend of one and passionate admirer of the other, hovering in the back of their minds? Did Mary feel she was being unfaithful to Martin, even though she had not been going out with him for some time? She later said there was an intensity in Peter which made her uncomfortable, a vehemence in their togetherness which was disturbing to her. She decided not to phone him but to wait for his call. It never came. Towards the end of January she discovered that Peter had called several times, but thanks to a Leneghan conspiracy in favour of Martin, she never knew. She called him and told him she would not be going out with him any more.

Her friends and family were careful to say they were advising her, as distinct from pressurising her, not to let Martin McAleese go. All they wanted, they said, was her own good. But she had had enough of men. She had had enough of well-meant advice. She was not prepared to be a prize in a competition between two men. "Bad cess to the both of them," she said to herself, "and bad cess to all the well-meaning do-gooders." The only advice she would take would be her own.

Chapter Nine

The McAleeses of East Belfast

And can they stop awhile to laugh
Who live in diagram and graph?
(John Hewitt: "Mathematics")

Like the moth that is attracted back again and yet again to the candle, Mary Leneghan kept returning to Martin McAleese. He was the one who understood her. He would be prepared to set aside his own ambitions and his own professional future for her, and she knew that. Despite the spats and the quarrels, the clashes and the conflicts, she knew that he would take on the world for her if only she would be his wife.

He was born on the 24 March 1951 in the Mater Hospital on the Crumlin Road and raised in 219 Albertbridge Road in East Belfast, the second of five children born to Charlie McAleese of Portglenone, County Antrim, and Emma McElgunn of Lisnaskea, County Fermanagh. Charlie and Emma met during the Second World War. She was working in a drapery shop in Irvinestown, and he was a fitter in the aircraft manufacturing firm of Short and Harland, in their seaplane factory at Kesh on Lough Erne. In 1945 Emma moved to Derry to work in a clothes shop, but the romance continued as Charlie regularly made the journey to visit her. In 1947 the couple married in the Long Tower Chapel in Derry. When Charlie was transferred to the main Short and Harland Aircraft Factory in Belfast, the couple moved there to live. They had none of the worldly sagacity of Paddy and Claire Leneghan, no understanding of the sectarian geography of Belfast and no idea that certain areas would be considered unsafe for Catholics. Charlie's only priority in looking for a house was to get one within walking or cycling distance of the aircraft factory. So it was that the McAleeses found themselves in the heart of East Belfast, surrounded by Protestants, many of whom were loyalists.

Their first child was stillborn in 1949, a little girl who was buried in an unmarked grave in Aughnahoy Cemetry in Portglenone, close to where her parents would subsequently be interred. Their first son, John, was born in 1950 and Martin in 1951. After them came Cathal, Kathleen and Kevin.

Martin does not remember a time when there was not sectarian tension in the area. His family were often the butt of insults. "Papish bastards", "Fenian scum" and much worse were regular greetings from street corners as the McAleeses passed by. Martin says about his early days: "I soon learned what side of the road to walk on. Every time I left the house I was wary. Every group I saw I eyed with suspicion. It was an awful way to live, a terrible way to grow up, but I knew no better."

The McAleeses never had a penny to spare. During all the years they lived in East Belfast, they never had a car or a phone. They got their first television set, a fourteen-inch black and white model, in 1967. Charlie worked six and a half days a week in the aircraft factory, his only time off being on Saturday afternoons. The factory operated a seven-day week, but in those days, only Catholics worked on the Sabbath in Belfast.

Martin McAleese was baptised in the Church of St Anthony in Willowfield and got his primary education in St Joseph's School, Ballyhackamore. His primary school days were not marked by any great academic achievement, as he explains: "On the morning of the eleven plus exam I found out that there was always a question on the paper based on alphabetical order. I had never learned the alphabet, and I spent the morning trying to learn it off by heart. I was as far as 'M' when the test started."

There were probably several reasons for the cavities the future dentist was trying to fill in his primary education that morning, and among them his enduring fascination and preoccupation with Gaelic football must take its share of the blame. The eleven plus examination was the only passport to grammar school, and in those days, the only hope anyone had of a possible third-level education. Martin failed the exam, and the headmaster of St Joseph's told his mother to keep him at primary school until he was fifteen years old and then set him to a trade.

Fr Peter McCann, a curate in the parish, was friendly with the Christian Brothers in St Mary's Grammar School in Barrack Street, at the bottom of the Falls Road. He had successfully pleaded a case with the principal, Brother McGee, for Martin's older brother John, and now, at Emma's request, he asked the Brothers to afford the same opportunity to Martin. He would be allowed to attend St Mary's for one year; at the end of that year his work would be reviewed, and if the results were favourable he would win a scholarship for the remaining six years.

Martin worked as if his life depended on it and won his scholarship at the end of the year. He says he will be eternally grateful, not only to his mother for her intractable determination that he would get the best education, but also to the Christian Brothers who made an act of faith in the boy who did not know the alphabet.

"I did my day's work and left the rearing and the educating of the family to Emma," said Charlie McAleese in later years. In this regard he was like many Belfast fathers of the time. Although his interest in his children's education was not always apparent, he followed Martin's sporting accomplishments with avid attention. His son's footballing prowess, which had caused him so much difficulty in his eleven plus, was now a great asset to him in the secondary school. St Mary's had a long-established Gaelic football tradition, and it was not long before Martin's talents were spotted and he won a place on the school team. A friend of his, Aidan Hamill, introduced him to the O'Donovan Rossa GAA Club, where Martin played at all levels. By the time he was sixteen he was representing County Antrim on the minor football team. He played for the Antrim minors in 1967, 1968 and 1969, and was captain of the team in that final year. Nineteen sixty-seven was a particularly busy year for the young Gaelic star as he played under-16, minor, under-21, junior and senior football all in one season for Rossa! He was usually in the midfield position but sometimes played centre-half forward or centre-half back. He was fast, full of adrenaline and nervous energy, and had a habit of constantly bouncing on the soles of his feet. He likes to compare this habit to the practice made famous by the great heavyweight boxer of the time Mohammed Ali. Some of his friends, with scant regard for Martin's desire to be associated with one of the greatest sporting heroes of all time, likened his constant hopping to that popular character of 1970s television fame, "Skippy the Bush Kangaroo".

He often played three matches in one weekend, but he had long ago learned his lesson about neglecting the books. No matter how hard he played or trained, he never fell behind in his studies. The Christian Brothers did not miss the opportunity to hold him up as an example to the other boys, and Martin was regularly embarrassed by references to him as a young man who could successfully balance the demands of study and sport. He explains his less than brilliant O level results by the athletes' adage that he did not want to "peak too early". He certainly peaked for his A levels: top grades in physics, chemistry, pure mathematics and applied mathematics, a remarkable achievement for someone who did not pass the eleven plus. It is not surprising that

Martin expresses an abiding abhorrence at the idea of children sitting such a fateful examination at such a young age.

In the summer of 1969, the Antrim County Board of the GAA and the Rossa Club agreed to pay the air fares so that Martin could fly home from London to play in the championship matches that year—a very unusual practice at the time. When he went to Queen's University, he was chosen to play for the college in the Sigerson Cup and the Universities' League. The pinnacle of his football career was reached in 1971 when he played on the Queen's team that won the Sigerson Cup for only the third time in the history of the competition. Although Mary Leneghan was well known as the most avid of all Queen's GAA fans, she was not present at that famous final in Galway. Her parents, having heard of the notorious after-match activities associated with the Sigerson final, had forbidden her to travel. Fr Ambrose McAuley, chaplain of Queen's University and great GAA supporter, rang Mary that night to assure her that Martin was perfectly safe from the advances of the Galway girls. He said that when he was leaving the ballroom of the hotel, Martin was busy dancing with a certain Kerryman among whose many talents dancing could not be numbered. The certain Kerryman in question was one Moss Keane.

Mary followed Queen's University GAA team up and down the country, and her voice from the sideline was an integral part of Queen's GAA matches during those years. She urged on Martin and the other players, reproached referees, reprehended opposing teams and rebuked anyone who saw any fault in her favourite players. On one famous occasion, at a match between Queen's and UCD, Martin received a kick in the groin from a UCD player. When the referee ignored the incident, Mary ran on to the pitch to tackle the offending player with her umbrella. Amidst a volley of hoots, jeers and cheers, Mary was removed from the field by the officials. On the way back to Belfast on the bus that night, the players, by a unanimous decision, voted her "Man of the Match".

When Mary missed that Sigerson final between Queen's and UCC in Pearse Stadium in Galway, she missed a very special occasion. She missed the equalising point Martin scored, the heart-lifting moment of the final whistle and the celebrations afterwards. She missed the big dinner in the Great Southern Hotel in Eyre Square and the opportunity to see Martin McAleese dancing with Moss Keane, who went on to be one of Ireland's great international rugby players. He is still a good friend of the McAleeses.

The occasion was very special for the university and for Martin especially. Inter-county senior footballers have a great respect for the Sigerson competition. Enda Colleran, that hero of Galway football who won three all-Ireland medals in a row from 1964 to 1966, said that the Sigerson Cup medal he won in 1960 was the sweetest of them all. Around 90 per cent of university players at that time were inter-county senior players, a status never achieved by Martin McAleese, thanks to a knee injury. That same injury put paid to an ambition he had nurtured since his childhood: to become a professional athlete. He says the fact that he never got the opportunity to test his ambition is one of the few regrets of his life.

Martin carefully selected a beautiful gold chain for his Sigerson medal and presented it to Mary. She wore it very proudly . . . until the day she lost it. Martin was inconsolable.

"When I found out that Mary had lost my Sigerson medal, I thought I would rather have it the other way round: that Mary would have got lost and I'd still have my medal."

Years later, when Mary was president, she told this story to Joe Lennon, former captain of the Down football team and author of several books on Gaelic games. Joe showed a great interest in the story and contacted the members of Bord na gColáistí, the Colleges' Board of the GAA. On the occasion of Martin's forty-seventh birthday, two months later, he was overwhelmed when a replica of his Sigerson medal was presented to him by P.J. McGrath, the chairman of the Colleges' Board.

Martin's whole social life centred around the GAA Club in Queen's, and love for Gaelic games was the biggest single interest he shared with Mary. As each new academic year started, the pair were less concerned with timetables and courses than with the new influx of students. Their priority was prospective footballers. Both were also active in the affairs of the Students' Union. The Union often invited politicians to address the students on areas of current interest, and among those who were invited was Tomás Mac Giolla, at that time president of Official Sinn Féin.

Mary and Martin were present on an evening in November 1971 to listen to a debate on membership of the European Economic Community, a topical question as the electorate in the Republic would be voting in a referendum on the issue in the spring of 1972. Mac Giolla was among those who was speaking against membership, and Michael Sweetman of Fine Gael was among the speakers in favour. Tomás Mac Giolla describes what happened that night:

There were up to five hundred students gathered when Máirín de Búrca and I arrived in the hall in Queen's University. The event had been organised by Eilis McDermott and the debate was very lively. At the end of the night I was ready to leave, heading back to Dublin, when I discovered that the air had been let out of the tyres of my car. One of the students located a foot pump and the tyres were re-inflated. Once again I was ready to leave when it was announced that British soldiers were waiting in the car park to arrest me. About four hundred students accompanied me to the car park. One of these students warned me not to let the British officer put a hand on my shoulder, as he would then have the right to use violence if I refused to go with him.

A brawl ensued in the car park as the students prevented the soldiers from getting near Mac Giolla, who lost his spectacles in the affray. The politician did not know where he was going as a group of students led him back into the hall and locked and barricaded the doors. Mary and Martin, in common with all the students, were incensed that the invitation they had given to a person to come and address them had been used as an opportunity to arrest him. A committee of students was formed there and then and immediately set to work. It was agreed that a phone call should be made to Jim Callaghan, the British minister of home affairs. Mac Giolla says that all the other politicians left Queen's at that stage, with the exception of Michael Sweetman, who phoned Garret FitzGerald at home. At two o'clock in the morning, one of the students announced that he had been talking to Jim Callaghan and that he had been assured that the British soldiers would be gone within five minutes. Half an hour later everyone went out to the car park. Mac Giolla was about to get into his car when several armoured Land Rovers full of RUC men arrived to arrest him. Everyone rushed back into the hall and the calls began again.

By seven thirty next morning, Mary and Martin were propped against a wall, trying to keep their eyes open, when it was announced that orders had been given to the British army and the RUC to withdraw and allow Mac Giolla safe passage. Out to the car park went the crowd again. This time their way was blocked by a crowd of loyalists who had surrounded Mac Giolla's car. The RUC were forced to return to scatter the loyalists. In the middle of the morning, he eventually left, accompanied by two RUC Land Rovers and a British army helicopter, which maintained their protective presence all the way to the border. Mac Giolla is full of praise for the students in their determination to protect the right of free speech. Mary says she was proud to be associated with the student group, a gathering representative of all shades of political opinion. It was a long and harrowing night for all of them, but Mary and Martin, like the rest of the students, took great satisfaction from being able to use the system. Both agree that it was much easier for a group of four or five hundred clever, articulate, third-level students to contact the appropriate people and demand their rights than it would be for the majority of Belfast people.

Apart from their passionate interest in Gaelic games and their involvement in the Student Union, the couple had a lot more in common. They both came from traditional, Catholic, nationalist, first generation Belfast families: families that had both lost their homes to sectarian violence, families which had both suffered under the old unionist regime. Mary and Martin were both clever, eloquent young people who enjoyed studying and loved sport. They were the thorn and the rose on the one branch: he subtle, quiet and patient; she unambiguous, forthright and passionate. Martin's people were very fond of Mary and Mary's family loved Martin. Both families saw the qualities in both of them and hoped they would soon settle down and marry. Martin was certain this would happen sooner rather than later, but Mary was not so sure.

Chapter Ten

A Coming of Age

"Religion's never mentioned here," of course.
"You know them by their eyes," and hold your tongue.
"One side's as bad as the other," never worse.
Christ, it's near time that some small leak was sprung
   (Seamus Heaney: "Whatever You Say Say Nothing")

Mary was one of eleven women from the group of fifty students who entered the Queen's University School of Law in 1969. There were twenty Catholics in her year group, by far the biggest percentage ever on the law course. It was a comparatively small class, and the students of all backgrounds soon became friends. They worked in a seminar system, with groups of ten or so students, which helped them to get to know each other particularly well.

In Belfast it has always been considered important to establish the religion of the person you are getting to know. The question would seldom be put directly, but the people of the city are adept at using oblique queries to check whether their new acquaintance is Catholic or Protestant. The school attended, though nowadays not always significant, was formerly of critical importance in determining religion. A person's name was another clue. A Protestant would hardly be called "Seán" or "Séamus", and few Catholics would go by the names "Shirley" or "Daphne". People would listen carefully for pronunciations. A Catholic would say "haitch" whereas a Protestant would be more likely to pronounce the letter as "aitch". There were ways and means to find out what was considered by many as the answer to the vital question. The Leneghans were reared to ignore the religion of prospective friends or acquaintances, and in this they were exceptional.

Mary's student friends were a mix of Protestants, Catholics and Jews, and it was a healthy mix. All had come from denominational schools, except the foreigners, and most were anxious to find out about each other, from each other. Curiosity soon dismantled the barriers, and friendships among them never broke down along religious lines. Membership of certain groups was the only aspect of student life that was denominational: St Vincent de Paul, the Unionist Association, the Ulster Association, the Christian Union, etc.

While she was still in secondary school, Mary was introduced to the Queen's Student Union by Dominic Burke and Declan Kerr. There was a particularly good debating society in the university at that time, and her two friends often brought Mary along to listen to the most eloquent and most famous of the speakers. Among them were Bernadette Devlin, Michael Farrell, Rory McShane, Kevin Boyle, Derek Davis, Tom McGurk and Eamonn McCann. Mary says that Bernadette Devlin, later McAliskey, was the cleverest and the most articulate speaker she heard during that time.

Queen's School of Law had a very strong teaching staff and was famed as one of the best schools in Europe. William Twining, the first lecturer Mary met, made a particularly strong impact on her. "The law is a blue cow," he wrote on the blackboard that first morning, meaning that a person could make the law into the summation of justice, a pink pig, beauty and truth, or whatever they wanted, depending on where they started their argument. He was a well-known and highly respected academic lawyer, a great thinker, a humane man with a sardonic sense of humour who taught legal systems and methods and the philosophy of the law. Mary was having her thinking and arguing skills refined and sharpened by one of Ireland's leading teachers of jurisprudence.

She and her friends were lucky to catch the crest of a great wave of academic lawyers. There were people like Claire Palley from South Africa, Leon Lysaght from America and lecturers from nearer home like Harry Calvert, Kevin Boyle and David Trimble, who taught land law. Lee Sheridan, David Myers and Eddie Veitch all taught in Queen's School of Law at that time, as did Abdul Palawallah, who was ahead of his time in the early 1970s in his understanding of the importance of computers in the legal system.

As it became clear that the Troubles were not going to fizzle out, many of the foreign lecturers left Queen's. Twining and Palawallah went to Warwick University, where the School of Law had a reputation as an avant-garde, experimental institution. Cardiff was another place that had a growing reputation, and some of the lecturers gravitated towards the School of Law there. Queen's was the poorer for their going. On the introduction of internment without trial, Palley and Twining formed a group of students and staff to debate the issues involved. The staff actively led and invited discussion on current legal issues and engaged with the events that were shaping the world around them. Many of these events had serious legal implications: the Diplock Courts, military curfew, powers of search and arrest. There was nothing that was not up for discussion. In the 1980s, Queen's University was accused of running away from issues, but such an accusation would have had no foundation in the early seventies. Mary and her friends understood how privileged they were to be able to discuss with, and learn from, a group of lecturers who had international standing as academic lawyers.

If the law lecturers were considered progressive, the same could not have been said of some of the textbooks they were using. Mary was moved to complain about one of the core texts, *Learning the Law*, by Glanville Williams, when she read the following extract: "It is not easy for a young man to get up and face the court; many women find it harder still. A woman's voice, also, does not carry as well as a man's."[‡]

Another passage that drew Mary's wrath read: "The technical Bar Qualification is a good enough stepping-stone to posts that do not demand actual practice at the Bar. Most women barristers, if they do not marry, take this way out."[§]

The Ardoyne woman had no intention of taking that way out. She was serious about her studies and determined about what she wanted to do with her qualification. The work was hard, as she explains: "The law is a tyrannical subject. The amount of reading to be done is enormous. I spent more time in the Law Library during the four years of the degree course than in any other room in the university."

It made more sense for Mary to study in the library than at home, where the peace and quiet required for serious reading was at a premium. She was exceptional on the course in the number of siblings she had. Most of her fellow students had one or two brothers or sisters at home, and their families were financially better off than the Leneghans.

Most of her days at college started with a look at the notice board on the landing in the Law School building, 19 University Square. The morning the first year results were posted was no exception. The woman who would later be characterised by her supreme self-confidence would not be recognised in the timorous young student who stood in trepidation at the top of the narrow stairs that morning, staring at the list of names posted in order of their results. She says that for several

‡   Glanville Williams, *Learning the Law* (London: Stevens, 1943), p. 192.

§   *Ibid*.

seconds she gazed unfocused before starting at the bottom and reading her way up the names. When she had reached halfway and had not found her name, she started again at the bottom. She had not got very far when two of her friends, Robert McKay and Ronnie Jaffa, lifted her and placed her face level with the top of the list. There it was in black and white: top of the list, top of the class—Mary Patricia Leneghan. Up until then she had no yardstick against which to measure her study and had little confidence in her abilities, apart from her debating skills, but from then on she was more comfortable in university and was in the top ten in every examination.

Mary was soon in the heart of all that was going on in the School of Law. She was elected on to the Consultative Committee for Staff and Students and through that body got to know many of the lecturers and students from other faculties and year groups. She became involved in the Law Society and later was elected its president. She loved the atmosphere of the School of Law and the academic life, was comfortable in the company of academics and was happy that she had found her niche.

Shortly after the SDLP was founded, Tom Connolly brought her along to a meeting of the South Belfast Branch, and she became a member of the party.[‡] She became a regular attendee at branch meetings, and the SDLP was the only party she supported during the years she lived north of the border. Years later, when she and Martin were living in Dublin, they both attended a few meetings of an SDLP support group in the city, but there was little scope for them to be of help and they drifted out of active politics.

Mary's grandfather, John McManus, had been an absolute and unapologetic de Valera supporter. If Dev did not agree with the conditions of the Treaty, then the Treaty was wrong. If he moved into constitutional politics, then that was the way to go. If he founded a political party, then Fianna Fáil was the only party worth supporting. John McManus was very proud of the medals he had won in the War of Independence, and the McManus house was always strongly nationalist and republican. But, as the family grew, it seemed that each of them had a different political viewpoint.

Claire, Mary's mother, would never have considered herself republican minded. Her attitude to politics was purely pragmatic. To her, politics was something external, a part of life that she had very little time for, that had very little to do with her reality. She had nine children

‡   SDLP: Social Democratic and Labour Party.

to rear. John was deaf. Damien had a cancer in his face, a tumour that was removed when he was very young but that entailed regular visits to the hospital during his childhood.

I remember one day I was in the Children's Hospital on the Falls Road to get some tests done on John. Damien was already in the hospital for treatment and Phelim was in my arms. As I waited outside a doctor's door, Damien came along the corridor in a wheelchair, being pushed by a nurse. I was very worried about the pair of them. In the middle of all my worries, I was trying to plan the dinner and work out would I make it back to Ardoyne before the chemist closed. Those were the interests and the worries I had. I had no time for politics, no interest in it, except where politics, or lack of political action, affected any member of my family.

Although I was very proud of my father, it never meant a lot to me that he had medals from the War of Independence. When I think of the stories he used to tell us about those days at the start of the twentieth century, all I can see is the suffering, just as it is only the suffering I have seen during the past thirty years. My own people suffered terribly during the pogroms in County Down in the 1920s. Because of those Troubles they were scattered as far away as Canada. As a family we have had our fill of violence and hospitals. Human life was always highly valued in this house. God help anybody who tried to talk to us about the morality of violence.

Mary has always been a constitutional nationalist. She believes passionately in the republic as a political institution, in the principles of republicanism and in the teachings of Tone and Rousseau, as does her father. The political influence of Paddy Leneghan is very evident in her. The effect of the years he spent as a trade unionist is apparent in her tendency towards social democracy. The pulse of the labour movement beats strongly in her, a pulse that never beat in time with the Labour Party, but which found its tempo in the ideals and aims of the SDLP. She was always rebellious, and the sharp, clever, quick retort was for ever hovering at the tip of her tongue. When one of her primary school teachers asked the class one day "Where are the British Isles, girls?" she could not resist the barbed reply: "Somewhere between Ireland and the European Continent, Miss."‡

---

‡   When Mary was young, her father gave her a copy of *Speeches from the Dock*. She says the book had a great influence on her political development, particularly the transcript of Robert Emmet's famous speech from the dock of Green Street Courthouse in Dublin in 1803, before being sentenced to death by Lord Norbury.

While she was attending Queen's University, Paddy Leneghan had very little interest in politics. The Long Bar and the rearing of the family were taking up all his time. It was called the Long Bar because the front door was in Leeson Street and the back door was in Cyprus Street, two streets that ran perpendicular to the Falls Road. The long narrow tavern was one of twenty or so pubs in the Lower Falls area, a dangerous area for any business premises. In the early seventies, gun battles between the British army and the IRA were a regular occurrence, and the nickname for the .38 Special Colt revolver, a favoured weapon of the IRA, was "the Leeson Street Special".

The people of the area were very fond of the gentlemanly publican from south of the border. "He keeps a good house," they used to say, meaning that not only was the place clean, but there was never a row or a fight in the pub. One of Paddy's friends and customers was Jim Sullivan, the chairman of the Central Citizens' Defence Committee. Another good friend was Paddy Devlin, the man who was with Mary in the offices of the CCDC during the curfew, a local councillor, an MP in Westminster and one of the founders of the SDLP. In Paddy and Claire's sitting room in Rostrevor, there is a painting of a British army patrol aiming at snipers in Leeson Street. The Long Bar is clearly to be seen, with a car parked across the street from it. The car is Paddy Devlin's, and that was its usual parking place while the revered socialist was holding meetings upstairs in the pub.

The people of the area had many sleepless nights, between British army and RUC searches, riots, gun battles and bombings. Sometimes the Long Bar was searched. Soldiers would block both doors and the place would be ransacked, every customer and bar worker, Paddy included, lined up against the wall, frisked and questioned, but nothing was ever found. This did not prevent the soldiers taking one or two of the drinkers with them for interrogation to the notorious Castlereagh Holding Centre. Even during daylight hours the area was seldom free from trouble of one sort or another. Paddy and his staff and customers became so used to the shooting that they began to accept it as part of life.

One day Paddy and the Guinness representative, Paddy McCaffrey, were standing talking at the bar. Paddy had just turned on the television for the horse races. The first race was due to start at two o'clock, and the attention of all the customers was on the screen. A burst of machine-gun fire came from Leeson Street and everyone went down on the floor. Just then the back door opened and in came Fran McGuigan, a regular customer who was more interested in the two o'clock race than in the shooting outside. While everyone else lay on the floor, he stood in front of the television, his attention alternating between the set and the newspaper in his hand as he made his choice for the first race. Having made his decision, he had to go next door to the bookie's to place his bet. As he walked towards the front door, everyone in the bar called for him to come back. He paused, looked around, consulted his watch and opened the door. The machine-gun opened up again. As everyone ducked Fran went back to the television to check the betting forecast. He was getting worried because it was almost two o'clock and he would not be able to place his bet. Once more he opened the door and once more the machine-gunner fired. At the stroke of two o'clock he made one more valiant effort but was once again foiled by the gunner. At last in utter frustration he turned to Paddy.

"Jesus Christ, Paddy, isn't it an awful country we're living in, when a man would need a white flag to go and put two shillings on a horse!"

Mary heard about the gun battles around the Long Bar on the radio, she saw the searches on the evening news, and every report of trouble in the Lower Falls only added to her worry and stress. She found it increasingly more difficult to apply herself to her studies. Her stress levels were elevated to new heights after an incident that happened on Saturday, 7 October 1972.

It was a typical Saturday afternoon in that part of Belfast: men in and out between the pub and the bookie's; a pint and a bet. Tradition and strict rubrics applied. The privacy of the bet was sacrosanct until the race was over, each man slipping out from the company in the bar and making his way next door. The crowd usually thinned out after the last race of the day, and Seamus Hanvey, one of Paddy's barmen, would go for a break around five o'clock. On this particular Saturday the favourite won the last race, and the pub was packed around half past five, most of the customers having an extra pint or two from their winnings.

The clamour suddenly stopped as the front door crashed open and two youths rushed in. One of them shouted at Paddy, "Mister, there's a car at your door and there's smoke comin' out of it!"

Paddy wasted no time on questions. He ran to the back door, threw it open and shouted, "Everybody out. Car bomb at the front door!"

Everyone ran out the back door into Cyprus Street, except one stubborn customer who insisted on finishing his pint. "An awkward auld git at the best of times," Paddy used to say about him. No matter what Paddy said the man would not move from his seat. Eventually Paddy grabbed him and dragged him along the floor and out the back door. They were no sooner out than the car bomb exploded.

Olive McConnell lived on Cyrella Street, one of the side streets which ran off Leeson Street. She was twenty-three years old and had one child, a little girl whom she could not find when everyone started shouting about the car bomb. She ran from Cyrella Street into Leeson Street looking for her daughter. The Ford Cortina had been left outside the Long Bar, but when the two UVF bombers jumped out of the car to make their escape, they had not engaged the handbrake properly, and the car was slipping slowly down the hill. It had moved four doors away and was outside the People's Co-op shop when it exploded. Olive McConnell was killed instantly when she was hit by a piece of the car, and twelve others were injured in the blast. The following morning there was a photograph in the *Irish News* of Olive's daughter being comforted by neighbours. She had been playing safely in the back yard of her own house all the time.

Later that same evening, as Paddy and the local people were still devastated by the atrocity, two men paid a visit to the Long Bar. Paddy did not recognise them and never saw them again. They asked him if he intended opening the pub again that night.

"I have no intention of opening tonight or tomorrow or the next day. We have to show some respect for the poor woman that has just been killed," said Paddy.

"Do you not realise that that's what those bastards who murdered her want you to do?" asked one of the men.

Paddy was confused and upset. It was clear to him and to everyone else that the Long Bar had been the target of the bombers. He did not know what he should do. Eventually, reluctantly, he opened the pub for one hour that night as a sign of defiance. His heart was never in the place after that. A year later he sold it to James O'Hare, a shopkeeper from the Falls Road. During the 1980s the famous bar, which for years had been run by Hugh O'Kane, and which Paddy had bought from his widow Ellie O'Kane, was demolished during redevelopment.

Paddy had a share in another business in Belfast. In 1971 he and a friend, Tom Hunt, bought a public house on Rosemary Street in the city centre. It was really three pubs in one: the Rosemary Rooms, the Red Barn and the Star and Garter. They had rented the premises to John McKenna who owned the Centre Half Bar on the Falls Road. At the start of November 1974, two parcel bombs of twenty pounds each were left there. When they exploded the whole place caught fire. Paddy got a call from the RUC late that night to go down to Rosemary Street with the keys. There were steel doors throughout the premises, and the firemen were unable to break them down. The keys on the big bunch were all very similar, and they were having difficulty sorting them out. Eventually they put protective clothing on Paddy and took him with them through the burning building. He says it was the most frightening experience of his life. The ceiling above him was a mass of flames, and pieces of blazing timber were falling all around him as he struggled to open three steel doors. He says, "When I got the last of the doors opened I walked on out the far end of the place and I never looked back at it. I just kept on walking."

Mary says she never saw her parents really angry, and Paddy and Claire acknowledge the truth of that statement. They say there was never an ounce of hatred in them. They were often hurt, confused and distressed, but never felt any malice. Mary says that a terrible change came over her parents during the first few years of the 1970s, that the sparkle went from their eyes, the *joie de vivre* that had been so much a part of them as she was growing up disappeared. As young parents they were always full of fun, always easygoing, always facing each new challenge with confidence and determination, but within that period of three years the spark of boldness and self-assurance was extinguished in them.

Years later Mary was driving home from Belfast to Rostrevor one night. She was listening to a radio programme in which a doctor was speaking about post-traumatic stress disorder. The doctor was Peter Curran, a psychiatrist in the Mater Hospital in Belfast, and as he described the symptoms Mary found herself driving slower and slower. Eventually she pulled into the hard shoulder. When he had finished speaking and Mary was parked on the side of the main road, she thought to herself, "Isn't that what we have, every one of us in our family, and my poor father a thousand times worse than the rest of us?"

As she sat in the darkness and thought back over those years, she recognised immediately when her father began to display the worst of the symptoms: after the bombing of the Long Bar. The whole family knew that the death of Olive McConnell was an awful blow for Paddy, but maybe they never realised just how heavy a blow it was. That murder came between him and his contentment. He was never able to ease his conscience after her death because he knew in his heart and soul that he had been the intended target of the UVF bombers and that Olive McConnell had died in his place.

Each member of the Leneghan family had his or her own way of dealing with the trauma. Mary's way, at the time, was silence: to keep her troubles to herself. She was studying hard at university, but the uncertainty was taking its toll on her. Their family home was gone. Her brother John had emigrated to England. The sale of the Long Bar and the insurance money from the Rosemary Rooms had not realised very much, and with the two businesses gone there was no income. The family was scattered. Paddy was ill and no one really knew why. For the first time in her life Claire was uneasy. Mary herself felt crushed, but like her parents she was not going to think too hard about all the difficulties.

Although she had thrown herself fully into the life of the School of Law and the university, it was obvious to all around her that there were difficulties at home, but none of her lecturers ever alluded to them or asked if anything could be done. By the autumn of 1972 she was falling behind in her work; she had too much to do at home and she had begun to be late with essays and assignments. Being fourteen years older than Phelim and eighteen years older than Clement, she was more of a mother than a big sister to the younger children and was, in a sense, complicit with her parents in trying to keep the worst aspects of their harsh reality from the younger children. Between these responsibilities, trying to study and trying to come to terms with her own trauma, she was like a juggler trying to keep too many things in the air at the one time. Something had to crash.

That autumn she spoke to one of her lecturers, Des Greer, a man who was afterwards made a full professor and who would influence an important decision Mary would take in years to come. He told her not to be worried about her studies, that everything would be all right, that it was not terribly important that the essays be finished on time, that he and the other lecturers understood. It seemed that the weight of the world was lifted from her shoulders, and she floated out of the meeting. Why, she rebuked herself, had she not gone to him sooner? She had been unsure how she would be received. She also admitted later that she was reluctant to share her problems with another person, and that pride had a part to play in that reluctance.

Life in the year 1972 was not all stress and strain. That summer she went to America for the first time, on a working holiday. It was usual for Queen's students to cross the Atlantic in the summer, in search of the dollars, the night clubs and the normality of life outside Belfast. A friend of Mary's who had worked the previous year in St Louis, Missouri, selling ice cream from a van, told her she could arrange for her to do the same work. Mary enjoyed driving and was looking forward to the summer work. When she reached St Louis she discovered that the ice cream van was more like a juggernaut than the little Mr Whippy vans that go round the streets of Ireland. No one told her before she tried to manoeuvre the truck through the streets of St Louis that her permit to sell ice cream was restricted to certain areas. She found out soon enough when she was arrested and taken to the police station. The sergeant, of course, was Irish himself . . . only fourth generation, hardly settled yet in the States, as he proudly told her. They settled down for a chat and he put all the blame on the ice cream company. He asked had she any relatives in America, and when he found out about Uncle Dan, Paddy's brother, who worked for TWA in San Francisco, he took it upon himself to ring him. He advised Dan Leneghan to bring Mary to California where she would surely get a more suitable job.

Mary celebrated her twenty-first birthday in Pacifica, San Francisco, in the house of her Uncle Dan and his wife Dorothy. Although she was a little bit homesick at first, she enjoyed the easygoing atmosphere of California, the sea and the sun and the freedom to come and go where and when she pleased. Life in the City by the Bay was very different from life in the City by Belfast Lough.

Dan got her a job in a catering company at the airport, and she wasn't long there when she became friendly with one of her co-workers in Club Catering. Paul was older than Mary, in his thirties, a handsome, gentle, refined, quiet man. She was delighted when he invited her to a concert and later to a couple of films and a play. Mary enjoyed his company immensely. One day Agnes, another Club Catering employee, took Mary aside: "Don't get too interested in him," she said. "He's gay."

As the weeks went by Mary recognised more and more the loneliness in her amiable and gracious friend and the pity shown to him by others because of his sexual orientation. Thoughts of her homosexual friend were very much in her mind some years later when she co-founded a campaign for the rights of the gay community in Ireland.

All too soon she left behind the sun and the sand and came home to the bombs and the bullets. Mary says that the mainstay on which she relied during those dark times was her faith. The Catholic Chaplaincy of the university was on Camden Street at the time, and she was a regular visitor there. When she went there first the chaplain was Fr Patrick Walsh, later Bishop of Down and Connor. Another later chaplain, who also became a bishop, was Anthony Farquhar.

Bishop Walsh says Mary was exceptional among Belfast students: "The Chaplaincy was attended mostly by students from the country. Belfast-based students did not normally frequent the place, but Mary was the exception. She was a loyal visitor. I remember her as a person of deep faith, a person who took her religion very seriously, but enjoyed life to the full."[‡]

Mary found another spiritual shelter during her college days; one not much frequented by Catholic students. It was the Church of Ireland Chaplaincy beside the university, and she visited it before she ever called into its Catholic equivalent. During Freshers' Week she was strolling along the Elmwood Avenue when she saw a sign in the window of number 22: "Come in and Have a Cup of Tea." Mary went in, had a cup of tea and a chat with the chaplain, and so began her lifelong friendship with the Revd Cecil Kerr. He was from County Fermanagh, one of four brothers born on a small farm outside Enniskillen. He founded the Christian Renewal Centre in Rostrevor, a haven of tranquillity, which Mary often visited in later years, renewing there not only her Christianity but also her friendship with Cecil and his wife Myrtle. His ecumenical work got public acknowledgement in 1986 when he was honoured during the People of the Year Awards in Dublin.[§]

During those years at the start of the seventies, Mary took consolation wherever she could get it. Apart from the troubles of her own immediate family, she lost several friends and acquaintances in the bombings of the Abercorn Bar, McGlade's Bar and especially McGurk's bar.[†] Paddy Leneghan and Paddy McGurk had been friends for many years, two publicans from the same mould: open, quiet and friendly, admired by their customers and neighbours. The Tramore Bar, as Paddy McGurk's pub was called, was on North Queen Street. On Saturday evening, 4 December 1971, a UVF man left a bomb containing fifty pounds of gelignite in the hallway of the pub. When it exploded a few minutes later, it killed fifteen people; among them Philomena, Paddy's wife, and his daughter Maria. John Colton, his brother-in-law, and James Cromie, a

---

‡   Interview with the author.

§   Cecil Kerr received one of the ESB/Rehab People of the Year Awards for his work in the area of cross-community relations.

†   The IRA bombing of the Abercorn Bar and Restaurant is considered by many to be one of the worst atrocities of the Troubles. Two women were killed and over seventy people seriously injured, many of them badly mutilated. The Royal Victoria Hospital's Disaster Plan was put into effect for the first time.

friend of Paddy's son John, were also killed. The events of those years stretched even Mary's faith to its limits.

"I became fed up with the old traditional piety that many people found comfort in. There was a battle going on inside me at that time between deep faith and dreadful doubt."

Terrorist violence was not the only kind of brutality that was bothering her at the time. In 1974 she read Erin Pizzey's new book, *Scream Quietly or the Neighbours Will Hear,* and it opened her eyes to the problem of domestic violence. In 1971 Pizzey had opened the first women's refuge in Chiswick, West London, and had subsequently written the first book on the topic of battered wives. Mary was appalled at the stories of cruelty within families and even more horrified by the statistics. She realised it must have been going on all around her. The women's movement and the fight for equality had not been as strong north of the border as it had been in the Republic, because of the emphasis in the North on civil rights. In 1970 Dr Thekla Beere had chaired the Commission on the Status of Women, whose report in 1972 became the charter for women in the modern Irish state. In 1973 the Council for the Status of Women was formed as an umbrella organisation for women's groups. In that same year, the Irish government appointed its first ever woman ambassador, Mary Catherine Tinney, to Sweden and Finland. Late in time as these events occurred, the women's movement in Northern Ireland had achieved little by comparison.

Mary has always been vocal on the question of women's rights. She has criticised colleges, denounced local authorities and rebuked political parties she found to be lacking in providing or protecting those rights. Within the structure of the Catholic Church, she has taken on priests and bishops and even the pope on the rights of women. Despite this record, she was never a signed-up member of the women's liberation movement. She explains that she had a problem with the narrowly rigid attitudes, the restraints and restrictions that were part of the movement in the early seventies:

> To become a fully signed-up member of the movement at that time you had to proclaim your beliefs in A, B, C and D, and suddenly you were subjected to the tyranny of these awesome orthodoxies. Suddenly the intellectual freedom which people had fought so hard to achieve started to be closed off. Soon people were coming under the yoke of an autocracy, which was in some ways as tyrannical as the anti-woman practices that had spawned the movement in the first place. In order to comply fully you could not

be a practising member of a church, especially the Catholic Church in Ireland. My own views on faith would have marked me out, in the eyes of some people, as the product of an unthinking convent school education. Few would have realised that my views were forged the hard way: that my faith was the product of a fight, a constant struggle. Despite the views of the more hard-line membership, faith was never going to be an obstacle to woman becoming liberated in her mind and in her views.

Erin Pizzey had a similar distrust of absolute compliance, as witness this account of the early days of the Women's Movement in London:

We, the mothers, sat around the kitchen table rearranging the world according to Marx. I, who had enjoyed men's company enormously, had the feeling that these women, underneath all their political chatter, really disliked men . . . Useless to tell these women that Marx never did anything for women, was unkind to his family and refused to have women in the Politburo.[‡]

Nuala Fennell had been a founding member of the Irish women's liberation movement in Dublin in 1970. When she saw a programme about battered wives in London and found that many of the women in question were Irish, she was moved to write a letter to *The Irish Times* asking for help to found a shelter in Dublin. The response was overwhelming, and a shelter was founded in 1974. A group of people from Queen's University went to meet her with a view to setting up a women's shelter in Belfast. Mary had been drawn into the issue by another Queen's student who got her inspiration in London, Patricia Irwin (now Montgomery), who was a year behind Mary in the School of Law:

I was doing a dissertation on battered wives and went to visit the refuge in London. When I came home I spoke to several women whom I felt would be interested in founding a similar refuge in Belfast. Among them were Betty Craig, who worked for the Belfast Festival; law student Nora O'Boyle; Sheena Flynn, a librarian at Queen's; Colm Fitzpatrick, a social worker who dealt with battered wives on a regular basis and Mary McAleese. Mary and I worked very hard and very well together. She persuaded some friends of her family to furnish and carpet the refuge in Camden Street, but more importantly, she put a lot of time and

---

‡ Extract from an essay by Erin Pizzey entitled: "How the Women's Movement Taught Women to Hate Men"; http://www.angryharry.com/reAnEssaybyErinPizzey.htm.

energy into the place and was a regular worker there until she moved to Dublin in 1975.[‡]

Bill Wright from Rostrevor, who owned a carpet factory in Newry, was a friend of Mary's family. Mary asked him to supply carpet for the refuge at a reduced price. "Bill carpeted the place from top to bottom and never took a penny," says Mary. She then asked her father to ask the Knights of Columbanus for some financial help, and they responded readily, supplying all the furniture for the building.

In 1973 Queen's University Belfast awarded Mary Leneghan an honours degree in law. Her family and relatives were very proud of her, with just cause. Philomena Lucy Bateson, another former pupil of St Dominic's, had been the first woman called to the Northern Ireland Bar for several years. With the exceptions of Kate O'Brien and Sheelagh Murnaghan, no woman had made a serious attempt to practise law for about twenty-five years. Now Mary Leneghan and two other women were about to assault the citadel of male domination. But first they had to do the Bar Year, and to do this they had to have a master, a barrister with whom they would work for a year while studying for the bar examination.

Mary did not know any barristers, but Kevin Boyle arranged that she would work with Peter Smith.[§]

> When Peter Smith accepted me, a Catholic woman, as his pupil, it was a brave and radical act. He was a quiet, private man, an honest man who was unshakeable in what he believed in. He was a straight man also, outspoken, and even though his pupil was also outspoken, I held him in a kind of awe during that year. In spite of the differences in our religious and cultural backgrounds, we found out, after a while—remarkably, we both thought—that we could work very well together while respecting our differences. I will always be grateful to him for his help and guidance as I was trying to make my way as a young lawyer.

Three Belfast Catholic women were called to the Northern Ireland Bar on the same day: Mary Leneghan, Eilis McDermott from the Glen Road in West Belfast, who later became the first ever woman QC in Northern Ireland, and Pat Kennedy from Fruithill Park, an old neighbour of Mary's.[†] The Bar year was a difficult year. There were

---

‡   Interview with the author.

§   Peter Smith was later chairman of the South Belfast Unionist Association and subsequently represented the interests of unionists on the Patten Commission.

†   QC: queen's counsel, the equivalent of senior counsel in the Republic.

fifteen students on the course, half of which was held in the School of Law and half in the Inns of Court. Some of the lecturers, including David Trimble, they knew already from the degree course.

While Mary, Pat and Eilis were working to qualify as barristers, the turbulent world around them was becoming even more chaotic. On New Year's Day 1974, the Northern Ireland Executive, the power-sharing experiment between unionists and nationalists, was established with Brian Faulkner as its Chief Executive. Many of the more obstinate unionists were unhappy with the idea, and eight RUC men were required to remove a protesting Ian Paisley from the Stormont Assembly. Unionists of all shades of opinion came together under the umbrella body of the United Ulster Unionist Council, whose aim was to stand firm against the implementation of the Sunningdale Agreement.[†] At the end of March a new organisation emerged: the Ulster Workers' Council, a coalition of loyalist groupings which threatened civil unrest unless the Stormont Executive was disbanded and the Sunningdale Agreement revoked.

These events, as usual, had serious consequences on the streets of Northern Ireland. Every event or major utterance on events provoked riots. During riots buses were burned. When a bus was burned, all public transport was taken off the roads. With no public transport, people were driving cars where they would not normally do so. Hijackings were rife. It was difficult and very dangerous to travel in Belfast after dark. Quite often Mary did not travel and consequently missed several lectures and seminars.

She was about to sit her final Bar exams when the Ulster Workers' Council Strike began on 14 May and she had to study by candlelight. The strike lasted a fortnight, and the electricity supply, public transport, the postal service, the telephone service, food, milk and fuel supplies were all affected. On the third day of the strike, the bombs exploded in Dublin and Monaghan, killing thirty-three people, the biggest number of lives lost in any one day during the Troubles.

In Belfast, Sammy Smyth, the press officer of the UDA and the

---

† On 6–9 December 1973 the Taoiseach Liam Cosgrave, the British Prime Minister Edward Heath and members (designate) of the Northern Ireland Executive met in Sunningdale, England. The Irish government agreed that the status of the Northern Ireland state would remain unchanged unless the majority of the people of Northern Ireland expressed a desire for change. All parties agreed on the formation of a "Council of Ireland" in which the Republic of Ireland would have a consultative role in some of the affairs of Northern Ireland.

Strike Committee of the Ulster Workers' Council said, "I am very happy about the bombings in Dublin. There is a war with the Free State and now we are laughing at them."‡

The bombings and Sammy Smyth's statement ensured that tension and trouble would reach new heights in the North. There were bombings and shootings, protests and riots, roads were closed and schools and work places emptied. On Sunday, 19 May, Merlyn Rees, the secretary of state, announced a state of emergency in Northern Ireland, but still the strike went on. Eventually, on 28 May, Brian Faulkner and his colleagues withdrew from the Assembly. The power-sharing Executive was dead, the Sunningdale Agreement was dead, and the strike was over.

Seamus Heaney wrote this about the tension in the city:

> There are few enough people on the roads at night. Fear has begun to tingle through the place. Who's to know the next target on the Provisional list? Who's to know the reprisals won't strike where you are? The bars are quieter. If you're carrying a parcel you make sure it's close to you in case it's suspected of being about to detonate. In the Queen's University staff common room, recently, a bomb-disposal squad had defused a bundle of books before the owner had quite finished his drink in the room next door. Yet when you think of the corpses in the rubble of McGurk's Bar such caution is far from risible.§

In Queen's University there was no talk of postponing examinations. Mary had an exam on the day Michael Gaughan died after sixty-four days on hunger strike in Parkhurst Prison in England. No one moved very far in any nationalist area that night. She sat her last exam on the day her old schoolmate Dolours Price and her sister Marian came off their hunger strike in Brixton Prison in England, where the authorities had been force-feeding them for six months. Many people, including Mary, say they "just got on with life" during those terrible days, and so they did. But getting on with life during a time of peace is not the same as getting on with life when there is a gun battle going on outside your door. The passing of time can soften the memories of horror and assuage the fear, but there is no doubt that those days in the 1970s were horrific and fearful for Mary Leneghan and for all those who lived through them.

---

‡   Sammy Smyth was shot dead by the IRA on 10 March 1976. UDA: Ulster Defence Association.

§   Seamus Heaney, *Preoccupations* (London: Faber and Faber, 1980), p. 31.

But through all the panic and dread people kept their sense of humour. The memory of an incident that happened during the year of the Bar course still brings a smile to Mary's face. She and some friends from the course were at a party hosted by Rajeev Dhavan when she was introduced to a well known lawyer who later became an equally well known politician. It was obviously a source of amazement and amusement to him that a Catholic woman thought she would pass the Bar exam and thereby be unleashed on the courts of Northern Ireland.

"Well, my dear, when you have failed the Bar you can always open a little bordello at the back of the Law Library," he said.

Mary says her hand was itching to slap his face. No one, except her close friends near by, noticed the effort it cost her to control herself as she replied in an unruffled tone: "I have no intention of failing the Bar. But, if I do, and if I open a little bordello at the back of the Law Library, you will never be a customer. Unlike the bordellos you obviously frequent, this one will have a sign outside saying 'Gentlemen Only'!"

The riposte was the talk of the Bar Library the next day.

Sexism wasn't the only reason why life as a Bar student was difficult; lack of money had its effects, too. During the four years of the degree course, she often worked in the Rosemary Rooms or the Long Bar, but such work was prohibited during the Bar year by the rules of the Inn of Court. She had declined a place on a PhD course in Edinburgh out of concern that the grant available to her would not be adequate. Mary was anxious not to ask her parents for money, and she never considered a bank loan as she had a dread of debt.

Some aspects of law were more attractive to Mary than others. She was attracted by the idea of research. The academic life, teaching the law, also attracted her. She had had her fill for the time being of Belfast life, of, as she says "the conflict, the hypocrisy, the pure naked sectarianism". She wanted out but first had to complete her year's pupillage after her call to the Bar. She gives her own account of her first day in court:

> I had all the unimportant paraphernalia, law degree, practising certificate, wig, gown, law books; I even had a client, God help him, but there were a couple of essential things missing. The first thing of paramount importance that I lacked was any idea of where I should sit. Even my client, a regular it seemed on the court circuit, knew where he should sit. He threw himself into the public gallery with the air of a man who owned the place, but I, the advocate on whom he was relying to impress the court, hung awkwardly around

the lawyers' benches in the hope that an obvious place would open up to which I could lay claim. It didn't. The longer I stood the more I wished a black hole would open up in the floor and swallow me. The second thing I lacked was the wit to ask someone to help me. Within minutes I no longer wanted my chosen vocation or my client. All I wanted was my mammy. Everyone else seemed so confidently busy, so at home, so known. I would have settled for feeling invisible, but actually I felt like a pair of Rosary beads in an Orange Lodge. Suddenly one of the busy lawyers looked up and caught my eye. Immediately he was at my side. "Sit beside me and I'll keep you right." He did. Gently and kindly he introduced me to everyone. They moved over on the bench and made room for one more. I now belonged. I was one of their own.[‡]

She now had her passport, and a valuable passport it was. It would take her anywhere she wanted, as long as she used it right. But who would go with her on her journey? There was no doubt about that in the summer of 1974 as she had been engaged to Martin McAleese since the springtime.

‡ Mary McAleese, *Reconciled Being*, p. 13.

Chapter Eleven

On Again, Off Again

I stepped out and she stepped in again
She stepped out and I stepped in again
("Lanigan's Ball"—traditional)

The engagement did not bestow any immediate stability on their relationship, nor did it convince Mary that all storms were now in the past. In Martin's mind, they were well set on the path he had always wanted, and now it was time to concentrate on another matter—namely employment. He had spent three years studying physics in Queen's, and although he had an honours degree in science, he had decided to work as an accountant.

In March 1972, before Martin's final year degree exams, Mary had driven him to Dublin for an interview with Stokes Kennedy Crowley, Ireland's biggest accountancy firm, where he was offered a position as an articled clerk to Laurence Crowley, a senior partner. That summer he moved to Dublin and started work. At first he lived in a single bedsit on Merrion Road and subsequently shared a flat with John McCrory, another old St Mary's boy from Belfast, in 7 Sydney Parade Avenue. This house was owned by Eileen Davitt, a daughter of Michael Davitt, founder of the Land League. Martin spent many an evening enthralled by the stories of "that lovely, lovely old lady", as he called her.

He was serving his articles over a three-year period, during which time he would submit for parts 2, 3, 4 and 5 of the examinations of the Institute of Chartered Accountants in Ireland. Those who had a degree in economics or commerce needed only to do parts 4 and 5; but as Martin's degree was not relevant to accountancy, he was exempt from only part 1. He says he did not attend a single lecture or any accountancy course, and the results of his first exam lend credibility to his claim: in the summer of 1973, he failed part 2. After that debacle he decided to buy a couple of books on the subject and successfully passed the repeat exam before Christmas. He then passed part 3 in summer 1974 and part 4 before Christmas of the same year. He still did not attend any courses, because any extra money he had was spent on travelling to Belfast at weekends to be with Mary.

In October 1973, Martin was joined in Stokes Kennedy Crowley by his old friend from Queen's, Seamus Mullan. Mullan's arrival coincided with the beginning of Martin's quest for new accommodation. Before the two friends found a suitable place for themselves, they shared a riotous house with Martin's old dancing partner Moss Keane and some other Kerrymen, Jim Coughlan and Denis Coffey among them. They all lived a comfortable bachelor life, and they often met after work in Madigan's or the Rathmines Inn for a drink and a chat about sport and the day's events. Seamus and Martin eventually moved into a less unruly apartment on Rathgar Road. Seamus was at that time playing inter-county football with Derry, and Martin often referred to him later as "one of the most talented footballers and perhaps the best free-taker that I have ever seen".

Despite the fact that Martin assiduously cultivated the image of the thoroughly modern man, he was old-fashioned in some areas. For example, he asked Paddy Leneghan's permission before he asked Mary to marry him. Luckily for him, both said yes. By the autumn of 1974, he found himself able to spend a lot more time with his fiancée because, to his delight, Stokes Kennedy Crowley had opened a new office in Belfast, in the Russell Court Hotel on the Lisburn Road, and Martin was transferred to his native city.

Mary was, by this time, finished with her Bar course and was busily trying not to feel like "a rosary beads in an Orange Lodge". She had moved out of the family home in Fruithill Park and was staying where she had previously spent six weeks, with her old friends Margaret and Pat Campbell. The Leneghan family would not be spending much longer in Fruithill because Paddy was anxious to find a new pub, outside Belfast if possible. On opening the *Irish News* one morning in late 1974, he saw an advertisement: "public house for sale in South County Down". He did not know which town the pub was in or how much the owners wanted for it, but he was interested. He and Claire loved that part of the country and had driven every road through the Mournes and around Carlingford Lough. Patrick and Damien were at school in St Colman's College in Newry and Kate was in the Louis Convent in Kilkeel. Claire started a novena.

When Paddy rang about the advertisement, he found that the pub in question was the Corner House in Rostrevor, owned by a man called Jim Flynn. Paddy remembered meeting Flynn years before, and both he and Claire had nice memories of the Corner House, where they had stopped for a drink a few times. It was a fine bar in a beautiful place. They had often said they would love to live somewhere like Rostrevor. Now they had the chance.

They bought the place in November, and in December Paddy and Martin started spending every weekend there, painting and hanging wallpaper and preparing the upstairs rooms so that the family could move in immediately after Christmas. Paddy did not want to lose the holiday business by closing the pub, so he and Martin decided to continue the repairing and decorating after closing time over the Christmas holidays, often working until breakfast time before falling into bed for a few hours. On Christmas Eve, Mary came to help them.

Paddy and Martin agree it was another strange Christmas. When Mary left them that night, they stayed working in the bar until three o'clock. After mass they had their Christmas dinner in the Great Northern Hotel and then started back on the work.

Charlie McAleese had this to say about Martin and Christmas: "When Martin was young there was never much celebration in our house on birthdays and even at Christmas. We always enjoyed those days but they were quiet. We never went out of our way to do anything special."‡

That was not the case in the Leneghan house according to Paddy: "They often concocted reasons for celebration in our house. Birthdays and Christmas weren't enough for them, and God knows there were plenty of birthdays. They would have a party at the drop of a hat, but Christmas Day was the most special of all."

On 3 January the Leneghans moved in. It was the end of a long and eventful association with Belfast, a connection that had cost them a home and two businesses and almost their lives. They were glad to leave it all behind. Claire was back in her own people's county and was content now for the first time since they left Ardoyne. Mary moved into an apartment in Ulsterville Avenue, close to the university, and had the pleasure, for the first time in her life, of having a bedroom of her own. For Martin, it was as if he were already part of the family. His happiness could not have been more complete as he looked forward to marrying the girl he had fallen in love with at first sight. To add to the contentment of all, the IRA announced a ceasefire on 9 February. The IRA peace agreement was short lived, but the accord between Mary and Martin was even shorter.

---

‡   Interview with the author.

On a Saturday evening at the beginning of April, they were at a dinner hosted by Mary's master, Peter Smith, when the rift happened. They spent the evening trying to be civil to each other in front of their host and the other guests, but inside they were furious with each other. Martin later blamed it on the brandy but Mary was taking no excuses. To her way of thinking, a remark Martin had made was mortally insulting to their host and extremely embarrassing to her. As he had no car Mary had to drive him home. By the time they reached the McAleese's new house in Ashton Park in Finaghy, the engagement was off and Mary never wanted to see Martin McAleese again. Not only was their relationship over, it was in tatters with never a hope of repair. Martin's mother came to the door when she heard the raised voices outside and found her future daughter-in-law, flames in her eyes, battle-rage in her every movement, berating her son on their doorstep. Her son was looking very cowed as he stood at his own hall door. When Mary saw Emma McAleese her anger evaporated. She says she felt terribly sorry for Martin's mother that night, but there was to be no going back on the decision. Goodbye, Martin McAleese.

When the Troubles started in 1969, Radio Free Belfast, a pirate station, was broadcasting to huge audiences all over West Belfast. As the transmitter was constantly moved around, the British army and RUC wasted a lot of time and effort trying to discover its whereabouts and who was behind it. One of the transmission bases was an upstairs room in the Long Bar, and Paddy Leneghan has many stories about the trouble they had with the makeshift equipment. John Gray, later of the Linenhall Library in Belfast, was one of the prime movers behind the station, and Rory McShane from Newry was one of the broadcasters. McShane had been president of the Student Union in Queen's University in 1968, was one of the founders of People's Democracy and was on the executive of the Northern Ireland Civil Rights Association. He was to be the principal speaker, with Lord Fenner Brockway, at the aborted meeting after the Bloody Sunday March in Derry in 1972. He and Sean Hollywood organised the massive protest march in Newry a week later, an illegal march which attracted 100,000 people, including Michael O'Leary, leader of the Labour Party in the Republic, the actress Vanessa Redgrave and the theatre director Joan Littlewood. McShane also stood as an independent candidate for the Northern Ireland Assembly after the Sunningdale Agreement and was narrowly defeated.

While Mary was still in secondary school, she often heard the fiery young socialist speaking at debates and meetings, and he was one of her heroes. She looked on him as someone who always knew the right thing to say and was not afraid to say it. He obtained his degree in 1968 and was gone when Mary arrived there the following year. But he had left a huge impression, and both staff and students often spoke of his eloquence and his courage. Everyone knew Rory McShane.

He was very different from Martin McAleese. An only child, he came from a well-to-do business background and had the self-assurance and aplomb that such a background confers. Martin's fame was limited to followers of Gaelic football in County Antrim, whereas Rory was seen regularly on television, his voice was instantly recognisable on the radio, and his photograph was often in the newspapers. To the nationalist people in the early days of the Troubles, he was one of their icons, and many listened carefully to his every word. One person, at least, in the nationalist community had no interest in Rory McShane or in any man. That person was Mary Leneghan. In fact, Mary was interested in very little. It was as if she were going around in a dream, blind to many things that were going on around her, and blind to the interest Rory was showing in her.

He was carving a successful career as a solicitor when he became seriously interested in the young barrister. He met her in Newry Courthouse one summer day in 1975 and invited her to lunch. The next evening they went for dinner and began to go out together.

She had no experience of going out with anyone other than Martin, and he was gone, never to return. Peter O'Keeffe, the only other man in whom she ever showed any real interest, was two years married by then. There was an emptiness in her life, and Martin was not the man to fill it. She had thought of him as being less mature than herself. Here, however, was a man who was older than her, not only in age but in the ways of the world; a sympathetic man, polished and confident. He had money and that assured air that goes with the well-filled wallet. He had fallen in love with her. He had mesmerised her with his charm, and Mary gladly capitulated.

Was she infatuated or in love or on the rebound? Was she attracted to the man or his image, or maybe a combination of the two? His money meant nothing to her, as was obvious when she repeatedly refused his offer to buy her a sports car, saying she was perfectly happy with the little yellow second-hand Fiat her father had bought her. Could it be that she was so out of tune with her emotions that she thought she was in love? Could the previous five years of trauma and tragedy have had a bearing on her reluctance to effectively analyse her situation? Whatever else happened during this time, one thing is certain: she turned her back on the old self-assertive, decisive, sanguine Mary and donned a different cloak. For the next few months she would be retiring and vacillating, fragile and vague. For the first time she would sit back and let someone else steer her life, and she would be happy to do so—or so she thought. She may have been ready for all the attention, devotion and kindness, but she was ill prepared for the speed and the intensity of the courtship. Three months after she had broken her engagement to Martin, Rory asked her to marry him and she agreed.

Rory wanted to give Mary the moon and the stars. He wanted to show her and give her the good life, the life of "the beautiful people". One evening he arrived at her house to bring her out for dinner. He had reserved a table at Number 10, a fashionable and expensive restaurant in Hillsborough. Mary had no idea where they were going to eat and she was dressed casually in a loose shirt and jeans. Rory asked her to change into a dress, but she refused. He then asked Claire to try to persuade her, but still Mary refused. "My ordinary clothes will do me well enough," she said. Eventually, when it was explained that the restaurant had a strict dress code, she reluctantly agreed to change, but as usual she had the last word. As she and Rory were shown to their table in the stylish restaurant, she looked around at the clientele, the décor and the expensive fittings and remarked, "Not a bad place for a socialist, Rory!"

Rory McShane had no chance with the Leneghans. No one except Martin McAleese would have had a chance. Martin was the boys' hero. For six years he had been letting them use his Brylcreem, his razor, his aftershave, had taught them football skills and timed their races. For six years he had been telling Mary's younger sisters how beautiful, how clever and how talented they were. He had charmed Claire from the outset, and Paddy knew him as a great worker and a true friend. One evening, as Rory was sitting in the Leneghan house waiting for Mary, Clement asked his mother, aloud, whom she would prefer: Rory or Martin. Claire tried to distract him by talking about a television programme that was due to start, but Clement, undeterred, announced to all present that he would much prefer Martin. Martin! Martin! Martin! It seemed to Rory that every time he came to the house he heard nothing but "Martin".

To Martin it seemed that he heard nothing from his friends but "Rory McShane and Mary Leneghan". On the day Rory proposed to Mary, Martin was sitting his part 5 accountancy exam. He says, "I was destroyed. I couldn't believe what I heard. Within three months of leaving me, she was engaged to another man. It was very hard to take."

In his heart he knew that Mary was never as taken with the idea of marriage as he was. He also understood that, for the sake of their relationship, they probably should have spent some time apart. He heard that Rory had bought a house in Rostrevor, Quay Cottage, right on the coast, a romantic nest for which they both had chosen the furniture, carpets and curtains. This news was the hardest to bear. There was only one way to deal with this: to become cool, indifferent, imperturbable—at least outwardly. That was the clever way, the McAleese way. He worked out his two-point strategy: priority number one, no direct contact with Mary; priority number two, Mary must have no idea how upset he was. He straightened his shoulders and stuck out his chin. He would brazen it out. He let it be known to their mutual friends that he was in great form, that he was enjoying life to the full.

Then came the day in mid-July when he turned the corner from University Road into Camden Street and had to stop suddenly or he would have bumped into Mary. There they were, face to face, and neither had any option but to be civil.

"Well, Martin, how are you? It's ages since I've seen you."

"I'm great, Mary, thanks very much. It's nice to see you again. I believe yourself and Rory McShane are going to tie the knot. I wish you both the very best."

"That's nice of you to say so, Martin. Any news from your end?"

"Never better, Mary, rarin' to go. I've itchy feet. You wouldn't know what part of the world I'd be in this time next year. Talking about travel, have you any plans for the summer?"

"Rory and I are going to honeymoon in Italy."

"That will be very nice. I'm off to Tenerife myself for a fortnight, along with a few friends."

The conversation continued for about ten minutes, Martin doing his best to maintain the nonchalant image, hoping that Mary was being duped by his apparent insouciance. He contends that when the conversation ended he was certain that he would get Mary back again.

"I understood that a lot of difficulties stood in the way of a reconciliation, but when I said goodbye to her that day on the corner of University Road, I walked on with a lighter step and a much lighter heart."

He claims he was able to read her, even then, as he would read a book; that he knew by her body language, her face, the things she said and the things she left unsaid, that he couldn't lose her. He says the meeting was an epiphany, a fateful episode that "bounced her back from whatever sort of catatonic trance she was in".

Martin's was a strange sort of certainty, according to his father: "For somebody that was so sure of himself, his heart was in his mouth every morning until he had flicked through the *Irish News* to see was there a picture of the wedding of Mary and Rory McShane."

Mary admits to only a very hazy recollection of the meeting on University Road and maintains that she can't remember what she and Martin talked about. "It was definitely no epiphany," she says. There were signs to be read if either of them had the eyes to read them. Mary had applied for a job in Dublin and was anxious to go there to live. Rory had a thriving solicitor's practice in Newry and would not consider moving. Would the married couple live happily separated by a border and seventy miles of road? Mary had not allowed Rory to buy her an engagement ring, but she still had the ring Martin had given her.

It was a sunny evening at the start of September, three weeks before the wedding, and Mary was extolling the virtues of her husband-to-be to her close friend Jo Thompson. She spoke of his gentleness, his kindness, his courtesy and charm, the respect with which he treated her, the care and attention . . . Then Jo started asking the hard questions. She wanted to know if Mary was certain in her heart of hearts that Rory was the man she wanted to be with for the rest of her life. How and where did she imagine herself and Rory in twenty years' time? Was she totally, utterly, entirely happy with their relationship? Had the relationship developed as she had hoped since they started going together? Mary's eyes began to moisten as Jo was speaking. Her vision began to mist as she considered her answers to the questions. Now she started to shake her head from side to side and the first tear slid down her face, unchecked. A stammering sob shuddered through her body as more tears forced their way from her tightly shut eyes. Soon she was shaking from head to toe and her handkerchief was sodden. She choked at first as she tried to talk through the racking sobs: first words, then phrases, eventually whole sentences as the self-recrimination erupted and the stark reality of her situation convulsed her.

Jo stood beside her as Mary phoned her mother.

"Why are you crying, Mary? What's wrong with you?"

There was a terrible tension in Mary between the need to talk and the fear of talking.

"Oh God, I'm very upset, Mammy. I don't know if I can go ahead with this wedding."

"And who says you have to go ahead with the wedding? Who says you have to if you don't want to?"

"Nobody but myself, I suppose. The whole thing is all my own fault. I've let this happen, and now I'm going to make an awful mess of Rory's life as well as my own if I don't go ahead with the wedding. I think this whole thing with Rory just happened on the rebound from Martin McAleese."

"Come on home, Mary, and we'll talk about it. If that's the way you feel about it, it's time to examine the whole thing from top to bottom."

The priest, the chapel and the hotel were already booked, the invitations sent out, some presents already received, travel arrangements made. There were hundreds of people who would not understand this turn of events. In spite of all this, by bedtime that night the wedding was off.

Claire was happy that Mary had changed her mind, even at the last minute, and the young Leneghans were even happier. They all thought that maybe Martin would have another chance. Paddy said nothing and would not be drawn. Years later he admitted that he was very angry at Mary for letting things get so far advanced before breaking off the engagement. But he also said it was a great relief to him that the wedding was cancelled.

Mary perfectly accepted her father's attitude, as expressed years later, and she understood and correctly interpreted his stolid silence at the time. For a woman who is usually capable of managing her emotions efficiently, she seemed unable to articulate all that was happening to her during her engagement to Rory McShane, and especially as their wedding day loomed nearer. She knew that the decision she made was the right one, although it would shake a very decent and loving man to his core. She says she thought it would have been easier to deny the harsh realities and to let herself be carried along with the excitement of the preparations. It might have been easier in the short term, but could she have lived with it? A good, brave and loyal friend was required to set her straight, and she found that friend in Jo Thompson.

Martin was just about to go to Tenerife when he heard the news. He says he was so overjoyed that he could almost have flown there without the help of the aeroplane. He enjoyed the holiday much more than he thought he would, and his friends never suspected that the contented expression he wore day and night had little to do with the sunshine and the relaxation.

When he arrived home his mother greeted him with news that made his smug smile wider still: "Mary's sister has phoned a couple of times to complain about you being off enjoying yourself on a foreign holiday while Mary is sitting at home depressed and broken-hearted. And it's all your fault. She wants to know what you are going to do about it. What are you going to do about it, Martin?"

"I'm going to have a cup of tea, Mammy. Is the kettle on?" replied Martin with a satisfied grin.

In the middle of October, Rory asked Mary to be his hostess at a Halloween party in Quay Cottage. Before they broke up they had planned to have a house-warming party in the cottage around Halloween. Now Rory wanted to go ahead with it under a different guise: a party for their friends and families on the Saturday after Halloween, to show the world that they were still friends. Mary thought it was a great idea and gladly accepted the role of hostess. The novelty of the whole idea helped to diffuse a lot of the tension surrounding the break-up. Everyone thought Mary and Rory were dealing with their difficult situation in a very sensible and mature way. A few times in the course of the evening, Mary noticed that her father had a pale and sickly look. She asked him if he was all right but could get no other answer than "Of course, I'm all right. What would be wrong with me?"

Next morning Paddy and Claire were hurrying up the hill to the chapel, a couple of minutes late for ten o'clock mass. They had almost reached the chapel door when Paddy collapsed with a massive heart attack. Mrs Bell, a nurse with years of experience in coronary care, who was also late for mass, managed to keep Paddy alive until the ambulance came and rushed him to Daisy Hill Hospital in Newry.

A week later Martin McAleese was in the Student Union in Queen's when he heard about Paddy's heart attack. He was shocked and upset. He had always been very fond of Paddy and would never forget the help and encouragement and financial support Paddy had given his family when they were put out of their house on internment day. He decided he would go and visit him in Daisy Hill. When he walked into the ward, it was immediately obvious how delighted Mary's father was to see him. The talk came naturally to both of them, and soon they were chatting away like the old friends they were. Later on, when Claire came in with two of the younger children, it was like a family reunion: Claire hugging him fiercely and telling him how well he looked, the children pulling him and vying for his attention with their stories of school and sports. Paddy lay back in bed and enjoyed the whole scene. When Martin was invited back to the Corner House for dinner, Claire did not have to ask him twice.

As Claire's car was approaching Rostrevor, Martin's nerves would not let him sit still. He was turning back to the children, pretending to listen to them, scratching his head as Claire kept up a constant commentary on every place they passed. He says he heard nothing. When the car pulled up outside the Corner House, Martin let Claire go in first, but it was the children who announced him as they rushed past their mother and shouted into the kitchen, "Look who's here for dinner, Mary!"

He stopped in the doorway and looked at her. Slowly and shyly he took a couple of steps into the kitchen, not knowing whether he should reach out to shake her hand or stretch out his arms to give her a hug. Mary solved his predicament by opening her own arms, and both of them fell into an embrace.

The story was all over the town like smoke, and friends started to call. Mary is strongly of the opinion that the conspiracy in favour of Martin was more widespread than the immediate family circle. Sometime after dinner Patti Power arrived to invite Mary and Martin to a party in her house the next evening. Patti afterwards maintained that the party had been planned for weeks, but that she only thought of inviting her dear friend Mary on the evening before the well-arranged event; and now that Martin was back in Rostrevor on a visit, well . . . ! The Leneghans begged Martin to spend the night with them rather than travel to Belfast and back again. Martin did not need much persuasion. He did not want to let Mary out of his sight again. At the party they danced and talked, whispered and reminisced. Towards the end of the evening, the dulcet tones of Paul Simon and Art Garfunkel singing "Bridge Over Troubled Waters" wafted from the stereo. It was always their special song, and it worked its old magic as it had done on other occasions. Before Martin left Rostrevor on Sunday night, he and Mary were once again engaged to be married and the date of the wedding was fixed!

This time both were satisfied in their minds that the decision was the right one. They agreed, one somewhat more wholeheartedly than the other, that the year apart had done them nothing but good. They visited Mary's dear old friends and neighbours, Tony and Myles O'Reilly, in their restaurant, the Golden Pheasant, outside Lisburn. The brothers were married to two sisters, and although the O'Reillys were close friends of Mary's, Martin had also come to know them and their wives very well.

When the brothers heard the news of the upcoming wedding, they opened a bottle of champagne.

"It'll be a small enough wedding," said Mary. "Around seventy guests. We'd love to have it here in the Golden Pheasant if that's possible. Can we have a look at the reservation book?"

"No problem, if you're talking about seventy or eighty guests," said Myles. "But I can't imagine your mother being satisfied with a wedding of that size. Look, we'll pencil in the date, but I bet you'll be back to me soon to tell me the place isn't going to be big enough. I know your mother."

Myles was correct in his prediction. Mary and Martin had to start asking around about a bigger venue for their reception. They took advice from friends and relatives and eventually settled for the Ardmore Hotel in Newry. This hotel was owned by the Scallon family, one of whom, Damien Scallon, was a friend of Mary's. Damien later married Dana, the singer who first won the Eurovision Song Contest for Ireland and would be one of Mary's four competitors in the campaign for the presidency twenty-one years later. The Ardmore Hotel had no Saturday free for a wedding reception until after the summer, and so the big day was changed to a Tuesday.

The month preceding the wedding was one of the busiest in Mary's life until then. She was living and working in Dublin and travelling North two or three times a week. Like any other young woman approaching her wedding, she found that the number of tasks seemed to increase by the day and the number of hours available to complete them seemed to decrease proportionately. She made the hats for the bridesmaids and the green velvet dress for her sister Claire. She would have made her own honeymoon clothes, but her mother and father insisted that they would buy an outfit for her. On the day appointed for the purchase of this outfit, Mary and Claire left the long-suffering Paddy waiting for an hour and a half under the famous Clery's Clock in Dublin's O'Connell Street, as they inspected every viable alternative outfit in Dublin city centre before returning to their first choice, where they had left Paddy, at Clery's. The following evening Mary set aside some time to pen what she considered a long overdue letter of thanks to her parents:

Dear Daddy and Mammy,

A word of thanks for the beautiful outfit you bought yesterday. I didn't expect such an outcome to a day's shopping and I really appreciate not just the clothes but the spirit in which they were bought. As always you want the best for me and for all of us. I hope I will be able to give the best in return, though I'll never be able to repay, even in a small way, all that you have done for me. But I want to stop now and say thank you to you both for simply everything before the panic sets in and the words are said in haste on our way out the door.

I don't always communicate my love and appreciation but I want you to know that few things give me as much strength and comfort as the knowledge that I have good, caring, loving parents. It means a lot in times of anxiety and loneliness particularly as there were always times like that in the past. This last year was an anxious one in many ways but for the sake of reassurance I'd like you to know that the step I'm now taking was well-considered and is one of the surest decisions I've made—mainly because it was made from a position of more critical and enlightened self-knowledge! I intend to work hard to keep that sureness and to build something good from it.

It's hard to find a minute's peace at home to say things that should not be left unsaid. I'll shortly be leaving a home in which I have been happy and well cared for; most of what I am was made and moulded there, just as what I will be when I leave will be directed and conditioned by all that I have seen, felt and experienced there. I hope I will be able to create with Martin a firm bond, wholesome and sharing, as I know you both want me to.

So before it becomes hectic as we get organised for the Final Whistle, thank you both for being so good to me, not just now but always. I hope the next three elope or become nuns.

All my love,
Mary

Mary Patricia Leneghan and Martin Philip McAleese were married in the Star of the Sea Church in Rostrevor on 9 March 1976. Fr Ailbe Delaney CP, an old friend of Mary's, made the journey from the monastery in Ardoyne to celebrate the nuptial mass. Mary's bridesmaids were her sister Claire and her first cousin, Bernadette Rogan. Martin's brothers John and Cathal were his best man and usher. Mary's friend from Rostrevor, Eibhlís Farrell, played the violin at the mass, and Eibhlís's sister, Siubhán Uí Dhubháin, played the organ.

At the reception in the Ardmore Hotel the meal was beautiful, the speeches witty and clever, and Mary and Martin and all the guests were in great form. Barnbrack, consisting of Jimmy McPeake, Alec Quinn and Owen McMahon, played the music. When the band started with "Will You Go, Lassie, Go?", the song made famous by the McPeake Family, the newlyweds did a slow dance in the middle of the floor as everyone sang the chorus again and again.‡ They were all looking forward to a long night of fine music, singing and dancing, but gradually the mood of the wedding party seemed to change. By the early evening Mary and Martin were sure the noise level of the guests had considerably decreased, and they noticed the odd furtive glance in their direction from friends who were busily engaged in serious conversation. Their families started to put pressure on them to leave and start their honeymoon.

"It's a long old journey to Dublin in the dark," said her mother to Mary, as if Mary did not know every yard of the way. "You had better be going now, and don't go near your granny. You can see she's crying. That's because you were always her pet and she's missing you already. I know she's been crying for a while. She's been very sentimental all day."

Mary knew it was not sentimentality that brought tears to her granny's eyes, but she did not get the opportunity to find out what the real reason was. As they were changing into their going-away clothes in the bedroom, they questioned each other about the change of mood at the reception.

"What's going on down there? Is there a row? Did one of your crowd insult one of ours? Something's wrong. They can't get us out of the place quickly enough. By the way, did you see Myles or Tony? I didn't see either of them all day?"

Mary threw her bouquet and the crowd sang "Now Is the Time When We Must Say Goodbye", but it was plain to the honeymooners that there was no heart in the singing. As they passed through the tunnel of guests on their way out to the car, they noticed more guests crying than they would have expected.

As the were settling themselves in the car, Claire spoke to them: "You are on your honeymoon now. Don't be depressing yourselves by buying newspapers or watching news for the next fortnight. Off you go now and enjoy yourselves."

They were entering Drogheda when Mary said, "Wasn't that a strange thing Mammy said about not watching news or reading the papers? She knows we both love to keep up with the news."

"She just doesn't want us to be listening to more bad news from home every day. She was just hoping we could leave all that behind us for a fortnight," said Martin, who did not believe a word he was saying.

---

‡ Often claimed as a Scottish song, it was first recorded by Francis McPeake in 1957 for the series *As I Roved Out* on BBC.

They were to spend their honeymoon in the Aghadoe Heights Hotel in Killarney, but had been invited by Hugh Tunney to spend their first night in his new hotel in Dublin, Sachs on Morehampton Road. Martin had done some accountancy work for him, and as a wedding present he had arranged for the couple to spend the night in the brand new bridal suite, although the only parts of the prestigious hotel which were officially opened were the bar and restaurant.

When they reached the hotel, Mary could not contain her anxiety. As soon as dinner was finished, they went up to the room so that Mary could ring home. Her sister Claire answered the phone, and Mary immediately knew that something was very wrong.

"Is Mammy sick? Did Daddy have another heart attack? Look, I know something is wrong and you had better tell me. Otherwise I'm going home."

"Myles and Tony were killed today," said Claire between bouts of sobbing. Cold sweat broke out on Mary's brow and her throat contracted. The hand-piece of the phone shook in her slackened grip as she listened to the broken pieces of the story coming down the telephone line from Belfast to Dublin. She had heard only a couple of sentences when she fell into the chair and the phone fell from her hand. She had difficulty breathing, and every time she closed her eyes she saw the ravaged bodies of the two men who had been like big brothers to her when she was growing up. Martin had to ring back and find out the details, trying all the while to comfort Mary.

Three UVF gunmen had entered the Golden Pheasant Inn shortly after opening time. They had forced everyone into a storeroom in the rear of the premises—thirteen people in all: men, women, girls and a six-year-old child. One of the women was Tony's wife. After ordering everyone to stay in the storeroom, they picked out Tony and Myles and, having warned the rest of the prisoners not to move, ordered the brothers to crawl out on their hands and knees. A couple of minutes later four shots were heard, and some minutes after that the building shook as an explosion ripped through the restaurant. The captives disregarded the orders of the gunmen and ran for their lives through a choking cloud of smoke and dust. Their defiance saved their lives. They had just emerged into the car park when a second explosion brought the whole building crashing down. The bodies of the two brothers were later found in the ruins of the restaurant.‡

---

‡ A member of the UVF was later sentenced to two terms of life imprisonment for the

Mary wanted to go home. She wanted the comfort of her family and she wanted to try to give some comfort of her own to the wives and families of the dead brothers, but the pressure coming from the North to go on with their honeymoon was overwhelming. Martin was prepared to do whatever she wanted. They deliberated and pondered and eventually made the mistake of succumbing to the pressure from home. They travelled to Kerry and tried to enjoy themselves, but it was impossible. Mary was blind to the beauties of Killarney, to the majesty of the Reeks and the magnificent setting of the hotel, and Martin spent all his time trying, to no avail, to comfort his new wife. One morning in the Aghadoe Heights, Mary and Martin were listening to the news before going down to breakfast when they learned that their wedding hotel, the Ardmore in Newry, had been damaged by a bomb. Another addendum to the tragic story of their wedding day concerns a holiday they spent in Florida in the early eighties. Members of the band Clubsound and their families were staying in the same resort. They were a Protestant group from home, led by George Jones, who later became a well-known broadcaster. Mary spent quite a lot of time with Ann McKnight, wife of one of the band members, Davey McKnight.

> One day we were talking about honeymoons and I began to tell Anne about our "honeymoon from hell". I had not said very much when the blood began to drain from her face and she started to cry. After a while she recovered enough to tell me why she had become so upset. The day after Myles and Tony were murdered, Anne's father was sitting having a pint in a pub near Lisburn when two men with pistols burst into the bar and began shooting indiscriminately. Anne's father was killed and six people were wounded. The murderers said the shooting was in retaliation for the murders of Myles and Tony.[‡]

Ann told Mary, "There was my daddy, an innocent man, sitting having a pint and minding his own business, killed in retaliation for the death of two men he would have liked and admired had he ever met them."

murders. He is said to have told police that he regarded the restaurant as "a military target". At the trial the judge described the murders as "among the most abominable committed by terrorists in recent years".

‡   A man was later tried and convicted for the murder of Robert Dorman in the Homestead Inn, near Lisburn, and for membership of the IRA. It was claimed during the trial that the shooting was in retaliation for the murders of Tony and Myles O'Reilly and other Catholics.

Some time later Mary was in the Law Library in Belfast when she was approached by a barrister who had been poring over a pathologist's report.

"Aren't you from Ardoyne? Did you know these people?" he asked as he spread some pictures in front of her. They were photographs of the corpses of Myles and Tony, burned and broken and barely recognisable. She turned and staggered from the room, her eyes burning. Every year, on the anniversary of their wedding, the memory of the tragic deaths of the O'Reilly brothers casts its shadow on Mary and Martin. They both agree that there are some memories from which we can never escape.

No one who has lived through the thirty years of the Troubles has been untouched by the horror of violent death or terrible injury. They all have their memories, and the memories have left their mark on them all. The memories have left their imprint on the life of Mary McAleese: on her coming of age, on her times of celebration and happiness. She had said, in all innocence, on occasions, that she would love to leave it all behind, to go South where she would be among her own; where, since her youth, she had felt a spiritual affinity with the people; where she would feel welcome. She felt that only south of the border would she be able to leave behind the sectarianism, the hatred, the daily struggle between her cultural identity and her fear of revealing it. Only in Dublin would she at last have peace and comfort and serenity.

Chapter Twelve

The Rocky Road to Dublin

In Dublin next arrived I thought it such a pity
To be so soon deprived a view of that fine city.
Then I took a stroll all among the quality,
My bundle it was stolen in a neat locality.
("The Rocky Road to Dublin"—traditional)

In September 1881, Richard Touhill Reid made a bequest to Trinity College Dublin in the form of a professorship of law, which became known as the Reid Trust in memory of the benefactor. Richard Reid, a Kerryman, also bestowed on Trinity College a sizarship, or grant, which would be available to certain undergraduates from Kerry. Brendan Kennelly was among those who availed of the Reid Sizarship.

One of the conditions attaching to the Reid Professorship was that the lecturer who would fill the part-time, temporary position would have the status of professor. Normally a professorship is a position achieved by a senior lecturer after years spent teaching a subject, after years of academic research and publication of scholarly works. The Reid Professorship did not work that way. It was to be bestowed on a junior academic lawyer of outstanding ability. Among the more famous Reid Professors in recent times were Eldon Exshaw and Matt Russell. Mary Robinson was appointed to the position at the age of twenty-five, the youngest ever Reid Professor at the time of her appointment.

In 1975 Trinity College went to the High Court to request a change in the terms of the Reid endowment. On 18 March that year the appeal was granted, and so, when Mary Leneghan applied for the job in the summer of 1975, she was seeking a position which was full-time and permanent.

In fact, Mary's original application to Trinity College Dublin was for a different position, but her research interests were not compatible with its requirements. Professor Robert Heuston said as much in a letter he wrote to her in the early summer. In that same letter he suggested that she might be interested in applying for the Reid Professorship, as her background and interest in criminology and penology seemed to suit the position. Under the revised terms of the job, the Reid Professor would be permitted to practise law, but it was hoped that the activities of the successful applicant would be confined to the purely academic. This expectation suited Mary. She was applying for the post in order to teach, not to practise. Off she went to Dublin for the interview, and two days later she was offered the position: the youngest ever Reid Professor at the age of twenty-four.

At the time of Mary's appointment, Yvonne Scannell was the only other woman employed full-time in the School of Law in Trinity College. Mary's immediate predecessor, Mary Robinson, would be remaining in the college to teach European law, but only on a part-time basis, as she was also a member of Seanad Éireann and had a successful law practice. The new Reid Professor paid a visit to Dublin that summer to meet Senator Robinson and also to find somewhere to live. The flat she rented on Waterloo Road was very small but had one great compensation: it was within walking distance of Trinity.

Shortly after her appointment, Mary received an invitation to the home of Justice John Kenny to discuss her new employment. She says he had a particular interest in the Reid endowment and explained its history and the reasons for its existence, emphasising that the use of the title "Professor" was one of the stipulations of the endowment: "That was why the Reid family instituted a professorship and not a lectureship." He said he understood that as a modern young person she might not want to use the title; that the world was changing rapidly in Ireland and due respect was not always paid to venerable institutions, and he asked her to play her part in maintaining the status of the Reid bequest.

In saying that Irish life was changing rapidly, Judge Kenny may have been guilty of understatement. Ireland, Britain and Denmark had signed the Treaty of Accession to the European Economic Community on New Year's Day 1973. One of the major social changes that came about in Ireland as a result of joining the EEC was an end to the so-called "marriage bar", which had prevented women from continuing to work in the public service after marriage. For the first time in many years, the economic situation of Irish farmers was improving considerably. In January 1975, they received £17,000,000 from the EEC, the first of many grants that would be coming their way. By the end of the 1970s, the Republic of Ireland would break the connection with sterling, the first step on the long road to being part of a single European currency. In January 1978, the Well Woman Centre for information and advice on family planning opened in Dublin. A group called Mná na hÉireann picketed the centre to display their outrage at such a blatant disregard of Catholic Ireland's traditional antipathy towards any form of contraception. These were not, of course, the same Mná na hÉireann so beloved of the future president Mary Robinson!

Eamon de Valera died on 29 August 1975 at ninety-two years of age. The date marked not only the end of a life but the end of an era. Under the leadership of Seán Lemass in the 1960s, the people of the Republic of Ireland had moved away from the de Valera-inspired introspection of the 1950s. Membership of the EEC sounded the death knell of the go-it-alone attitude, which could trace its roots back to Arthur Griffith's *Sinn Féin* policies at the start of the twentieth century. As de Valera's death coincided with the state's beginning to flex its economic muscle and strengthen its international ties, some historians thought the time opportune to begin a reappraisal of Irish history.

Foremost among the revisionists was Conor Cruise O'Brien, an intellectual, a journalist and a historian, husband of the highly acclaimed Irish poet Máire Mhac an tSaoi. As a Labour Party TD he became minister for posts and telegraphs in the Labour-Fine Gael coalition under taoiseach Liam Cosgrave. In later years he became a member of Bob McCartney's United Kingdom Unionist Party. However, in 1975 O'Brien's involvement in McCartney's party and the right wing of Northern unionism were far in the future and would have been unimaginable to many of those in the Republic who came under his sway in the 1970s. Mary has this to say about his teachings:

> When I first arrived in Dublin, Conor Cruise O'Brien was at the height of his political power and influence. I found it difficult to believe I was listening to an Irish government minister when everything he said about the North and about the nationalist people had the ring of unionism to it. His arrogance, as he blatantly rewrote Irish history, was almost frightening. He created and nourished an attitude to Northern nationalists which some people in the Republic are still trying to grow out of.

In the year 1975 a lot of that growing was still to be done by a lot of people, and Mary was very disappointed in what she found to be the prevalent attitude in Dublin to Northerners. It is possible that she was naïve in expecting the people she met in the city to show an interest in her story or in that of any person who was associated with the conflict in the North. Many people with Northern accents in Dublin found themselves treated with varying amounts of misgiving. There was a suspicion abroad that Northern nationalists must, by definition, be supportive of the Provisionals, tacitly or otherwise, by proximity if not by desire. Some people feared that any conversation with a Northerner about the Troubles would result in an attempt to seduce them into a particular party political perspective, or worse. Mary was amazed and pleased by the amount of worthwhile causes being espoused by the people of the capital city: anti-apartheid, the plight of the Vietnamese people, the Palestinians, animal rights, the Campaign for Nuclear Disarmament, civil rights for black people in America . . . But it was a constant source of grievance to her that many Dubliners were giving the deaf ear to the victims of violence in their own country.

Less than a decade had passed since the Irish state had celebrated the fiftieth anniversary of the 1916 Rising with parades, pageants and specially commissioned television programmes. Every school had been issued with a copy of the Proclamation of 1916, and the leaders' faces had appeared on stamps, postcards and commemorative coins. Railway stations in Dublin were renamed after Pádraig Pearse, James Connolly and Seán Heuston. Many of those who had so recently commemorated the dead of the Easter Rising with reverence and passion were, by 1975, rowing back on such overt nationalism. Many of them were now questioning the value of the commemoration, querying the morality of the leaders and doubting the merits of the Rising.

Three years before, the Irish government had announced a national day of mourning for the dead of Bloody Sunday, but between 1972 and 1975 a semi-official bad taste had attached itself to the word "nationalist".

The daily litany of atrocities which assaulted people from television, radio and newspapers was having a desensitising effect, particularly on those who knew none of the victims and were not familiar with the places that featured regularly on the daily news bulletins. Ardoyne, the Lower Falls, Andersonstown, Crossmaglen, the Bogside, the Creggan . . . all became synonymous with death and terror, and some people were afraid that the terror would spread south and land on their own doorsteps. Still more did not care what happened "up there" as long as the insanity stayed "up there".

Mary's knowledge of Ireland's Civil War and its fallout was academic. She had no clear understanding of the tensions and animosities that had lain unresolved since Partition and that were bubbling once again to the surface because of the Northern conflict. The feelings ranged from "We

144

let our people down in 1922" to "Sure, they're all British up there anyway." Many of those who were equivocal on the subject thought it best to remain aloof from all controversy. Even Jack Lynch, when he was taoiseach, displayed a certain ambiguity about Northerners in a remark he made to Sir John Peck, the British ambassador, in 1970: "People in the North are different—that's all."[†]

Mary now admits that she was somewhat innocent and immature in her expectations when she arrived in Dublin:

> Through all the sufferings and hard times of the Troubles, I kept a clear vision of Dublin as the spiritual home, the capital, a place of refuge where I could be among my own, where people thought and felt as I did. It is not unusual for people who live in a cultural netherworld—like the society in which I lived in Belfast in the seventies—to gather their sensitivities and their cultural ambitions and attribute the ideal of them all to a place that has iconic status in their lives. For us that place was Dublin. We bristled at the very idea of Belfast as a capital city and had long defended Dublin as our Mecca. It housed the headquarters of every organisation we held dear. It was where the national flag flew freely and proudly, where the pillar-boxes and the buses were green, where the harp was on every coin. In defending Dublin we persuaded ourselves that we knew it very well.

Northern Protestants are inclined to view Catholics as quintessentially Irish and "green". Mary sometimes met unionists who tried to persuade her to a unionist point of view, she met a few Protestants who said they were offended by her cultural identity, but no Protestant or unionist ever questioned her identity. Like many other Northern Catholics in the seventies, her Irishness was never challenged until she came to Dublin.

Wherever else in Dublin this happened, Mary was generally safe from ideological insults in Trinity College. When she started teaching in the School of Law it was located in the New Square. There was a shortage of rooms in that part of the college, and she shared an office for a while with Bill Vaughan. When she got an office of her own it was on Pearse Street. Her small room at the top of a narrow stairs contained only an old desk, an old chair and a large brand new cabinet. On the cabinet was a sticker which proudly proclaimed that the article was made in Ireland.

---

† State Papers relating to the year 1970, released in the year 2000 under the thirty-year rule.

She was pleased to see such a fine-looking, new piece of Irish furniture—until she opened the door and it fell off and hit her on the head. She got an early taste of the acerbic wit of the Dubliner after she had phoned to complain about the offending article. A man arrived at the bottom of the stairs and shouted, "Hey, Missus, are you still aloive?" She certainly was still "aloive" and well and even happier when she got a better office in the Arts Building shortly afterwards.

The Department of Law in Trinity was small, the atmosphere snug and cosy in some respects and forbiddingly formal in some other areas. She was working with people for whom she had great respect. She found that, unlike Queen's University, where faculty members and students mixed freely and comfortably and social mores were very relaxed, the traditions of Trinity were more rigid. It was not the sort of place where the teaching staff went out for a couple of pints after a day's work. She says this about her first few months in the college: "I was very happy in my work and with my colleagues, who were all very professional and academically supportive; but the atmosphere of the place did not particularly lend itself to close friendships. It could be a lonely place at times."

Concern for her family, and for Martin and his family, added to her sense of isolation. Martin was still in Belfast, and his parents had just been forced out of their second home. The intimidation in Rathcoole had become so bad that Charlie McAleese asked the local RUC sergeant to help him get a house in another area. The sergeant wrote a letter to the Housing Executive to the effect that the police were unable to protect the McAleese family and that they would be unable to continue living in the area. The letter resulted in an offer of a house in Finaghy, a suburb south-west of Andersonstown and bordering a Protestant area on the Lisburn Road—another dangerous place to live, but nominally safer than Rathcoole. Martin's mother, Emma McAleese, had not been in full health since the family was forced out of the Albertbridge Road. Now she was diagnosed with multiple myeloma. Mary's grandmother, Cassie McManus in Ardoyne, was failing also, and Mary missed not being able to call to see her as regularly as she would have liked.

She went back to Belfast as often as she could and returned to Dublin full of stories, opinions and insights. She walked the length of the Shankill Road with Mairéad Corrigan and Betty Williams, the "Peace People". She and her family and Martin and their friends often deliberated long and hard on what everyone around them saw as the burning issues of the day and the landmark events that would have a bearing on their lives: the end of internment, the conviction of the

Birmingham Six, the Balcombe Street Siege and the death on hunger strike of Frank Stagg—all incidents that would have serious repercussions on the lives of ordinary people in Northern Ireland. She used to return to Dublin anxious to discuss these issues, to hear the views of people who were not as intimately involved, but she found it difficult to attract people into a serious conversation on the issues, or even to get them to reveal an opinion. It was difficult to leave a situation where people regarded certain issues as momentous and hugely significant in the shaping of the future, and to be mixing, a few hours later, with people to whom such issues were problems that existed outside their reality, topics to be glossed over in the newspaper.

Sinn Féin supporters in Dublin had plenty to say on these issues and on the day-to-day problems of people in the North, but Mary had no interest in Sinn Féin, in their opinions or in their policies. She admits that lack of interest in what was going on in the North was not widespread south of the border. She says she felt more at home discussing developments in Northern Ireland with people from places outside Dublin and with people who were not totally absorbed in academic life.

She was interested in many causes and soon got deeply involved in several of them. Considering her background, her devotion to the Catholic Church and the manifest depth of her faith, she would have been considered by many as a conservative Catholic. However, in this, as in many other aspects of her life, people found it increasingly difficult to label her. It was not so difficult to put a distinctive label on Irish society in those days: the Irish state was very conservative in terms of sexuality. Contraceptive devices were banned in the Republic until Charles Haughey, as minister for health, relaxed the ban in the 1970s. It was not a total relaxation, however, as only married couples were allowed to avail of them. Sex education was not very widespread. Nudity in film, on television or on stage was unheard of. Although John Charles McQuaid, the Catholic Archbishop of Dublin, had died in 1972, the shadow of that giant of Catholic orthodoxy and social conservatism still lay dark and impenetrable over many institutions in Ireland.

Mary became very friendly with a colleague of hers in Trinity, David Norris, a world authority on the writings of James Joyce. Norris had founded the Irish gay rights movement and was seeking to repeal the archaic law that prohibited sexual intercourse between people of the same sex. Mary thought of her friend Paul in San Francisco and remembered the difficulties he faced in a so-called enlightened society because of his sexual orientation. When Norris invited her to be co-founder with him

147

of the Campaign for Homosexual Law Reform, she readily accepted. It was a radical cause, and many people were surprised when she fronted the organisation. The cause of homosexual law reform attracted many famous and influential people to the campaign team. Among them were Noel Browne, the former Clann na Poblachta minister for health, of Mother and Child Scheme fame; Dean Victor Griffin of St Patrick's Cathedral; Catherine McGuinness, the judge; Victor Bewley, the champion of travellers' rights; and Hugh Leonard, the playwright.

The committee met regularly in David Norris's rooms in Trinity College or in Buswell's Hotel in Molesworth Street, opposite Leinster House. It was a small group, but each member was strong and articulate. Mary was often the spokesperson for the campaign, speaking on behalf of the committee on television or at press briefings, launching pamphlets or doing interviews. She was comfortable with the group, with the job, with the image. It bothered her not at all when they were damned by certain powerful people, when they were condemned as a dissident group whose aim was to destabilise Irish society! In spite of the claims about their treasonous nature, they were joined by Dónal Barrington, senior counsel, who later became a judge of the Supreme Court. It was he who steered their case through the High Court. When he was appointed judge, Mary Robinson took over the case and brought it as far as the European Court of Human Rights.

When Mary and Martin McAleese married they bought a house, 31 Eglantine Avenue, in Belfast and lived there when Mary went North. She still had her little bedsit on Waterloo Road in Dublin, and they lived there when Martin went to Dublin. For the first ten months of their marriage, they were together only at weekends.

John O'Neill was financial controller of Blueskies Ltd, a subsidiary of Aer Lingus, that was located in Westmoreland Street in Dublin. He asked Martin McAleese to do some accountancy work for a consortium called Enterprise Travel Ltd in Belfast. When O'Neill resigned his position with Blueskies at the end of 1976, Martin applied for and got the job. He took up his new position in Westmoreland Street in January 1977, and he and Mary were now living in the same city for the first time since they were married. They found it difficult to sell their house on Eglantine Avenue in Belfast. This was a problem because they needed the proceeds to acquire a more suitable Dublin home than Mary's tiny flat. Marie Louise Tallon, a friend of Martin's who worked in Blueskies, came to their rescue, and they rented her house in Scholarstown in Rathfarnham until they had saved enough money for a deposit on a house of their own.

As it happened, they subsequently bought a house not in Dublin but in County Meath, close enough to the city and less than two hours from Rostrevor. The house was a modern bungalow on Lagore Road, in the townland of Mooretown. It was situated in the middle of the countryside, a few hundred yards off the road between Ratoath and Dunshaughlin. What else would they call their oasis of tranquillity but "Rostrevor"? It was a strange collection of houses on that little country lane: the McAleeses lived in "Rostrevor", beside them was a house called "Ardglass" and further down the road was a house called "Portaferry"—three place-names from the coast of County Down within half a mile of each other in the heart of County Meath! No wonder the McAleeses soon felt at home in their new location.

Because of Martin's job with Blueskies, the couple had access to free travel and were able to fly to many parts of Europe whenever they felt like it. Martin would spend a lot of time entertaining clients, and Mary often joined him on these occasions. Although they enjoyed it at first it soon lost its gloss.

Although Mary was Reid Professor her salary was that of a junior lecturer, and Martin's salary was modest enough. When Mary was studying for the Bar exams in Belfast, she had been heavily dependent on the financial support of her parents, a fact that bothered her a lot at the time. She knew that when she started practising law there would be a lean time ahead of her in the early years. She knew her parents could not afford to support her, and even if they could, it would be unfair on the younger members of the family. She was delighted to get the job in Trinity because she could repay some of her parents' generosity and even help some of the younger members of the family.

Thanks to the influence of her mother and grandmother, the habit of thrift was deeply ingrained in her. She and Martin saved for whatever was required in the way of furniture or fittings for the house. A year and a half after they moved in, there was still no carpet on the floor. Sheila and Eugene Tinnelly had given them an electric frying pan as a wedding present, and they had been doing all their cooking on that. They had put a deposit on a cooker, and only one more salary cheque was required before it was theirs. On Friday night Martin came home with a set of golf clubs, an out-and-out bargain at £100! Complete with bag! Wasn't he the lucky man to get such a . . . Martin admits he was a lucky man not to have the entire set broken over his head. There was war that night in the oasis of tranquillity in Mooretown, the only row the couple ever had over money, as they claim. It may have been the only time they let

149

finances come between them, but neither of them will ever forget it. Martin never got any good out of the clubs due to the maledictions she called down on them and on him that night. He claims Mary's imprecations as an excuse for his golfing handicap not dropping below sixteen.

In the mid-seventies there were rigid barriers between legal practitioners and professionals such as police, the probation service, social workers and especially the prison service. Mary felt her students should have some practical experience of the penal system they were learning about, but first these barriers had to be breached. She contacted the Department of Justice with a view to asking an official to come and address her classes. Dermot Cole agreed to pay them a visit and was asked back several times. On the third occasion Mary discovered he was a cousin of her good friend Eibhlís Farrell from Rostrevor. Cole introduced Mary to Martin Tansey from the Probation Service. The barriers were beginning to fall. Before long the students were benefiting from the combined experience of a whole cohort of guest lecturers from the Department of Justice, the Probation Service and the Prison Service. The next logical step was for the students to visit the prisons, and Mary was facilitated in this by the web of contacts she had established. Some members of An Garda Síochána were doing an Institute of Public Administration course in association with Trinity College and, as part of it, were attending Mary's classes. Among her students was Michael Ringrose, who was a garda inspector at the time. Lecturer and student became good friends, and Michael proved to be very useful in opening doors for Mary in her efforts to make her courses more interesting and practical for the students.

Spending on the prisons during the seventies had increased by 600 per cent, but the system was worse than ever. Use of illegal drugs, particularly heroin, had increased significantly, as had the suicide rate among prisoners. Recidivism was becoming the norm. People had started to ask fundamental questions about the prison system: why send people to prison? Was it for the sake of punishment? Retribution? Reformation? Correction? Was a prison term always the most effective means of dealing with convicted criminals? Foremost among the questioners was Joe Costello of the Labour Party and the Prisoners' Rights Organisation.

Costello approached Seán MacBride with a view to setting up a commission of inquiry into the Irish penal system. MacBride fully understood the problems, and in the absence of any official government inquiry he agreed to chair an independent commission. Dr Louk Hulsman of the University of Erasmus in Holland, chairman of the Committee on De-Criminalisation of the Council of Europe, agreed to co-chair one of the public hearings. The members of the commission represented a broad sweep of Irish public life. There was Michael D. Higgins, chairman of the Labour Party and lecturer in sociology in NUI Galway; Senator Gemma Hussey; Patrick McEntee, one of the country's foremost senior counsels; Fr Micheál Mac Gréil, SJ, lecturer in sociology in NUI Maynooth; Matt Merrigan, general secretary of the ATGWU; Una O'Higgins O'Malley, barrister and committee member of the Glencree Reconciliation Centre, daughter of Kevin O'Higgins, minister for foreign affairs and minister for justice who was assassinated in 1927; Muireann Ó Briain, barrister and secretary of the Association of Irish Jurists; Michael Keating, TD, Fine Gael spokesman on human rights and law reform. When the young Reid Professor of Law in Trinity College was asked to join the group she readily agreed.

Seán MacBride used the famous words of Ramsey Clark, not only as an introduction to the report, but as a mantra for the group: "No activity of a people so exposes their humanity, their character, their capacity for charity in its most generous dimension, as the treatment they accord persons convicted of crime."[‡]

The aim of the group, in the words of MacBride, was "the promotion of true and just social order in our society".[§] Was this not the very thing that Mary and her people had always sought? Here was work that suited her abilities and her interest, and she decided to give it her all.

Public hearings were conducted in the Jesuit house in Milltown Park, Dublin, during April 1979. At these sessions several ex-prisoners, including Eddie Cahill, brother of Martin Cahill, "the General", had the opportunity to describe their experiences of prison life. Among the lawyers who made submissions were Senator Mary Robinson, Pat McCartan, Ciarán Mac an Ailí, Michael D. White and Séamus Breathnach. Joe Costelloe likewise had his say. There were group submission also from such diverse organisations as Pax Christi, the Simon Community and the Irish Republican Socialist Party.

The Commission had eleven members, and they came together regularly in Seán Mac Bride's home, Roebuck House, in Clonskeagh. For almost two years they researched, read submissions, listened to

‡   Mac Gréil, p. vii.
§   *Ibid.*

arguments and prepared their report. When the Report of the Commission of Inquiry into the Irish Penal System was published in November 1980, the Irish government did not receive it with enthusiasm. Gerard Collins, minister for justice at the time, having refused to co-operate with the Commission, was in no mood to welcome the report.

The Garda Commissioner Patrick McLaughlin also refused to co-operate, as he explained in a letter to MacBride: "As Commissioner of An Garda Síochána, with responsibility for law enforcement, it does not fall within my area of competence to discuss or otherwise comment on the prison system and treatment of prisoners. Accordingly, I don't feel that it is appropriate that I or any of my Officers should attend, as requested in your letter."[‡]

The report contained sixty-eight recommendations, one of which was that the care of prisoners no longer be the responsibility of the Department of Justice. The Commission suggested that a Treatment of Offenders Board should be set up, the majority of whose members would be experts in the fields of education, religion, medicine, social sciences, etc. and independent of the prison system or civil service. They also recommended the establishment of hostels for those on bail, the introduction of community service and an end to solitary confinement. They further urged the government to raise the age of criminal responsibility to fourteen and to establish an independent inquiry into the abuse of drugs in Irish prisons. Although the report got no official government approbation, it had an impact on Irish society. Shortly after its publication, the Catholic Church was moved to establish its own inquiry. That was followed by the official Whitaker Inquiry. The members of MacBride's commission were the pioneers who prepared the way, who asked the hard questions and who made the recommendations that government was forced to listen to.

Mary had an enormous respect for Seán MacBride, a man whose life was inextricably linked to the cultural and political development of Ireland in the twentieth century. His father was Major John MacBride, who fought with Thomas McDonagh in Jacobs' Factory during the 1916 Rising, who was convicted by a British court martial and executed by firing squad in Kilmainham Jail on 5 May 1916. His mother was the beautiful and bewitching Maud Gonne MacBride, the inspiration for some of William Butler Yeats's best known poems. Seán MacBride lived

‡ MacBride, Appendix 3.

a full and an extraordinary life: as a revolutionary, a senior counsel at the Irish Bar, a politician and humanitarian. He was at one time chief of staff of the IRA, and at other times founder of a political party, minister for foreign affairs, tánaiste and general secretary of the International Commission of Jurists. He founded Amnesty International and won the Nobel Peace Prize in 1974, the Lenin Peace Prize in 1977 and was awarded the American Medal of Justice in 1978.

To Mary McAleese he was a hero, a savant and an exemplar, and she treasured the friendship that developed between them during the time they worked together on the Commission of Inquiry. Their mutual regard was largely based on their common areas of interest and the ease they felt in each other's company. He was always available to her as a counsellor and good listener. She describes the effective silencing of MacBride, during the seventies and eighties, when revisionism was at its height, as a source of great vexation to her.

"It was an appalling loss for this country that Seán MacBride did not get the hearing he deserved in those days; that the people of Ireland did not get a true flavour of his wisdom and the sharpness of his intellect and understanding when he was at the peak of his maturity."

One evening in 1988, Mary was at a dinner in Queen's University with a group of people who were celebrating the introduction of equality legislation in Northern Ireland. Roy Wallace, who was a pro-vice-chancellor of Queen's at the time, was the host, and apart from Mary and a couple of civil servants, most of the other guests were members of the Alliance Party. There was a lot of congratulatory talk at the dinner, people complimenting each other on the work they had done to achieve parity of opportunity in the workplace for Catholics and Protestants in Northern Ireland. Mary put a question to the assembled guests: how significant was the work of Seán MacBride, particularly his MacBride Principles, in preparing the way for the passing of the legislation that had been enacted in Westminster earlier that day? The senior civil servant, Sir David Fell, a man respected by all present, took it upon himself to answer the question: "If it were not for the MacBride Principles, and the ameliorating influence they had on the British government, this legislation would not be in place today."[‡]

Mary describes MacBride as a man of the utmost humility, the modesty that comes from having nothing to prove. He had a deep understanding of the problems of Northern Ireland, and he and Mary

‡ As given by Mary McAleese from memory.

often discussed and dissected the finer points of Northern politics. They were not always in agreement. McBride's proposed federal solution, for example, did not sit well with her. He had gone the road of violence and had long since turned his back on it, resolutely and for ever. He understood not only the mindset of the people of violence but the suffering of the victims. He also comprehended the inner conflict between passion for justice and the desire for peace.

Seán MacBride died on 15 January 1988, while Mary was in hospital and unable to attend the funeral of a man whose company she remembers as very special, almost magical. She says she never heard him utter a cynical word. The strongest expression in his lexicon was *slíbhín*.[‡] Mary says she remembers him using the word frequently. She adds that she remembers many occasion on which he could have used it, but refrained.

---

‡ *Slíbhín*: a sly, shifty person.

Chapter Thirteen

A Conscientious Conscience

> When I landed in the republic of conscience
> it was so noiseless when the engines stopped
> I could hear a curlew high above the runway.
> (Seamus Heaney: From "The Republic of Conscience")

"I never stopped believing in God," says Mary. She may not have denied God, but she often quarrelled and fought with him (or *her,* as she might say herself). Certain injunctions laid down by the representatives of God on earth—the hierarchy of the Catholic Church—caused her some distress during her early years in Dublin. In the spring of 1993, she gave public expression to some of her grievances in a long interview with Gay Byrne on *The Late Late Show.* She admitted that she, in common with many Irish people, had a difficulty in reconciling her conscience with the teachings of the Catholic Church on some of the major moral issues of the day. During the interview she also alluded to what she called "the erosion of the reasoning capacity of the Church, in the person of the pope, on a matter that has been a cause of concern to me for years—the status of women". At the end of the 1970s, the attitude of the Irish state to certain issues of morality—namely contraception, divorce and abortion—was being carefully scrutinised and monitored by many intellectuals, particularly in Dublin. Shortly after her arrival in Dublin, Mary was being counted among this group, and with good reason: she was airing her views as strongly as many of them.

When she joined David Norris in co-founding the Campaign for Homosexual Law Reform, she was going against the will and authority of the Catholic Church. However, the Church authorities were not taking a very rigid or public stance on the issue. In fact, Mary had the support of several members of the clergy for her stand.

She says her touchstone in matters of conscience was her old soulmate, Fr Justin Coyne. She often reminded herself of what he considered the most important commandment of all: to love unconditionally. She says his words were a guiding beacon for her in the darkness of those days of spiritual turmoil. In her own book Mary analyses the reasons for the Troubles and comes to the conclusion that the only way out of the morass of hatred and hostility is the way of the Gospel, the way of reconciliation and forgiveness, the way of love.

At the beginning of 1980, she brought Martin along to a housewarming party hosted by friends of hers, two homosexual men. Martin was not sure how comfortable he would be at the party. Mary assured him that if he became very uneasy they would leave early. He reluctantly agreed and off they went. As they were approaching the house, he was several steps behind Mary, carrying the large Yucca plant that was their housewarming present for two men he had never met and with whose situation he could not agree. He was dumbfounded when the door was opened by a well-known priest, a friend of theirs, who bade them welcome with the words "Come in. You're just in time for the blessing." Martin spent much of the evening chatting to some elderly relatives of the newly blessed couple and soon realised that his discomfort was slight compared to that of the couple's parents and grandparents. Martin sympathised with them as they were trying to come to terms with what was going on, and doing their utmost to learn "unconditional love".

The way of love was very clear to Mary in the case of homosexuality. It was a broad, clear highway with a distinct sign that proclaimed: "Here Is the Way of Love." The teaching of the Catholic Church on the question of conscience is fundamentally simple: let your conscience guide you in all things. The only condition is that the person, and thus the conscience, must be fully informed of the teachings of the Church on the issue in question and fully conversant with all sides of the argument before making a decision. This uncomplicated teaching throws the responsibility back on the person who has to make the moral choice and thus, sometimes, makes the way of love somewhat vague. Mary understood that the whole question of conscience was simple enough to be accurately summarised in one sentence, but could be complex enough to drive a person demented.

The complication can be exemplified in a paragraph from a pastoral letter written by Mary's former bishop in Belfast, Dr William Philbin of Down and Connor: "As Christians we have already exercised our conscience on the larger and more fundamental question of whether we accept Christ and his Church as holding authority from God to teach. Once we have made this acceptance we are obliged, and obliged by our conscience, to follow the authoritative guidance that comes from these sources."[‡]

Ironically, in 1979, when Mary was struggling with her conscience, Sir Peter Medawar published the book *Advice to a Young Scientist*, in which he wrote the famous sentence: "The intensity of a conviction that a hypotheses is true has no bearing on whether it is true or not." His words were cold comfort to Mary.

She has often referred to the faith she practised at the end of the 1970s as "a faith born of desperation". Her belief in God was never in question, but her allegiance to the Catholic Church was very suspect at times. She stopped going to mass and found that prayer and the Scriptures were food enough for her soul. Many a Sunday morning she left the house in Mooretown to drive to mass in Dunshaughlin, but instead of turning left for the church she turned right and drove to the Hill of Tara. There she would sit with her back to the *Lia Fáil*, the Stone of Destiny, her New Testament in her hand, reading and meditating. She found a certain satisfaction in what she was doing. She felt close to God, but it was not the intimate, familiar bond she experienced at mass. Undoubtedly Mary was sorely missing the warmth and comfort of the Church. In her diary she describes some of the difficulties she experienced at that time:

> Sitting in Mass, week after week, desperate for a glimpse of Christ, hoping for a feeling of union, of amity with those beside me. But we're so inhibited that even the sign of peace is ignored, as we sit in nervous, anxious, time-conscious silence, as a man gabbles his way through the ritual and offers some words, which may or may not strike a chord . . . The restless desires and hopes, which have so often in the past simply pestered me, and which I have not seen my way to tackling, now positively upset me: the dogma, the duty, the institutional framework geared to mass consumption of unchallengeable fact—pity poor Galileo! Why am I a less valid, less articulate part of the Church than the clergy and the pope? Why were we always fed dogma? Why were we not introduced to the gentle fullness of Christ's love—why instead did we see only Christ confused, Christ twisted into *Humanae Vitae*, transubstantiation, the Virgin Birth, all manner of things of little moment to daily life and love of each other . . .[§]

---

‡   *L'Osservatore Romano*, weekly edition in English, 20 June 1968, p. 3.

§   Mary McAleese, Diary.

The visit of Pope John Paul II to Ireland at the end of September 1979 was a watershed for her. Her initial reaction was that she would not go to see him, but the more she thought about it the more she felt she could not stand the isolation outside the flock. She decided that although it would be difficult for her to bend the knee completely to the Church authorities, she felt the need of the comfort and solace that came from Church discipline. When a friend jokingly told her that "It would be great to discover a wee Protestant sect that believed in transubstantiation," it was purely that—a joke. No other Church appealed to her. No other Church could ever satisfy her. The Catholic Church was what she was reared to, what suited her, what had called to her since her childhood, what formed and shaped her faith. It was the Church to which her life and her destiny were inextricably linked because, deep down, she really believed in it. She was hooked.

Mary chose the visit of the pope as the occasion at which she would subject herself once more to the discipline of the Catholic Church. Poor Galileo, to whom Mary referred in her diary, surrendered very reluctantly to Church authority. His only alternative was to be burned at the stake, but Mary's submission was heartfelt and made with full determination and volition.

Being back in the flock was a great comfort to her. Years afterwards, when she was studying Irish and came across the poetry of Seán Ó Ríordáin, she recognised herself in the following lines from his poem *"Saoirse"*—"Freedom":

> I'll go down among the people
> I'll go on foot
> And I'll go down tonight.
>
> I will go down bondage-seeking
> From the venom-liberty
> That's howling here:
>
> And I will tie the thought-pack,
> wheeling
> And snarling around me
> In my solitude:
>
> And I will seek the ordered temple
> That is full of people
> At special times:[‡]

‡   Kiberd and Fitzmaurice, p. 41.

Like Ó Ríordáin, she was seeking the freedom that is to be found in regulation and restriction, in the conventions and etiquettes of organised religion, in what she often referred to as "the old rigid orthodoxies". She recognised in the poem the naked honesty that allowed Ó Ríordáin to say at the end of his life that *"Saoirse"* was the only poem he had ever written that he did not grow to hate at some time; the only poem that was not drafted beforehand; the only poem which he did not really create, but which grew out of his pain. The words resonated with her:

> For now and ever my hate has deepened
> For the goings-on of freedom,
> For independence.[‡]

Mary was not saying she would never again have another independent thought in her head. In submitting to the authority of the Church, she was not saying she would tie up for ever the howling pack of unrestrained thoughts that had bothered her so much. Her conflict with the Church over the status of women was not going to disappear overnight. She had decided to continue the fight from the inside.

There were other struggles going on in Mary's mind, and the question of divorce in Ireland was a case in point. She says she never saw it as a black and white issue. She understood and empathised with people who wanted a legal, civil, Irish divorce, as is evident in what she had to say on the subject to the annual meeting of the Law Society in Galway in 1979:

> We need to stop thinking of marriage as a rigid structure alien to and isolated from the couple who make it function. We must stop thinking of divorce as an inhuman monster who creeps in through open bedroom windows, disseminating huge dollops of marital disharmony . . . Anti-divorce lobbyists often argue that divorce damages children, yet the truth is that what damages children is not the de jure dissolution of the marriage but the process of rows, scenes, violence, bitterness, recrimination and upheaval which de facto break it up.[§]

However, in the run-up to the divorce referendum of 1986, seven years later, when Mary voted against the introduction of divorce, she spoke every bit as passionately against its legalisation as she had spoken

---

‡   *Ibid.*, p. 45.

§   Mary McAleese, private papers.

for it in 1979. Her words at that meeting in Galway are sometimes used to attest to a U-turn in her views on divorce. In relation to this, Mary has previously quoted the words of John Cardinal Newman—"To be human is to change"—and has described her change of attitude as "more of a left turn than a U-turn".

"The issue was never black and white. Divorce is a grey area with many pluses and minuses. Sometimes the scales will dip a bit one way and sometimes the other. But when a decision is to be made, the scales cannot remain perfectly balanced. That does not mean you are 100 per cent in favour of that direction."

Apart from any consideration of U-turns or left-turns, one essential difference between the proposal of 1979 and that of 1986 was the type of divorce on offer. No-fault divorce was the proposal put before the electorate on 26 June 1986. She says that even in 1979 she would have been opposed to such a form. She looks on divorce as a civil facility, pointing out that it is not listed in any United Nations document as a human right. Even in the 1970s, when she was arguing in favour of divorce, she understood that it couldn't be argued on the basis that it would have no social ramifications. Looking back, she says her views in those earlier days were eclectic, a little bit over-sophisticated, and that they matured and tightened up since that weekend in 1979 when she locked horns with Eamonn Barnes at the debate in Galway.

Children's rights and the interests of both parties are nowadays taken fully into account in divorce settlements, but such was not always the case. Mary sees the divorce culture in England, for example, as resulting from the triumph of the rights of the individual over the welfare of society during the first half of the last century. On the question of individual rights, Martin McAleese agrees totally with his wife. He describes himself as conservative in his thinking on social issues and on morality, and believes that the rights of children take precedence over his own rights or happiness.

In an ecclesiastical annulment, a person who has been found guilty of ill-treatment of a partner or of the children in a marriage becomes subject to an impediment. The impediment goes on record, and if that person ever wants to remarry within the Church, the offences are made known to the prospective partner. Mary believes the state has something to learn from the Church in this regard, particularly in the area of no-fault divorce. A partner could be a child abuser or a spouse beater, but if the divorce is on a no-fault basis, knowledge of that fact does not have to be made known, and the guilty partner is free to commit the same crimes again in another marriage. "Are you in favour of divorce?" she says, was not a question that could be simply answered.

For quite a while before 7 September 1983, the date of the first referendum on the subject of abortion, Mary had been speaking forcefully on the rights of the unborn. This positioned her squarely to the right of centre in the eyes of those of the liberal left to whom she had been a champion in the days of the first divorce referendum. She argues that as far as she was concerned there was no left or right on these issues—just the issues themselves. She also says that the way of love was her only guide in all her soul-searching. As Emily O'Reilly said in 1984, "McAleese was probably the victim of the Irish myth machine which assumes that any articulate, intelligent person, working in either the law, the media or both, must therefore be a ranting liberal leftie, supporting divorce, abortion, etc. etc."

As more information and further possibilities were piled on the scales of her conscience, the abortion question became even more complicated for her when she found herself opposing the stance of the pro-life movement before the second referendum, in 1992. In 1983 the question facing the people was straightforward: do we want legalised abortion in the Republic of Ireland? Two thirds of the voters said "No". But between then and 1992, the Supreme Court ruled on what became known as the X Case, and the question was no longer so simple. A fourteen-year-old girl had been raped and left pregnant. When her parents decided to bring her to England for an abortion, this was brought to the attention of Harry Whelehan, the attorney-general, who took the case to the High Court. There it was decided that the girl could not leave the state with the intention of seeking an abortion. The case was appealed to the Supreme Court. There, based on evidence that the teenage rape victim was threatening to commit suicide, it was decided that she had the right to leave the state to seek an abortion. In giving its judgement, the Supreme Court criticised the government for the lack of legislation on the question of abortion.

The Taoiseach Albert Reynolds was forced to announce a second referendum, which was to be held on 25 November 1992. This time the people would be asked to decide on three separate issues: the availability of abortion, the right to travel to seek abortion and the right to distribute information on abortion services. On the substantive issue, the government proposed that no one would have the right to terminate the life of a foetus except where it was necessary to save the life of the

161

mother, as distinct from preserving the health of the mother. The wording was not fully satisfactory to either side and there was further polarisation between pro-life and pro-choice groups.

Mary's position was that the mother and the unborn child had equal rights, but even that seemingly straightforward position was not without its complications. What happens in the case of an ectopic pregnancy, where the fertilised egg develops outside the cavity of the uterus? What happens if a pregnant woman has cancer of the womb? On these questions, the pro-life movement made a crucial distinction between treatment which was targeted towards the mother, even if such treatment had a lethal detrimental impact on the foetus, and direct targeting of the unborn. Mary's position was that the mother was entitled, as of right, to all treatment necessary to save her life, including direct termination of the unborn foetus. The irony was that her stance now put her in conflict with people whose cause she believed in wholeheartedly and allied her to people with whom she shared little.

She also felt very alone in her stance until she learned that Patricia Casey, professor of psychiatry in UCD and the Mater Hospital, and Cornelius O'Leary, professor emeritus of political science in Queen's University Belfast, agreed with her. All three were in accord that women should not have the right to abortion except to save their own lives. They believed that abortion was unlawful killing and was not permissible except in self-defence. They wrote a letter to *The Sunday Tribune* and to the *Irish Press:*

> We welcome and support the forthcoming referendum on the substantive law of abortion. We hope that those who are pro-life will feel as we do and vote "yes" . . . The Supreme Court Decision in the case of the Attorney General–v–X contradicted the express will of the Irish people as well as decades of medical and legal practice by permitting the direct abortion of the unwanted child . . . No wording is perfect, but we believe the wording offered by the Government is pro-woman and pro-unborn.‡

Mary was friendly enough with Cardinal Cahal Daly that he would sometimes call on her for advice. When he did so before the second abortion referendum, Mary advised him to accept the government's proposal. Some time later she received a call from him during a meeting of the bishops in Maynooth. He told her that the hierarchy was seeking

---

‡   Mary McAleese, private papers.

a small change in the proposed wording of the constitutional amendment, and that if they could get this change they would recommend the government's proposal. If the government was unable or unwilling to change the wording, the hierarchy would remain neutral on the issue. Mary was asked to convey this message to the government. Her first question was, "Where does Archbishop Desmond Connell stand on this?" When she was told that the bishops were unanimous in the decision, she said she would rather hear from the archbishop himself. She says Archbishop Connell came to the phone and confirmed what Cardinal Daly had told her. She then contacted the Attorney-General Harry Whelehan, who passed the message on to the Taoiseach Albert Reynolds. Whelehan came back to Mary with the message that the government could not change the wording because of the difficulty they had already had in devising an acceptable formula of words.

The Conference of Catholic Bishops advised Catholics to vote according to their consciences. The leaders of the pro-life campaign were angry at this neutral stance and at what they saw as the influence of Cornelius O'Leary, Patricia Casey and, particularly, Mary McAleese. O'Leary had been vice-chairman of the campaign during the 1983 referendum, and now his opposition to the views of the leadership rankled, particularly with John O'Reilly, one of its founders. Senator Des Hanafin, papal knight and chairman of the pro-life campaign, was incensed. He blamed Mary McAleese's influence for what he saw as the hierarchy's lack of proper leadership, and he and his wife Mona flew to Rome to ask the pope to interfere. The pope did, and Cardinal Daly was summoned to Rome. Meanwhile, the Archbishop of Dublin Desmond Connell was the first to break ranks with his episcopal brethren on the decision of the Bishops' Conference. His pastoral letter, which was to be read at all masses in the Archdiocese of Dublin, advised the faithful to vote against the proposed amendment. His example was soon followed by Bishop John Magee of Cloyne and Bishop Tom Finnegan of Killala. The members of the laity who looked to the hierarchy for direction were bewildered by it all.

On the Friday before the referendum, *The Late Late Show* studio was set out like a courtroom, and the programme was dedicated to helping the public to understand the intricacies of all that was involved in the referendum. The mock courtroom had a judge and lawyers for and against the amendment. Mary was a witness for the pro-choice side, and former Justice Peter O'Malley was the judge. Fidelma Macken and Niall Fennelly, both of whom were later appointed to the bench, were the legal team for the proposal. Against the proposal were the barristers Felix McEnroy and Garrett Cooney. In the studio that evening Mary met Patricia Casey for the first time. They felt an immediate rapport which later developed into a strong friendship. The psychiatrist was to be one of Mary's pivotal supporters during the election campaign for the presidency.

Although the proposals on travel and information were passed, the proposition on the substantive issue of legalisation of abortion was rejected. Monsignor Denis Faul berated Mary and those others who supported the proposal: "Ireland would have become the first country in the world to have abortion enshrined in its constitution."[‡] She says that two principles guided her in all questions of public morality: that the moral teachings of a Church should not be forced on the people of the country; and that the responsibility for accepting or rejecting any moral teaching lay with each individual.

---

‡   Interview with Monsignor Denis Faul.

Chapter Fourteen

The Flying Anchor

I know where I'm going
And I know who's going with me
("I Know Where I'm Going"—traditional)

Martin McAleese is not the type of person to let questions of public morality come between him and his night's sleep. He is basically a traditional Catholic for whom the normal obligations of his Church and the routine demands of Christian life are quite enough. At the end of the 1970s, he was more interested in the hierarchical structure of Aer Lingus than that of the Catholic Church. In 1978 he left Blueskies and went full-time to Enterprise Travel as financial controller and company secretary. The business involved ten travel agents in Northern Ireland in a consortium with Aer Lingus. The headquarters of Enterprise Travel was in Belfast, but they maintained an office in Dublin, and Martin regularly travelled between the two cities.

Aer Lingus had four subsidiary travel companies like this at the time, each with its own chief executive and its own financial controller. It made no economic sense, a fact that he understood very well. He also understood that the situation could not endure and that his own job, sooner or later, was going to be at risk. This caused him no great concern, for he was sure he would easily get another job, but the evident impermanence of his position set him thinking about his future and about what he really wanted to do with his life. He had always been attracted to minute and detailed mechanical work, but also relished intellectual challenge. He thought back to a profession he had been interested in when he was sitting his A levels: dentistry, a profession that incorporated his work interests and which would be financially rewarding. What started as a notion began to take form as a desire for career change, specifically an urge to go back to college and qualify as a dentist. Such a drastic move would entail living solely on Mary's salary for some years. He decided it was time to discuss the possibilities with her.

Meanwhile, Mary went flying, not as a passenger in a Boeing all over Europe, but as a pilot in a Cessna all over the east of Ireland. She had long been interested in learning to fly, and in the autumn of 1977 she took a trip to Weston Aerodrome, on the plains of Kildare, where she first met Darby O'Kennedy. Darby was captain of the flying club there and was also her teacher for most of her lessons. She had little support from her family or her husband for her new hobby as they thought it unnecessarily dangerous. It was nice to have people concerned about her, but their worries did not stop her enjoying the freedom, the tranquillity and the pure thrill of piloting a plane through empty skies. She flew mostly Cessnas or Pipers during her time at Weston, little two-seater, one-engine planes. It may not have been terribly dangerous, but it was certainly expensive as a hobby, and Mary spread her lessons over a long period of time, relishing the prospect of each visit and each flight.

The Department of Transport and Power granted a learner pilot's licence, number 1440, to Mary Patricia McAleese on 3 March 1978, and she was soon flying solo. She was very proud of her achievement, and evidence suggests she had good reason to be proud, as she was a good pilot. Darby O'Kennedy told her as much and said that, when she had the requisite licence, he would give her a job as an instructor in Weston. She thanked him kindly but had no interest in his invitation. Her only interest was in flying. It was not uncommon for a group of four or five student pilots, once they were sure their fascination was not merely a passing whim, to combine their resources and buy a plane. Mary had become interested enough to start looking around for a few partners with a view to buying a second-hand Cessna.

In the spring of 1979, Mary was between two worlds. She had been reading the works of Fyodor Dostoevsky and Hermann Hesse, whose books deal with dislocation and the incompatibility of different areas of people's lives. Maybe the books had a bearing on the yearning that was tormenting her, or maybe her own dislocation had drawn her to those books. She loved working in Dublin and she loved living in County Meath. Although she had no great desire to return to Belfast, she missed the comfort of her friends. In January that year, after receiving a letter from Pat Montgomery, her friend from the days of the Belfast Women's Refuge, she wrote in her diary: ". . . renewed nostalgia for Belfast . . . still this feeling of not belonging, the desire to return to the warm, bosomy comfort of familiar Belfast. But must muster all the mental anti-bodies, the

166

realistic approach and console myself with assurances of the need to move and grow and learn . . ."[‡]

If she could feel the same warmth and cosiness around Dublin as she felt around Belfast, the same friendliness and sense of belonging, her life would be complete. After the report on the Irish Penal System was published, after the Campaign for Homosexual Law Reform was well established and the connections made for her students with the Department of Justice, Mary's life was becoming quiet again. She needed to be busy.

She decided to join the Irish Council for Civil Liberties. One of her colleagues in Trinity College, Kadar Asmal from South Africa, was prominent on the Council, as was Pat McCartan, the lawyer who later became a Democratic Left TD before being appointed a judge. Asmal was to become president of the Council for Civil Liberties in 1980, but at that time he was better known as leader of the Irish Anti-Apartheid Movement. In later years he returned to South Africa as a government minister under Nelson Mandela.

Although the ICCL was to the forefront of many worthwhile causes, and although Mary found her work with the Council fulfilling, it always bothered her that the organisation was not an all-Ireland body. The National Council for Civil Liberties, a British organisation, was the group that operated in the North. Ironically, the first annual general meeting of the ICCL that she attended, 15 and 16 June 1979, was convened in the All-Ireland Club.

Mary's reputation as a civil rights lawyer was growing apace. In June 1978, she had a difference of opinion with Rory O'Hanlon, a senior counsel at the time and later a judge. The occasion was a conference on changes in the law governing the admissibility of confession statements in Northern Ireland. The new law governing terrorist offences was taken from the European Convention on Human Rights. O'Hanlon argued that the new law would not dilute the very strong protection of the accused already afforded by the common law. Mary argued the opposite: that the common-law protections were obviated by the new law and that the latter would now permit the use of force to obtain confessions. As practice and case law subsequently showed, she was right. When the first case under the new law was brought before Ambrose McGonigle, judge of the Northern Ireland High Court, he commented that a prisoner could suffer a lot of physical and

---

‡   Mary McAleese, Diary.

mental abuse before it could be deemed "torture or inhuman and degrading treatment".

Apart from legal quarrels such as this, the academic life was a comfortable and quiet one for Mary, too comfortable perhaps for a spirited woman who was constantly generating new ideas and formulating new approaches to problems. She was looking for a fresh challenge, one that would stretch her intellectual capabilities and satisfy her eagerness to gain a deeper understanding of people and of life in general in the Republic. Help was at hand.

When Muiris Mac Conghail was appointed head of television programmes in RTÉ in 1977, he set out to make the national television station a more intellectual place. In some departments he found that "new" was not necessarily "better" and in others that "new" was sometimes "too new". Pádhraig Ó Giollagáin was commissioned to write a television series set in an inner city school, *The Spike*, but RTÉ soon discovered that they had misread the tolerances of the Irish viewing public. As Ó Giollagáin says, "Ireland was just not ready for programmes in which sexual content was less than subtle, and so *The Spike* was spiked."[‡]

In the Current Affairs Department, Mac Conghail followed the example of Jack Whyte and enticed some very talented people from academic life. One academic who had already proved his worth in front of the camera was David Thornley, a gifted and popular presenter of political programmes, who later left RTÉ and became a Labour Party TD. Thornley's colleague on the political programmes was another academic, Brian Farrell, who was sharing his lecturing duties with his on-screen political analysis and cross-questioning. Mac Conghail attracted people like Justin Keating, Maurice Manning, Paddy Geary and Mary Redmond from college life to studio life, and RTÉ Current Affairs was the richer for them. The formula was working.

Mac Conghail was delighted to see an application from Mary McAleese for a position as reporter/presenter in the Current Affairs Department. He had already seen the young law professor smoothly handling the hard questions on television. He thought she might be every bit as effective in putting the hard questions on his new current affairs programme, *Frontline*.

She was no stranger to television studios. Apart from her experience as a guest on many programmes, she had done a television training

‡   Interview with author.

course ten years previously. When she was a first-year student in Queen's, the St Vincent de Paul Society decided to send two of their members to what was then the Catholic Communications Institute in Booterstown, in Dublin. The Society, like many other organisations, was becoming media-conscious and felt that some of its members should learn how to handle themselves in front of a camera. The people chosen to go on the communications course were Mary and Ruaidhrí Higgins, who later became a well-known solicitor in Belfast.

As an academic working exclusively in her own subject area, Mary missed out on the feeling of being part of a team. In the School of Law in Trinity College, she felt a little insulated from political forces, both local and national, and from the ebbs and flows of ordinary life outside the groves of academia. As she looked around she saw people operating as members of teams in all walks of life, and she wanted to experience the kinship and interdependence of co-operative work. She wanted to be part of a jigsaw. She also needed, as she says herself, "to get under the skin of life south of the border". She thought there was no better way to achieve both of these aims than to accept the offer that was made to her on 21 March 1979: presenter/reporter in the Current Affairs Department, RTÉ Television, starting on the fourth grade of the incremental scale at £6,729 per annum.

To Mary the work was like a dream come true. She uses the Irish word *"meitheal"* to describe the ethos of *Frontline*, and she describes her producer, Peter Feeney, as more of a *"meitheal"* leader than a taskmaster.[‡] She also says: "Peter Feeney was one of the most decent people I have ever met. I learned a lot from him about handling people. He was not a push-over boss, but he respected others and respected their judgement. He was a great listener, and it was a genuine pleasure to work with him."

In that same year, George Waters succeeded Oliver Moloney as director general of RTÉ. On the same day that Mary started her new job, Colum Kenny also started. He and Mary remained friends when he later became a lecturer in communications in Dublin City University and a journalist with the *Sunday Independent*. Forbes McFaul was part of the team, and Joe Little and Colm Keane also joined around that time.

All during the summer, autumn and winter of 1979, she made her weary but satisfied way home each night to Mooretown. The tiredness did not bother her in the least. She loved company, not only at work but at home also. She wanted her first home to be like her mother's and her

---

‡   *Meitheal*: a working party, usually of neighbours, gathered to do a specific job.

grandmother's, a *céilí*-ing house where visitors would always feel welcome. Relations from the North regularly stayed with them. Friends from Dublin often came for dinner and sometimes stayed over. She loved entertaining.

The McAleeses were welcoming hosts, Mary's cooking was good and the dinner parties were easy, comfortable occasions. The house was in good shape by that time. The new cooker was living up to her expectations and every floor had its carpet. Their financial circumstances had also changed for the better since the night they had the row over the golf clubs. Their friends called them DINKYs—Double Income No Kids Yet.

In the spring of 1980, Martin decided that he really wanted to study dentistry. Apart from the fact that he wanted to be a dentist, there were other reasons for the change of career. They knew they were both travelling too much to have a proper life together. The constant journeys abroad had been part of Martin's life for some years, but now Mary was travelling also. Over a period of two months, they examined every aspect of the proposed change. They discovered that because Martin already had a degree in physics he could get an exemption of one year from the five-year dentistry course in Trinity College. Three questions were going around and around in his mind as the time came for him to make the final decision. Would he be burning the bridges behind him as he left the comfortable line of work he was in? Would he do well on the course, if he were accepted? Would he make a good dentist?

True to their nature they had some money put aside. Between that and Mary's salary, they thought they could just about make it through the four years. A few nights after Mary handed Martin's application form into Trinity, they were watching the nine o'clock news when the taoiseach Charles Haughey made his famous speech, telling the people of Ireland that they would have to tighten their belts. Mary and Martin were staring at the television set as he was speaking, nodding their heads sagely and listening to his every word as if he were talking directly to them. They knew that, in their case, he were absolutely right.

Mary never said a word to Martin about the Cessna, and the flying lessons were forgotten about.

"It was Martin's determination to do dentistry that knocked Mary's plans on the head," says Mary's mother Claire. "Because of Martin McAleese they had to sell a car instead of buying a plane."

She was speaking in jest, of course, the sort of banter that can only work properly between people who have great respect for each other.

She and Paddy both knew that the young people were never afraid of hard work, and because of that they would struggle through any financial difficulties that would come their way. Although the members of both families knew that Martin had Mary's full backing for what he was doing, they could not fully understand why anyone would give up a successful career and go back to college for four years. Mary understood.

Martin knew he would be called into Aer Lingus head office sooner or later, either to be let go or to be offered a job in the new amalgamated Aer Lingus travel concern, Aer Lingus Holidays Ltd. He got the call on the day he received his acceptance letter from Trinity College. As Mary was on a short break in Donegal with her cousin Marian Bradley from Philadelphia, she had to wait until evening to contact him, and when she eventually made contact from a phone box in Lettermacaward, she found him agitated. At the age of twenty-nine he had just been told he was being seriously considered for the position of chief executive of the new company. The job came with a very good salary and an attractive package. He told her that the Aer Lingus people were taken aback when he explained what he intended to do. When they asked him to consider his decision further, he explained that he had already thought seriously about it. He had enough of the life of constant travel and entertaining. He wanted a job from which he could come home at night. He wanted to be a dentist. He started his course in Trinity in October 1980.

He was the second oldest in a class of twenty-nine dental students, of whom five were mature students. There was no comparison between his life as a single, carefree student in Belfast and this life in the School of Dentistry in Dublin. Every word that fell from the mouths of Professor Diarmuid Shanley or Professor Robert McConnell was like a seed dropping into fertile ground. He never missed a lecture, was never late with an essay or an assignment. Fear of failure spurred him on. Nothing was going to come between him and his study. Although he found the course hard, the pace of life was now much slower for him. The days and the weeks took on a shape he had almost forgotten. He was able to distinguish morning from afternoon and Tuesday from Friday. He was also at peace.

"Pride and determination motivated me to work hard. I became obsessed with succeeding in that course. In contrast, the liberating aspect of having made such a life-changing decision gave me great peace of mind. I kept saying to myself, 'If I did it once I can do it again.' That gave me great confidence, and from that comes great contentment."

That year Mary had her second miscarriage. Both happened a few short weeks after conception and she had no physical ill effects. She was young, healthy and strong. She also had a positive attitude and did not begin to worry that she might be prone to miscarriage. She wanted children, but was, as she says, "prepared to leave it in God's hands". She focused on her new job.

The producer of *Frontline*, Peter Feeney, says: "We very soon recognised her ability and promoted her to studio presenter. She was quick-witted and articulate and had all the qualities necessary to be a very good studio presenter. Off camera I found her to be a courageous person, never afraid to tell things as she saw them. She had the ability to pull debates back to reality."[‡]

Because *Frontline* went out only once a week, there were obvious difficulties with the topicality of the programme. It was impossible to tackle news items properly if they were five days old by the time the programme was broadcast. Despite that, *Frontline* was held in high regard in the days before RTÉ viewers became accustomed to current affairs programmes going out four nights a week.

During her time on *Frontline*, Mary interviewed Mary Robinson on the subject of the Diplock Courts in Northern Ireland, a topic on which both civil rights lawyers had strong opinions. Before Christmas 1979, she and Charlie Bird worked on a programme on abortion; she covered the PAYE workers' strike in January 1980 and the Fianna Fáil Ard Fheis in February. She did a programme on the Irish Deaf Society in March and another on the proposed women's prison in Clondalkin in April. She loved the work and she loved all she was learning.

She was not blind to the internal politics of RTÉ. She feels that the station had come heavily under the influence of Conor Cruise O'Brien in the seventies, particularly after the publication of his book *States of Ireland*, a treatise that was particularly effective in propagating the gospel of revisionism. At the start of the Troubles, RTÉ accurately reflected the view of the majority of the people in the state, in that it was sympathetic to the plight of the nationalist people in the North. In 1972, the RTÉ Authority was dismissed when the station broadcast a report of an interview between Kevin O'Kelly and the then chief of staff of the Provisional IRA Seán Mac Stiofáin. O'Kelly was sentenced to three months in prison for contempt of court when he refused to give evidence about the interview at the trial of Mac Stiofáin some time later.

‡ Interview with author.

The prison term was reduced to a fine, but not before O'Kelly had spent some time behind bars. He was feted as a nationalist hero by some people at the time, but his courageous stance was surely motivated more by the protection of his journalistic integrity than by any nationalist or republican leanings.

Seán Mac Stiofáin claimed that an anti-nationalist bias in RTÉ pre-dated the Fine Gael–Labour Party coalition government of 1973–1977: "The anti-Nationalist views of some members of Fianna Fáil were responsible for the change of sympathy within RTÉ. It was Gerry Collins, as minister for posts and telegraphs, who introduced Section 31 of the Broadcasting Authority Act in October 1971. He did that to silence me, and others like me, and to conceal the republican version of the struggle in the North from people in the South."‡

Even by the early 1970s, it had become clear that the IRA's role had changed from being defensive to offensive. Mac Stiofáin maintained that neither the policy change within the IRA nor their subsequent bombing and assassination campaign had any influence on the change of attitude towards Northern nationalists within RTÉ that later characterised their current affairs programmes. RTÉ, like most of the country, was bitterly opposed to the Provisional IRA's campaign; but by dint of a bewildering logic, RTÉ was becoming not only increasingly indifferent to the predicament of ordinary nationalists who gave absolutely no support to the IRA but were, in fact, positively suspicious of them.

Mary claims that there was a definite and tangible anti-nationalist, anti-Catholic and anti-intellectual atmosphere in RTÉ by the time she went to work there. She was able to ignore it during her first year, as it did not affect her work or her relationship with her colleagues, but all that was to change. A terrible silence fell over the Current Affairs Department of RTÉ in September 1980. On the ninth of that month, Mary wrote in her diary, "Last edition of Frontline transmitted—no-one has any idea what the future holds for them. No communication from anyone at all."§

It was not long before Mary discovered what the future held for her: in her own words "the most difficult, the darkest, the worst time of my life".

‡   Interview with author.
§   Mary McAleese, Diary.

Chapter Fifteen

It Was the Worst of Times

> You coasted along.
> And all the time, though you never noticed,
> the old lies festered;
> the ignorant became more thoroughly infected.
> (John Hewitt: "The Coasters")

On 6 October 1980, *Today Tonight* was screened for the first time. Viewers saw Mary McAleese standing outside Dublin's Gate Theatre, reporting on the opening night of Brian Friel's new play, *Translations*. She says that until shortly before that first programme was made she had no idea what her role in RTÉ would be and that she first learned of her involvement in *Today Tonight* from a newspaper. It was probably the only time in her life that a deficiency in the Irish language could have been considered advantageous to her. She says she was told that if she had been able to speak Irish she would have joined colleagues such as Michael McCarthy and Éamonn Ó Muirí on the Irish language programme *Féach*. Such a move was considered a demotion, but in the light of what was ahead, it would probably have been a happy demotion.

It was a bad start to a bad year. According to Mary, and to many of her colleagues, she was treated like an IRA fellow-traveller. In 1981 she wrote, "I was a Catholic, a Northerner, a Nationalist and a woman—a quadruple deviant in the eyes of many influential people in RTÉ."[‡]

Regarding that year, from the autumn of 1980 to the summer of 1981, she now says, "That year was the most difficult, the darkest, the worst time of my life. In saying that, I am taking into account the years of the Troubles in Belfast. Without a doubt, it was the most traumatic period of my life—bar none."

Her new editor, Joe Mulholland, had joined RTÉ in 1969, and soon made his mark by winning a Jacobs Award for a documentary on Frank

---

‡   Mary McAleese, Diary.

Ryan.[‡] Mulholland, who would later become managing director of television in RTÉ, was born in Donegal, trained as a teacher in England, furthered his education in France and gained a doctorate in medieval theatre in the University of Nancy. He was, at one time, a contributor to the French newspaper *Le Monde.* In 1980 Muiris Mac Conghail appointed him editor of the new current affairs programme, *Today Tonight,* and also gave him a free hand to recruit his own team. This was to be a flagship programme, a highly professional, innovative show in its coverage and analysis of breaking news and issues of national importance. There were ten producers and ten reporters, but only two full-time researchers, Fintan Cronin and Mary Curtin, as most of the reporters did their own research. "The general consensus was that the previous programme was not working. I wanted a clean sheet and new presenters. There was a lot of pressure on me to put *Today Tonight* on the map. I did it, but not without some casualties," Joe Mulholland says.[§]

The pressure on Mulholland was understandable. RTÉ were investing a lot of money, resources, time and talent in the new programme, which would be broadcast four evenings a week. In many ways their hopes for *Today Tonight* were realised. In the years to come it would win acclaim as a progressive and enterprising programme, and its consistently good TAM ratings would prove its popularity. Jobs on the *Today Tonight* team were in great demand among reporters and producers. Anyone would expect Mary McAleese to be exhilarated by the flurry, the challenge, the intensity of this working environment, but such was not the case. She says that from the outset her professionalism, her integrity and her cultural identity were not only questioned but also disparaged. She and many others who worked in RTÉ at the time say that members and supporters of the Workers' Party were responsible for the anti-nationalist atmosphere that was cultivated in the national television station.

The roots of the Workers' Party can be traced back to the start of the Troubles. The IRA split into two factions in December 1969, and Sinn Féin followed suit a month later at its Ard Fheis. The immediate cause of the rupture in republican ranks was the attempt by some members to allow recognition of the parliaments in Stormont, Westminster and

---

‡   Frank Ryan: republican and socialist; fought in Irish and Spanish Civil Wars on republican sides; death sentence in Spain was commuted; died in Germany, 1944.

§   Interview with author.

Dublin. It was felt that most of the supporters of this proposal were also promoting a socialist rather than a republican agenda. Those who opposed the motion walked out of the Ard Fheis and became known as Provisional Sinn Féin, and those who remained were called Official Sinn Féin. Republican sympathisers have traditionally worn a paper replica of an Easter lily at Easter time, in commemoration of those who died in the Easter Rising of 1916. At Easter 1970, the supporters of the Provisionals wore lilies that were fastened with a straight pin while the Officials' lilies were gum-backed. Since then Official Sinn Féin and their supporters have been know by the nickname "Stickies". The sobriquet has clung to them over the years despite several official name changes and several re-inventions: the Republican Clubs, Sinn Féin the Workers' Party, the Workers' Party, and Democratic Left (which has since been subsumed into the Labour Party).

After the republican split, nationalist areas of Belfast became sub-divided into "Sticky" areas and "Provo" areas and an internecine war erupted. Leeson Street, where Mary's father owned the Long Bar, was a "Sticky" street, albeit right on the unofficial border with "Provo" territory. Since Mary often worked in her father's bar, she has long experience of the "Stickies" since the time of the split.

Not only were the Officials turning their backs on republicanism and nationalism, they were also turning to Marxist communism in great numbers. To them the priority in Northern Ireland was the class struggle. Eoghan Harris was prominent among those who promoted this idea. According to socialist author Pat Walsh, "In early 1974, Eoghan Harris, who even then was becoming the dominant ideologue in the party, delivered a paper called From Civil Rights to Class Politics. This argued in effect that Civil Rights had been achieved in Ulster, and that now the way was open for political development aimed at uniting the workers on class issues."[‡]

Harris spent many years working in RTÉ, and even though Mary was working there during his time, the pair never met. Harris's ideas influenced some of those in middle management in the station. Some people who worked in RTÉ when Mary joined the station maintain that there were up to fifteen members of the Workers' Party in key positions in RTÉ: editors, reporters, researchers, etc., and up to fifty ardent supporters. Others say there were no more than six members and between twelve and fifteen supporters there at any one time. It is said

‡   Pat Walsh, *Irish Republicanism and Socialism* (Belfast: Athal, 1994), p. 71.

Judge Patrick Flanagan,
Mary's great grand-uncle.

Frank Leneghan (Mary's grandfather)
and Willie Leneghan (Mary's uncle)
Roscommon.

Bridget Leneghan (Mary's grandmother), Carroward, Co. Roscommon.

*Frank Leneghan, Dan Leneghan (uncle), Brigid Leneghan (grandmother),
Paddy Leneghan, Roscommon.*

Mary on 'Bronco' the donkey, Paddy Leneghan standing, Carroward 1955.

Standing: May Cassidy, Kevin Cassidy. Seated: Ann Trainor (2nd from left).

Claire Leneghan, Nora McAreavey (holding Mary), May Fitzpatrick, Ardoyne 1951.

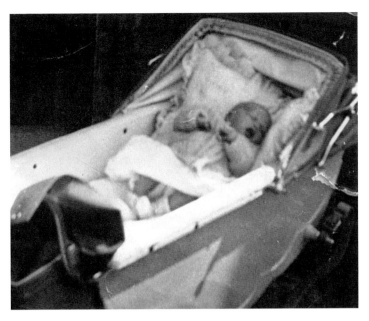

Mary, Ladbrooke Drive, Belfast 1951.

Claire Leneghan, Mary, Nan Bradley, Anne Bradley.

McAleese family (L-R): John, Emma, Cathal, Kathleen, Charlie, Martin (aged 9).

Mary, Kevin Cassidy (first cousin) on the donkey, Carroward 1955.

Mary and Nora Leneghan, Ardoyne 1957.

(Top left) Mary, First Holy Communion 1958.

(Top right) Mary aged 8 with the prize she won in the talent contest in Butlins.

Mary, Mercy Convent, Crumlin Road, Belfast 1958.

The 11+ Class, Mercy Convent, Crumlin Road, Belfast 1961-62 (Mary front left).

St Mary's CBS Belfast Football Team, 1966. Martin McAleese with cup.

*(Above left) St Dominic's Badminton Team. Back row, left to right: Maureen Totten,
Mary, Frances Lucas. Front row, left to right: Patricia Gilfedder, Kathleen Boyle.
(Above right) Mary and Martin, 1970.*

Back row (L-R): Mary, Nora. Front row (L-R): Patrick, Phelim, Claire, Damien.

Mary and Martin at their first formal dance.

*Open Day in Dromantine, 1971: Pat Leneghan (standing), Kevin McAleese,
Damien Leneghan, Kathleen McAleese, Claire Leneghan, Mary (with Clement
Leneghan), John Leneghan, Martin (with Pheilim Leneghan).*

Martin's graduation. Charlie, Martin, Emma, QUB 1972.

(Above left) Mary is conferred with LLB, Queen's University, July 1973.
(Above right) Called to the Bar, Belfast 1974.

Old Corner House, Rostrevor, in the seventies.

Wedding Day, 9 March 1976.

"Rostrevor", Mooretown, Ratoath.

The McAleese house, Mooretown, Ratoath, County Meath, 1977–87.

Mary, RTÉ 1979.

that in many cases membership of the party was shrouded in secrecy, in keeping with the Marxist strategy of placing activists in strategic positions in the media and trade unions. There was no place in such a plan for nationalism. On the other hand, the courting of unionists was a key element, as witness the frequency of interviews with unionist as distinct from nationalist spokespersons on RTÉ current affairs programmes at the start of the eighties.

Monsignor Denis Faul from Tyrone and Fr Raymond Murray from Armagh were bitter enemies of the IRA. They denounced them at every turn, but also condemned some of the activities of the RUC and British army, including their interrogation methods. Denis Faul had been saying mass every Sunday in Long Kesh, later known as HM Prison the Maze, for twenty-five years. He and Raymond Murray knew more about prisons and the treatment of prisoners than most public figures in the Northern nationalist community, yet their voices were seldom heard on RTÉ. Monsignor Faul says:

> I was never invited to be interviewed or to speak on *Today Tonight* during those years—neither myself nor Fr Murray from Armagh. The BBC often invited me to speak on their programmes, and I was regularly on *Newsnight*. Our impression of RTÉ journalists was that they never did their research, never did their homework. They would come to Belfast and head straight for the bar of the Europa Hotel. They used to get their information, or a version of the information, from the RUC Press Office.[‡]

Michael McCarthy, the producer of *Féach*, the popular Irish language current affairs programme of the time, has this to say about the perception of bias in the reporting of *Today Tonight:*

> We, in *Féach*, would have resented the serious misreading of the political landscape in the North by *Today Tonight*. There is no way we would have fitted into their cosy editorial consensus on the North. For the very few who held different views, life was difficult if they voiced them. But we, as a programme, did have to deal with the fallout from *Today Tonight* when working in the North, particularly among nationalist and republican communities. Frequently a measure of distrust, and sometimes of open hostility towards RTÉ, had to be contended with because of the perceived bias within our major current affairs programme.[§]

---

‡   Interview with author.

§   Interview with author.

When *Today Tonight* was starting, Joe Mulholland recruited Fintan Cronin as a researcher. Cronin, who had an MA in political science and was an expert on the politics of the left, soon got to know Mary McAleese as they were working side by side in the office on the first floor of the Administration Building:

> Mary McAleese was highly intelligent, sharp and extraordinarily articulate. She was also very open and friendly and liberal in the best sense of the word, but she would not suffer fools gladly. In contrast to the very public Catholic stance she took in 1981, I have no recollection of her saying much about her Catholic views or beliefs in 1980. She was much more interested in what was going on in Northern Ireland at that time, particularly the hunger strikes in the Maze Prison, and more especially the effect those strikes were having on the lives of ordinary people.[‡]

The horror of the hunger strikes, the deaths of the ten men in the Maze and the seventy people who were killed outside during the hunger strikes—these events formed the backdrop to Mary McAleese's troubles in RTÉ during her second year working there. There was hardly a man or woman in the country who did not have a strong opinion on what was going on in the Maze at that time. RTÉ was a microcosm of this, at times a seething microcosm. The hunger strikes polarised people's views. Wherever there was a political or ideological crack before 1981, there was a chasm afterwards. Barry Cowan, a Protestant, born in Coleraine and brought up in Ballymena, was one of Mary's colleagues on the programme. He had worked for the BBC in London before joining RTÉ as a presenter/reporter on *Today Tonight*. According to him the polarisation that was so evident in RTÉ was needless. He claims that some people, including Mary McAleese, took what people said too seriously:

> Mary wasn't really part of the group from the North, the Northern Mafia as we were called. The group took quite a ribbing at the time. I was often called a "Black Northern Prod", and I usually gave back as good as I got. There was a core of strong nationalist opinion on the programme in those days. At the time of the Falklands War, for instance, a lot of time was spent discussing what the islands should be called. These people were insisting the Falkland Islands should be referred to as the "Malvinas". Mary was not part of that group either. I found her

---

‡ Interview with author.

178

a bit distant at first but got to know her much better later on. In 1985, my production company, Bridge Productions, was making a series of programmes called *God Knows*. She was the first person I asked to present the programme, and that is an indication of my respect for her.[‡]

Peter Feeney agrees with Barry Cowan that opinion in RTÉ was very polarised: "We were brought up with a very simplistic view: a view of 'us and them'. These ideas began to be challenged in the 1970s, partly by the intellectual arguments of, for example, Conor Cruise O'Brien and partly by some people in the media. The escalation of the Troubles polarised opinions in RTÉ, and this reached a peak with the hunger strikes of 1980 and 1981."[§]

Exactly three weeks after the first *Today Tonight* programme was broadcast, seven republican prisoners went on hunger strike in the H-Blocks of the Maze Prison. Back in 1976, Merlyn Rees, secretary of state for Northern Ireland, had announced that the British government had decided to put an end to the special status that had been afforded to prisoners who were convicted of politically motivated crimes. The change was to come into effect from the first day of March that year. From that date, political prisoners would be treated like ordinary criminals. This decision would entail five main changes in the prisoners' circumstances. They would have to wear prison clothes. They would have to do prison work. They would no longer be allowed to organise their own educational programmes. There would be no remission of sentences for good behaviour. They would no longer have free association, which spelt the end of the old prison camp structure, as the prisoners would now be held in cells. The abrogation of these five changes later constituted the five demands of the prisoners in the subsequent hunger strikes.

What had previously been known as Long Kesh was demolished and the H-Blocks were built: a series of cell blocks in the shape of the letter "H". The prisoners protested vigorously about the changes. On 15 September 1976, Kieran Nugent was the first person to be convicted under the new prison regulations. When he was not allowed to wear his own clothes, he refused to wear any clothes, except a blanket. Within a year there were eighty prisoner '"on the blanket", as the protest was called. Within another year, many prisoners were refusing

---

‡　Interview with author.

§　Interview with author.

179

to use the toilets in protest against alleged brutality by warders as they were going to and from the toilet blocks. The "dirty protest" had started, and prisoners began to smear the walls of the cells with their own faeces.

In August 1978, Cardinal Tomás Ó Fiaich paid a visit to the H-Blocks. When he came out he spoke frankly and bluntly to the waiting reporters: "One could hardly allow an animal to remain in such conditions, let alone a human being. The nearest approach to it I have ever seen was the spectacle of hundreds of homeless people living in the sewer pipes of Calcutta."

This statement, combined with the work of the Relatives' Action Committees, succeeded in creating a lot of sympathy for the prisoners among the nationalist community, among republicans and also among people who gave no support whatsoever to Sinn Féin. Still there was no move from the British government. The prisoners had brought their case to the European Commission on Human Rights, and in June 1980 they received their judgement. The Commission said the prisoners had brought their condition on themselves, but it berated the British government for doing nothing to resolve the situation. On 27 October, seven of the prisoners went on hunger strike.

Fintan Cronin claims he was sent to Belfast shortly afterwards to do some research on this first hunger strike. He says Joe Mulholland told him to interview two people in Belfast: Mary McMahon, a Workers' Party councillor in Ballymurphy, and John McMichael, second in command of the UDA. It is alleged that McMichael was also commander of the UFF, a paramilitary group that has been responsible for the deaths of hundreds of Catholics.‡ Cronin says he refused to interview either of these people on the subject of republican hunger strikes in the H-Blocks.§

Joe Mulholland says he did not keep a diary of those years and does not remember the incident. He says he was never a member of the Workers' Party, a claim accepted even by his critics. He says of the political scene during 1980–1981: "Emotions were running very high on both sides: nationalist and unionist. My intention was to steer a middle

---

‡   UFF: Ulster Freedom Fighters, a cover name for the UDA.

§   Although John McMichael was closely associated with UDA and UFF violence for many years, he is now acknowledged as one of the pioneers of the political rethink among loyalists. He wrote two books, *Common Sense* and *Beyond the Religious Divide*, both of which earned high praise from Cardinal Tomás Ó Fiaich.

line between them, and I was determined not to allow the programme to be used for political propaganda."[‡]

On 21 November 1980, Mary McAleese wrote the following in her diary:

> Consistently H-Block coverage is biased at worst, misguided at best. Discussion tends to be unsatisfactory for the decision and the editorial line have already been stipulated and decreed and it is difficult to make the other case without people getting shirty, pompous or downright nasty. It would be so refreshing to have a genuinely open, intellectual discussion, a search for objectivity. But the membership doesn't really allow for that. Too many wear the blinkers of half-thought-out prejudices wrapped up in the voices of knowledgeable authority.[§]

At the *Today Tonight* team meetings, Mary and the small number of people that were of a like mind on these issues failed again and again to put the case for the ordinary nationalist. She was repeatedly accused of being a "Sinn Féiner". As that first hunger strike maintained its momentum, so the unease in the country, and the tension in the *Today Tonight* team, intensified.

The hunger strike ended after fifty-three days, five days before Christmas, due to the intervention of Cardinal Ó Fiaich. One of the hunger strikers, Seán McKenna, was critically ill at that stage, and he was moved to Musgrave Park Hospital in Belfast. Controversy still surrounds the ending of the 1980 hunger strike. The prisoners always maintained that they ended the strike on foot of a promise that their five demands would be met, a claim that was denied by the British government.[†]

Some days after the ending of the strike, the British Prime Minister Margaret Thatcher made a speech in which she referred to the prisoners in the H-Blocks: "The government will never concede political status to the hunger strikers, or to any others convicted of criminal offences in the province."

That Christmas was a tense one in the North. Every time Mary travelled to Rostrevor and Belfast—which was nearly every weekend— she became more and more certain that a bad situation was growing steadily worse. At the start of February, the prisoners issued a statement

‡   Interview with author.

§   Mary McAleese, Diary.

†   It was widely believed by nationalists that elements in the Northern Ireland Office objected to the government's intention to allow the prisoners to wear their own clothes.

saying that, unless the five demands were met, they would have no option but to begin another hunger strike. On 1 March 1981, the most tragic hunger strike in Ireland's history began, a strike that would leave ten men dead in the H-Blocks and seventy people dead on the streets of Northern Ireland. The date was chosen carefully: it was five years to the day since the British government had made their five changes and ended political status.

As a strategy and a weapon of protest, the hunger strike has always had a special place in the hearts and minds of Irish people. Even in pre-Christian times it was considered the ultimate protest, and people were known to have fasted to death at the doors of those who had wronged them. In the history of Irish republicanism, solemnity, reverence and even a degree of mysticism have attended the deaths of hunger strikers, and the sacrificial and redemptive aspects of the death of Christ himself have been the inspiration for some of them. Thomas Ashe, for example, before his death by force feeding while on hunger strike, wrote a poem entitled "Let Me Carry Your Cross for Ireland, Lord". Terence MacSwiney, the Lord Mayor of Cork, wrote on the example of the early Christian martyrs in his prophetic *Principles of Freedom* shortly before he died on hunger strike in Brixton Prison. Martyrs have always been venerated in Ireland, and those who die on hunger strike are the most revered, the person who fasts unto death for a cause being regarded as a noble and courageous victim. Death by hunger strike is seen as the most noble, the most heroic death of all. Nobody knew all this better than the IRA. The emotional outpouring, and the subsequent violence, engendered by any death in the H-Blocks was going to be catastrophic.

Fr Alex Reid, the priest who did so much to bring an end to the Troubles, understood the inevitable consequences. He now goes so far as to say, "Without a doubt, the hunger strike of 1981 added ten years to the Troubles."[‡]

Bobby Sands, the officer commanding the IRA in the Maze Prison, was the first to refuse food. From the time he went on hunger strike, he was represented by Pat Finnucane, the solicitor who was murdered by loyalists acting in collaboration with security forces in 1989. Sands had joined the IRA at the age of eighteen. He was sentenced to fourteen years in prison after being convicted of travelling in a car containing arms and ammunition. When Brendan Hughes went on hunger strike in

---

‡　Interview with author.

1980, Sands succeeded him as commander of the republican prisoners in the Maze. Likewise, when Sands refused food in 1981, he relinquished command and was succeeded by a former neighbour of Mary's from Ardoyne, Brendan "Bic" McFarlane, who was to retain command throughout the hunger strike.[†]

The hunger strike was only a couple of days old when it was condemned by Bishop Edward Daly of Derry, the "priest of the white handkerchief" of Bloody Sunday fame. The leadership of the IRA was not in favour of the hunger strike at first, as they later made clear. The impetus for the strike came from the prisoners themselves. On 2 March, the blanket protest was ended in order to focus attention on the hunger strike. In the McAleese house, in the Leneghan house, and in many other houses, it was obvious that this would be a death fast and would have terrible consequences. The cause of their certainty was the immovable stance of "the Iron Lady of Downing Street", as Margaret Thatcher had been dubbed. She had misread the end of the 1980 hunger strike; and Sands and those who would follow him would not end their fast without gaining political status.

On Thursday, 5 March, the H-Block hunger strike was the lead item on many of the world's newspapers. The reason for the sudden international interest was the death of Frank Maguire, the independent Westminster MP for Fermanagh-South Tyrone. Three nationalists had declared their interest in contesting the by-election for the vacant Westminster seat: Noel Maguire, a brother of the dead politician; Austin Currie of the SDLP; and Bernadette McAliskey, who said she would withdraw in favour of a candidate chosen by the prisoners in the H-Blocks. The Sinn Féin leadership decided they would nominate Bobby Sands, and by the end of March, Austin Currie and Noel Maguire had also withdrawn. The Fermanagh-South Tyrone by-election would now be a straight fight between the H-Blocks candidate, Bobby Sands, and the unionist candidate, Harry West. By election day, 11 April, two IRA men, Francis Hughes and Raymond McCreesh, and the INLA prisoner Patsy O'Hara had joined Sands on hunger strike.[§]

Mary understood what the British government had effectively done

---

[†] McFarlane, who was a former clerical student, remained in command for the duration of the hunger strike. He had been convicted of taking part in a bomb attack on the Bayardo Bar on Belfast's Shankill Road, in which five people were killed. He escaped from the Maze in 1983 and was extradited back from Holland in 1986. He played a central role in the talks which preceded the ceasefire of 1994.

[§] INLA: Irish National Liberation Army.

and the price that would be paid for the lack of intervention in the hunger strikes. Despite their refusal to regrant political status to the prisoners, they had bestowed on them a legitimacy and an eminence in the eyes of many people in Ireland and throughout the world. On that Thursday of the by-election, Mary spoke at a *Today Tonight* team meeting in Dublin. She said she had been doing her sums, and that based on her simple calculation of the Catholic and Protestant voting populations in Fermanagh–South Tyrone, she reckoned that Sands would win by around 700 votes. As *Today Tonight* was not normally broadcast on Friday evenings, she suggested that provision should be made for an exceptional programme the following evening . . . There was uproar in the room. She says she was attacked by speaker after speaker and that they were "menacingly angry". She was told that she did not know what she was talking about, that her calculations were inaccurate and that Harry West was sure to win. The occasions on which Mary McAleese was reluctant to defend her position have been very few, but this was one of them. Some who were present maintain that the vehemence and the intensity of the attack left her speechless, and that she was shaking as she left the room.

When news came through around noon the following day that Bobby Sands had secured 30,492 votes and Harry West 29,046, *Today Tonight* was the only major current affairs programme in this part of the world without a presence at the count centre in Enniskillen. Mary describes a senior colleague coming into the office where she was sitting at her desk. She says his face was red as he glowered at her and said, "I see your man won!"

Her response was immediate and forceful: "How dare you describe him as 'my man'? I've never been a supporter of violence in my life. Is Harry West your man? Is that what this is all about? As a person who can do maths, I did the sums yesterday. I told you, as a journalist, not what I wanted to happen, but what I believed would happen. Now that it has happened, don't take your anger out on me."

A film crew was hurriedly gathered. Deirdre Younge and Joe Little, as producer and reporter, were dispatched by helicopter to Enniskillen. Mary McAleese said she was not available to travel. When the film crew reached the count centre, they discovered they had travelled without a production assistant: Monica Cowley had been left at home. By agreement with the unions, a producer could not operate outside the studio without a production assistant, and Cowley was sent from Dublin to Enniskillen in a taxi while RTÉ negotiated permission to broadcast on the understanding that she was on her way. Michael McCarthy was at the count centre that day, working with *Féach*.

"On the day of the count the *Today Tonight* team arrived late in the afternoon or early evening looking rather foolish. There were many UK television crews there, as well as crews from other parts of the world, and here was our flagship current affairs programme nearly missing the occasion altogether. It was a desperate professional gaffe. Rather than having all of us look stupid, I conceded some of our time to them."‡

Meanwhile, the situation in the North was deteriorating. Three TDs went to talk to Sands in the Maze. They sought a meeting with Margaret Thatcher afterwards, but she refused to meet them. On Tuesday, 21 April, while on a visit to Saudi Arabia, she issued the famous statement: "Crime is crime is crime. It is not political."

If sound advice on the situation in Belfast was available to her, she did not recognise the wisdom of it. Not long after the hunger strike ended, most British newspapers reflected the opinion of the journalist David McKittrick: "Since that awesome display of sacrifice and resistance no one has really believed that Republican and Loyalist prisoners are the same as non-terrorist inmates: they may be regarded as better, or as worse, but they cannot be viewed as indistinguishable."§

Despite the efforts of the European Commission on Human Rights, despite the intervention of Monsignor John Magee, private secretary of Pope John Paul II, despite the persistent attempts of Cardinal Tomás Ó Fiaich to intercede, Bobby Sands died at 1.17 on the morning of Tuesday, 5 May 1981. He was twenty-seven years old and had been on hunger strike for sixty-six days. In Armagh, the ecclesiastical capital of Ireland, the responses of the Catholic and Protestant archbishops were very different. Cardinal Ó Fiaich criticised the British government for their intransigence. Dr John Armstrong, the Church of Ireland primate, referred to the death of Sands as "one of the most calculated pieces of moral blackmail in recent times". The divergent views were reflected in many places outside Armagh, not least in RTÉ.

The election and death of Bobby Sands was a turning point in the history of the Troubles, as it marked a shift towards constitutional politics in republican strategy. In the Northern Ireland local elections that month, the National H-Block/Armagh Committees won thirty-six seats. These committees had no direct connection with Sinn Féin, yet

---

‡   Interview with author.

§   *Independent*, 29 December 1997.

the support for them represented a large block of political sympathy that Sinn Féin might tap into for their own benefit. They decided to seek that support through the ballot box and found that it was available to them. Many of the voters who comprised this new, broader constituency may have been previously ambivalent about violence, but would never have stood resolutely behind the IRA or their political representatives.

These were the people who pressurised Sinn Féin into taking constitutional politics seriously and by so doing made Northern Ireland more politicised than it had ever been. The huge broadening of the support base for Sinn Féin led to a fear in Irish and British government circles that Sinn Féin would soon overtake the SDLP as the party most representative of Northern nationalists. This fear was one of the reasons for the signing of the Anglo-Irish Agreement in November 1985. Ironically, the deaths of the hunger strikers laid the foundations of the Peace Process of the 1990s, a process in which Mary McAleese played no small part.

On the morning of 5 May 1981, there was very little talk of a peace process or the political development of Sinn Féin. As the news of the death of the first hunger striker spread, the British government was denounced in newspaper editorials in many parts of the world. This was accompanied by a huge international swell of sympathy for the cause of the hunger strikers. Even Ronald Reagan felt the need to put some clear political ground between his administration and that of his personal friend and closest foreign ally, Margaret Thatcher. He issued a statement of sympathy on the death of Sands. Messages of condolence were pouring in from all over the world, from individuals, from groups, from city councils and corporations and even from governments.

As foreign news crews packed every available flight into Belfast's Aldergrove Airport, senior members of the *Today Tonight* team were strongly of the opinion that the funeral of Bobby Sands would be a small affair. They did not want to send cameras to Belfast in case they might give some recognition and encouragement to the Provisional IRA. Mary was just back from Belfast, and she realised that the death of Sands was bigger than the IRA, bigger than Sinn Féin, bigger than any group or faction. Even members of the SDLP were caught up in the groundswell of emotion. The ordinary nationalists of the North would be at the funeral in their thousands. When she voiced this opinion at the team meeting in RTÉ, she was met with the rejoinder, "There will be more cameras there than mourners."

On the morning of Thursday, 7 May, the body of Bobby Sands was taken from his house to St Luke's Church in Twinbrook. After the requiem mass, his coffin was carried down the Andersonstown Road to Milltown Cemetery. The long stretch of road between Twinbrook and Milltown was lined with mourners, and there was a strange and solemn silence all over West Belfast, a hush that was broken only by the plaintive sound of the solitary piper who led the cortège and the shuffling of thousands of feet. The RUC estimated the attendance at 100,000. "Did you count the hundred thousand cameras?" Mary asked her colleague the next day.

From the time the hunger strike started, Mary had worked as a sort of roving reporter on programmes that covered areas of interest like child welfare and the Leisure Show in the RDS. It was obvious to her that she was being kept well away from anything as controversial as Northern politics. There was a reason for this, according to herself, a reason that had its basis in the long, contentious team meetings of the *Today Tonight* staff. On Fridays particularly, a meeting which started at ten in the morning might not finish until seven in the evening. These sessions would sometimes be attended by more than twenty people, and Joe Mulholland promoted dispute and controversy. People who were regular attendees say that team members were encouraged to speak their minds freely on all manner of subjects. One of them describes the tone of the meetings with the following quip: "The meetings were always democratic at the outset, but at some point Mulholland would insist that pure democracy give way to democratic centralism."

Fintan Cronin has this to say about the team meetings:

Mary McAleese suffered at those meetings. It seemed that no matter what she said she was attacked. She often made the point that the nationalist voice was not heard on the programme, and in this she was correct. Week after week people like Harold McCusker were guests on the programme, and we listened to them condemning the hunger strikers and the people who supported them.‡ No other point of view was aired on *Today Tonight*, even though most nationalists in the North supported the demands of the hunger strikers. That support was much more widely based than support for Sinn Féin or the IRA.

Mary McAleese was no Sinn Féin supporter. It would be almost impossible to put a label on her political point of view. She

‡ James Harold McCusker: Ulster Unionist Party MP for Upper Bann. When he died in 1990, his seat was won by David Trimble.

187

had high principles, but I don't think she had any fixed left or right ideology. If I had to describe her politics, I would say she was a nationalist social democrat of some sort, liberal in outlook. I never heard a shred of Sinn Féin policy in anything she ever said. In spite of this, because she questioned the obvious lack of balance on the programme, she was accused of being a "crypto-Provo", and her professionalism and her personal integrity were called into question. She was deeply hurt by remarks such as these.[‡]

Studio interviews were usually conducted by people like Brian Farrell or Olivia O'Leary. Mary was amazed when she was told to go to Belfast and conduct a studio interview with Bernadette McAliskey and Glen Barr, on Wednesday, 30 April.[§] On 16 January that year, UDA gunmen had attacked and wounded Bernadette McAliskey and her husband Michael in front of their children. She had received seven bullet wounds in the attack and was not fully recovered at the time of the interview. Barr was to be interviewed in his capacity as chairman of the New Ulster Political Research Group. It was widely known that this group was connected to the UDA, and RTÉ was prohibited, under Section 31 of the Broadcasting Act, from broadcasting an interview with a member of the UDA, or any other proscribed organisation.

Mary raised the question of a potential breach of Section 31 with the producer Tish Barry before the programme: "I strongly questioned the wisdom of interviewing Barr live on air and warned the producer, in unequivocal terms, that they ran the risk of infringing Section 31. My complaints were ignored."

During the programme, Barr began talking about UDA plans in terms of "us" and "our plans". McAliskey interrupted angrily, pointing out that Barr had just admitted that he was speaking on behalf of the UDA and could therefore not be interviewed under the current legislation. Mary turned her attention completely to McAliskey, ignoring Barr for the duration of the interview.

"Immediately after the programme, I protested vehemently at the impossible position I had been put in, and I wrote to Joe Mulholland in straight-talking terms," she says.

On the following Monday morning she received a letter in reply:

---

‡ Interview with author.

§ Glen Barr had been commander of the UDA in Derry during the Ulster Workers' Council strike

. . . As I said to you Glen Barr was invited on to the programme as Chairman of the New Ulster Political Research Group. He has been a political representative in the North and has been involved in talks with the Taoiseach, members of the opposition and with politicians in the United States. His voice is that of the urban Loyalists and as such, cannot be ignored in the present circumstances. That he has clearly identified himself as being quite close to the UDA was unfortunate and must exclude him from broadcasts forthwith. Let me emphasise that at no time did I seek clearance from Andy Tyrie for Barr's appearance.[‡]

On Wednesday, 13 May, six days after the funeral of Bobby Sands, trouble erupted in the Republic when nearly two thousand people attempted to break into the British Embassy, after the announcement of the death of a second hunger striker, Francis Hughes. Baton charges and rioting ensued. According to people who were present at the *Today Tonight* meeting that day, the atmosphere was even more unrestrained than usual. One of the journalists had returned from Belfast, where he had interviewed Fr Des Wilson for a programme about the H-Blocks. Some members of the team did not like what Fr Wilson had to say, and they were attacking the journalist for broadcasting the priest's views. Each time he started to defend himself, he was attacked again. Eventually one of the members of the team called him "a fucking Provo". A silence fell on the room.

The voice that broke the stillness was that of Mary McAleese. In astonished horror she asked, "Is no senior member of management willing to say that calling a colleague an 'effing Provo' is highly libellous and is creating a hostile working environment?"

When no one answered her she erupted. Back went the chair as she came to her feet and bent forward, knuckles white on the table top. Everyone present was taken aback as the pent-up frustration caused by months of insults and innuendo poured out in a torrent of anger. She told the attacker that he could not distinguish the message from the messenger and said she would gladly be a witness if there were to be a slander case. She described the journalist as a diligent professional who took his obligations under the Broadcasting Act very seriously and did not deviate from its provisions; who told the story just as he got it,

---

‡ Andy Tyrie was the commander of the UDA. It was an open secret in the North of Ireland that the UDA had close ties with the New Ulster Political Research Group and the Ulster Political Research Group that succeeded it.

without adding to it or taking from it, without twisting it to fit a preconceived political point of view. She was not finished. She said senior members of the programme staff were blind to the realities of life north of the border. She accused them of letting their hatred of the IRA—an antipathy that she shared—blind them to the political implications of Sands' death. She told them that people in the North no longer had any faith in the reporting of *Today Tonight*. She finished with a warning: if anyone ever called her such a name, they would be defending themselves in a court of law.

Knowing that she would probably be the next victim of a slanderous attack, she wanted to put down a marker, and the marker worked. Some people started to defend the journalist, but Mary was deaf to what was being said. She was upset. There were tears of hurt and anger and frustration in her eyes as she left the meeting and drove down to Donnybrook, seeking solace in the dusky stillness of the church at the crossroads.

Some years later, a person who was present at the meeting was asked, "Did it nearly get physical?"

His reply was, "If you had heard Mary McAleese, you would understand there was no need to get physical."

Mary has this to say about the meeting:

A professional journalist was treated shamefully at that meeting. He was a victim of bigotry. The bigotry in RTÉ was an extraordinary phenomenon. It was very different from bigotry in the North: bigots in RTÉ were the most righteous self-styled liberals. It was bad enough when the revisionists in the seventies were telling us that nationalism was dead, but then the Provisionals came along to tell us that they, and only they, were the real nationalists, the super-nationalists. Whatever ordinary poor nationalists were left after all that were now being attacked by *Today Tonight*, a programme of our national television station.

Peter Feeney says succinctly about those years, "RTÉ got it wrong."[‡]

"I erred in not interpreting correctly the depth of feeling among Northern nationalists at the time," says Joe Mulholland.

When speaking about the system in RTÉ Current Affairs at the start of the eighties, Mary uses words like "Machiavellian" and "Kafkaesque". She goes further still when she compares working there to working for the Stasi, the East German secret police, whose job it was

---

‡   Interview with author.

to ensure that everyone followed the same political doctrine. Before Christmas 1980, after three months working on *Today Tonight*, she wrote in her diary:

> I'm sure few of them are fully attuned to our statutory function in these matters. It is not our role to be doctrinaire or to adopt one side. We are statute bound to be objective. Apart from the innate wrongness of using their powerful position in the media to promulgate party, rigid party politics, they are also far, very far off the mark in their assessment of public feeling—hardly surprising when one remembers that the political views they represent rarely find their way into Dáil or Seanad. These meetings are like trips to Never Never Land where people have become self-appointed apostles for an irrelevant cause.[†]

[†] Mary McAleese, Diary.

Chapter Sixteen

A New Ireland

Tell me now that hate lies sleeping,
Tell me now the flag is furled,
Sing to me an end to weeping,
Bring to me visions of a brave new world.
(Dominic Behan: "A Brave New World")

Mary was always very fond of her Aunt Bridget, her mother's sister, who spent years working in the kitchen of St Joseph's College of Education, close to her house in Ramoan Gardens in Andersonstown. She was working there in the summer of 1981 as more prisoners were joining the hunger strike in the H-Blocks. One of the last to join was her son, Mary's first cousin John Pickering.

Bridget says that when her son was a teenager he was going through Divis Street, at the bottom of the Falls Road, on his way home after buying new shoes, when a riot started. He was captured by a British army "snatch squad" and arrested. People arrested during riots could be charged either with disorderly conduct, for which there was no mandatory sentence, or riotous behaviour, which carried a mandatory six-month sentence. He was convicted of the latter and spent six months in St Patrick's Training School on the Glen Road. When he left the reformatory, he was a fully fledged IRA man, and the half year that he spent there was the start of a total of seventeen years he would spend behind bars.

He was later interned without trial. When he was released, he and Mary met at a funeral. When she questioned him on his employment prospects and his plans for the future, he replied that he was "a freedom fighter". Mary had no sympathy with his paramilitary ambitions, and he got the sharp edge of her tongue. She told him that his idea of freedom was short-sighted and reminded him that his own mother was breaking her health trying to rear a family of twelve children and working in the college at the same time.

When the 1981 hunger strike started, John Henry Pickering was in the H-Blocks, serving two sentences in connection with two incidents that happened on the same day, 19 August 1976. He was one of two men convicted of murdering a seventy-seven-year-old Protestant man, William Creighton of Church Avenue, Dunmurray, who owned a filling station at Finaghy Crossroads on the Lisburn Road. The man was shot dead when he grappled with the four masked men who entered his premises. After the shooting the gunmen placed a bomb in the filling station. When it exploded, causing widespread damage to the property, the security forces rushed to the scene. Pickering and another man escaped to a house in Cranmore Gardens, further along the Lisburn Road, but they were followed. During a siege they took an elderly gardener as hostage. John Pickering received a life sentence for the murder of William Creighton and a twenty-six-year sentence for his part in the siege.

The leader of the IRA active service unit to which Pickering was attached was Kieran Doherty, who would later die on hunger strike after being elected to Dáil Éireann for the constituency of Cavan–Monaghan. Pickering was for some time the boyfriend of Bairbre De Brún, who was later to become Sinn Féin minister for health.

John Pickering went on hunger strike on 7 September 1981, eight days after the death of the tenth hunger striker, Michael Devine, who was also the last to die. Six days after Pickering joined the strike, James Prior was appointed secretary of state for Northern Ireland. Four days later, on 17 September, Prior visited the H-Blocks, where he had a three-hour meeting with Pickering and the other prisoners who were still on hunger strike, in an attempt to get them to take food.

Another man who had been trying to put an end to the hunger strikes was Fr Denis Faul. From the time Sands started his fast, Denis Faul had worked tirelessly in an attempt to avoid what he feared would be the deaths of many prisoners and the resultant deaths of many people outside the Maze. He organised meetings of the families of the hunger strikers in an attempt to persuade them to intervene in the event of a striker going into a coma. In doing this he was going against the whole strategy of the hunger strikes and interfering with the political aims of Sinn Féin. He says he understood all that very well, but that human lives were more important to him than political strategies. He also made repeated efforts to persuade the British authorities to allow the prisoners to wear their own clothes, which he felt was the critical issue. He understood the mentality of the prisoners better than most and was convinced that if the British government had acceded to that one demand many lives could have been saved. Fr Faul knew Bridget Pickering long before her son went on the death fast.

I used to have my lunch in St Joseph's College every Sunday, after saying mass in Long Kesh, before I'd go home to County Tyrone. Bridget Pickering worked in the college, and that is how I go to know her. She is a very special woman. She demonstrated great strength and bravery when she stood up and spoke in front of a large gathering of relatives of hunger strikers in the Lake Glen Hotel in Andersonstown. She said that if her son John went into a coma she would ask for medical intervention. That took some courage.[‡]

On his weekly visits to St Joseph's Fr Faul always gave a report on her son. He did not know Mary McAleese at the time, although he knew who she was from her appearances on *Today Tonight*. He says he considered that programme completely pro-unionist and had no way of knowing that Mary's views were any different from those that were represented by the content of the programme.

Bridget Pickering has this to say about Fr Faul and the ending of the hunger strike:

> On my way home in the car from visiting John in Long Kesh, I used to get a lump in my throat, and I literally wouldn't be able to talk for hours. Quite often I wouldn't be able to go to work the next day, but the priests in the college were understanding and very good to me. When John went on hunger strike, I used to phone Fr Faul every day. I don't know what I would have done without him. He organised meeting for the relatives of the hunger strikers. I remember talking to Mrs McCloskey from Dungiven at a meeting in the Lake Glen.[§] Her son Liam was blind and far gone. When I asked her would she sign or let him die, she said she would ask for help, but it hadn't come to that yet. Kieran Doherty's girlfriend asked Fr Toner to marry them before he died. If they were married she could have intervened, as next of kin, to save his life.
>
> I remember that Sunday in the Lake Glen Hotel when I spoke up. It was the first time in my life that I ever spoke at a meeting and I was shaking. I was really terrified, but I knew I had to say it. I told them that if my son fell into a coma I would ask for his life to be saved. The Kesh men blamed me for breaking the strike, and John didn't speak to me for five months. He was the very last man to

---

‡   Interview with author.

§   Mrs McCloskey: the mother of Liam McCloskey, who took food after fifty-five days on hunger strike.

come off the hunger strike. He had been on it for thirty-one days, but he was alive.[‡]

Bridget Pickering had to try to balance her love for her son with her abhorrence of his activities. She paid dearly for both. Every time she visited him in the Maze, she was treated abominably by the warders, as if she was fully supportive of all he had done.

On 3 October the H–Block strike was officially declared over. Ten men had died, but despite the official ending, six men were still fasting. Since it was clear that their relatives would intervene to keep them alive if they fell into a coma, a joint statement was issued on 4 October: "Mounting pressure and cleric-inspired demoralisation led to [family] intervention and five strikers have been taken off their fast."

The only striker still fasting was Mary's cousin John Henry Pickering, "Pickles" as he was known to his friends. He maintained his hunger strike for several more days. As his mother said, he was the last of the H–Block hunger strikers to accept food.

Fr Faul knew that no politician could have done what he did. He had spoken to Gerry Adams, Martin McGuinness and Joe Cahill, but he knew, as he says himself, that "the man who ended the hunger strike would be committing political suicide". He felt he had nothing to lose and everything to gain. He cared little for what Sinn Féin or the IRA thought of him. He was in the business of saving lives. With the end of the hunger strike, the tensions in the country eased somewhat.

In Dublin, Mary McAleese was as relieved as anyone. She was especially relieved for her Aunt Bridget and the Pickering family. Her own situation in RTÉ was not improving, and she began to think it was time for her to look for some other work. She did not have to look very far because, soon after she began to consider moving, she got a phone call from her old friend, Professor Robert Heuston. He told her that her successor in Trinity, Mark James Findlay, from Sydney, Australia, was about to leave the Reid Professorship and that her old position would be once again vacant. This set Mary thinking. After the year she had just spent working with *Today Tonight*, the peace and quiet of the academic life seemed very inviting.

She maintains that no pressure was ever brought to bear on her to leave RTÉ and that her difficulties with her colleagues on *Today Tonight* were not insuperable. Michael McCarthy holds the opposite view:

She came from Ardoyne and had first-hand experience of politics

‡ Interview with author.

in the North. "Sticky" ideological claptrap just would not wear with her, nor would a version of "benevolent unionism" which was being naively peddled around the place. She was a challenge too big to handle, and so began the smear, ridicule and use of invective to isolate and eventually silence. Mary left. She had no option. It would have destroyed her to stay. The "Stickies" were ideologically buoyed up for a war of attrition. They were ruthless and determined. With them unilateral decency did not pay. Unfortunately, Mary became the victim of a caucus that was personally vicious and territorially vengeful. She, being the biggest threat to that caucus, took the biggest hit.[‡]

Whether Mary had an option or not, she left. In the autumn of 1981, she returned to the relative tranquillity of Trinity College as Reid Professor. There was not a trace of dampness on her cheeks as she left RTÉ, although she missed her friends and many of her colleagues in Current Affairs. She and Martin were now able to spend more time together. They were even able to travel together each morning from County Meath into Trinity. The professor drove and the student studied: Mary, with the car radio at low volume, trying to listen to the news; Martin with his head stuck in a book, not prepared to waste a minute of learning time. Martin was equally dogged about his studies when visitors came to the house. He and Mary would welcome them, but Martin would then explain that he was engaged with his studies and that Mary would be entertaining them. He might see them later for a cup of tea! Mary says, "I was often embarrassed. But that single-mindedness was part of his personality and I accepted that. I was also very proud of him."

In those days before the children came along, home life for Mary was, more often than not, a solitary existence. She joined a keep fit class, started attending evening classes in German in Dunshaughlin Community School and joined the local church choir. She also began to attend the prayer meetings that attracted large crowds in the Friends' Meeting House in Eustace Street, in Dublin, at the end of the seventies and the early eighties. Once or twice a week, Mary, with some friends or relatives, would make her way there or to another prayer meeting in a convent near the Royal Hospital in Donnybrook. Her usual companions were her sister Nora or her cousins, Mary and Evelyn McKenna, or Frances Lynch.

---

‡ Interview with author.

Many smaller prayer groups evolved from those larger meetings: little groups of people from all walks of life and various social and economic backgrounds, coming together to read and study Scripture and join in shared prayer. It was a small group such as this that gathered in Mary's own house in Mooretown. At first the group changed its venue every week, each member taking a turn at playing host, but finally it settled on the McAleese house as its permanent home. Mary got great enjoyment and satisfaction from these meetings. The people in the group were a disparate lot. There was a university lecturer, a shopkeeper, some students, teachers, a nurse, housewives, a priest, an elderly bachelor, a post mistress and an official from a semi-state body—all secure in each other's company and happily praying away together.

Mary was once again fully involved in college life and had been appointed registrar of the School of Law. She was also receiving offers of part-time work on various programmes in RTÉ. The idea appealed to her. Apart altogether from the boost such offers gave her self-confidence—that she was considered good enough to be sought out—she found the idea of the work attractive. Money was another consideration: the small amount they had saved before Martin left his job was long since exhausted, the mortgage was a burden, and the interest rates were very high at the time. She decided to accept one or two of the offers.

She had been invited by the television producer Noel Smyth to co-present a new programme, *Europa*, with Conor Brady of *The Irish Times*. *Europa* was due to go out once a month and would earn her £65 per programme. It was to be a magazine programme about Irish ex-patriates in various European cities and would involve a bit of travelling. The pace of the programme was slow, sociable and intimate—in perfect contrast to the pace of *Today Tonight*. Each month a piece was to be filmed abroad and another piece at home. Because of Brady's commitments with *The Irish Times*, Mary did the travelling. She usually went straight to the airport from Trinity College on a Friday afternoon. The crew would meet up in Paris, Copenhagen, Madrid or Milan on the Saturday morning and work would commence. Mary was normally home again on Sunday night and back in Trinity on Monday morning. The schedule was tough and she was usually weary after a weekend away, but she loved it. She says she really enjoyed the team work with Noel Smyth, Conor Brady and Michael Ryan, who later featured as the presenter of *Nationwide* after the *Six One News* on RTÉ One television.

Her dual backgrounds in broadcasting and the law were perfectly suited to another position she was offered on the *Pat Kenny Show* during the summer. Ed Mulhall, the producer, was looking for someone to do radio court reports. Why look further than a professor of law with a background in broadcasting? Mary would give a word picture of the court or of an on-going case and would describe the atmosphere and give a lawyer's perspective on all that was going on. When Mulhall was put in charge of a new radio drive-time programme, *Studio 10,* Mary was his choice of co-presenter with Colm Keane. At ninety minutes long, from five o'clock to half-past six every Friday, it was the longest talk-only programme, without music, RTÉ had broadcast up until then. During the six months Mary worked on *Studio 10*, she got to know people like Dermot Morgan, later of *Father Ted* fame, Breandán Ó hEithir, Hugh Leonard and Colm Tóibín.

Within a few months of her going back to Trinity, the travel arrangements in the McAleese car had changed completely. Martin had to drive because now Mary was reading: preparing lectures or programmes. Martin has an interesting account of those journeys from Mooretown to Trinity College:

"Mary had a weekly book review spot on one of the radio programmes with Myles Dungan. She had always been a speed reader. I remember on a few occasion we left the house in Mooretown with me driving and Mary starting to read a book she was to review live on radio an hour or two later. Invariably the book review was a great success, Mary speaking with great authority on the subject, the author and the style. No one ever knew she had not spent days and nights poring over it."

During her broadcasting work Mary interviewed a few bishops. She had met Cahal Daly, who was Bishop of Down and Connor at the time, at meetings in Belfast and had also met Bishop Peter Birch of Ossory. These contacts, combined with her experience on the MacBride Commission and her background in teaching law, made her a perfect candidate for a new commission on the Irish Penal System which was being set up by the Catholic hierarchy.

The group came together for the first time on 19 May 1981, under the auspices of the Council for Social Welfare, to undertake their new study. The bishops wanted to further the work MacBride had done in 1980 and also that of Justice Eileen Kennedy in the 1970s on the juvenile penal system. Bishop Peter Birch had been appointed chairman, but when he died before the group came together, he was succeeded by Peter Keehan.

Justice Seán Delap and Dr Maurice Hayes were members, as were three prison chaplains: Harry Gaynor, Dermot Leycock and a man who was to become a lifelong friend, Breffni Walker of the Holy Ghost Order. This working group had considerably more success than MacBride's group in their dealings with the Department of Justice and the prison authorities. Officers of the department and prison governors gave them their full support, spoke candidly to them and gave them access to the prisons. Mary's relationship with the officers of the Department of Justice, carefully nurtured during 1979 and 1980, was certainly instrumental in achieving this new-found rapport with officialdom.

The group studied the prison system, the daily lives of the prisoners and warders, the culture and subcultures within prisons, the rights and lack of rights of prisoners, the prospects of rehabilitation, public perceptions and the role of the Church.

Much of Mary's professional life was spent teaching penology, and she and her penology students visited every penal institution in the Republic, but she found the visits difficult.

"The lack of liberty, the abasement, the utter humiliation, the deprivation of dignity and the failure to put the time in prison to constructive use—these are aspects of prison life that I have always found deeply troubling. The saddest thing about prison is that many people just can't cope with the loss of freedom. I know that for the good of society we have no option but to remove some people from that society, but other methods of punishment should be considered before a person is locked up."

She never visited her cousin John during the seventeen years he was incarcerated.

The Bishops' Commission studied many of these alternative methods of punishment that were in use in other countries. When the Commission's report, *The Prison System,* was published, it was obvious that there was no great difference between their recommendations and those of the Commission that had preceded it: "Essentially, the policy of using alternatives wherever possible is based on the belief that these avoid the personally destructive aspects of imprisonment; therefore on these grounds alone their use is justified."[‡]

Mary worked on several reports for the Council for Social Welfare before she actually joined the Council. Some of these publications dealt with issues as diverse as the travelling community, the status of

---

‡   Council for Social Welfare, p. 71.

199

children, public health policy and the papal encyclical *Laborem Exercens.*[‡]

The following year, 1983, Mary was invited to join the Council for Social Welfare. It had been founded in 1970 to advise the Catholic bishops on matters of social concern in Ireland. Dr James Kavanagh, Auxiliary Bishop of Dublin, was its president, and under his stewardship they had published several major reports: *A Statement on Social Policy*, *A Statement on Family Law Reform* and *Planning for Social Development*. When Mary joined the Council they were preparing a report on illegitimacy.

In that same year Mary attended, for the first of many times, the Annual Ecumenical Conference in the Ballymascanlon Hotel, outside Dundalk. She also went to Corrymeela for the first time.[§] During that year she got to know many people, including Bishop Cahal Daly and Dermot Herlihy, who shared her deep interest in peace and reconciliation and the promotion of cross-community understanding.

Towards the end of 1983, Garret FitzGerald's Constitutional Crusade was in full swing. John Hume had advised FitzGerald to convene a forum which would re-examine the concept of nationalism and at which ideas concerning the re-unification of the country could be aired. In January 1984, the New Ireland Forum sat for the first time. Various groups, north and south, were invited to make oral or written submissions: political parties, the churches, trade unions, voluntary organisations and other interested parties. Colm Ó hEocha, from NUI Galway, was appointed chairman.

The Catholic hierarchy made a written submission, which was not well received. The principal author of the document was Bishop Jeremiah Newman, and many of the bishops thought it a very conservative statement of the Catholic Church's position. The hierarchy decided to make an oral submission in order to clarify some of the points made in the original document, and it was decided that a woman should be a member of the group that would attend the sitting of the Forum. Gemma Loughran, a lecturer in St Mary's College of Education in Belfast, was invited to sit with the bishops on the panel, but when she was unavailable, they decided to invite Professor Mary McAleese.

At the end of January, after a long week in college and a weekend

---

‡ Pope John Paul II, 1981.

§ Situated on the North Antrim coast, near Ballycastle, the Corrymeela Community promotes the healing of social, religious and political divisions.

spent filming in Amsterdam, Mary wrote in her diary: "Though I hate the pressure, I wonder could I live without it?"[‡] She was on her way to bed when the telephone rang. The caller was Dermot Ryan, Archbishop of Dublin, who extended to her the bishops' invitation to join their representatives on the panel at the New Ireland Forum.

It was not an easy decision for Mary. She had been very disappointed with the bishops' written submission. She felt it had set back the cause of cross-community understanding and could promote diffidence among Protestants to future reconciliatory gestures from Catholics. She explained to Archbishop Ryan that her acceptance of his offer would be subject to two conditions: if Bishop Jeremiah Newman were on the panel she would not sit with them, and neither she nor the other representatives could be tied to the written submission. The archbishop agreed.

Mary knew it would be an enormous personal statement if she accepted the invitation; that she would at last be saying, in the most public of ways, that she was prepared to stand shoulder to shoulder with the guardians of the institutional Catholic Church. She understood the courage it took for the bishops to approach her: she was, in the eyes of many people, strongly in favour of some things the hierarchy vigorously opposed. In the year 1979, for example, at a debate organised by the Law Society in Galway, she had spoken publicly and trenchantly in favour of divorce. In March 1981, she had chaired a meeting on the subject of abortion in Liberty Hall, in Dublin. It was a public meeting with speakers such as Anne Speed, Anne Marie Hourihane and Mary Holland. She afterwards said she had been assured it would be an open forum and was unaware that the mood of the meeting would be significantly pro-choice. Regardless of any misunderstanding, many people thought at the time that she stood for the pro-choice side of the debate. If Mary's decision to sit with the bishops was a brave one, their decision to invite her was an equally courageous move.

On the evening of 1 February 1984, Mary had a meeting with the other members of the delegation in Emmaus, the Christian Brothers' retreat house in Balheary, outside Swords. Several bishops were present: Cahal Daly of Down and Connor, Joseph Cassidy of Clonfert, Edward Daly of Derry, and Dermot O'Mahony, Auxiliary Bishop of Dublin. Fr Michael Ledwith from St Patrick's College Maynooth and Matthew Salter, a lecturer in education from Queen's University, made up the

‡   Mary McAleese, Diary.

panel. Mary says she was not asked to agree with anything the panel had to say, either at that meeting or at any other time. She had a completely free hand to agree or disagree, but as Bishop Cahal Daly laid out the general lines of their position, she found herself in accord.

The following morning, the tables in St Patrick's Hall in Dublin Castle were laid out in a large hollow oval. The hall would look very different thirteen years later when she would be inaugurated there as President of Ireland. At the New Ireland Forum there was no top table and no podium. Everyone was on the same level and had the same status. On one side were the representatives of the political parties: Fianna Fáil, the SDLP, Labour and Fine Gael. The politicians were allowed to question the speakers.

Colm Ó hEocha introduced the members of the delegation and asked Seamus Mallon of the SDLP to formally welcome them. After Bishop Daly's opening remarks, the politicians were free to question the delegation, and they focused their queries on the contents of the document that had been previously submitted to the Forum. They asked about the role of the Church vis-à-vis the role of the state. Mary McAleese answered that question: "Its sole jurisdiction is in relation to its flock. It does not seek to have any jurisdiction beyond that. It is not entitled to, nor does it seek to, tell any Government that the Catholic view of marriage should be enshrined in legislation because it is the Catholic view, but it does reserve the right—the same right accorded to any group, any individual in a democracy which holds freedom of speech as a central element, as a matter of public interest—to comment in relation to issues of public morality."[‡]

She continued on the question of peace and reconciliation: "Many people who put their vote in the box for Sinn Féin would not give their vote to violence but give it out of a sense of frustration . . . I wonder how far off is the day when these same people's ambivalence about violence may be resolved fully in favour of violence, which it most certainly will be if this Forum, for example, is not successful; if constitutional politics are not successful."[§]

She spoke on the question of "pluralism", saying that the Church was committed to the advancement of pluralism, that striving to achieve tolerance and harmony amidst diversity was a welcome ideal. She stressed the importance of an agreement on the meaning of the word

‡   Proceedings of New Ireland Forum, 9 February 1984.

§   *Ibid.*

"pluralism" when discussing minority rights, asserting that it could not mean an insistence that society live by the morality of the lowest common denominator. She explained that pluralism had to involve itself in balancing the claims of competing groups and must devise ways of handling value judgements, and that in order for pluralism to work there had to be areas of shared consensus.

Representatives of the Labour Party then had an opportunity to question the panel, and it was Mary's colleague from Trinity College, Senator Mary Robinson, who raised the question of integrated education in Northern Ireland. Mary McAleese feels that the question was aimed at the delegation in general, but some of those who were present feel that it was aimed at the woman from Ardoyne. In any event, it was the woman who had been educated in denominational schools in Belfast who answered the question in terms of her own experience:

> The notion that consensus comes from contact, or even that understanding comes from contact, is wrong. It is a dubious and simplistic notion. It would be nice if it were right. There are very many levels of contact in Northern Ireland between people, which do not demand honesty in relationships. I myself lived in an area which is often described as a flashpoint area, known as Ardoyne. It was a mixed area as I was growing up. I had tremendous contact with Protestant neighbours, played with them. They were in and out of my home, but it did not stop one of them from becoming a member of the UDA and now doing a life sentence for killing five Catholics . . . I have very grave doubts, from my own direct experience, about the ability of the school to break down sectarian prejudice. In fact I am convinced in my own mind that an awful lot depends on the nature of the contact and on the honesty of the relationship involved.[‡]

The bishops were delighted with her eloquence and her frankness. She herself was happy that the delegation had succeeded in putting the case for the Catholic Church in a modern Ireland very clearly and very well, that they had redeemed whatever could be redeemed, and that they had portrayed the Church as an organisation that was alive, open and forward looking. There were, however, some people who were not happy with Mary's performance, who were not happy that Mary had taken a stance with the Catholic bishops. Among them were some of her colleagues in RTÉ.

---

‡ *Ibid.*

One month after she walked into St Patrick's Hall with the bishops, a special meeting of the Dublin Broadcasting Branch of the National Union of Journalists was convened. They were called together to discuss one motion: a proposal to suspend the membership of one of their members, namely Mary Patricia McAleese. She was accused of breaching one of the rules of the NUJ, which stated that members must earn at least two-thirds of their salary from journalism. A letter from Mary McAleese was read out at the meeting. In it she said she could perfectly understand the union's concerns about those who had another job outside broadcasting, but she could not understand why the meeting was called to discuss her situation only, and not all the broadcasters who had two jobs.

Des Cryan, who was working in the News Department in RTÉ at the time, was present at that meeting. "Mary McAleese had been quite a mute member of the NUJ, so it was all the more astonishing to witness the sudden antagonism towards her. It was pointed out by some members present that Brian Farrell, among others, was also double-jobbing. It was obvious to me and to several other members of the Broadcasting Branch that the motion to suspend her membership was sheer prejudice. It was evident that there was a hidden agenda and that it stemmed from her appearance with the bishops at the New Ireland Forum."

Almost two years later, when Mary was asked in a newspaper interview if she thought the officers of the NUJ were prejudiced against the Catholic Church, she replied: "I have no doubt whatever about it. I think only a tiny minority are responsible. It could be that there is a personal prejudice against me but my own opinion is that if I had gone to the Forum with a Church of Ireland or with a Jewish delegation there would not be a word about it."‡

Patrick Kinsella was chairman of the Broadcasting Branch of the NUJ at the time. He dismissed Mary's assertions as being groundless. When he was questioned on the case of Brian Farrell he replied, "Yes, there are anomalies."§ When Mary read this in the newspaper, she sent Kinsella a letter in which she remarked: "You were not correct when you said there were anomalies. There is only one anomaly—and I am it."†

---

‡　*The Irish Times*, 10 February 1986.

§　*Ibid.*

†　Mary McAleese, private papers.

Mary's cause was not helped by the fact that she had "insulted the profession of journalism", as some journalists read it, around the time that she appeared at the Forum. In the course of an interview she had said: "I don't play sport or have any other hobbies. I find you need some kind of relief from law, so broadcasting has become my hobby."

Her own explanation of what she said is that broadcasting, because she enjoyed it so much, was akin to recreation for her. However, some journalists read it as a disparagement of their profession, saying that her statement was a clear inference that broadcasting could not compare, in intellectual terms or in importance, with the legal profession.

It is not clear for what reason, or list of reasons, the National Union of Journalists suspended Mary McAleese. The double-jobbing issue was the only one raised publicly, and it is clear that Mary was treated unfairly in that regard. That issue was the only one referred to in an official letter she received from Roberta Wallace, secretary of the Broadcasting Branch, on 31 March 1984:

> Your letter was read at the branch meeting and members said they appreciated the spirit of your views and it was also felt that there was to be no question of singling out one person on the issue. However, the motion calling for your suspension was not taken and it was ruled that the branch is forced, by rule, to suspend your membership. A special committee has now been set up to look into the whole matter of double jobbing and freelance employment and the branch expects its first report in two months.[‡]

That committee never met. A year and a quarter after that first letter from Roberta Wallace, another one arrived: "At the branch annual meeting I mentioned your letter again and the branch passed a motion instructing the double jobbing committee to produce its report. We await developments."[§]

They are still waiting. Mary has this to say about her suspension: "It was a case of absolute bigotry. I was given no opportunity to defend myself at that meeting. I am convinced that the whole issue arose out my appearance with the bishops at the New Ireland Forum. It was a disgraceful act on the part of those who initiated it. The worst aspect of it is that nothing was ever done to rectify the situation, or to bring it to a proper conclusion."

Mary's membership was never rescinded, and she is still a suspended

‡   *Ibid.*

§   *Ibid.*

member of the Dublin Broadcasting Branch of the National Union of Journalists. Fourteen years after her suspension, as President of Ireland, she attended a media awards ceremony in the Berkley Court Hotel in Dublin. John Bowman introduced her as the first journalist, and the first member of the NUJ, to be elected President of Ireland. When Mary corrected him with the words "the first suspended member", the laugh from the assembled members of the media shook the rafters of the hotel.

In 1984, although she was suspended, she was not prevented from continuing her part-time work in RTÉ. She worked away as she had always done, with one little difference: she was somewhat better off financially, as she did not have to pay her annual subscription to the NUJ.

Chapter Seventeen

Mother Mary

The sap of another generation
fingering through a broken tree
to push fresh branches
towards a further light, a different identity.
(John Montague: "The Living and the Dead")

Mary had an aunt, two first cousins and a good friend who were all called Mary and who were all childless. When after five or six years of marriage Mary showed no sign of imminent motherhood, her mother began to worry that her eldest daughter had "the curse of the Marys". "A lot of auld baloney," was Mary's stock reply to such worries. The aunts were also getting anxious. "E'er a whisper yet?" was a regular question. Long before they were married, Mary and Martin often spoke quietly together of their hopes and plans for a family. If they ever had a girl, she would be called "Emma Claire" after both grandmothers. They often whispered together, as in a secret lovers' code, about how life would be with "EC". By 1982 they had been married for six years and there was still no sign of "EC". In spite of all their blustering and their smooth dismissal of Claire's concerns, they were getting just a tiny bit uneasy.

On 30 December 1981, Martin's mother Emma McAleese died. At the start of February, Mary began to feel that maybe, just maybe, she might be pregnant. She also had a feeling that if she were indeed carrying a child, then things would go right this time. She went to the doctor for a pregnancy test and was told to ring for the result around five o'clock that afternoon. She and Martin were just passing the County Club in Dunshaughlin, on their way home to Mooretown, listening to the car radio, when the five o'clock news started. Although they were only five minutes from home, Mary was not prepared to wait. They stopped at the County Club and used the public phone. When she and Martin got the good news from the doctor, Mary felt an irresistible urge to tell someone, anyone. One person would be enough, and then she and

Martin could savour the glad tidings on their own for a while. Paddy Peters, the owner of the County Club, was the chosen recipient of Mary's secret intelligence report, and he was delighted for "the three of them". They decided they would not share their news with Claire just yet, just in case.

Emma Claire McAleese was born in Mount Carmel Hospital in Dublin on 21 September 1982, and Martin and Claire were present at the birth. Mary says it was not a difficult birth, but afterwards she was more anaemic than would have been expected. The doctor was not particularly worried about that. In the normal course of events she would have been given some blood, but since her blood type, B negative, was scarce it was decided not to bother with a transfusion. She was, however, given the blood product Anti-D immunoglobin. Mary was later among the group of women tested for hepatitis C, but her tests were negative. She says she will always be grateful for the scarcity of her particular blood type, because if she had been given a transfusion, her chances of contracting hepatitis C would have been greater.

Martin's close friend Seamus Mullan and Mary's sister Claire were the godparents at Emma's christening. After six weeks Mary went back to work—too soon, as she now says, because she was extremely tired. Martin was still a full-time student, so they decided to take the baby into Trinity with them each morning and leave her in the college crèche. This system was working very well until the crèche closed, due to a strike, and was not expected to re-open in the immediate future. They decided to ask Charlie McAleese, Martin's father, if he would like to come and stay with them for a while and look after Emma. Charlie was lonely in Belfast after the death of his wife, and the thought of staying with Mary and Martin appealed greatly to him. He also loved children. Charlie spent the autumn and the start of the winter with them, getting to know the locals as he wheeled Emma in her pram around the roads and lanes of south Meath. The crèche re-opened after Christmas, and in January Charlie went back to his house in Finaghy.

One evening a short time later, Mary and Martin were talking about how easy it was to get on with Charlie, how well he fitted into their lives and how much he loved Emma. They both agreed that they missed his quiet, cheerful presence around the house. Martin said, "I think Emma misses him, too."

Mary agreed and voiced the question that neither of them had yet asked, although it had been in their minds for some time: "Do you think he would like to come and live with us?"

They decided to ring and ask him how he would feel about it, but they never got the opportunity. Charlie rang them that evening to ask would they mind if he came down for the weekend.

"How would you like to come and live with us?" asked Mary. He did not need a second invitation. He moved in and lived happily and contentedly, as a much loved member of the McAleese family, until his death in Áras an Uachtaráin eighteen years later.

Although his culinary experience was severely limited, Charlie said he would like to do a bit of cooking now and again. A couple of weeks after he moved in, he rang Mary in her office and asked, "Mary, how do you make stew?"

Mary enumerated the ingredients and carefully explained the method. Before very long she was regretting that she had ever told him. They had stew every evening for a fortnight. When autumn came his query was, "Mary, how do you make apple tarts?"

When Mary discovered she was pregnant again in the early autumn of 1984, she had a disagreement with her doctor, Robert Brennan. He told her that her dates were wrong, but she was convinced she had them right. The dispute was settled when she was sent to the Rotunda Hospital in Dublin for a scan.

"There are two babies in there," the nurse told her. "You're having twins."

Mary was right about the dates and the doctor was correct in his measurements. She never imagined she might have twins, but as soon as she was told, she thought about her own godchildren, the twins born to her Aunt Bridget after her tenth child.

Mary left the Rotunda and walked down Parnell Square. It was a bright, breezy day, as she remembers, the first leaves blowing off the trees inside the railings of the hospital. Although the swelling of her tummy was totally insignificant, she closed her coat so that no one would spot her bump. This time she did not want to share her news with anyone . . . not just yet. She was enjoying it too much, taking immense satisfaction in her secret condition—twins! She had never dared to hope for twins. She was finding it hard to believe. She had asked the nurse to confirm it in writing on hospital stationery in case Martin had the same difficulty believing it. She says that as she walked along O'Connell Street towards Trinity College, her little grin of gratification broke into a beaming smile of pure happiness every time she thought of the two little lives inside her that were due to come into the world after Easter.

Both their financial and their domestic circumstances were changing, for Martin was about to complete his training as a dental surgeon. His graduation was only a few weeks away and he had a job already organised. His position in a dental practice had been influenced by a little bit of serendipity the previous July. Mary had gone to Dublin to the press conference for Fr Niall O'Brien, the priest who had been held captive in the Philippines and who had just arrived home in Ireland. Martin was at home in Mooretown. He was stripped to the waist and covered in dust, busy scraping polystyrene tiles from the bathroom ceiling and trying to entertain a daughter who steadfastly refused to be entertained, when the doorbell rang. The caller told him, "The big man from Armagh is out in the car and would like to come in."

The caller was a chauffeur and "the big man" was none other than Cardinal Tomás Ó Fiaich, who had also been in Dublin to welcome home Fr O'Brien and who had called to see an old friend in the nursing home in Ratoath on his way back to Armagh. Realising he was near the McAleese home, he decided to call to thank Mary personally for her contribution at the New Ireland Forum.

As the driver went back to the car to collect the Cardinal, Martin ran to don a shirt and grab the crying Emma. He was embarrassed. There was neither a biscuit nor a bun left in the house to offer the Cardinal with a cup of tea. He and his friend Seamus Mullan had drunk the last drop of alcohol in the house the night before, so there was not even a drink to offer him. As the "big man from Armagh" took the crying baby from the flustered father, Mary arrived home, complete with bags of shopping, to retrieve the situation.

She was amazed to see Cardinal Ó Fiaich dandling Emma on his knee, both of them obviously delighting in each other's company. In the course of the ensuing conversation, over tea and biscuits, the Cardinal mentioned that he knew Martin was soon to graduate as a dentist, and he also mentioned that his home town of Crossmaglen did not have a resident dentist. When Martin heard this, a seed was sown.

He had arranged to work as an associate dentist in the practice of Des Casey in Bessbrook, County Armagh, with a view to getting some experience of high-volume National Health dental work in the North. He did not intend to stay there very long before looking for a position in the Republic. Casey, from Bray, County Wicklow, had trained in the Royal College of Surgeons in Dublin and had worked in Armagh city as an associate dentist before starting his own practice in Bessbrook. By the time Martin joined him, he had been working with just a dental nurse and a receptionist for twenty years and was looking for a partner. The two men soon became firm friends as well as good working companions. After four months Martin decided to accept Casey's offer of a partnership and bought 50 per cent of the practice. A month later they opened the first permanent practice in Crossmaglen, much to the delight of Cardinal Ó Fiaich.

Casey was delighted to leave the administration and the handling of the finances to the former accountant, a decision he would never regret. Within a year they had two busy practices, served by themselves and two associate dentists, and by late 1989 both practices were fully computerised. Within two years both parties in the Casey-McAleese partnership were prepared to admit that their business was "financially very rewarding".

Martin rented a house in the town of Warrenpoint, between Newry and Rostrevor, and often stayed in it when he was too tired to travel back to County Meath. The twins were due to arrive at the start of May, so Mary brought Emma to spend Easter in the rented house. They would be only a couple of miles from all the Leneghans in Rostrevor, and Martin would not have far to travel to be with Mary and Emma each evening. The plan was that Mary would spend the first part of her maternity leave there and travel back to Mooretown a week or ten days before the date she was due, so that she would be near the Rotunda Hospital for the birth of the twins. She was tired. She had been working very hard until Spy Wednesday and was looking forward to a rest over the Easter holidays. On Good Friday, a month before her time, the labour pains started. Martin rang Carmel Browne, a friend who was a midwife in Daisy Hill Hospital in Newry. Carmel strongly advised Martin to bring Mary straight into Daisy Hill rather than make the journey to Dublin. It was good advice. Saramai and Justin McAleese were born the following morning, Holy Saturday, 6 April 1985.

Mother and twins left Daisy Hill two weeks later. Martin had to go back to work, and it was a great relief to him and to Mary that Charlie was there to look after Emma. When Mary was discharged from hospital, she took the twins to the house in Warrenpoint for the duration of her maternity leave. There was plenty of family support on hand. Her mother and the rest of the relations were in and out every day from Rostrevor, and Martin was home every evening.

Pauline McCormack, a first cousin of Mary's on her mother's side, and her husband John were Justin's godparents. Saramai's godparents were Nuala Lowe, a first cousin of Mary's on her father's side, and her husband Séamus. Saramai was called after an aunt of Martin's and a grandaunt of Mary's, who were both called Sara. The "Mai" part of her name, pronounced "May", was for Nuala Lowe's mother, Mai McGreevy. Justin Charles, of course, was named for Mary's *anamchara*, Fr Justin Coyne, and her father-in-law. Years before she was married, she had said that if she ever had a son she wanted to call him Justin.

Charlie's affection for the twins was exceeded only by his devotion to them. He was a grandfather of a very special kind: gentle, sympathetic and loving and totally dedicated to his grandchildren. He loved them all equally, but there was always a special bond between Charlie and Emma. He later said: "Emma never went to bed any night without calling in to have a wee word with me and give me a goodnight kiss."

They all shared their joys and their sorrows with him. Granda Charlie had to be shown each cut and scratch and each baby tooth that fell out. In him they found a good listener, and they poured out their difficulties and secret worries to him. He was scrupulously fair in the affection he showed to the three of them, but the affinity between him and Emma was similar to that between Mary and her own grandmother Cassie.

From the day Emma McAleese was born, Mary swore that no one would ever be allowed to raise a hand to her, or to any other child of hers. She was reared with the help of an odd slap on the bottom, and a stinging slap from a ruler was to be expected in school. Her thoughts on corporal punishment are very firm: "I have never seen an adult strike a child except in anger. Corporal punishment often promotes fear and even cowardice in children who witness it: they are afraid to speak out against it for fear of suffering the same consequences."

Mary's own parents chided her for forbidding physical punishment in the house. She had to warn Charlie that he would never be allowed to smack the children, and although he had often smacked Martin and his other children when they were young, he had no problem with the veto. Years later he spoke of how his attitude changed during the rearing of the young McAleeses.

"At first I thought Mary was wrong, but I wasn't long changing my mind. Those children were always at their ease with everybody, especially with their own family. They would be in trouble sometimes, the same as any other children, but there was never any tension between them and their mammy and daddy or between them and me. I never in my life saw children so relaxed."

When Charlie said, "They would be in trouble sometimes, the same as any other children," he was perfectly correct. There were times when Mary herself felt like shaking them, or worse. When Emma was three years old, Mary was invited by Fr Dermod McCarthy to give a talk in the Pro-Cathedral in Dublin. Mary says, "I was not humble enough to refuse his request because I'd say I was the first woman to stand in that pulpit without a rag in one hand and a tin of Mr Sheen in the other."

The night before she was due to preach to a packed church in Dublin, she still had no idea what she was going to say. Panic was beginning to rear its ugly head. She was sitting at the kitchen table, asking God for some inspiration and staring at that most intimidating of all writers' implements—a blank page—when the plaintive cry came from Emma's bedroom, "Mammy! Mammy! I want Coca-Cola!"

Martin, who was comfortably ensconced in the sitting room watching snooker on the television, reminded Mary that the child wanted her mammy, not her daddy. There was not a drop of Coca-Cola, or even anything that would pass for it, in the house, and the local shop was closed. Mary tried to interest Emma in milk, water, orange juice . . . Emma wanted Coca-Cola. When it had been patiently explained, for the twentieth time, and still to no avail, that the requested refreshment was simply not available, Mary was drumming her fingers with increasing rapidity on the offending blank page, as a prelude to tearing out her hair. Suddenly an apparition manifested itself in the doorway: Emma, complete with anorak zipped tightly over her nightclothes and teddy dangling from her left hand. She stared at her mother as she announced, "I running away!"

Patiently but firmly, Mary accompanied the would-be runaway back to her room, tucked her safely into bed, and recommended to her—both as her mother and her lawyer—not to put a foot on the floor again before morning. Mary returned to the kitchen table and to the page which was still as blank as ever. Once again she prayed for inspiration, reminding God that women didn't often get the opportunity that had been dropped in her lap to preach in a major church. Like many inspiration-seekers before her, she took down a copy of the Bible and let it fall open. She was amazed at first, taken aback, before she burst out laughing at what she saw as God's sense of humour.

The Bible had fallen open at the First Letter of St Paul to the Corinthians, chapter 14, verse 34: "Let women keep silence in the churches; they must stay in the background as the Law itself lays it down. But if they would learn anything, let them ask their husbands at home, for it is a shame for a woman to speak in the church." At least she had the start of the sermon.

The children did not always share Mary's faith in divine intervention. Several years later, on 8 December, she was attempting to inveigle Sara into going to mass. But first she had to get her out of bed.

"This is the Feast of the Immaculate Conception. On this day, many years ago, the Blessed Virgin kept our family safe when men with machine-guns came to murder us in our beds. We should always be grateful to Our Lady and at least go to mass on the Feast of the Immaculate Conception."

The child's response was not exactly what Mary wanted to hear. "Sound more like the Immaculate Coincidence to me," said Sara, before turning over and going back to sleep.

As the children grew, their interests did not always reflect those of their parents. Mary had never been an avid pop music fan. She had a friend whose father was able to get tickets for the Grand Opera House in Belfast, and by the time she was in her mid-teens she had been to all the major operas. "Thank God the children didn't take after their mother," says Martin, who was a competent jiver in his younger days. He often regaled the children with stories of his prowess on the dance floors of the "hops", as the discos were called in those days. Although Mary was not an aficionado of the music of the Beatles or the Rolling Stones, she liked the Beach Boys and was a devotee of Roy Orbison. When she was young, the singing of John McCormack was the family's staple musical diet, from the old gramophone in the Leneghan house. Claire had a large collection of McCormack 78 records of which she was very proud—until her eldest daughter learned from a *Blue Peter* programme on BBC how to make interesting pots by immersing such old records in boiling water and bending them to the required shape!

Both Mary and Martin were anxious that the children would share their own love for Irish music. During the years they were going out together, they were familiar faces at the *céilís* in the Ardscoil and at the sessions in Cumann Chluain Ard. As a teenager Mary had participated in *Slógadh Gael Linn*, singing a Beatles song translated into Irish, and she was a member of a ballad group that sang in the GAA talent competition *Scór*. During the years she lived in Belfast, she never missed a concert at the Belfast Folk Festival. It was there that she heard the Chieftains and the Dubliners for the first time. Both she and Martin were members of the Rossa GAA club and attended many a good session in the clubhouse. The taste in music there was not exclusively Irish, they say, and visitors to the club were as liable to hear the music of Frank Sinatra as the music of Frank Patterson, or even Frankie Gavin.

214

When Mary was a child, the *Lives of the Saints* featured strongly in the reading material provided at home. Although she and Martin had long since decided there would be a broader required reading in the McAleese house, some of those saints about whose lives she had read at an early age held a fascination for her. She was enchanted by the life of the great mystic St Catherine of Sienna and by the story of St Thomas More, lawyer, writer, scholar, counsellor and friend of King Henry VIII. A relation of Mary's, Br Bede McGreevy, first introduced her to the life of the canonised English lawyer when he gave her a present of his biography. She developed a great respect for the saint whose rhetorical skills had been honed at the Inns of Court, a regard, she says, that was instrumental in her choosing the law as her way of life. Shortly after she read that particular book, Fred Zinnemann's famous film *A Man for All Seasons* was released, starring Paul Scofield as Thomas More. The film only served to consolidate her esteem for the man. Apart from a few classics of this type, Mary's favourite films are notable for the fact that Omar Sharif seems to feature in most of them. It is not clear whether the Egyptian's acting ability was the attraction, or his good looks.

The McAleese children proved to be musical and were given the opportunity to develop their skills from an early age. Mary has a fine mezzo soprano voice and loves singing. She was not a total nerd when she was young. Apart from her visits to the Grand Opera House, she didn't really discover the beauties of classical music until she was in university. It is interesting to note her favourite composers: Frédéric Chopin, Bèla Bartok, Bedrich Smetana and Jean Sibelius—nationalists all, who used their music to nationalist effect in their various countries.

One night, when she went into Justin's bedroom to say goodnight, she found her son lying in bed reading poetry, just as she had often done when she was young. She says she was glad to see him discovering for himself the wonderful world of verse and hoped that it would always hold an attraction for him. She found that the pressures of school examinations spoiled the enjoyment of so much poetry for her, especially that of William Butler Yeats. She discovered Patrick Kavanagh's poetry after she had left school and found it all the fresher and more appealing for not being required reading. She still quotes her old teacher May O'Friel on the subject of poetry in school: "Don't agonise over it. Read what the critics say. Regurgitate it. Don't try to impose your own grain on the poetry. You'll have plenty of time to educate yourselves when the A levels are over."

One of her problems with the poetry of Yeats is that when she was learning it she was comparing it to the poetry of Lorca. There was no contest, in her mind, in terms of the pleasure she got from them. Creena O'Farrell was the Spanish teacher in St Dominic's. During Mary's last year in school, Creena took the class to a seminar in Queen's to hear a talk by a young lecturer called Ian Gibson. Mary had never heard of him and had no idea that he would be one day recognised as a world expert on the poetry of Lorca. Neither could she suspect that he and she would become good friends in later years. At some point during that seminar Mary fell in love with the poetry of Federico Garcia Lorca. She always reads it in the original, as her Spanish has been fluent for many years. Of some of her favourite poets—John Hewitt, W.R. Rodgers and John Montague—she says, "I never learned a word of their poetry in school. I think, somehow, I was the better for it."

Sport, of course, had to play a big part in the rearing of the McAleese children. None of them have so far shown any indication that they have inherited Martin's expertise on the football pitch, but they have all shown an eagerness for athletics and games since they were very young. Emma was the first to display an interest in rowing. When she became good at it, she said she would like to do a summer course to hone her rowing skills. She was twelve years old when she first went to Eton, the famous English public school, where, according to her trainer, she would find the best summer course in rowing. As Emma was setting off from home that morning, her mother noticed a hurley sticking out of her bag.

"Where are you going with the hurley?" asked Mary.

"I hear they have great playing fields in Eton," replied Emma. "I'll be able to play camogie there."

"Rugby!" exclaimed her mother. "It's rugby pitches they have in Eton. But it doesn't matter. They've never heard of camogie in Eton. There will be nobody else there with a hurley to play with you."

Emma excused herself, went back into the house, and when she came out again there was a second hurley sticking out of the bag.

"If they've never heard of camogie in Eton, then I'll teach them."

She hugged her mother and off she went. Mary was left staring after her, imagining her daughter playing camogie where "wars were won on the playing fields of Eton" and imagining the dead generations of English nobility turning in the marble tombs. The apple doesn't fall far from the tree.

Chapter Eighteen

A Cautious Candidate

What kind of turmoil has come
between me and my night's sleep?
Such foolishness! Wake up!
Damn and double damn him,
the funk, the lousy turncoat,
skulking from all I stand for.

(Micheál Ó Siadhail: "Psalm in the Night")

When Paddy Leneghan owned the Long Bar, he was often annoyed by young people running in one door and out the other, using the pub as a short-cut between Leeson Street and Cyprus Street. One of those cheeky teenagers was a girl by the name of Anne Smyth, who lived in Abyssinia Street. Many years later, while Mary McAleese was taking so much joy in her family life and watching in fascination as her children grew up before her eyes, Anne Smyth, who was by then Anne Maguire, was in prison in England, separated from her children and her husband, serving a sentence for a crime of which she had no knowledge and of which she was totally innocent.

Anne Maguire is a gentle, soft-spoken woman who never showed an interest in anything other than caring for her husband and four children. She had five regular cleaning jobs in various shops near her home in the Third Avenue area of London. These jobs were badly needed because her husband Paddy had been out of work for several years. Anne never had a minute to herself. She spent her life cleaning shops, doing her housework and rearing her children. She was a member of only one club: the Paddington Conservative Club. She and her husband Paddy were always vehemently anti-republican. On the evening of 4 December 1974, Anne was washing clothes and preparing dinner for her own family plus three neighbouring children and Giuseppe Conlon, her brother-in-law from Belfast, who was staying with them. Giuseppe was married to Sarah, Paddy Maguire's sister, and he had come to London to find a solicitor for his son, Gerard

217

Conlon, who had been arrested in connection with the bombing of two pubs in Guildford, in Surrey. Unknown to anyone in the house, Gerard had signed a false confession in which he had implicated Anne in terrorism. In the confession, he stated that his Aunt Annie Maguire had taught him, in her own house, how to make bombs. Conlon later retracted his ludicrous statement, but it was too late. As Anne was sorting clothes for the washing and keeping an eye on the stew, a heavy banging was heard at the front door. Anne asked her daughter Anne-Marie, who was eight years old at the time, to answer it. Before Anne-Marie reached it, however, the door was shattered from its hinges and in poured armed police, in riot gear, preceded by large dogs on chains.

The Maguire Seven, as they came to be known, were arrested: Anne and Paddy and their two sons, Vincent (sixteen) and Patrick (thirteen), Giuseppe Conlon, Anne's brother Sean Smyth and a family friend, Pat O'Neill. The seven people were convicted of handling explosive material, sentenced and imprisoned. To Mary McAleese and many others in Ireland, it was obvious that the wrong people were in prison, not least because of the lack of evidence against them. A seventeen-year-old apprentice technician in RARDE administered the infamous Thin Layer Chromotography Test on the Maguires.[‡] It was claimed that this test detected minute particles of nitroglycerine on their hands. When Dr John Yallop, former director of RARDE and the man who devised the TLC test, appeared for the defence and said the test was inconclusive, his evidence was given scant regard. When scientists in Dublin and Glasgow later proved conclusively that the test was worthless, because many ordinary everyday household products gave the same result as nitroglycerine, the original samples from the Maguires' hands had mysteriously disappeared.

The conviction based on this lack of evidence was condemned out of hand in Britain, but very little was said in Ireland. The English scientist Brian J. Ford, who wrote the best-selling *Cult of the Expert,* went so far as to say, "Instead of the Forensic Science Service offering independent expertise, it was acting as a state-run service to get prosecutions."[§]

The Archbishop of Westminster Cardinal John Basil Hume said, "Anne Maguire was caught up in a terrible situation not of her making, accused unjustly of a crime she never committed."[†]

---

‡   RARDE: Royal Armament Research and Development Establishment.

§   *Laboratory News*, 18 July 1991.

†   Anne Maguire, with Jim Gallagher, *Why Me?*, (London: HarperCollins, 1994), Foreword.

Sir John May, former Appeal Court judge in England, said it was the worst case of injustice he had ever seen.

Gareth Pierce said, "It's very disturbing that when science has gone so wrong and been responsible for wrong convictions, that it hasn't been taken to task in this appeal."[‡]

Mary McAleese had something a little bit stronger to say: "British justice at its nastiest, murkiest, most disgraceful."

On 3 March 1976, Anne Maguire was sentenced to fourteen years in prison. She had already spent time on remand with Carole Richardson in Brixton Prison and in Holloway, but when she was convicted she was sent to the high-security Durham Prison, where she met Anne and Eileen Gillespie and Judith Ward. She was released on 22 February 1985, and she and her husband Paddy came to Dublin the next day, courtesy of RTÉ. Among those who were at Dublin Airport to welcome them home to Ireland was Mary McAleese.

Two years previously, a priest called P.J. Byrne decided to form an association to look after the interests of Irish people imprisoned abroad. Fr Byrne was secretary of the Bishops' Commission for Emigrants in England. Among those he asked to help him in forming the group were Stasia Crickley, Fr Breffni Walker, John O'Connell, who was a priest at that time, and Mary McAleese. With the help of Bishop Éamonn Casey, they eventually succeeded in getting the patronage of the Irish bishops for their new association, offices were acquired in Parnell Square, and Nuala Kelly was appointed secretary of ICPO, the Irish Commission for Prisoners Overseas.

ICPO had a particular interest in the cases of the Birmingham Six, the Guildford Four and the Gillespie sisters, Anne and Eileen. Their objective in the case of Anne Maguire was to get the case re-opened with a view to her being found innocent. Mary took Anne Maguire to meetings all over the country, telling her story and seeking support for those who were still in prison. She became very taken with the quiet, unassuming woman who prayed every night for those who were responsible for her imprisonment.

"Anne Maguire is an exceptional woman, one of those who have most impressed me during my life. Her integrity, her faith and her gentleness amazed me. I never heard her utter a bad word about anyone, although God knows she had reason. She is steeped in the love of God and the love of her neighbour."

---

‡ *Laboratory News*, 18 July 1991.

It bothered Mary that the people of Ireland had not done more for Anne and her family when they were in prison. Both Mary and Anne say that David and Niall Andrews were outstanding among the politicians who took an interest in her case. Other politicians got involved after it became obvious that the Maguires were innocent and when they had already won people's sympathy. But when people were suspicious of them, seduced by headlines in the English tabloid newspapers, and blind to the concerns of reasonable people about the flimsiness of the case against them, the voices of Irish politicians were very muted. In the preface of her own book, *Why Me?*, Anne thanks upwards of sixty people for their support, including Mary McAleese of Queen's University and Joe Mulholland of RTÉ! Many members of the British parliament are mentioned, but not a single Irish politician.

When she was due to appear before the Appeal Court in an attempt to get her original conviction overturned, Anne Maguire was almost penniless. When she was released from prison, her home was gone and her family scattered. She had immediately looked for work and had got a job as a school cleaner, but her wages were very small. In her own words:

> Mary McAleese was one of those people who made me feel like a human being again. When we were at meetings, we always stood shoulder to shoulder and she would introduce us both: "I am Mary McAleese and this is Anne Maguire." As if to say, "It's both of us or neither of us—take us or leave us." She always believed in me. She was more than a friend—a very special person—and all my family feel the same. She was always very generous. When I went to the Court of Appeal to try to get the conviction quashed, she sent me money so that I could get a new outfit. We could go on a holiday to her home any time we wanted. Mary was afraid of nobody. She brought me to see an Irish government minister to look for his support in trying to get my name cleared, but he said he couldn't help. When he was explaining his position he said, "This woman has been tried and convicted." Mary answered him, "So was Jesus Christ!"[‡]

The Irish are the largest ethnic group in British jails. When Mary was working for the ICPO, 80 per cent of the prisoners on their books were in prison in England. She was delighted when Cardinal Hume spoke publicly on behalf of Anne Maguire and she saw the effect his statements

---

‡   Interview with author.

had on public opinion. She was strongly of the belief that other influential English people should be encouraged to campaign on behalf of Irish prisoners in England. She felt that people like Robert Kee or Tony Benn or Sir John Biggs-Davison would be effective in increasing public awareness of the injustices being perpetrated on Irish citizens in England, and in creating more sympathy for their cause. Mary was in regular contact with members of parliament in Britain and got to know some of them very well. One of those parliamentarians with whom a strong mutual respect was established was the Labour Party MP Chris Mullen, the man who worked hard for the release of the Birmingham Six. When he wrote his book on Irish prisoners in England, he asked Mary to launch it in Dublin. Mary McAleese and Anne Maguire are still friends, and Anne was an honoured guest at the presidential inauguration.

Nuala Kelly, secretary of ICPO, has this to say on Mary's involvement with the organisation:

Mary was a very useful person to have on board. She was steady, never operating on an emotional whim, even when highlighting the suffering of prisoners' families. She never accepted information without questioning it fully. She had extensive contacts all over the world and used them for support and to check the smallest details. She also provided an important social setting for our work—at times feeding us and entertaining us. Her work in persuading the Irish government to ratify the Convention on Transfer of Sentenced Prisoners was probably her most important contribution. She left the board of ICPO when she went north in 1987, but continued to help us as a consultant. Any time I went to Belfast for meetings, she made herself available to me for advice and support. I don't know where she got the time."[‡]

Nobody, including Mary, seems to know where she got the time for all she was doing. She was writing a regular column for *The Sunday Tribune*. She was invited to go on the board of *Focus Point* by Sister Stanislaus Kennedy, where her work ranged from devising strategies to lobby government for support for the homeless to fund-raising and interviewing prospective employees. Although she had campaigned for the rights of prisoners, she was conscious of the rights of the victims of crime. She attended meetings of the Association of Garda Sergeants and Inspectors and addressed them on this issue. She was invited by Derek

---

[‡] Interview with author. The Convention on Transfer of Sentenced Prisoners was ratified by the Irish government in 1995.

Nally, a man with whom she would have no little difficulty in years to come, to be a committee member of a new organisation he had just founded: the Association for Victim Support. She took a particular interest in and worked in support of the Rape Crisis Centre. She publicly denounced the practice of strip-searching in Northern prisons, especially in the Women's Prison in Armagh, where both inmates and visitors were regularly subjected to such searches. When Fr Raymond Murray of Armagh organised an Anti Strip-Search Conference in Trinity College, Mary and the psychiatrist Dr Ivor Browne were two of the main speakers. She had not forgotten her old acquaintances in Trinity College and supported her friend and colleague David Norris in his ongoing work for the rights of homosexuals.

She was one of those who nominated David Norris and Catherine McGuinness when they sought seats in Seanad Éireann. She also helped Norris in his campaign, lobbying on his behalf and canvassing university graduates who would have a vote in the Senate elections. She did this during both campaigns in 1982. When the 1987 election campaign was getting under way, she heard that some of his supporters had expressed reservations about her being on the campaign team: that she was now perceived as being too Catholic and as having too much Catholicism in her politics.

David Norris says: "If any of my supporters were unhappy with Mary's Catholicism, they certainly never said it to me. I have always had the utmost respect for her and always found her to be a person of courage and integrity. Some of my followers may have voiced objections to her, but not in my presence."

Fintan Cronin has said he found it almost impossible to put a political label on Mary and described her as "a nationalist social democrat of some sort, liberal in outlook". Her support for the SDLP in the North would be consistent with that analysis, but what was her party of preference in the South? She says only one party ever received her serious consideration: Fianna Fáil. Before she became a member of the party, she was active in the Fianna Fáil Women's Committee, and when she made contributions to draft papers on subjects such as divorce, it was obvious that what she had to say was in perfect harmony with the philosophy of the party.

When she had her first dealings with Fianna Fáil, they had been in opposition to a Fine Gael/Labour Party coalition government led by Garret FitzGerald that had been in power since 1982. Mary made many friends and many future allies in the Fianna Fáil Women's Committee.

222

Among them was the public relations consultant Eileen Gleeson, who would later be appointed special adviser to the president. She also became friendly with the future Minister for Education Mary O'Rourke, sister of the former Minister for Education Brian Lenihan (who would later run as Fianna Fáil candidate for the presidency) and aunt of the future TDs Conor and Brian Lenihan. Mary renewed her acquaintance with Veronica Guerin, whom she had first met at the New Ireland Forum, and she became friendly with Catherine Byrne and many others in the party. She describes these women as "highly intelligent, fun-loving, hard-working people" and obviously enjoyed their company. Mary O'Rourke was the chair of the Women's Committee, and it was she who asked her new friend to give a speech at the upcoming first-ever Fianna Fáil Women's Conference.

Nearly five hundred delegates, including the leader of Fianna Fáil, C.J. Haughey, packed into the ballroom of Jury's Hotel in Dublin for the occasion. Haughey had been impressed with Mary McAleese at the New Ireland Forum, but he now found himself exhilarated by the freshness of her delivery and fluency as her speech ranged over the multiplicity of issues affecting women in the Ireland of the 1980s. The more he listened the more he was convinced that this woman would be a great asset to the Fianna Fáil parliamentary party. By the end of the conference the word had gone out: Mary McAleese was to be on the Fianna Fáil ticket at the next general election.

Ironically, the person who actually invited Mary to join the ranks of the "Soldiers of Destiny" was none other than the future Tánaiste Mary Harney. A few short months after persuading her that Fianna Fáil was her true spiritual home, Mary Harney left the party and, with the former Minister Des O'Malley, drew many other disaffected Fianna Fáil people to their ranks and founded a new political party, the Progressive Democrats. On 16 January 1985, Mary McAleese sent an application for membership of Fianna Fáil to Brian O'Malley, the secretary of the Peadar Macken/Constance Markievicz Cumann, near Trinity College in the constituency of Dublin South-East. She was proposed by Tom Cosgrove, seconded by Michael Sweeney, welcomed into the Fianna Fáil fold and soon appointed cumann secretary.

With the tenure of the Fine Gael/Labour coalition government due to expire in a year, the political parties were beginning to choose their candidates for the next general election. When the Fianna Fáil selection convention for the Dublin South-East constituency assembled on 26 January 1986, Mary was one of several contestants for two nominations.

The first to be chosen that night was the sitting TD Ger Brady, who got forty-eight votes. The former Lord Mayor of Dublin, Councillor Michael Donnelly, was chosen on the second count. Mary did not show much concern when she received only seven votes. She knew she had not been around the constituency long enough to have a realistic chance of gaining a nomination against two successful incumbent public representatives. She also knew that the National Executive had the power to add the name of any candidate they chose to the list of nominees in any constituency. If Charles J. Haughey really wanted her as a candidate, he would ensure her candidacy. In the memorable words of the Fianna Fáil press officer P.J. Mara, "nothing was certain": several other candidates were being considered for a place on the Dublin South-East panel. Among them were the Councillors Eoin Ryan, Mary Hanafin, Michael Mulcahy and Ellen Gunning.

Referring to Mary's poor showing at the selection convention, Haughey later said, "She was shafted."[‡] This is doubtful. Her lack of support certainly did not reflect a lack of political involvement, but it may have reflected a lack of engagement with local as distinct from national issues. In matters of national import, she was totally engrossed, particularly in Fianna Fáil's opposition to Garret FitzGerald's "Constitutional Crusade". In an attempt to make the Republic of Ireland less of a "cold house" for Northern unionists, the FitzGerald government attempted to introduce divorce by referendum in 1986. A few days before the referendum in June of that year, Mary spoke trenchantly against the proposal:

"Divorce, we are told, will make us liberal, democratic, tolerant, pluralist. Terrific! We can proudly join the other liberal democracies of the world: Russia, South Africa, Poland, Northern Ireland."[§]

This was one of many attacks she made on the pro-divorce campaign, each more scathing and more caustic than the last. It was the sort of straight-from-the-shoulder fighting talk thought by many, including Charles Haughey, to be characteristic of Northerners. Chieftains of the Haughey sept were kings of Ulster until the twelfth century, a fact not lost on the future taoiseach, who had many relations in the North.[†] Among them was Monica McWilliams, future leader of the Women's

‡   Justine McCarthy, *Mary McAleese: the Outsider* (Belfast: Blackwater Press, 1999), p. 79.

§   Mary McAleese, private papers.

†   Edward MacLysaght, *Irish Families: Their Names, Arms and Origins* (Blackrock, Co Dublin: Irish Academic Press, 1957), p. 115.

Frontline, RTÉ 1979.

Back row: far left, Kevin Cassidy;
far right, Mary Fitzpatrick
holding daughter, Sinead.
Front row (L–R): Albert Dolan,
Mary Dolan, Eileen O'Hara
(grand-aunt), Mary Cassidy
(grand-aunt), Nora McDrury
(grand-aunt).

Charlie McAleese.

Mary and Eibhlis Farrell.

Cassie McManus and John McManus (Mary's grandparents), at their fortieth wedding anniversary.

Claire Leneghan, Martin, Mary, Dermot McQuaid, Pat Leneghan, Pauline McQuaid in Miami, 1981.

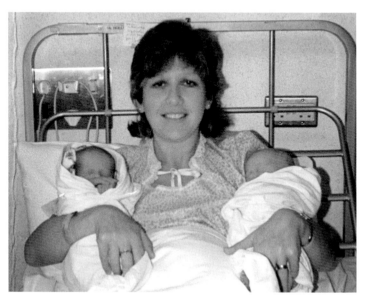

Mary, Justin and Saramai, Daisy Hill Hospital, Newry, 6 April 1985.

Called to the Bar, The King's Inns, Dublin, 1986. Mary and Martin with Claire and Paddy Leneghan.

(Left) Martin's graduation as a dentist, TCD, November 1984.

Mary, Martin and Emma at Martin's graduation.

Mary and Emma, Fatima 1986.

*Mary McAleese flyer, 1987
General Election Campaign
in Dublin South-East.*

MARY McALEESE

DÁIL CANDIDATE
DUBLIN SOUTH-EAST

Please Vote 1, 2, 3, and 4 in
order of your choice for
Fianna Fáil Candidates —
Gerard Brady T.D.,
Cllr. Michael Donnelly,

MARY McALEESE

and Cllr. Eoin Ryan.

**Thank You For Your
Support on Feb. 17th.**

Charlie and Emma, Rostrevor 1988.

Mary and Martin, Oliva, Valencia 1990.

Sara, Justin and Emma, 1992.

Martin after the London Marathon, 1990.

Father Paul McNellis, Sara, Mary, Martin, Justin, Harry Casey, Rostrevor 1992.

The family with Charlie McAleese, Rostrevor 1993.

The Sam Maguire Cup on a visit to St Mary's Boys' School, Rostrevor 1994.
Pete McGrath (the Down coach) and Justin McAleese.

Martin, Mary, Maria Moloney and Denis Moloney.

President Mary Robinson, Eibhlís Farrell, Siubhán Uí Dhubháin
Children (L-R): Sara, Rós Ní Dhubháin, Christchurch Cathedral 1993.

Paddy Leneghan, Emma, Justin, Martin, Charlie,
Petra (former girlfriend of Phelim), Mary, Sara, Monaghan Barracks.

Behind The Commons, St Stephen's Green,
during the presidential election campaign, October 1997.

Leneghan family. Back row (L-R): Nora, Claire, Damien, Phelim.
Front row (L-R): John, Kate, Paddy, Mary, Claire, Clement, Pat.
Evening of presidential election count.

The morning of the inauguration,
Portmarnock Hotel and GolfLinks, 11 November 1997.

Coalition. He always had a strong empathy with the nationalist cause in the North, particularly at the start of the Troubles. In 1970 the Taoiseach Jack Lynch fired Haughey and Neil Blaney from their ministerial posts. They, along with Irish Army intelligence officer Captain James Kelly and Belfast republican John Kelly, were charged with conspiracy to import arms with a view to distributing them among the nationalist people of Northern Ireland. Although he was found not guilty, the allegations raised enough doubt to have him cast into a political wilderness until Lynch appointed him minister for health in 1977. Two years later, Haughey was taoiseach, a post held by Seán Lemass, Haughey's wife Máirín's father, between 1959 and 1966.

By the time Mary joined Fianna Fáil, Garret FitzGerald and Margaret Thatcher had signed the Anglo-Irish Agreement. One of the provisions of this agreement was the establishment of a permanent conference under the joint chairmanship of the Irish minister for foreign affairs and the British secretary of state for Northern Ireland. Civil servants from both jurisdictions were appointed to a secretariat located in Maryfield, just south-east of Belfast. For the first time, the Republic of Ireland would have a say in the internal affairs of Northern Ireland. The reciprocal concession was that, also for the first time, the Irish government recognised the right of the people of Northern Ireland to determine their own political future. In the North the loyalists, and many unionists, opposed the agreement. In the South, loyalists of a different colour opposed it also: those who adhered steadfastly to the doctrine that only the people of the whole island of Ireland should decide the future of Northern Ireland. Haughey and most of the membership of Fianna Fáil were amongst these. Mary McAleese, although she had serious doubts about the Agreement, says she was not opposed to it on this basis:

> I was not totally opposed to the Anglo-Irish Agreement, but I was morally certain that it would not work. Here we had two irreconcilable philosophies, nationalism and unionism, and the Irish and British governments were trying to persuade both sides that they could achieve their political ambitions. No conflict can result in a win-win situation, but it is possible to achieve a willingness to facilitate a reasonable compromise on both sides. This is what happened at the Good Friday Agreement. The big weakness of the Anglo-Irish Agreement was that the governments did not seek the opinions of the people of Northern Ireland, both unionist and nationalist, beforehand.

In unionist and loyalist areas all over the North, posters appeared carrying the words "Ulster Says No!" An appendix inspired by a popular television advertising campaign for orange juice appeared on many of these posters: "But the Man from Del Monte Says Yes! And He's an Orangeman!" The most prominent and most famous of the anti-Agreement banners was stretched above the magnificent colonnade of Belfast's City Hall. It proudly proclaimed, "Belfast Says No!" Shortly before Christmas, a person gifted both artistically and acrobatically climbed up and added the letters "-el" to the message, changing the political slogan to a Christmas greeting: "Belfast Says Noel!"

Having made a fruitless attempt to amend the Anglo-Irish Agreement in the Dáil, Haughey announced in October that Fianna Fáil would try to change the terms of the Agreement if they were returned to power. This was not the only agreement to which they were opposed. The coalition government was loud in its praise of the Single European Act as an instrument which would bring great benefits to Ireland by facilitating freer commerce among the member states of the European Union. The government had decided that Ireland's ratification of the treaty would be by means of a vote in the Oireachtas rather than a referendum. To Haughey and the majority of Fianna Fáil, the signing of the treaty was to be resisted for two main reasons: the possible compromising of Ireland's neutrality and the negative implications for the country's indigenous industries.

Some people were of the opinion at the time that Mary McAleese's opposition to the Single European Act was based on the premise that abortion could become freely available under the terms of the act that provided for the free movement of services within the European Community. She says she was, in fact, opposed to the act for two other reasons that had nothing to do with abortion or social policy. Firstly, she feared the curtailment of the sovereign powers of the Irish people in the formulation of their own foreign policy, and secondly, the act was not to be ratified by the people of Ireland but by their elected representatives.

Haughey, McAleese and the Fianna Fáil party were clearly of one mind on the subject: they would vigorously oppose the ratification by the Oireachtas of the Single European Act. In October, Haughey announced that his party in government would also seek to amend the terms of this treaty if they were returned to power. He asked Mary to write an anti-Single European Act speech for him, and once again he was delighted with her thoughts and her words. This woman had a bright future in Fianna Fáil.

A year and a day after the selection convention in Dublin South-East had refused to select her as a Fianna Fáil candidate in the upcoming general election, the National Executive of the party announced that they were adding the names of Mary McAleese and Councillor Eoin Ryan to the Fianna Fáil ticket in that constituency. Three days later Mary received a congratulatory letter from an old friend, Paschal O'Hare, the Belfast barrister: "Sometimes I feel that the people in the Republic of Ireland take for granted their political institutions. Would that we Northern Nationalists had an arena to which we could give our full unqualified support."

Mary agreed wholeheartedly with the latter sentiment but would soon find that, whatever about political lethargy among the electorate in the Republic, the politicians and prospective politicians were taking nothing for granted. The day after she received this letter, the twenty-fourth Dáil was dissolved. According to Charles J. Haughey, she now had a great opportunity to prove herself politically. Mary did not agree with him. Haughey had offered her a choice of five constituencies, including Dublin North, Wicklow and Dublin South-East. She told him she was not in a position to make a choice and asked him to make the decision. Dublin South-East was his choice. She later said that she understood that she would have no chance of winning a seat in any of them, but in Dublin South-East she would have the best opportunity to put down a marker, to build up a profile which would give her a more realistic chance in a subsequent general election. She saw it as a first instalment and was probably correct in her estimation: although Eoin Ryan did not fare as well as Mary in 1987, he was successful in the next general election, in 1989.

Dublin South-East was a four-seat constituency and was home to some heavyweight political contenders. It was generally accepted that the taoiseach Garret FitzGerald would be re-elected for Fine Gael. Ger Brady, the incumbent Fianna Fáil TD, was considered a safe bet, as was Ruairí Quinn, the minister for labour and future leader of the Labour Party. Realistically, there was only one seat that was remotely winnable for Mary: that of Joe Doyle, who had been a Fine Gael TD in the constituency since November 1982. The date of the general election was set for 17 February, which left the candidates seven weeks in which to prove themselves to their constituents.

As election day approached, the mood in Fianna Fáil headquarters was buoyant. Ironically, the reason for their confidence was the appalling state of the economy. The number of people unemployed in the state had just, for the first time ever, exceeded a quarter of a million; there was a record budget deficit, and thousands of well-educated young people were leaving the country to find employment elsewhere. Although the people were obviously dissatisfied with the performance of FitzGerald's government, they were also a little wary of Charles J. Haughey. However, the electorate had a new choice in 1987: the Progressive Democrats, the new party that had been founded by Des O'Malley and Mary Harney. No one could have forecast the success they would enjoy in their first outing.

Harry Casey, a close friend of the McAleeses, was Mary's election agent. Despite his abiding interest in politics, North and South, Casey had never been a member of a political party. His support for Mary in the 1987 election was purely that—support for Mary McAleese, as distinct from support for Fianna Fáil. Apart from Harry Casey's input, the electioneering was mainly a family affair. Martin travelled from either Crossmaglen or Bessbrook after work each evening, and he and Paddy Leneghan, Mary and Harry canvassed door to door the length and breadth of the constituency.

Their canvassing took them from some of the poorest parts of Dublin to some of the wealthiest: from the crowded inner city flats to the leafy avenues around the foreign embassies. They chatted with the people whose main concern was the advancement of Garret FitzGerald's Constitutional Crusade, and they sympathised with those whose concerns were far more basic: unemployment, health cuts and social welfare benefits.

Paddy Leneghan's experience of canvassing was not a happy one. However, his problems did not arise from any difficulties with the electorate.

"I didn't like her brief involvement in politics. I always knew it was a rotten game, but until then I didn't know just how rotten it was. Our greatest enemies were within the Fianna Fáil party. I had better relations with the Fine Gael people than with Mary's own party colleagues in the HQ in Harold's Cross."

In a constituency where four Fianna Fáil candidates were vying for what was realistically one seat, Martin's experience was certain to be similar to that of his father-in-law.

"We got more hassle from the Fianna Fáil supporters than from Fine Gael or Labour. One Sunday morning, for example, I was shouldered out through the gates of Rathgar Church by Michael Donnelly's supporters who were trying to prevent us handing out Mary's campaign literature. We were told to go back where we came from, that we were not wanted."

Mary says: "I was very uncomfortable about being imposed on the constituency. I did not ask to be added to the running order; I was invited, and thinking back on it I don't think I should have accepted the invitation. Although we had some difficulties with supporters of the other Fianna Fáil candidates, I must say that Ger Brady, particularly, acquitted himself like a perfect gentleman at all times. I could find no fault with him or with his supporters."

By election day, 17 February, Mary and Martin had spent more than £5,000 of their own money on the campaign, a substantial sum in 1987. The people of Dublin South-East were classified as the most reluctant electorate in the state that day: just over 56 per cent of the 68,286 on the electoral register turned out to cast their votes. The quota was 7,655, and Garret FitzGerald was elected on the first count with more than 8,000 votes. Mary McAleese was in seventh place out of sixteen candidates, with a total of 2,243 votes, at the end of that first count. As the counting continued, Ger Brady and Ruairí Quinn were elected. Having received few transfers, Mary was eliminated after the eleventh count. She got 503 votes when Eoin Ryan was eliminated, 90 from Aengus Ó Snodaigh and 152 from her "old friends" the Stickies.

The day after the general election Mary said, "I was prepared to do it this time but I'm not sure if I would be prepared to do it again in four or five years time. It is very unlikely that I will ever contest another Dáil election."[‡]

This is a particularly negative view of a campaign which she never expected to win. By way of explanation she says: "I never realised the commitment of time that was involved until the campaign was in full swing. Morning, noon and night I was knocking on doors, meeting constituency workers or preparing speeches; family life was almost non-existent. I also hated the continuous in-fighting. One journalist remarked to me afterwards that he never saw anyone so delighted to lose an election."

The fourth seat in Dublin South-East was eventually won, on the fourteenth count, by Michael McDowell of the Progressive Democrats, a victory which brought the total of the new party's TDs to fourteen. Mary did not spend much time at the count centre that night when it became obvious that she would not be elected, but she was there in plenty of time for the announcements and congratulated those who had succeeded.

---

‡ *The Irish Times*, 18 February 1987.

Although Charles Haughey did not get the numbers required for a single party majority, he managed to form a government with the support of independents like Tony Gregory and Neil Blaney. As Mary had polled well enough to be still in contention by the eleventh count, and as the Fianna Fáil vote in Dublin South-East had increased by 1.5 per cent, Haughey had every reason to be happy with the performance of his new candidate. Senate elections had to be held within ninety days of the dissolution of the Dáil, but Mary showed no interest in fighting another election. It was rumoured at the time that the new taoiseach was considering her as one of his nominees to the Senate, but even this possibility held no interest for her, as was evident from her unwillingness to avoid conflict with the leader of her party. The Single European Act was the political issue that effectively parted the paths of Charles Haughey and Mary McAleese.

Chapter Nineteen

A Farewell to Dublin

But for all that I found there I might as well be
Where the Mountains of Mourne sweep down to the sea.
(Percy French: "The Mountains of Mourne")

The Constitutional Rights Campaign was founded in November 1986 to oppose the ratification of the Single European Act. The two people most closely associated with the embryonic campaign were Raymond Crotty, an agricultural economist who was a part-time lecturer in statistics in Trinity College, and Anthony Coughlan, a sociology lecturer in the same university. They and their supporters were concerned about the implications of the act for Irish neutrality and sovereignty. Crotty and Coughlan were well-known Euro-sceptics; Mary McAleese was a committed European; but it was no secret that Mary and many members of Fianna Fáil had serious reservations about the SEA. When Anthony Coughlan invited Mary to join the campaign she agreed. She and John Carroll, the leader of the Irish Transport and General Workers Union, became joint chairs of the Constitutional Rights Committee.

The committee was not acting in a vacuum. In Cork another group had formed with the same basic objective of blocking the ratification of the Single European Act. This group, People First—*Meitheal,* was led by a husband and wife team Joe Noonan and Mary Linehan, both solicitors. Among the people who were active with them was a woman whose path would later cross that of Mary McAleese in 1997, a young anti-nuclear activist called Adi Roche. Mary's recollection is that she and Adi got on well together. In fact, despite their political differences, of which there were many, the opponents of the SEA all worked very well together.

The Single European Act had already been ratified by every other member state of the European Union, and the Irish government was anxious to endorse it and lodge it with the Italian government by New Year's Day, 1987.‡ The immediate common objective of the Dublin and

---

‡   Italy held the presidency of the European Union at the time.

Cork based groups was to obtain an injunction preventing the Irish government from ratifying the act before Christmas. On their behalf, the Senior Counsel Paul Callan made an application to this effect to the High Court in the name of Raymond Crotty. Justice Dónal Barrington heard the application. On Christmas Eve, the McAleeses and the Leneghans were sitting down to dinner in Rostrevor when the phone call came from Dublin to let Mary know that the injuction had been granted. As in the case of the Nice Treaty several years later, Ireland alone of all the member states of the European Union had obstructed the enactment of a European treaty.

On 18 February 1987, the day after the general election, the High Court decided that the Constitutional Rights Committee's argument in favour of a referendum had no legal basis and that the government was free to ratify the SEA in the Oireachtas. All was not lost, however; the High Court granted the Committee leave to appeal to the Supreme Court. But before the appeal could be lodged, a visiting dignitary to Dublin unwittingly hammered home the wedge that had been loosely lodged between Haughey and McAleese. This visitor was Jacques Delors, the president of the European Commission, who, chequebook in hand, was anxious to persuade the taoiseach-elect of the value of the SEA to Ireland. He did so admirably. Charles Haughey, with the ardour and eagerness of a recent convert, let it be known that the ratification of the SEA was now one his priorities. One member of Fianna Fáil who was not influenced by this sea change was Mary McAleese.

At the start of April, the Supreme Court decided that the government was obliged to put the ratification of the treaty to the people by means of a referendum. In was a victory in principle only for the Committee as the result of the referendum was a foregone conclusion. On 24 May the ratification was carried by a sizeable majority. Mary afterwards consoled herself with the words: "The battle was lost, but at least it was the people who decided."[‡]

Charles Haughey was not impressed with the activities of the woman he had envisaged as a rising star in the Fianna Fáil firmament. After he was elected taoiseach, he changed his mind on some other matters, principally the question of extradition and the Anglo-Irish Agreement. Mary had no great difficulty with extradition.

---

‡ Forty-four per cent of the electorate voted in the referendum on 24 April 1987: 70 per cent for the amendment and 30 per cent against it.

"Permitting extradition is a political decision, but the responsibility for the proper implementation of it, for the protection of the rights of the accused—particularly of those to be extradited to Britain—lies with the courts."

Her attitude towards the Anglo-Irish Agreement—apart from the fact that she did not think it could work—was that she saw nothing wrong with the people of Northern Ireland being granted self-determination. This had been the unionist dictum all along and was now the official position of the Irish government. Presumably it would remain so after unionists ceased to be in the majority in Northern Ireland. She says there will be a special satisfaction to be gained from reiterating the principle of self-determination when there is a nationalist majority in the North.

Although Mary and the Fianna Fáil leader saw eye to eye on these issues, the breaking of ranks on the question of the Single European Act opened a wound that refused to be healed. The festering of the wound became obvious to everyone when a reporter asked Charles Haughey if he had any comment on the obvious disagreements between himself and Mary McAleese, referring to her as ". . . one prominent member of the party clearly not following the party line". Haughey turned to the reporter and asked, "Did you say prominent?"[‡]

The Fianna Fáil party made no attempt to censure her during this time, and she remained a member of the Macken/Markievicz Cumann until she went back to live in the North. Her political activity was very limited after the general election of 1987, and her involvement with Fianna Fáil was almost non-existent. She now had time to concentrate on her studies. She had been conferred with an MA by Trinity College and was working on a PhD thesis on the subject of women in prison. She was content to be finished with party politics and happy to be able to spend her time once again in academic pursuits: researching, writing, teaching and reading; but such tranquillity was not what life had in store for her.

Martin had settled into his dental practice. Although his original intention had been to spend no more than six months working in the North, he was by then a full partner with Des Casey in an expanded and lucrative practice and gave no further thought to working in Dublin. He began to talk of moving the family further north, to somewhere nearer the border. He suggested that if Mary could squeeze her work in Trinity College into a three-day week, she would not have to do much travelling.

---

‡   *Sunday Tribune*, 24 May 1987.

233

This proposal was bolstered by the suggestion that she could spend one or two nights a week with her friend Margot Aspell in Raheny. She would have time and space to herself and could continue her work on her PhD. Mary was not enamoured of these propositions. She was happy where she was, and Martin's partnership in County Armagh had never been part of their plans. But as Martin continued to maintain that his plan was the only sensible solution to a difficult situation Mary capitulated. They put their house in Mooretown on the market with an asking price of £42,000, but there was no immediate interest in it.

There were many reasons why Mary was happy where she was. In Mooretown they had the best of both worlds: they were close enough to Dublin, but lived in the heart of the countryside, and the feeling of leaving the stress of city life behind in the evenings was a tonic in itself. She had her night classes and she had her choir, the people with whom she went to Lough Derg each year. The prayer group that met each week in her house had a central role in her life, although she knew that her husband was not terribly taken with the idea of shared prayer. When they had gone, as a couple, to the big prayer meetings in Eustace Street, Martin had found the singing strange and the handholding and praying in tongues bizarre. When the smaller prayer group began to meet in the McAleese house, he tried it for a couple of weeks, but decided that displays of emotion or the revealing of intimate thoughts, even within the security of a group of friends, was not for him. He refers to it as "hands, knees and bumps-a-daisy Christianity". His own preference was for religion in its more traditional form. He felt that the prayer groups laid too much emphasis on the "God of Miracles", the God who would cure the blind and the lame and the person dying of cancer. Mary, who was more comfortable with miracles, was also comfortable with resignation.

She had accepted the inevitability of an upheaval in her life and had resigned herself to leaving her friends and the house where she had spent ten happy years. When they first began to think seriously about a new place to live, they confined their quest to places south of the border. They were very interested in the coastal village of Blackrock in County Louth, but no suitable house was on the market there. They searched in Carrickmacross, in Castleblayney, Ravensdale and Dundalk, but of the houses that were available none really appealed to them. If they had to cross the border, there was only one place they would consider: Rostrevor. Mary's mother and father and most of the family were living there already.

Paddy and Claire had sold their pub, the Corner House, to Pat Traynor and had bought Glen Villa, a house situated between the Corner House and the chapel in the middle of the town. Paddy had not returned to full health after his heart attack, and for the first time in their lives, he and Claire were taking it easy. When he began to feel stronger again, he worked part-time for Brian O'Hare in the Old Kilowen Inn, not a hundred yards from the Corner House. Later again he and Claire moved into a modern bungalow in the Greendale development in the town.

Mary's deaf brother John had a hairdressing salon in Rostrevor at that time and was living in a rented cottage. He later moved into an apartment owned by Mary and Martin, near his parents' house, when, after he had suffered a stroke, it became obvious that he could no longer work for a living. Kate, who at that time was living in New York, would eventually settle down with her family in Rostrevor. Mary's sister Claire was a nurse in Daisy Hill Hospital in Newry, and she and her husband Brendan Connolly also lived in Rostrevor. Clement was studying law in Queen's University in Belfast, and Phelim was in the Air Corps in Baldonnell, outside Dublin, but their parents' house was still their headquarters. Pat lived a couple of miles away in Warrenpoint and Damien was teaching in England. Nora was not at home at the time but would soon have her own place in Rostrevor. It seemed that you couldn't throw a stone in the town without hitting a Leneghan.

Apart from these family connections, Rostrevor had its own attractions. It is a small, quiet town—a village almost—in a snug, sylvan, south-facing setting between Carlingford Lough and the Mourne Mountains. Mature forests surround it and sweep down the slopes of the hills almost as far as the shore. The gigantic boulder known as *Cloch Mhór* stands stark in a clearing on Slieve Martin to the north, and the Cooley Mountains form a magnificent backdrop to the vista over the lough to the south. Rostrevor even has its own glen, the Fairy Glen, with its stream that tumbles down the mountain, over the Salmon Leap, and through the town to the sea. Although it is a tranquil spot, it has not been unaffected by the Troubles: two members of the RUC and one civilian lost their lives there. But as a place to live and to rear a family, it is safer than most in Northern Ireland, a necessary consideration for Mary and Martin when they had three children under the age of five.

Rostrevor gave Mary her first taste of village life, and she loved it. In many ways it was in complete contrast to her years in Ardoyne and Fruithill Park. Sectarianism, if it existed at all, was never discernible there. Catholics, Church of Ireland, Presbyterians and Methodists all had churches there, but unlike many other places in Northern Ireland, their congregations presented a united face to the world: all one people; a caring, welcoming community. People could be reasonably sure of their personal safety on the streets of Rostrevor, day or night. It had a boys' primary school for Justin and the girls could go to the Mercy Convent, and both schools were close enough to the centre of the town. Among the town's more famous sons are Dr T.K. Whitaker, the former governor of the Central Bank and recipient of the "Greatest Living Irish Person Award" in November 1992, and Ben Dunne, founder of the supermarket chain that bears his name. Rostrevor was about to have an even more famous daughter.

In the month of June 1987, Mary and some of her friends from the prayer group were on a visit to the Revd Cecil Kerr's spiritual sanctuary, the Christian Renewal Centre. As Mary was chatting with Cecil, he mentioned that Dr Wilson's house in the town was for sale. He knew that Mary was considering a move to Rostrevor, and he suggested that she might like to have a look at the house. As soon as Mary saw it she knew it would be too small for a family of five. Dr Wilson mentioned that the next house on the avenue, a house called Ros Ard, was for sale, although there was no sign to that effect outside. Mary liked it as soon as she saw it. When she rang the bell she was invited in by the owner of the property, Mary Carty, and as they moved through the hallway she saw a photograph on the wall.

"Isn't that Brian Carty?" she said. "He was two years ahead of me in the Law School in Queen's. Are you his wife?"

"I'm his widow," replied the woman.

She had four children and wanted to move back to Belfast to be closer to her own family. Over a cup of tea the two women discussed the price of houses, and Mary Carty said she wanted £68,500 for Ros Ard. When she arrived home in Mooretown the next night, Mary told Martin she had found the house they wanted, in Rostrevor. If he was surprised at her news, she was equally surprised at what he had to say: they had been offered £42,000, their asking price, for their own house, and he felt they should accept. Martin was not as immediately taken with Ros Ard as Mary was. Against Mary's better judgment, he asked his friend Seamus Mullan to bargain on their behalf, but Mary Carty would not budge from the price she had originally asked. Eventually the McAleeses accepted. On 15 August, the Feast of the Assumption, bonfire night in the Catholic areas of Belfast, the McAleeses moved into their new home in Rostrevor.

Martin McAleese maintains that there was never a family as clannish as the one into which he married:

> Family gatherings in our house were always Mary's family gatherings. I never met the likes of them for closeness. Every Saturday morning Mary would bake, and it was as if all her family could smell the baking. They would leave their various houses and apartments all over Rostrevor and find their way to our kitchen. They would spend the morning talking and eating brown bread and scones and then go off for the afternoon to do their own shopping. By five o'clock they would be having withdrawal symptoms, and they would have to get together again, back in our kitchen. They are very demonstrative in their love and affection, but all this does not guarantee harmony. The Leneghans would have as many rows as any other family.

Mary did not mind the odd family spat. The Leneghans were a very close-knit group, and spats were merely that—short-lived quarrels. Like her mother and her grandmother before her, she felt a deep joy and sastisfaction at being back among her own people. She also delighted in the unhurried tempo of life in the picturesque seaside town. The speed with which she lived her life and the intensity that she brought to her work found their perfect counterpoint in this slower pace of life. She renamed the house Kairos, a Greek word meaning "opportunity, time, season".‡ It was well named. An opportunity for a new beginning in her life had just presented itself.

Shortly before they moved into Kairos, an old friend of Mary's rang and said he would like to pay her a visit. The caller was Des Greer, professor of law in Queen's University Belfast, the sympathetic counsellor to whom she had brought her worries when she was a student. Former lecturer and former student had met many times over the years as Professor Greer was external examiner for Mary's students in the School of Law in Trinity College. He told Mary that a new director was being sought for the Institute of Professional Legal Studies attached to Queen's University. Mary had read the advertisement for the position months beforehand and had presumed the post was filled. Mainly because she was happy where she was, in Trinity, but also because the advertisement had mentioned that the successful applicant would be a practising lawyer, she had not considered applying.

---

‡ *Chronos* is time itself, *kairos* how the time is used. From a bronze allegoric statue in Sikyon, by the sculptor Lysippos.

Des Greer explained that the selection board had not appointed any of the applicants; that they were now putting together a list of suitable candidates and that they were reserving the right to change the advertised criteria. In other words, in the process of headhunting they might decide to choose an academic lawyer for the position. When he asked her if he could to put her name forward, she replied that she would like to think about it and discuss it with Martin. Since returning to Trinity from RTÉ, she had been much happier in the job and more content in herself; but in the light of the move to Rostrevor, they decided that applying for the directorship would be, at least, another option. Mary rang Des Greer and said she was prepared to let her name go forward.

She then set about finding out as much as she could about the Institute and the post of director. She met the staff and the influential members of both professional legal bodies: the Law Society of Northern Ireland and the Honourable Society of the Inn of Court of Northern Ireland.[‡] After meeting the two solicitors representing the Law Society, she felt that they had set their faces against the appointment of any academic lawyer. She argued her case: that she had read all the reports on legal education; that her area of expertise, pedagogy, was a significant element of the job; that the Institute was a teaching institution and that her forte was teaching the law. She spoke of course construction, of management, of dealing with students, but afterwards she felt that all her talking was to no avail.

The interview panel was chaired by Turlough O'Donnell, lord justice of appeal and chairman of the Council for Legal Education. The selection committee comprised twelve members, and among them were the two solicitors, representatives of the Inn of Court and the university. Even the interrogation she had got from those two men had not prepared her for the quizzing she received from the panel. They questioned her on every aspect of the qualifications and aptitude she would bring to the job, on her work in Trinity College, on the initiatives she had taken there, on the changes she had introduced in the courses she had taught, on her ideas for the Institute . . . By the time she was finished she was exhausted, but she was happy that she had answered all their questions to the best of her ability.

She was at home in Rostrevor that evening when Turlough O'Donnell rang to offer her the job. She was delighted, of course, and said as much

---

‡   The body, as distinct from the professional body, representing barristers is the Bar Council.

on the phone. She also said that she could only accept the job in principle because she had to give notice to Trinity College. When Mary found out that Trinity wanted three months to find a suitable replacement for their Reid Professor, she informed the board of the Institute that she would not be able to work full-time until after Christmas, but that she would be prepared to work part-time until then. The members of the board were happy with this arrangement. Trinity College eventually appointed another Belfast-born Reid Professor, John Larkin.

The Institute of Professional Legal Studies had been set up by the British government on the recommendation of the Armitage Report on legal education and training in 1976. Under this new system, law students were required to spend a vocational year in a university environment, learning the practical skills of drafting, advocacy and client care that would stand them in good stead in their future careers.

Mary's predecessors in the Institute were both Protestants: James Elliott and James Russell. Since comparatively few Catholics held senior positions in the legal professional, and since the directorship of the Institute was an important post in legal circles in Northern Ireland, it was widely expected that a Protestant would be appointed.[‡] When the selection committee had refused to appoint any of the original applicants for the position, they had asked a senior law lecturer from Queen's University to fill the post in a temporary capacity until a permanent director was appointed. This caretaker director was a man who had taught land law to Mary in Queen's, a man by the name of David Trimble. Trimble was not happy when he learned of Mary's appointment, particularly since he also had been a candidate for the position. In fact, he and Mary were the only people interviewed for the job. He was not alone in his disappointment. In the unionist community there was widespread anger and frustration that a Catholic had been appointed to one of the most prestigious positions in the academic legal life of Northern Ireland.

David Trimble's life revolved around Queen's University, the Orange Order and unionism. He had been a lecturer in Queen's since he graduated there in 1968, and his wife Daphne Orr had been one of his undergraduate students. His rise through the unionist ranks was by way of the Vanguard Unionist Party, where he became deputy leader to James Craig. His political pragmatism allowed him to be at one time an

---

‡   In that year, 1987, 95 per cent of the professors in Queen's University were Protestant, and in most departments more than 75 per cent of the lecturers were Protestant.

advocate of UDI and at another time a staunch upholder of the union with Britain. Before he became known for his moderate views and before he became joint winner, with John Hume, of the Nobel Peace Prize, David Trimble was considered a hardline unionist. His militant reputation was greatly enhanced in 1995 when he and Ian Paisley walked shoulder to shoulder down the nationalist Garvaghy Road in Portadown and waved triumphantly to the crowd, their joined hands upraised in victory. His "not an inch" stance on that occasion probably won him the leadership of the Ulster Unionist Party on the resignation of Jim Molyneaux in that same year.

At the time of Mary's appointment, Trimble was chairman of the Lagan Valley Unionist Association, an influential member of the Ulster Unionist Party, and the candidate of choice of many members of that same party for the job as director of the Institute of Professional Legal Studies. There was speculation that the appointment of Mary McAleese was a political choice designed to pacify the Irish government. Unionists drew attention to the stipulation in the original advertisement that the successful candidate would be a practising lawyer, pointing out that Mary McAleese had practised for only one year in the North and never in the South, and neglecting to mention that David Trimble had never practised at all. The campaign of protest at Mary's appointment culminated in the tabling of a motion for debate in the British House of Commons. The four Westminster Unionist MPs who tabled the "early day motion" were all friends and colleagues of David Trimble: Cecil Walker, Roy Beggs, Clifford Forsythe and the man who would later be Trimble's deputy leader of the Ulster Unionist Party, John Taylor.[‡] The motion read:

> That this House, believing in the principles of merit, equal opportunity and fair employment, shares the concern among members of the legal profession and others regarding the appointment of Mary McAleese as Director of the Institute of Professional Legal Studies at Queen's University, Belfast; and calls for an early debate, to establish if the post was advertised for a semi-retired or retired practitioner of several years standing; if Mary McAleese has practical legal experience; if on graduating from Queen's University, Belfast, she went to live and work in another jurisdiction, namely the Republic of Ireland; if she has ever

---

‡ An early day motion is a device usually used to ensure that certain questions or statements go on the official record of the House of Commons. They do not normally generate much interest or publicity.

practised in the jurisdiction of the United Kingdom; if she now spends two days per week on average in Belfast and still lectures in Dublin; the level of salary afforded to the Director of the Institute of Professional Legal Studies at Queen's University, Belfast; the number of lectures given by Mary McAleese since her appointment at Queen's University, Belfast, to date; whether there is validity in the speculation that Mary McAleese was nominated by the Premier of the Republic of Ireland, Charles Haughey, and appointed for political reasons rather than merit; and the number of applications made for the position of Director of the Institute of Professional Legal Studies at Queen's University, Belfast, and the qualifications of each applicant.

As with most early day motions, it was never debated. The reference to the salary of the director of the Institute was an interesting one. The salary was very attractive as it was not linked to the lecturers' scale or even to the professors' scale, but rather to that of County Court judges. The rise represented a considerable increase in the McAleese family income.

Professor Gordon Beveridge, who was vice-chancellor of Queen's University, defended the appointment of Mary McAleese in a statement which effectively put an end to the public criticism. He said that in the opinion of the selection committee, a group representing various legal bodies and eminent institutions, she was the most suitable candidate for the post, and that their decision was final.

Mary has this to say about the whole commotion: "There is a certain type of unionist who cannot bear the thought of any Catholic getting anywhere on their own merits, who cannot abide the idea of any Catholic breaking out of the mould in which they have been kept for years. This was the case with my appointment as director of the Institute. Some of those unionists were choking themselves with bitterness."

At the time, Mary made no public utterance about her detractors' attempts to rescind her appointment, but an incident happened in August 1995 which forced her to break her silence on the subject. A UTV production called *If I Should Die* was being filmed. In the series the subjects—well known people in Northern Ireland life—were to imagine themselves dead, and guests on the show were given the opportunity to speak of them in obituary form. The presenter, the Revd John Dunlop, former moderator of the Presbyterian Church in Ireland, invited Mary to be one of the subjects, and he invited David Trimble to speak about her life and work. Trimble's political antennae must have

241

been suffering a severe bout of insensitivity that day. He raised the subject of her appointment as director of the Institute, saying that she should never have got the job as her qualifications were not good enough and repeating the allegation that her appointment was due to political pressure from the Dublin government.

Mary's response was as succinct as it was incisive: "There were two candidates shortlisted for the Institute. I was one and he was the other. I leave it to people to make up their own minds."

The pro-unionist newspapers in the North were not the only ones that were causing trouble for the new director. Shortly before Mary left Dunshaughlin for Rostrevor, she was interviewed by Fergus Pyle of *The Irish Times* about her move back to the North. She made no reference to work on the PhD but jokingly mentioned that she intended to catch up on her knitting, which she had been neglecting for too long.‡ Two days after that interview was published, on Sunday, 4 October 1987, a photograph of Mary appeared on the front page of the *Sunday Independent*. The headline of the accompanying article proclaimed: "Home Rules—So Mary Returns to Her Knitting".

The article was in the form of an open letter from the *Sunday Independent* journalist, Liam Collins, to Mary McAleese:

> So farewell then Mary McAleese, publican's daughter, self-publicist, professor and conscience of the "set menu" rather than à la carte Catholics.
>
> You who stood with the Bishops in the New Ireland Forum yet were humbled at the polls by a mere Sacristan, Joe Doyle (blueshirt persuasion).
>
> You, who constantly attacked the media, yet used it at every opportunity as a platform to further your own career.
>
> You, who were paraded as the Fianna Fáil answer to Dublin 4 yet failed CJH, while legal colleague and Progressive Democrat Michael McDowell went on to win fame and notoriety.
>
> With what legacy do you leave us, Mary? Is it substantial or will you forever be numbered among those famous for being famous, rather than famous for some achievement?
>
> You came to us in 1975 with the grand title of Reid Professor of Law. It is begrudging of us to say this was mere glorified lectureship. But with your girlish looks and your Northern lilt you made the most of it.

---

‡   *The Irish Times*, 2 October 1987.

Those nasty people in RTÉ called you "that Provo lady" and gave you the boot for double-jobbing, while more acceptable double jobbers (like Mr. Brian Farrell) continue to grin at us from the goggle box.

But soon you were opposing this, supporting that, writing letters to the papers, guesting as a "talking head" on behalf of the great unwashed.

In those confusing days of abortion, contraception, referendum your voice was always heard.

Though you have the knack of falling on your feet, it was something of a surprise to hear you were moving back to what you once described as "the most sectarian State in Western Europe".

As Director of the Institute Professional Legal Studies you will organise vocational courses for barristers in the North. Given the tie-up between the legal profession and politics some may find it surprising that you are swapping Ratoath for sweet Rostrevor.

As you depart with husband Martin and family we remember your words. "To accept that jibe (Home Rule is Rome Rule) from a people who deliberately created a Protestant (sic) for a Protestant people and who make no secret of the fact that they want to get back to that situation. I simply refuse to enter into debate with them."

When she returns home, the once vociferous Mary McAleese intends to confine herself to knitting.[‡]

A week later, on the letters page of the same newspaper, four letters were published in which the writers complained about the treatment of Mary McAleese in the article:

Those who, like Mrs McAleese, oppose the liberal agenda in this country can expect to be head-butted and kicked (metaphorically, of course) in our national media . . .

Observing a journalist venting his spleen is never a pretty sight, but when it is done to launch a personal attack and abuses a position of easy access to the media, it is seen at its most reprehensible . . .

Liam Collins' peevish and mean-minded article . . .

What an unpleasant display of jeering journalism . . .[§]

---

‡ *Sunday Independent*, 4 October 1987.

§ *Ibid.*, 11 October 1987.

243

One letter supported what Liam Collins had to say:

> I want to congratulate Liam Collins for his article on Mary McAleese. This woman came down here to meddle in the affairs of women—women who have not had the advantage of a free education all the way through to university, received from the British . . .[‡]

It was the only letter that did not have the writer's name attached. In the same edition of the newpaper, a small article appeared under the title "Mrs Mary McAleese":

> In relation to an article about Mrs Mary P. McAleese last Sunday, we wish to state that any possible inference from that article that Mrs McAleese had any connection or association with, or any sympathy for the Provisional IRA, or that she had been dismissed by RTÉ for double-jobbing, is totally without foundation. We wish to apologise to Mrs McAleese for any such possible inference.[§]

The apology was published after Neil Faris from the firm of Cleaver Fulton Rankin, solicitors in Belfast, had demanded such in a letter to the editor of the *Sunday Independent:* "We require you at this stage to publish a full and unequivocal apology and retraction on the front page of your next issue of 11 October to be given equal prominence with the original article."[†]

Mary says the demand was made because she was furious, hurt and, most importantly, fearful for the safety of her family and herself in the light of the "Provo lady" reference in the article, which was particularly worrying as they were by that time living north of the border. When the *Sunday Independent* replied that they would be unable to publish the apology on the front page of their newspaper, she instituted legal action against them. Compensation was not mentioned at that stage.

The legal proceedings were initiated in the Republic and in Northern Ireland, as the newspaper is read in both jurisdictions. Eugene F. Collins & Co. were her solicitors in Dublin, and Michael O'Mahony of McCann Fitzgerald Sutton Dudley represented the newspaper. In the statement Mary made to her lawyers, she said, among other things, that her professional capability had been impugned; that she had never been dismissed from RTÉ; that a connection between her and the Provisional IRA had been formed in

---

‡   *Ibid.*, 11 October 1987.

§   *Ibid.*

†   Mary McAleese, private papers.

244

readers' minds, and that her own safety and that of her family had been put at risk by the article.

The barristers John P. Trainor and John Farrell prepared the statement of claim for Mary. The legal teams, when they were assembled, were formidable: Garrett Cooney and Fred Morris (who would later become president of the High Court) represented Mary, and Niall Fennelly and Kevin Feeney represented the *Sunday Independent*. After a couple of months, Mary's legal team endorsed Neil Faris's original opinion that they would never get as far as the courtroom. The case was to be heard in the High Court in Dublin on 17 November 1988. Garrett Cooney, whom Mary met for the first time when they arrived in the Four Courts, was of the opinion that she could obtain a large sum in compensation, but Mary maintained that an apology, dictated by her, on the front page of the *Sunday Independent*, was more important to her than financial reparation.

Justice McKenzie empanelled the jury, and Kevin Feeney was the first barrister to speak. He asked the judge's permission for a short recess in an attempt to settle the case. During the interlude, the representatives of the newspaper said they would be unable to publish the apology on the front page as a meeting of the board of the paper would be required to sanction that. They were prepared to pay a large sum in settlement. Mary McAleese was not satisfied, so in they went again. Feeney asked for another pause in proceedings to consult with his client again. This time they agreed to an apology on the front page, but Mary McAleese could not dictate it. Mary was still not satisfied, so in they went again.

At last an agreement was reached in respect of the actions in both jurisdictions. An apology, dictated by Mary, would appear in a prominent position on the front page of the next issue of the newspaper, accompanied by a photograph of Mary, chosen by herself. In the apology, the editor accepted that the allegations in the original article were without foundation, and that they had caused Mary McAleese considerable distress. Costs were awarded to the plaintiff. Mary accepted the prohibition not to reveal the amount of the damages, but it was enough to buy all the Leneghans a present each and to give her parents, her aunts and uncles and their spouses a weekend in a fine hotel in Dublin. Some money went to Concern and some to charities for the deaf, and there was enough left to put a sizeable deposit on an apartment in Ballsbridge in Dublin 4. Shortly after the apartment was bought, one of the Leneghans christened it "Independent House".

Brendan Clifford, the publisher and editor of *A Belfast Magazine*, must have been paying scant attention, if any, to the proceedings of the libel case in Dublin. He published a libellous article about Mary in the August/September 1988 edition of his magazine. The two-page spread, entitled "The Knitting Professor", was remarkably similar to the offending article in the *Sunday Independent*, and Mary dealt with *A Belfast Magazine* exactly as she had dealt with the Dublin newpaper. Legal proceedings were instituted against Brendan Clifford, as editor and publisher of the magazine, and against Eason & Sons (Northern Ireland) Ltd, its distributors. Donal Deeney, the well known QC who would later become chairman of the Arts Council of Northern Ireland, represented Mary and cited nineteen grounds for defamation in the statement of claim. No apology was ever published because, although the damages were reputed to be small, they were enough to put the cheaply produced magazine out of business.

Mary had been attacked many times in print over the years but had never, until then, taken a libel case against any publication. In explanation of her actions at the end of the eighties, she says: "Going back to live in the North in 1987 marked a change in my life, a new beginning, and I decided that I was no longer prepared to be a victim. If people were going to attack me in public, they would have to be ready for a fight. Much more importantly, the articles in the *Sunday Independent* and *A Belfast Magazine* endangered more than me; they put Martin and the children at risk, and I was not prepared to allow anyone to do that."

Mary had good reason to be fearful for her personal safety. There were people on both sides of the political divide for whom rumour was justification enough for murder. In many cases, even rumour was not required. No profession was immune from the assassin's bullets and bombs, and lawyers and university lecturers suffered their share of casualties. Edgar Graham, a law lecturer in Queen's University and Ulster Unionist member of the Northern Ireland Assembly, was shot dead by the IRA as he got out of his car outside the university library. Miriam Daly, another Queen's lecturer and a H-Block activist who succeeded Seamus Costello as chairperson of the Irish Republican Socialist Party, was shot dead by the UDA. No one on either side of the divide was safe. Mary has often said that her best strategy in the face of such danger was "to keep my soul in a state of grace", and she attributes this defence tactic to the late Judge Rory Conaghan from Derry.

Conaghan was one of the very few Catholic judges on the Northern Ireland bench and the youngest, at forty-five years of age, when he was appointed in 1965. He was famous as the judge who sent Ian Paisley to prison. Mary was in his company in the Bar library one day when a colleague asked him if he had bullet-proof glass in his windows and steel sheeting in his doors. Conaghan replied that he did not. He felt that if terrorists wanted to kill him he could not stop them. He asserted that his only defence was to keep his soul in a state of grace. Mary laughed as loudly as anyone else in the library that day. Two months later the judge was dead, shot by an IRA gunman through a window of his home as he had breakfast with his wife and his eight-year-old daughter. He was the first of three senior judges to be killed, the others being Lord Justice Maurice Gibson and Judge William Doyle.[‡] After Rory Conaghan's death, Mary considered his words in the library and now describes them as "the most important lesson I ever learned".

On the question of death threats, Mary's abiding emotion was neither fear nor worry but disgust. Shortly after she started working in the Institute, she received an anonymous phone call. The unknown male caller reviled her with abuse and scorn and then stated unambiguously that she would be shot. Soon afterwards she received a similar call from the same man, and then a letter. The envelope contained a single A4 page of photocopying paper and contained, amid a torrent of invective, a death threat. By the time the third call came, Mary was as certain as she could possibly be that, despite the venomous tone of the messages, her life was not in danger.

She said nothing to Martin about the threats as she did not want to worry him unduly. She did not contact the RUC as she felt nothing could be proved, and the attention that an investigation would inevitably draw on her could only do her harm. Like many people who lived through the thirty years of the Troubles, the McAleeses are not easily frightened. Martin drove every day through the area that was once described by a senior British army officer as "the most dangerous part of Europe"—south Armagh—but neither he nor Mary was especially timorous about that. However, Martin was worried about Mary's security in view of the controversy surrounding her appointment as director of the Institute and because of the amount of night driving she did. Mary, however, had no intention of being an easy target for any terrorist. She never travelled exactly the same route to her office, nor arrived at the same time on any two consecutive mornings. She also examined her car carefully before opening it every day. Despite her assertion that she was in the state of grace, she was in no great hurry to shrug off her mortal coil.

---

‡   Several Northern Ireland magistrates were also killed during the course of the Troubles.

Chapter Twenty

God Save Queen's

O Lord our God arise, scatter her enemies,
And make them fall.
Confound their politics, frustrate their knavish tricks,
On thee our hopes we fix:
God save us all.
                    ("God Save the Queen"—anonymous)

The Institute of Professional Legal Studies had a chequered history of discontent with both legal professions. In the early years the professional bodies continued to operate their own separate education schemes in tandem with the Institute, but under the terms of its establishment the Institute was gradually to appropriate this role completely.

Problems arose when the professional bodies no longer had control over who would have access to their professions. Some of the more stolid and rigid practitioners of the law found it hard to accept that the old nepotistic system, whereby sons and daughters of lawyers and their friends often got preferential treatment, was inimical to any concept of justice or equality. The only solution was to devise an instrument that would objectively differentiate between students, and so Mary insisted on competitive entry based exclusively on an entrance examination. There was outrage when this was first mooted, but eventually common sense and common decency prevailed.

Some years before her appointment, the Law Society had effectively threatened to close the Institute by removing their imprimatur. When she took over, she asked them to address any complaints to her or to the Council of Legal Studies, the governing body of the Institute. They took her at her word. Many of their concerns were found to be groundless, but they were able to suggest some ways in which the work of the Institute could be improved. Mary wisely accepted their suggestions and was able to implement some worthwhile changes as a result of the open engagement. A year after her appointment, she was invited to lunch by the two solicitors who had quizzed her so vigorously prior to her interview.

248

She accepted the invitation with reluctance, only to find the men perfectly charming and magnanimous in their praise for her work in running the Institute. They also assured her that she could count on their full support in the future. Quite a while later, she learned the reason for their satisfaction and why her relations with the Bar Council had become so cordial. Basically, both professional bodies appreciated her willingness to lift the phone and ask their advice when she felt it was appropriate.

The next problem Mary had to overcome concerned the institution to which the Institute was attached, Queen's University itself. The Institute did not fit well into the Faculty of Law, was not situated on the university campus and was outside the faculty and department structures. It did not fit the usual academic shape of things. The students found themselves outside the normal information circuits and social networks, and the staff did not have the same advancement and promotion prospects as their colleagues in Queen's. For these reasons, and also to ensure their future security in the event of a serious dispute with the professional legal bodies, Mary set out to bond the Institute as closely as possible with Queen's University and to draw it completely into the mainstream of university life.

Her first steps in this direction were hobbled by an unforeseen problem with the Student Union and with its president, Tim Atwood, brother of the SDLP politician Alex Atwood. A rumour began to gain currency among the student body that candidates for the Institute would have to undergo psychological screening. The Student Union took up the case and demanded that the proposed testing should not take place. The officers of the union, who were predominantly nationalist, were convinced that the newly appointed nationalist director of the Institute would support them in their demand. Mary explained that the tests were not compulsory; that the Department of Psychology in the university was conducting a long term study on the correlation between the results of the admission test and the students' end-of-year results; that only general patterns were sought and that the tested students would maintain their anonymity. The tests did not impact on any student's admission to the Institute or to the legal profession. But the Student Union stood firm. They wanted no psychological tests. Mary also stood firm. She thought the tests would be worthwhile. The students took their case to the Board of Visitors. When their appeal was rejected, the Student Union were far from happy with the new director. The fact that Mary remained adamant on the question of the tests redounded very much to her credit with others, academic staff included.

She was not long in the job when she introduced an initiative that had not been seriously considered until then: job sharing for women members of the academic staff! For some reason the university authorities had long maintained that such a practice would be unworkable. When the Institute's teaching staff began to jobshare, and when the Institute did not fall into total disarray and anarchy, job sharing became easier throughout the university.

The Institute of Professional Legal Studies in Belfast was constantly enhancing its standing and became highly regarded for its teaching of client counselling, negotiation, mediation and its pioneering work in computer-based learning and the use of video as a training technique; it was soon leading the field in Ireland and Britain in the area of advocacy training. As its reputation grew, Mary was invited more and more to travel as a visiting lecturer to universities in other parts of the world. In the United States, she spent two weeks teaching in the William Mitchell School of Law in Minneapolis and also lectured in the George Washington University and Catholic University in Washington. She was guest lecturer at the Council of Legal Education's Institute of Advocacy in Oxford and the Lord Chancellor's Advisory Committee's Conference on Legal Education and Training. She also lectured at the Universities of Bristol and Newcastle. She was an adviser to the Joint Forum on Legal Training in Dublin and was external examiner for the School of Law in Nottingham and the Law Society of England and Wales. Visiting other legal training institutions was something of a symbiotic process, as Mary explains:

> I really enjoyed my visits to universities in other countries. I often learned as much as I imparted, and both the Institute and I benefited in many ways from some of the ideas I brought home. One of the more useful of these had its origin in England and was called the Plain English Campaign. Its aim was to persuade lawyers to use ordinary, everyday words instead of arcane phraseology. I once asked a class of about seventy students to draft a simple lease which would be of use to a person renting a flat, the lease being due to end on a certain date. Not one of them used the word "end". We had "the lease will terminate" and "the lease will determine", but no simple "the lease will end". After that I became an even more staunch supporter of the Plain English Campaign.

Mary's own institute was, by its very nature, progressive and innovative. It had to be. There was no place like it in Ireland, England or Wales, as a university-based institute for the training of both solicitors and barristers was a radical departure from previous models of legal training. One of the reasons often mooted for its success is its small scale. In Northern Ireland around seventy solicitors and perhaps twenty barristers are trained each year. In England there were law firms which took in twice that number of apprentices and ran their own in-house law schools. But England and Wales began to see the value of legal training institutes attached to universities, and Mary was called in as a course design consultant for a number of the new projects.

She invited lecturers from the National Institute of Advocacy in America to give seminars in Belfast, and she established a competition between the Institute in Belfast and the King's Inns in Dublin. One of her part-time lecturers was Brian Doherty, a government lawyer and Northern Ireland's leading expert on European law. In keeping with her belief in the importance of the European dimension in both the training of lawyers and in the practice of law, she invited him to devise a course with emphasis on his particular area of expertise. Also, at her instigation, the Law Society invited John Temple Laing, of the European Commission, to lecture on the importance of a broader view of European law among lawyers in Northern Ireland. She entered her students in the long-established Louis M. Brown International Client Counselling Competition, the biggest competition of its kind in the world, and one which attracts teams from every country that practises the common law. The Institute performed very well from the start, and year after year the Belfast students proved to be among the best in the world.

If it was her aim to make the Institute of Professional Legal Education the best of its kind in these islands, she was well on her way to achieving her goal. She also found time to realise her other ambition by immersing herself in the life of the university. As each year passed, Mary McAleese's name appeared on the register of more and more committees, councils and boards: the Academic Council, the Board of Curators, the Committee of Deans, the Council of Legal Education, the Executive Board, the Teaching and Learning Committee, the Planning and Resources Committee . . . With each new appointment, Mary, and the institute she directed, were becoming more and more well-known, and more importantly, the Institute and Queen's University were being drawn ever closer together. Of all the groups in which she served, one of the most important to her was the Equal Opportunities Group.

She had a deep interest in the subject and introduced the teaching of the law and practice of equal opportunities and fair employment into the curriculum of the Institute. She also attended several courses on the topic. They covered fields such as religion, race, disability, gender and age—areas where the potential for bias lurked. Education and training in equality were sorely needed in Queen's University. In 1989, the result of an investigation by the Fair Employment Commission showed that Queen's was guilty of unfair practices, and the authorities were warned to rectify the situation. An independent group of advisers made more than one hundred suggestions as to how the authorities could re-invent the university as a fair employer of nationalists and women. Big changes were in store for some of the deep-rooted customs of the place. The authorities decided that equality training would be compulsory for all university employees. Mary was among the small group of trainers selected to promote a new culture of inclusivity. Among them were lawyers, psychologists, human resource personnel and sociologists. Specialists were called in to train them in how to train others. The work was arduous at first but got progressively smoother as they toiled their way through the more than three thousand employees.

Mary was chair of a group that, among other things, heard appeals and complaints from students and staff. One appeal came from a man called Ronnie McCartney, who had spent seventeen years in prison for shooting at a policeman in Southampton. His counsellor at the appeal was the one-time Sinn Féin Councillor Máirtín Ó Muilleoir, who says that McCartney had obtained a degree in social science but was refused a place on the vocational course in Queen's which would have qualified him as a social worker. He quotes a representative of the course who spoke at the appeal: "As social work professionals, we have to ask ourselves if it is appropriate that offenders and ex-prisoners should be allowed to enter a profession such as social work, which we hold very dear."

Mary McAleese asked the representatives of the course if, in their opinion, McCartney would win a legal appeal against the university.

"I don't know," was the reply.

"I don't know may not be good enough in this case," she replied. The appeal was allowed.[†]

Mary remembers the case: "There was no legal basis for the decision of the course representatives. Apart from that, one would think that a person who has spent seventeen years in prison would bring a certain understanding to social work."

---

† From the notes of Máirtín Ó Muilleoir.

Although Mary was known as "Professor" while she worked in Trinity College, when she travelled to Belfast the title did not travel with her. As director of the Institute she had no academic title other than "director", but in 1993 Queen's University decided to make her a full professor of law. It was widely seen as due recognition for her and for the work she was doing, and it also added considerably to the status of the Institute, encouraged the staff and greatly pleased the Law Society and the Bar Council.

Mary enjoyed a very generous salary. Shortly after her appointment as director, the County Court judges, with whose scale her salary was linked, got a significant pay rise, and later got two retrospective rises. Her financial position was very comfortable, but more senior professors in some other departments were not earning as much as she was, a fact that caused a certain amount of resentment. Another difficulty with Mary's high salary was that it came from the Institute's purse, and their budget was not designed to allow for such a salary. She was embarrassed and uncomfortable with this situation, particularly as she was financial controller of the Institute. She spoke to the bursar of the university, James O'Kane, and proposed that she would link her salary to the professorial scale, a proposal that was heartily welcomed and a gesture that was worth making, she says.

James O'Kane, as bursar, understood her fiscal ability. Queen's University had its own travel company, QUB Travel, which was on the point of bankruptcy. O'Kane asked her to help him rescue the company. Mary obliged, and within a very short time the company was in the black again. Within a year they were able to sell it, for a nice profit, to USIT, the travel company of the Union of Students in Ireland. Very soon she was elected to several other groups and boards where her financial acumen was used to great advantage: the Finance Committee, the Remuneration Committee, the Deans' Business Group. She was also appointed representative of the university on the Belfast Strategy Group for Business in the Community.

As well as displaying a propensity for financial affairs, she was also adept at obtaining money from people, groups and companies to fund worthwhile educational projects. The Institute was located in an old building in Upper Crescent, just a couple of hundred yards from the university, but the accommodation was appalling and the surroundings were not conducive to study. The building itself was small, dark and gloomy, but the university was slow to acknowledge the need for a change. Mary's invitation to the Attorney-General Sir Nicholas Lyle to visit the decrepit building persuaded him of the value of moving into a more modern building. His views, along with pressure from Sir Basil Kelly, chairman of the Council of Legal Education, ensured that the Institute was relocated to a fine building in Lennoxvale.

Mary always had a particular interest in the education of deaf people, especially those, like her brother John, who were profoundly deaf from birth. She felt that few members of the deaf community got the educational opportunities they deserved; that most of them fell by the wayside in the secondary schools and that very few of them progressed to third level. Her eyes were opened to the educational possibilities for the deaf when she went to visit her brother John when he was in hospital in Germany after having a stroke while on holiday there.

John had suffered a heart attack three months previously in London. It had not been diagnosed as such, and he had been given medication for a stomach ulcer. The doctors in Berlin were mystified by the medication because they had discovered the previous heart attack but could find no sign of an ulcer. Because of the stroke he was unable to move his mouth properly, and because his right hand and arm were paralysed, he was able to sign with his left hand only. Neither the doctors nor Mary were able to understand what John was trying to tell them. All became clear when some of John's deaf German friends arrived. Not only were they able to understand two-handed and one-handed sign language, but they were also able to translate for the doctors in German and for Mary in perfectly fluent English. Mary was amazed by their linguistic skills and by the educational system that had developed them. She had already introduced a course of training in sign language for students at the Institute, the first of its kind in Europe, but now she saw a chance to do more.

When she came home from Berlin, she contacted Dr Roddy Cowie, a psychologist who had a special interest in the education of the deaf, and together they drafted a research proposal on deaf education which they presented to British Telecom. The latter's cheque for £100,000 gave birth to one of the most important educational initiatives Mary was ever associated with: Project Succeed.

Queen's University organised the first ever conference on the education of the deaf in Northern Ireland. As guest speaker they invited Professor Michael Schwartz, the deaf lawyer and lecturer from Rochester College in New York, where the National Institute of Technology for the Deaf is situated. He gave a superb lecture, in sign language, while his wife, Patricia Moloney, gave a simultaneous translation.

Despite her involvement in so many activities, Mary still found the time to engage in a significant amount of research: surveys on attitudes to imprisonment, studies on the incarceration of children, etc.— research that one might expect from an academic lawyer with a particular interest in penology. But her interest in the use of computers and information technology in the training of lawyers was reflected in a body of research she conducted in the early nineties, developing computer-based tutorials in criminal procedure. In 1992 Mary, in association with Dr Patrick Branningan and Dr George Munroe, published a document under the auspices of BILETA.[‡] She had conferred with Professor John Gardner, an educationalist and co-director of the Centre for Computer Based Learning in Queen's, and had also invited two other experts to join her group: John Sayle, a computer programming expert, and Barry Valentine, a barrister, author and tutor in the Institute. Valentine was also an authority on criminal procedure, the first subject they dealt with in their research. An excerpt from the foreword to the document gives an idea of what they set out to achieve:

> We chose Criminal Procedure (Indictment) for our first venture. Having taught Criminal Law and Procedure for nigh on seventeen years Mary McAleese was aware how great was the gap between the "L.A. Law" laden student perception and the reality of plodding through a minefield of rickety rules and regulations which could reduce the most sensational fact situation to something about as exciting as a dentist's waiting room. Yes, Criminal Procedure needed to be glamorised.[§]

The remarks in the foreword may be unascribed, but no great powers of deduction are necessary to identify the author. This work was not research purely for the sake of research. In trials conducted in the Institute, an average 6 per cent higher mark in the final examinations was attained by those who used the programme.

Within seven years the Institute had a fine cohort of young academic/practitioner lawyers, well trained in teaching the practice of law and with an attractive career structure. Formerly, the permanent senior lecturing posts had been held by senior lawyers who had joined

---

[‡] BILETA: the British and Irish Legal Education Technology Association. In 2002, Mary McAleese was appointed president of BILETA. Lord Saville of Newdigate, the judge who conducted the Second Bloody Sunday Inquiry, was her vice-president.

[§] Mary McAleese, private papers.

the Institute on retirement from practice. Younger people had, as a consequence, found promotions almost impossible. All that had now changed.

Before Mary became director, few people in Queen's, apart from those in the Faculty of Law, knew much about the work of the Institute, but within seven years the university itself was reaping the harvest of the Institute's work and good name. The authorities in Queen's recognised in her the same charisma and persuasiveness that would not be lost on Fianna Fáil elected representatives three years later. Exactly seven years after she took on the mantle of director of the Institute of Professional Legal Studies, the university honoured her with a position never before held by a woman, a post in which only one Catholic, her friend Professor Seán Fulton, had ever served.

It was a fine evening in September 1994, and Paddy and Claire Leneghan were driving home to Rostrevor. They turned on the car radio just in time for the first item on the *Ten O'Clock News*: "Professor Mary McAleese has been appointed pro-vice-chancellor of Queen's University, Belfast. She becomes the first woman and only the second Catholic ever to hold this position . . ."

Paddy remembers very well his feelings on hearing the news:

My first reaction was to ask, "Why?" I had more of a sense of surprise than a sense of pride or an urge to go and tell people about it. I was more amazed that Queen's would appoint a Catholic woman to that position than that my daughter had been appointed. Of course, when I got over the initial amazement it made a lot of sense. Nobody deserved it more than Mary, but Catholics in Belfast did not always get what they deserved. I was very proud of Mary's achievement, because it was an achievement. It was one of the great highlights of my life.

In the hierarchy of Queen's University, the Chancellor Sir David Orr was akin to the chairman of the board; the Vice-Chancellor Sir Gordon Beveridge was like the chief executive and the three pro-vice-chancellors acted as deputy chief executives. The decision to elevate Mary was a closely guarded secret. In spite of the quality of her contacts, both high level and low level, she heard not a whisper of her impending promotion. The first she knew was when Sir Gordon Beveridge asked her to pay him a visit in his office and officially informed her that she was to be offered the job. Mary's immediate response was that she would have to think about it. She said she would have to consult Sir Anthony Campbell, chairman of the Council for

Legal Education, to find out if he would release her from some of her duties in the Institute in order properly serve the university in her new capacity.

Sir Anthony Campbell and the Council for Legal Education were very happy to accommodate her by reshaping her duties in the Institute. The Law Society and the Bar Council were delighted, and there were wide grins of satisfaction on the faces on her two solicitor supporters. The Institute was now immersed as deeply as it possibly could be in the life of the university. Mary regretted that she would no longer be able to spend as much time as she used to in the Institute that she had moulded and nurtured. She would no longer be doing much teaching there, and this was the biggest regret of all.

In response to the new situation, Anne Fenton, a senior lecturer in the Institute, was appointed assistant-director. Her appointment was a great help, but Mary was still director and still had full responsibility. The situation was unlike her previous double-jobbing experience in two notable respects: firstly, no one was complaining this time, and secondly, she found the double responsibility onerous. Little by little, however, her teaching duties lessened, and eventually her functions were purely those of an administrator and policy maker.

Mary's principal responsibility as pro-vice-chancellor of the university was in the area of external relations, and it was an extensive brief. As part of her duties she was expected to explain university policy decisions to the public, when it was thought necessary. She was barely three weeks in the job when one of these policy decisions proved to be very controversial, and Mary McAleese was given a baptism of fire as QUB spokesperson. Ironically, although the decision to change the policy in question was made before Mary's appointment, she is still associated in the minds of many people with the university Senate's resolution to discontinue the routine playing of "God Save the Queen" at all graduation ceremonies.

By long-standing tradition the RUC band played the British national anthem at graduation ceremonies in Queen's University. Year after year, nationalist graduates faced the same dilemma: would they go against their principles and stand for "God Save the Queen" and perhaps earn the opprobrium of their fellow nationalists, or would they refuse to stand and create a tension that might spoil the special day for themselves and their families. Year after year, no matter what they did, the day was spoiled for many people. The fact that it was also the custom for the RUC band to play at all graduations only added to the controversy.

257

Before Mary's appointment as pro-vice-chancellor, and therefore as an *ex-officio* member of the Senate of the university, the Senate had appointed a working group, under the chairmanship of Robin Shanks, to examine the proposals of the Fair Employment Commission and the Advisory Group on Equal Opportunities. One of the strongest submissions of both groups was the creation of an appropriately neutral and harmonious working environment in the university. The main task of Shanks's working group was to identify any practices or procedures that militated against the desired ethos in Queen's. Their report was formidable and contained a range of propositions, including the suggestion that the British national anthem was overused. When they examined the practice in British universities, they discovered that the anthem was not usually played there except when a member of the British royal family was present. They advised that it should not be played if it could be perceived as partisan. In their report they also mentioned overuse of loyal toasts and a suggestion that the RUC band would be part of a rota of bands that would play at ceremonies. The presence of the RUC band demanded an armed RUC and British army presence, and the overweening militarism of the occasion was not conducive to a neutral and harmonious environment.

When the report went to the Senate it was robustly discussed and debated, but the vote eventually determined that the recommendations would be accepted. The media erroneously reported the abolition of the British national anthem at Queen's graduating ceremonies as well as the termination of the RUC band's connection with the university. In unionist circles it was seen as a nationalist plot and the "greening" of a great bastion of the Protestant unionist establishment. Coinciding as it did with the appointment of Mary McAleese, and the fact that she had the job of explaining these changes to the public, all connections pointed to a Catholic nationalist conspiracy. No matter what she said they would not listen. They saw her hand in the decision of the Senate, and nothing would convince them otherwise. On that occasion, and on that question, Mary's renowned persuasiveness seemed to count for very little.

It was the exception that proved the rule. The inequality issues in QUB had damaged the university's image, and financial support from within the nationalist population was at a low ebb. Mary was charged with changing that image and with finding ways of promoting good relations with some of the wealthier alumni and others who might be interested in donating much-needed funds. Gordon Beveridge had commissioned a report on external relations. The author of the report, a Scot by the name of Ian Moore, recommended that the university engage the services of a public relations firm to work on their behalf. Mary favoured this suggestion and was delighted when the university accepted the proposal.

A working group from Queen's selected Drury Communications Ltd from Clonskeagh in Dublin, a company that had recently successfully completed a similar assignment for University College Dublin. Tom Kelly, former deputy chairman of the SDLP and a director of the company, was the person who supervised the project for Queen's. As part of their work the company canvassed the attitudes of some well-known wealthy people in Northern Ireland to donations to Queen's University. Among them was Martin Naughton, founder of the Glen Dimplex Group. He and his wife Carmel had endowed the Martin Naughton Fellows Programme in Irish Studies, which allowed for the interchange of scholars between the University of Notre Dame in America, University College Dublin and Trinity College Dublin. Despite his obvious interest in academic funding, he had never, until then, been approached by Queen's University, and he let it be known that he was interested in making a substantial donation provided the monies were designated for use in the field of management studies.

The message was not graciously received at board level. Some members expressed the view that the university should be free to use the donation as it saw fit. Mary could barely contain her anger at what she saw as the churlishness which could so easily jeopardise a sizeable contribution. "Do you want his money or not?" she asked the members of the board. "It's his money. Should he not have a say in how it is used?" This time her persuasiveness held little of her distinctive charisma, but was tinged with a certain amount of intimidation. It worked. Word went back to Naughton that the university would be delighted to hear his ideas. Queen's received a donation of a quarter of a million pounds to part-fund, at the donor's request, a professorship of management. Martin Naughton also proved to be a generous contributor to Mary's election campaign two years later.

There were large parts of Northern Ireland, notably those places west and south of Lough Neagh, where the population had no easy access to higher education. As pro-vice-chancellor, Mary was given the task of addressing this situation by founding centres for distance learning. The first of these projects was to be situated in Armagh and would take the form of an Outreach campus of Queen's University. Once a suitable premises was obtained, lecturers from Queen's could travel there to teach, and students could join in lectures and tutorials in the university itself by means of videoconferencing technology.

Mary initially made some contacts in Armagh City Council. Des Mitchell, clerk of the Council, was particularly helpful in introducing her to the right people and in helping her to make her way through the maze of red tape. With the help of Gary Sloane and Sharon Steele, she found a suitable location at 39 Abbey Street, the former county infirmary, which was founded in 1774 by Archbishop Richard Robinson. This was only the starting point. The old building needed a makeover to make it suitable as a campus; interviews were to be conducted, staff appointed, a programme and syllabus constructed. A set of community-orientated, life-long learning programmes was designed to increase participation in higher education by women, part-time mature students and those with non-traditional qualifications. Incredibly, within a year the first students were enrolled in extra-mural and certificate programmes, primary degrees and masters courses. Among those who were amazed and delighted at the speed and efficiency with which the Outreach campus was established was one of the men who had complained about her in the Westminster parliament when she was appointed director of the Institute. In September 1995, exactly a year after Mary's appointment as pro-vice-chancellor, John Taylor, the local Unionist Member of Parliament, stood at the opening ceremony of the Armagh campus of Queen's University Belfast, proudly avowing his gratification that Mary McAleese had done a wonderful job of founding such a worthwhile institution in his own city. He would later be one of the first to congratulate her on her nomination by Fianna Fáil as their presidential candidate.

The Omagh project did not work along the same lines as the Armagh campus. Third-level students were already studying in Omagh College under very good teachers who were accredited to Queen's as part-time tutors and lecturers. The problem was that in order to complete their degrees the students had to travel to Belfast. Mary's aim was to build on what was there already and to ensure that degree courses could be completed in Omagh. This was one of the areas in which she was deeply involved when she was elected president.

Mary was President of Ireland when Omagh was devastated by that horrific bomb on 15 August 1998. She knew many people in the town through her work in the Outreach programme; people such as Seamus Devlin, the director of Omagh College, and John McKinney, chief executive of Omagh District Council. Such was her respect and affection for the town and the people of the town that she rejected security advice and insisted on travelling to Omagh the day after the tragedy.

The establishment of the Outreach programmes was an important milestone in the history of education in Northern Ireland in that it made third-level education accessible to many people outside the cities, people for whom it was previously only a fantasy. It was probably Mary McAleese's most important contribution during her tenure as pro-vice-chancellor.

Peter Froggat was vice-chancellor of Queen's before he became chairman of the board of directors of the Ulster American Folk Park, a few miles from Omagh. He and his colleague Eric Montgomery asked Queen's to consider establishing a degree course in emigration studies in the Folk Park, and because of her Outreach experience, Mary was asked to investigate the feasibility of the suggestion. As well as the famous Folk Museum, the park also boasts the finest library on emigration studies in the country. This, combined with a highly qualified academic staff, state-of-the-art lecture and seminar rooms and the most modern audio-visual equipment, made their case a strong one. Mary's comment on their request for an under-graduate module was that they were not ambitious enough. She saw it as a perfect location for a masters course in emigration studies and formed a steering group in Queen's University to support the idea.

By now there were Outreach programmes west of the Bann and south of Lough Neagh, but still Mary was not satisfied. The icing on her Outreach cake would be a cross-border venture, and she had her own ideas about that. She had read an article written by Ian Hughes, a young scientist from Queen's, about mobile phones and electromagnetic fields. She made a point of meeting him to compliment him on his ability to express the complicated scientific concepts in a well-written, interesting and straightforward manner. The result of her meeting with the young scientist was an insight into the number of science-based articles appearing daily in newspapers and popular magazines, on subjects such as agriculture, medicine, natural sciences, electronics, etc. He pointed out that most of these articles were written by journalists who had no science credentials, or by scientists who had no journalistic background. He spoke of the mutual benefits of a masters degree in science communication, and in Mary he had a keen listener.

One of the beauties of the idea was that it would not be unduly onerous on any of the justly famed QUB science departments. Each area would have a small input to make up an attractive package.

Unfortunately, at that time, Queen's lecturers were inundated with research assessment exercises and teaching quality assessments—they had little energy for new ideas and were in no mood for new visions, no matter how worthy. The responses varied from "We've no time!" to "We've no money!" and "We've no interest!" Mary eventually squeezed enough reluctant will to get the project off the ground, not in the Belfast campus, but in her own bailiwick in Armagh.

QUB was internationally renowned for its science faculty, but it did not teach journalism. A partnership arrangement was required. Mary knew that the Department of Journalism in the recently founded Dublin City University was gaining a good reputation, and so she approached the president of the new college, Danny O'Hare. His response was "Great idea! Let's make it happen." Just before she was elected president, Mary was involved in similar links between QUB and NUI Galway, and the University of Limerick.

As Ireland's first cross-border degree course was being established, Mary's engagement with some other groups was not gaining the same international recognition, although the involvement was important and revolutionary in its own right. She decided that a true external relations brief should not be confined to purely academic work, but should involve contact with the university's nearest neighbours—those who lived and worked in the immediate vicinity of Queen's. Most of the houses around the university had long since been turned into student flats, and most of the proximate external contact was confined to dealing with the owners of these houses on behalf of students. But there was one indigenous community left in the area: the people of Sandy Row.

Even more than the Shankill Road, Sandy Row has long been recognised as the most Protestant of Protestant areas in Northern Ireland. Shortly after the "God Save the Queen" squabble, Mary went to talk to the local community council, and through them met the teachers, pupils and parents of Blythe Street Primary School—the nearest educational establishment to Queen's University.

"We're not interested in anthems," one of the parents told the pro-vice-chancellor, "only in getting an education for our kids. Most of them don't even get the eleven plus, never mind getting into Queen's."

Through the schools, Mary organised visits to Queen's for the Protestant children of Sandy Row and the Catholic children of the Ormeau Road. The project was christened "Good Neighbours". The undergraduates organised homework clubs and helped the children with their studies. In encouraging the children and their parents to attend university activities, it took a lot of the mystique out of university life and effected the first crack in the glass ceiling that had kept generations of children from these areas in menial jobs or on the dole. Two years later the smiling faces of the children of Blythe Street Primary School, Sandy Row, would bring a lump to the throat of the new president on the morning of her inauguration in Dublin Castle.

In 1845, in the reign of Queen Victoria of England, three Irish Queen's Colleges were established in Belfast, Galway and Cork. The colleges in Galway and Cork were subsequently subsumed into the National University of Ireland, and the Belfast college became the independent Queen's University. The year 1995 was the 150th anniversary of the founding of the three colleges, and in Queen's University a committee was formed to direct the sesquicentenary ceremonies and to organise concelebrations with Galway and Cork. The main commemorative occasion was a reception in St James's Palace in London: a dinner for six hundred people from the universities, which was attended by Mary Robinson, President of Ireland, and Queen Elizabeth II of England. Seán Fulton was in charge of the organising committee. Remembering the adage which says that if you want a job done well you should ask a busy person, he asked Mary to help him with the organisation, and one of the many duties she undertook was the introduction of the guests to the Queen of England. It was the first time the two women met.

Some time later, Mary received a phone call from Sir Simon Cooper, the master of the Queen's Household, inviting her to lunch in Buckingham Palace. He explained that the Queen was anxious to meet her again at an occasion where they might have a proper conversation. One of the leading living symbols of Irish Catholicism and nationalism was about to have lunch with the apotheosis of English Protestantism.

It was a private lunch for seven people, including Mary McAleese and Queen Elizabeth. They were an eclectic group: General Sir Rupert Smith, who within a year would become General Officer Commanding British Forces in Northern Ireland, and within three years would become NATO's Deputy Supreme Allied Commander Europe; a probation officer from Manchester; a Maltese doctor who was working in Scotland; a black Church of England priest who was working in inner-city London; and a woman who had been the commander of WRAC, the Women's Royal Army Corps. Mary remembers it as a pleasant lunch. The discussion initially ranged over the multiplicity of interests represented by the guests, but as the table was cleared for the serving of tea and coffee, the Queen narrowed the focus of the conversation to the affairs of Northern Ireland. Mary says that, apart from herself, the black Church of England priest from inner London knew more about the people of Northern Ireland than anyone else at the table, including the general who would have command of the British forces there.

As Mary and the Queen of England were saying goodbye, they said, as people often say in such circumstances, that they hoped they would meet again sometime. Neither of them really thought it would happen, and neither of them could imagine that their next meeting would be as the heads of state of two sovereign nations.

Chapter Twenty-One

A Glimmer in the North

So today across the Irish Sea I wave
And wish him well from the bottom of my heart
Where truth lies bleeding, its ear-drums burst
By the blatter of his hand-me-down talk.
In fond memory of his last stand
I dedicate this contraceptive pill
Of poetry to his unborn followers,
And I place
This bunch of beget-me-nots on his grave.
(W.R. Rodgers: "Home Thoughts from Abroad")

In that same year, 1995, a conference entitled the White House Conference for Trade and Investment in Ireland was convened in Washington DC with the aim of attracting American investment into the island of Ireland, particularly Northern Ireland and the border counties. It followed on President Clinton's appointment of Senator George Mitchell as his special advisor on economic initiatives in Ireland and the sending of Commerce Secretary Ron Brown to Belfast to identify new business links.‡ Forty American companies already operated in the North, providing 9,000 jobs, and the International Fund for Ireland was funding a broad range of economic and social development projects. The message of the conference was simple: a Northern Ireland at peace is a Northern Ireland ready for business. The vice-chancellor of Queen's Sir Gordon Beveridge was unable to attend and he asked his pro-vice-chancellor to travel in his stead.

Mary saw the conference as an opportunity to promote the new campus in Armagh and possibly source new funding for some of the courses there. She contacted Professor Wallace Ewart, of the University of Ulster, and in conjunction with five American universities, they and

---

‡ Senator George Mitchell later came out of retirement at Bill Clinton's request, to become the president's special advisor to Northern Ireland—the job for which he is best remembered in Ireland.

some colleagues put together a package to establish a distance learning consortium. Their objective was to obtain some federal funding, which would help them to attract private contributions for their project.

Among those whom Mary got to know at the conference was Jim King, director of the US Office of Personnel Management, permanent chair of the National Partnership Council, and a close advisor to Bill Clinton. When Tom Kelly of the SDLP introduced them, King told Mary that his daughter was studying in Ireland and was engaged to a young Irishman whom he had yet to meet. As the conversation progressed Mary realised that she knew King's future son-in-law, Deiric Ó Broin. Just a week previously, her friend, Eibhlís Farrell, who was head of the College of Music in the Dublin Institute of Technology, had brought Deiric, as president of the Student Union, to the McAleese's apartment in Ballsbridge. She was able to reassure Jim that his daughter's choice was a good one.

King's people had originally come from the area around Boyle in County Roscommon, near the little cottage in which Paddy Leneghan had been reared and which was now owned by Mary and Martin. Mary was able to give him an account of all his relations in the area and what they were doing with their lives. By the end of the conference, the Kings and the McAleeses were firm friends.

In 1995 Bill Clinton was anxious to tap into the well of good will that resulted from the IRA ceasefire and to bolster the efforts of the governments of John Bruton and John Major in paving the way for a permanent peace. To this end, he decided to visit Belfast and Dublin at the end of November of that year. At the end of the summer, Jim King, his wife Eleanor and his sister came on a visit. They stayed with the McAleeses in Rostrevor before they all travelled to Roscommon, where they visited the King relations and found their ancestral home. Martin McAleese and Mary's cousin, Eugene McGreevy, were building a stone barbeque in the garden of the old cottage in Carroward. Jim King, who was watching them at work, told them they were using the wrong tools and said that a special stone-cutting hammer was required to do the job properly. He knew how to work with stone!

Off he went to Boyle where he found the implement he wanted in King's hardware shop. On his return to Carroward, he could not wait to demonstrate the proper way to shape stone for building a barbeque. The first blow left the special hammer in two halves. To his credit, King accepted with resigned amusement the ensuing ridicule and the inevitable jokes about Americans who know everything about everything. Shortly before the Clintons came to Ireland, Mary received a letter from King: "If you get a chance to talk to Bill Clinton, tell him you are a friend of mine."

On the 30 November, the Clintons arrived in Belfast. The main speech of the day was delivered in Mackey's factory, on the peace line on the Springfield Road. Clinton spoke eloquently of peace and reconciliation, of the need to leave old grudges behind and go forward together for the sake of the children. The audience responded with thunderous applause, with one exception. Cedric Wilson, the unionist politician, heckled the American president twice by shouting, "Never! Never!" His second interruption was caught on television and beamed all over the world, to the chagrin of all present. What was not broadcast was the response of another unionist politician who, in a moment of mad ecumenism, turned to Wilson and responded: "Go back to Jurassic Park where you belong!"

No one who was present in Belfast city centre that night will ever forget the spirit of excitement and optimism and joy that infused the crowd of 60,000 people who cheered when Bill Clinton lit the Christmas lights on the huge tree outside the City Hall. Catholics and Protestants held hands and sang and swayed as Van Morrison stood on the stage beside the first serving American president ever to visit Belfast and sang "Days Like This". When he reached the line "Wouldn't it be great if it was like this all the time?" the hills around Belfast seemed to echo back the enthusiastic hopes of the crowd.

That night the Clintons were due to attend a function in the Whitla Hall of Queen's University. The Northern Ireland Office, who was hosting the reception, had hired the hall for the occasion, and the guests were mostly politicians. The people chosen to represent Queen's were Gordon Beveridge and his wife Trudi Beveridge; Jim Kincaid, the former headmaster of Methodist College and a member of the university Senate; and Mary McAleese.

When the President of America met the future President of Ireland that night, an observer would have been forgiven for thinking they were old friends, as the pair stood and chatted, laughed and swapped stories.

"Mr President, Jim King told me to mention that I am a friend of his," said Mary, after she had welcomed him to the university.

"The hammer!" said Bill Clinton. "Tell me about the hammer! What is this story? He told me to ask you about it."

As the chat rattled on, the people in line to be introduced were becoming more and more curious about what the president and the pro-vice-chancellor had to say that was so obviously engrossing to both of them. All that night, and for a few days afterwards, her friends and people in the university pestered her about the nature of the conversation. Even Sir Gordon Beveridge was not above idle curiosity in the matter. Mary got a phone call from Martin O'Brien, who was working with the BBC. He said he had been watching everything on the various television monitors in the control room, but as there was no microphone near Mary and Bill Clinton, he was sorry he could not lipread. "What were you talking about?" Mary mischievously left the question unanswered. She was reluctant to ascribe the resolution of what was fast becoming an enigma to something as trivial as a broken hammer. Better to leave it a mystery.

Outside the life of the university, Mary was as busy as ever, as was Martin. The children were now at school, and Brigid Kerrigan, their then housekeeper, was keeping the house in order. Charlie McAleese was there with the children all the time, and Paddy Leneghan called every morning and evening, like a watchman, doing the rounds of his family's families. Paddy and Charlie had long since become firm friends and both enjoyed the daily visits.

Martin was working in both Bessbrook and Crossmaglen. He rose every morning at a quarter past six and was in work by eight o'clock. In the early days he sometimes did not reach home until nine o'clock at night. As well as his dental work, he had taken on the accountancy and the computer work for the practice. This extra load eased somewhat when he and Des Casey employed Margareta McAlinden as their full-time practice manager. Despite the demands of his work, Martin found time to run thirty or forty miles each week.

He also found time for domestic matters, and he and Mary ensured that they were able take delight in the various milestones of their children's development. Both maintain that family life was their priority and also agreed on the importance of inculcating a broadminded attitude in the children. Having suffered the consequences of bigotry, they were adamant that none of their children would ever hear a sectarian sentiment in their home.

Sectarianism was top of the worry list of many people in Ireland. John Dickinson, minister of Ballynahinch Presbyterian Church, says, "The fact that sectarianism exists in our community diminishes us as a people. That it is found in the life of our churches calls into question the credibility of our Christian faith."[‡]

---

‡ "Sectarianism: Root and Branch; Lion and Lamb", issue 10, ECONI—the Evangelical Contribution on Northern Ireland.

This was one of the reasons why, at the start of the 1980s, the Catholic Archbishop of Armagh Cardinal Tomás Ó Fiaich and the Church of Ireland Archbishop of Armagh Dr Robin Eames re-established the Irish Inter-Church Talks. They were familiarly known as the "Ballymascanlon Talks" because the delegates came together for the first time in September 1973 in Ballmascanlon, County Louth, at the instigation of Cardinal William Conway and the Church of Ireland Archbishop George Otto Simms. Archbishop Eames described the talks as "the first tangible collective response of the Irish Churches out of the cauldron of community suffering."‡

Mary attended her first Ballymascanlon Talks in 1983 and was a regular contributor to the proceedings of subsequent meetings, which were convened approximately every eighteen months. When it was decided, in 1990, to appoint a working group to produce a discussion paper on the subject of sectarianism, Mary was asked to be co-chair of the group, with John Lampen from the Society of Friends. They came together for the first time in February 1991.

The working party was a motley group representing the main Christian churches. Among them were the Revd Gary Mason, Methodist; Dr Kenneth Milne and Carrie Barkley, Church of Ireland; Revd David Temple, Presbyterian; Dr Joseph Liechty, Mennonite; and Sr Mary Duddy, Fr Denis Faul and Paul Rogers from the Catholic Church. Joe Campbell of the Scripture Union and Fr Michael Hurley SJ, of the Irish School of Ecumenics were also in the group, and Dr David Stevens, general secretary of the Council of Churches in Ireland, was their secretary. There was another Methodist in the group: Revd Sam Burch, director of the cross-community group Cornerstone, and a great friend of the Redemptorists in Clonard. Other members were Martin O'Brien, Seamus O'Hara and Muriel Pritchard. All were deeply committed Christians who were prepared to give generously of their time and talents because of their concern for the future of Ireland. They were all also human—very human at times.

For the first few months everyone was politely respectful of each other's views and perhaps just a touch too courteous for comfort. This soon changed. As the material mounted and they began to talk about history, education, confessionalism, triumphalism, people began to see offence where none was intended; some unwittingly said hurtful things about others; and some discovered things about themselves that they

‡ Address in NUI Galway, 28 June 2002.

found hard to accept. But they continued to work hard. As might be expected, the chapter entitled "Sectarianism—A Learnt Process" was written by Mary McAleese. In it she describes sectarianism as an evil which is often assimilated by children in family life. In this chapter Mary leaves aside her characteristic first person singular; there is no reference to her family or to their experiences, and the prose is unrelenting and terse:

"Back in our homes we quietly justify our failure to differentiate between Provos and Catholics, between UVF and Protestants. We teach sectarianism by shorthand. Collapsing down important distinctions is easy and it is treacherous."[‡]

Brian Keenan was just finishing his famous book, *An Evil Cradling*, while Mary was writing this chapter on learnt sectarianism. Although the words "evil cradling" do not appear in the report, that is the term she now uses when she speaks of sectarianism in the home: "Sectarianism starts from the minute the child can understand its parents' words. We are all guilty, even though none of us says, 'OK, kids, gather round now and we'll have half an hour of sectarian indoctrination.' The evil cradling is much more subtle than that. What a child learns is what a child does."

Dr Paul Connolly of the University of Ulster did some research on sectarian attitudes in Northern Ireland. His results, which were published in a report called *Too Young to Notice*, show that children as young as three years of age experience sectarian thoughts.[§] His findings served to confirm what some people had long suspected and what Mary had written ten years previously.

The working group on sectarianism had many difficulties in the course of their work, most of them arising from the straight-from-the-shoulder views of the American Mennonite, part-time history lecturer in St Patrick's College Maynooth Dr Joe Liechty. He was hard on both Catholics and Protestants in what he had to say and in the unbiased historical perspective he brought to the subject of the roots of sectarianism. If an Irish Catholic had said these things about Irish Protestants, or vice versa, the injured party would have found comfort in the familiar refrain: "What would you expect from the likes of them?" But here was a perceptive American, a trained historian, looking in from

---

‡ Inter-Church Meeting, "Sectarianism: A Discussion Document" (Irish Inter-Church Meeting, 1983), p. 71.

§ RTÉ *News*, 25 May 2002.

270

the outside with the chilly clarity of impartiality and absolute neutrality, and what he had to say left both sides embarrassed and bristling. Fr Denis Faul and Carrie Barkley were first into the fray and were soon followed by several others. Mary left Liechty and Kenneth Milne to the train that night. "Joe felt he was lucky to escape with his life," she says. Joe, however, was unbowed. He was unhappy with the way his assessment was received, or not received, but continued to work with the group, settling ultimately for the separate publication of his paper as part of a booklet entitled *Roots of Sectarianism.*

The group eventually agreed on the contents of their document. There were chapters on "Dealing with Religious Differences" and "Developing Trusting Relationships" and on the most common bones of contention between Catholics and Protestants. Mary McAleese and John Lampen, as co-chairs, presented the report at the next session of the Ballymascanlon Talks in Dromantine, outside Newry, in October 1983, and Mary addressed the assembled delegates:

> This is not a report about a problem which is out there somewhere. You won't be able to preach about this at a distance. The problem of sectarianism is foursquare in this room. We are all of us, and each one of us, responsible. How many of us sitting here today can say honestly that in every conversation, especially those in "safe company", we have never uttered a word which could be construed as hurtful to those of other denominations? How many of us are glad our conversations were not tape recorded for posterity? Yet posterity has a way of being affected by them anyway. How many of us have had the courage to contradict the myth that Catholics are all Provos, Protestants are all bigots?[‡]

The report was well received, and the delegates returned to their parishes and their people, full of good intentions and bent on wiping out sectarianism if it was the last thing they would do. The eagerness, however, did not last. Within a couple of years, the people themselves were complaining about the lack of diligence among the church authorities. For the next two years, Mary and John Lampen toured the country, talking and listening, explaining and helping, advising and supporting wherever they were asked to go.

What motivated Mary to leave her young family and her cosy home, evening after evening, to listen to the same arguments and complaints in cold parish halls and draughty chapels? Was it pure altruism or was

---

‡   Mary McAleese, private papers.

there any personal gain to be obtained from all this? Whatever esteem she was earning was confined to small groups. She was not even being paid mileage for her travels and her troubles. Was her work inspired by love for the people of God? A hunger for justice and peace? Or was it simply that her innate stubbornness would not allow her to let go until the job was completed? The truth is probably a combination of these reasons.

As Mary and John went about their work among those who were interested in closer cross-community relations, sectarianism and bigotry were having a field day in certain areas of the North; notably around the Garvaghy Road, near Drumcree, in Portadown, and in the Lower Ormeau Road area of Belfast. In the autumn of 1996 Mary was invited to be a member of an episcopal delegation which would make written and then oral submissions to the North Commission for Contentious Parades, a group that was chaired by Dr Peter North and on which the Revd John Dunlop and Fr Oliver Crilly sat. The other members of the episcopal delegation, which was led by Archbishop Brady, were Monsignor Denis Faul, Cardinal Cahal Daly and Martin O'Brien. Denis Faul was not too happy with Mary's contribution: "As a member of that commission she was not nearly tough enough. I was of the opinion that our demands should be as strong as we could possibly make them, but Mary was usually in favour of compromise."‡

Mediation and conciliation, rather than compromise, were the characteristics that were uppermost in the mind of Fr Brendan Callanan, provincial of the Redemptorist Order in Ireland, when he invited Mary to become involved in the Redemptorist Peace and Reconciliation Mission in Belfast in the spring of 1996. "She was invited because of her commitment to peace and her strong religious convictions."§

The Clonard monastery, and the large church beside it, are situated in Clonard Gardens, a couple of hundred yards off the Falls Road, close to the mixed Springfield Road and within a short distance of the Protestant Shankill Road. The "Peace Line" almost borders the Redemptorist property.

John Austin Baker, the Anglican Bishop of Salisbury, has said about the place: "The Church of Clonard is to me one of the holy places of the world. Every pew, every brick seems soaked in prayer, in the longing for

‡   Interview with author.

§   Interview with author.

grace to love God and man, to live in forgiveness and peace with all our neighbours."‡

The Clonard novena is by far the biggest of its kind in Northern Ireland and has been running since 1943. The church and car park are always overflowing during the nine days of this novena, which culminates each year on 27 June, the Feast of Our Lady of Perpetual Succour, and Mary McAleese's birthday.

Fr Alex Reid came to Clonard in 1961. He was born on the South Circular Road in Dublin in 1931, and his family moved to Nenagh, in County Tipperary, when he was quite young.

He says, "I joined the Redemptorists in 1949. In the tranquillity of the novitiate in Esker, outside Athenry, I never thought I would one day be wakened by the sound of gunshots." On that momentous evening in August 1969 when Mary McAleese was standing at the top of the hill looking at the destruction of Ardoyne, Fr Alex was helping the people of Bombay Street, near the monastery, as their homes were also being burned. During the years he lived in the monastery of Clonard, Fr Alex earned the respect and confidence not only of the Catholic people of the Falls Road, but of the Protestant people of the Shankill Road also.

His contact with Protestant paramilitaries started in the simplest of ways: "From the monastery we were able to read a clear message on the gable of Cupar Street: 'You are Now in the Heart of Protestant Ulster.' So one Sunday lunchtime I decided to make my first foray into 'Protestant Ulster'. Republicans had thrown two nail bombs into Cupar Street the previous night, and I was anxious to explain to our Protestant neighbours that this action was not representative of the Catholic people in Clonard. I walked along Cupar Street and knocked on a door at random. The woman who opened it was startled to see a man in the robes of a Catholic priest, but when I explained my mission she opened the door wide and invited me in. She was Liz Wallace, a saintly widow who subsequently became a great friend of mine. I met many Protestant people that day, including some of the hard men, and I promised them that I would confront the leaders of those who had thrown the nail bombs. As I was leaving, the residents stood at their doors and thanked me for coming around. I asked them to put their trust in my word and now I had to go and act on it. It was the only way to gain their trust. Trust from both sides is all-important. If I later told people it was OK

‡   Clonard Monastery, 24.

273

for X, who was on the run from paramilitaries, to come home again, I was putting a man's life on my word."[‡]

In the 1970s he spent a lot of time working as a mediator between the warring wings of the IRA during the bloody feud between the Officials and the Provisionals. He also spent time talking to Protestant paramilitaries. Through his quiet, powerful ministry, he has won the confidence of both sides to such an extent that he is now one of the very few people, if not the only person in Ireland, with whom both republican and loyalist paramilitaries will confer and cooperate. It will always remain a matter of conjecture just how many lives have been saved thanks to the intervention and the wisdom of this man. Although he was in poor health at the time, he was indefatigable in his attempts to work out a settlement of the hunger strikes of 1980 and 1981. During the 1980s and 1990s, he and some of the other priests of Clonard, especially Fr Gerry Reynolds, worked tirelessly with both sides to stem the rising tide of sectarian killings.

In an interview with Gorka Espiau, a journalist with the magazine of the Basque peace organisation, *Elkarri*, in 2002, Fr Alex is reported to have said that "IRA terrorism could have ended as early as 1981 if there had been more goodwill from other parties."[§]

However, he has said more recently, "It became apparent to me in 1986, from working with paramilitaries on both sides, that the conditions were falling into place, for the first time, to put a permanent end to the murders."[†]

He was one of the first to understand that many members of the IRA were becoming tired of the war and were beginning to look for other ways to realise their objectives. Through the good offices of Tim Pat Coogan, he visited Charles Haughey in his home in Kinsealy in Dublin to discuss his ideas. Haughey was very taken with both the man and his ideas and introduced him to his Northern adviser, Martin Mansergh. When Haughey was elected taoiseach the following year, he asked Mansergh to contact Alex again. The priest was back in the role at which he excelled, the role of intermediary, but this time it was between Martin Mansergh and Gerry Adams, the president of Sinn Féin.

In March 1988 a photograph of Fr Alex Reid appeared on the front page of many of the world's leading newspapers, as he knelt beside the

---

‡   Interview with author.

§   Reported by Liam Clarke in *The Sunday Times*, 21 February 2002.

†   Interview with author.

semi-naked, battered body of a British soldier, one of two who were beaten, stabbed and shot by a number of mourners at an IRA funeral in Andersonstown. The funeral was that of Kevin McBrady, one of those who had been shot by the loyalist Michael Stone in Milltown Cemetery.[‡] Two off-duty British soldiers, Derek Wood and David Howes, drove into the funeral procession as it made its way down the Andersonstown Road. By the time Fr Alex found them, both soldiers were beyond his help. Although his attempts to resuscitate them were too late for the young men, they served to increase the priest's standing in the eyes of all conflicting parties. The journalist Mary Holland, who was there that day, described Alex's actions as "hope for humanity in the midst of barbarity".

This was the man who was to become the working partner, close friend and confidant of the future President of Ireland. His Tipperary hurling background colours his speech in the following piece:

> We had a couple of very good women on the team that was dealing with the loyalists. I had always felt that the male-female dynamic was very important in the Irish peace process. I believe that men and women working together can see a much more complete picture and can work more efficiently. Mary McAleese had been in my mind for three years, but I never approached her. I never really thought we would be lucky enough to get her on the team. After Canary Wharf we felt our team needed to be strengthened in order to stop such a thing happening again. Thank God Mary came on board with no hesitation. She is an amazingly articulate woman, intelligent, sharp and intuitive. She is warm and affectionate, but when the circumstances call for it, she can be tough and uncompromising. She gave me great confidence. When I used to go to meetings, and had Mary with me, it was like having Christy Ring and Mick Mackey together on your team. Three minutes into the meeting, Mary would have the *sliotar* flying over the bar.[§]

Fr Reid took another big step along the road to peace when he invited John Hume and Gerry Adams to come together to compare and contrast their ideas on the future of Northern Ireland for the Hume/Adams Talks, as they are now known. He recognised Adams's intense interest in a peaceful solution, and that of Hume was apparent to the world. In

‡ At the funerals of Mairead Farrell, Danny McCann and Sean Savage, who had been shot dead by British army SAS personnel in Gibraltar the previous week.

§ Interview with author.

trying to achieve an understanding and a unity among nationalists, he was trying to create a political dynamic which would be as powerful, or even more powerful, than that represented by the IRA. The appointment of Peter Brooke as secretary of state for Northern Ireland in July 1989 helped to entice republicans to the discussion table, and a process was started, which was later continued by the next Northern secretary, Patrick Mayhew: the Brooke/Mayhew Talks as they are now referred to.

These talks were on three levels: among politicians within Northern Ireland, between Northern politicians and the Irish government, and between the Irish government and the British government. Fr Alex worked at each level of these talks. A lot of his work, both past and current, must remain secret to protect his own integrity and the absolute confidence which paramilitary groups still place in him. He says that although the IRA ceasefire did not happen until 1994, by the summer of 1991 most of what was necessary to facilitate the end of hostilities was in place.

However, more atrocities were in the offing. The IRA bomb in Warrington, in England, which killed the children Jonathan Ball and Tim Parry, led to the formation of Peace Initiative '93, fronted by Colin Parry, Tim's father. More children were among the dead when an IRA bomb killed ten people at a fish and chip shop on the Shankill Road in Belfast. The UFF retaliated by killing seven people and wounding thirteen in the Rising Sun Bar in Greysteel, County Derry. Eventually the Downing Street Declaration, signed on 15 December 1993 by Albert Reynolds and John Major, promised that Sinn Féin could join talks on the future of Northern Ireland if the IRA renounced violence.

During all the tit-for-tat bombings and shootings, and the slow and painstaking behind-the-scenes moves that eventually led to the 1994 IRA ceasefire, Fr Alex was tireless. He is best placed to describe his own work:

> When a conflict like the one in Northern Ireland has become violent and is causing suffering and bloodshed, the Church has a missionary and pastoral duty to intervene directly and to do all she can to bring its violent dimensions and their tragic consequences to an end. Here her role may be to facilitate the necessary dialogue between the relevant parties, especially when all lines of communication between them have broken down, and the tragic dimensions of the conflict cannot and will not be ended unless and until they are restored.

She must then use her political neutrality, her moral credibility and her own lines of communication to provide the kind of sanctuary setting where the parties to the conflict, who sincerely wish to use political and democratic methods to achieve justice and peace, can meet together for the necessary dialogue without damaging their own political or moral credibility and without compromising, or appearing to compromise, any of their own political or democratic principles.

He maintains what he considers a very necessary sense of humour in the face of all the tragedy: "Having lived so long in Belfast, I feel I can say I have been all around the world—and several other places besides!"[‡]

His work was not only stressful but often lonely. He was constantly meeting groups who refused point blank to have any communication with each other except through him. He was listening carefully to what they had to say, passing their ideas on to others; trying to strengthen weak conduits and trying to create means of communication where none had existed previously. His words and his message were regularly misunderstood, and he often came under extreme pressure. What he needed was a couple of people whose Christianity was very important to them, strong people who would look on the mission as a Christian service rather than a political operation, but who would have a deep understanding of the political pressures and the social dimensions that were particular to Northern Ireland.

The 1994 IRA ceasefire ended on Friday, 9 February 1996. A few minutes later a massive bomb exploded in London's Canary Wharf, injuring over one hundred people and causing millions of pounds worth of damage. Shortly afterwards, Mary McAleese and Jim Fitzpatrick were invited to join the Clonard peace mission. Fitzpatrick was the owner and editor of the nationalist morning newspaper, the *Irish News,* a man well known and highly respected for his work for justice and peace. Mary gives this account of her first meeting with the Clonard priests:

> One day, shortly after the Canary Wharf bombing, I got a phone call from Fr Brendan Callanan, the provincial of the Redemptorists in Ireland. He said that he and Fr Alex Reid would like to call to see me. Until then I had only a sketchy idea of the work of the peace ministry. By the time the two men left the house that night, I was amazed by the scope of their work and the extent of their contacts. Their commitment to peace and reconciliation was

‡   Interview with author.

absolute. They were prepared to talk to anyone who would listen and to listen to anyone who would talk. They were highly respected by paramilitaries on both sides of the divide, who felt they could talk freely to them, in total confidence, in a non-judgmental setting. In this way the priests were able to gain important insights into the mindsets and aspirations of the paramilitaries. The phrase "no boundaries" was a kind of mantra with them. The paramilitaries looked on the Clonard peace mission as a neutral and safe environment, and all understood that the priests' only agenda was the promotion of peace and the message of the Gospel.

From the time John Hume and Gerry Adams began their talks at the instigation of Alex Reid, they came under a lot of pressure both from outside and inside their organisations. Neither of the leaders was apologetic about the contact, and Hume famously remarked that he "did not care two balls of roasted snow" about reaction to his talks with Adams. Mary always had a great regard for Hume's ability to win people over in a one-to-one situation. His work in encouraging influential Irish-Americans to further the peace process was a powerful testament to this ability, and he was now bringing it to bear on the leader of Sinn Féin. Adams was only too aware of the necessity of bringing a speedy end to violence. His difficulty lay in persuading the republican movement to join him in the effort, not only to bring about another ceasefire, but to maintain the peace.

In 1996, with the seventeen-month ceasefire in tatters, the most urgent job facing the recently augmented Clonard peace ministry was to gain an insight into the reasons for the collapse of the ceasefire and a clear understanding of the necessary conditions that would facilitate another, and more permanent, cessation of violence. According to Mary McAleese, and many other commentators, the political vacuum that followed the 1994 IRA ceasefire was a sure sign that it would not hold. She was also of the opinion that that ceasefire was not called for any reason of morality, but because the IRA believed that there was a more effective way of realising their objectives. Hume and Adams had persuaded them to give political action a chance, and the Irish and British governments had pledged that political action would occur. It didn't.

During her work with the peace ministry, Mary, to her knowledge, never met a single paramilitary. Her work was confined solely to the people of politics. She, Jim Fitzpatrick and Fr Alex spent a lot of time in meetings with representatives of Sinn Féin and the SDLP. For many years, people outside Northern Ireland saw only one area of polarisation:

that between nationalists and unionists. But within the nationalist community there was a long history of acrimony between Sinn Féin and the SDLP, between their followers and between their leaders. With the increasing politicisation of Sinn Féin, the struggle for the hearts and minds of the nationalist people, and for their votes, intensified. Although Hume and Adams had spent a lot of time and effort increasing their understanding of and respect for each other's views, the resultant goodwill had still to percolate down to the grassroots members of the parties. Traditionally, SDLP supporters looked on Sinn Féin supporters as being, at best, ambivalent towards the violence of the IRA. To Sinn Féin supporters, the SDLP were not nationalist enough, not to mention republican enough. These attitudes needed to be analysed. It was too easy, and far too dangerous in the circumstances, to categorise and oversimplify the presumed characteristics of political rivals.

The feeling of the peace ministry group was that the peace process would be best served by seeking a meeting of minds, as far as was possible, among nationalists; the forging of a political force for peace that would be more powerful than any paramilitary force. In doing this they were meeting one group one night, another group another night, bringing messages and clarifications back and forward like bees bringing pollen; analysing what each had to say, asking each group to reflect honestly on what others had to say, and constantly seeking a common platform for both sides.

With John Hume's permission, the group was meeting senior members of the SDLP, encouraging them to become involved in this talks process, discovering their difficulties with Sinn Féin, and particularly with their followers at election time, and explaining the problems that Sinn Féin had with some of their political decisions. Apart from a forum in Derry, in which Mitchell McLaughlin had some contact with Mark Durkan, there was no real communication between the senior figures of the two main nationalist parties. Mary was amazed to discover that the two major nationalist political figures in West Belfast, Gerry Adams and Dr Joe Hendron, had never spoken to each other.

As part of this mediation process, Bríd Rodgers of the SDLP was invited to a meeting with Fr Alex, Mary and Jim Fitzpatrick. Everyone present understood the necessity for absolute discretion and the underlying peace-seeking reason for the meeting. As the meeting progressed, Bríd Rodgers passed on her concerns about the activities of some members of Sinn Féin and was made aware of the concerns of some members of that party. This is the conciliation process that was misrepresented a year later when it was alleged that "Mary McAleese had a Sinn Féin agenda". As well as causing distress to the presidential candidate and damaging her election campaign, the breach of confidence also endangered the work of the peace and reconciliation ministry. Mary was still heavily involved in the work of the ministry up until she decided to seek a nomination for the presidency.

Chapter Twenty-Two

Only Twenty-Four Hours in a Day

Well, there's another dozen done,
An' here's another lot begun;
When these are finished there are more,
My God, it's only just struck four!
(Richard Rowley: "The Stitcher")

Mary McAleese may never have contributed very much to the coffers of the major brewing or distilling companies, but she always enjoyed her food. She was reared on good plain fare. The Leneghans always had fish or champ every Friday, and on the other days they had meat or eggs.‡ Homemade bread, freshly baked every day, also contributed to a better than average diet for the time and place of her childhood. When she visited Spain for the first time in 1968, she discovered the joys of shellfish, and as she grew and began to travel more, her taste became more eclectic. Simple Italian dishes have long been among her favourites, but whether foreign or traditional, nothing, she says, can beat a good home-cooked meal.

During the 1990s, however, the opportunities to cook a favourite dish and eat a relaxed meal with her family were mostly reserved for weekends. Her already busy life became even busier after she became an active member of four major boards: BBC Northern Ireland, Channel Four Television, the Electricity Board of Northern Ireland and the board of the Royal Hospitals' Trust.

Back in 1984, a year before she began broadcasting *Just a Thought* on RTÉ Radio One, she was invited by the Revd Trevor Williams, head of Religious Programmes for BBC Northern Ireland, to write and read some pieces for *Thought for the Day*. She subsequently did several programmes for BBC NI and BBC Radio 4, among them *Prayer for the Day* and the very successful *The Protestant Mind*. She therefore had a good working knowledge of the station by the time she was appointed to

---

‡ Champ: mashed potatoes with chopped scallions and butter.

the BBC Broadcasting Council for Northern Ireland in 1992. The Council was not a board in the strict sense of the word, but it operated just like one, and Mary's role was akin to that of a non-executive director.

Among her fellow members was Anne Gibson, wife of Justice Terry Gibson and sister of Bishop Edward Daly. Jim Kincaid, a former colleague of Mary's from the Senate of Queen's University and former headmaster of Methodist College, was chairman at the time of Mary's appointment, but he was replaced shortly afterwards by Sir Kenneth Bloomfield, a senior civil servant. Fears of a new era of unwarranted government influence on local broadcasting were quickly assuaged by Bloomfield's disarming frankness and honesty. In fact, the changeover was seamless.

Colin Morrison, who was controller at the time, was soon replaced by Robin Walsh, a Belfast man who returned from a stint with the BBC in London to take up the position in his native city. The swingeing cutbacks began in earnest shortly after Walsh's appointment. Every couple of months, the controller was forced to let go more staff and axe another programme or two. When Walsh left, he was replaced by another local man, Pat Loughrey, whom Mary had known quite well when he was head of Educational Programmes. Despite his best efforts, and those of the Council, there were further redundancies. Reports within the broadcasting corporation in Britain suggested that the days of regional broadcasting might be numbered, and morale was very low. In the face of all the gloom, the new Blackstaff Headquarters Building in Belfast was planned, delivered and opened during Mary's time on the Council, but by the time she left, a lot of the employees of the station had moved to the freelance sector. The fact that during her two-year tenure BBC NI went through two chairmen and three controllers tells its own story. Her next broadcasting appointment was to a more successful area and a more positive environment.

In 1994 she was invited to join the board of Channel 4 Television as a non-executive director, and as she was unable to operate in a directorial capacity in two broadcasting organisations, she said goodbye to the BBC. The morale in the two stations could hardly have been more different. Mary came on to the board as Sir Richard Attenborough was retiring, and became the third Irish appointment on a board of twelve members: Frank McGettigan was already general manager and David Thompson was financial controller. The board was full of very talented, very capable people, but the person who impressed Mary most was Sir Michael

Bishop, the chairman. She says she learned a lot from his style of chairing meetings.

He was inclusive and caring, making sure that everyone on the board got space and time and never letting his own views be known until everyone else had an opportunity to say what they had to say. He knew little about television and made no secret of that fact, but he was prepared to learn and gave the professionals around him full credit for their expertise. The board was full of lively, feisty people, and he had the great gift of being able to bring out the best in them and pull everyone together.

The vice-chairman was David Plowright, the brother of Joan Plowright, the actress who was married to Sir Lawrence Olivier. Michael Grade was the chief executive, and when he resigned, Mary, Bishop and David Plowright were delegated to appoint his replacement. Michael Jackson from the BBC was their choice.

Channel 4 is a curious entity. It is a public service broadcasting body which must finance itself by advertising. It commissions most of its programmes, much the same as TG4 does, and operates effectively by the will of government within a very strict statutory remit. The Independent Television Commission is its immediate policing body, but it is also subject to challenge from the Broadcasting Complaints Commission and the Broadcasting Council. The board met once a month, but Mary was often back and forward to London more frequently than that. She says she is proud of her work on the board and makes light of Channel 4's reputation for late night risqué programmes. "My father described some of them as 'a cure for bad thoughts'," she says.

The board was not a censorship body. They did their best to ensure that the regulations as set down by the Independent Television Commission were observed, but they sometimes got their knuckles rapped. Mary claims that on these occasions there was a fine line and a judgment call one way by the ITC and the other by Channel 4. Only programmes which were thought to be controversial were flagged to be discussed by the board, and the occasions when programmes were stopped were very rare. Among the controversial programmes was *The Committee*, the famous documentary programme by Sean McPhelimy about alleged conspiracies in Northern Ireland. The board spent a lot of time dealing with the downstream consequences of the transmission of the programme, and a number of libel writs were issued.

Mary was disappointed in some of the programmes, however, including one on Mother Teresa. It seemed that her mother held her personally responsible for the programme and rang her several times after it was aired: "Is this what your father and I educated you for? A hatchet job on poor Mother Teresa?" Mary was particularly impressed with a major series on Bosnia and the Balkan war and also with a series on the homeless in Britain.

Probably the most famous film commissioned by Channel 4 while Mary was on the board was *Four Weddings and a Funeral*, and her most amusing recollection of her time with the station centres around the film's opening night in the Odeon Cinema in Leicester Square in London. It was a benefit occasion, hosted by Elton John, and in keeping with the theme of the film, the guests were asked to arrive at the premiere dressed as if they were going to a wedding. It was the famous occasion when Liz Hurley arrived in a dress that seemed to be made of safety pins. As Martin McAleese was unable to attend, Mary invited a friend, Fr Sean Carroll, to accompany her; and as Sean worked in a poor inner-city parish in London and lived on very modest means, Mary persuaded him to come in his everyday clerical clothes to save him the expense of hiring an outfit.

Channel 4 had hired a fleet of stretch limousines to ferry the guests to the Odeon. The poor priest could not remember the last time he had even been in a taxi. The cameras were rolling as Mary and Sean made their way into the cinema, and the priest was praying that Cardinal Basil Hume was not watching this on television. At last they took their seats and the film started. The opening sequence is a catalogue of swear words and bad language. In her embarrassment, Mary was unable to look at Sean, but as the film progressed she realised that he was enjoying the fun as much as she was. At the reception afterwards, people presumed that "the priest" was Mary's husband, and the poor man was complimented by many of the guests on the authenticity of his shabby clerical outfit. His protests of "I always dress like this! I'm the real thing!" served only to impress the guests even more.

The board of Channel 4 has a lifespan of three years, but Mary was asked to stay on for a further year. A new chief executive was to be appointed in place of Michael Jackson, and Michael Bishop was asked to stay on to facilitate the changeover. He, in turn, asked Mary to stay with him. She was unable to complete the year's service, however, because of the presidential election campaign.

On 29 July 1991, Richard Needham appointed Mary to the board of Northern Ireland Electricity, again as a non-executive director. NIE had, until then, been one of those monolithic Northern Ireland companies that had always been a bastion of male Protestantism. The time was ripe to do something about that because NIE was to be privatised.

Mary says, "It was my initiation into the world of big business and big money. Electricity is a complex industry, both in language and concepts, and I had to read my way into it very carefully. On an intellectual level, the work on the board was stimulating and very rewarding. As soon as I felt I had a good grasp of what was going on, the process of privatisation started. But I enjoyed that also. There was no place on that board for someone who was not prepared to give 100 per cent all the time."

Sir Desmond Lorimer, who was later replaced by David Jeffries, was chairman of the board at the time, but the position of chief executive was vacant, and that position had to be filled before the privatisation process could begin. Mary, who had been raising the question of equal opportunities in employment regularly, was adamant that the position must go to the person best suited to and qualified for the job, regardless of religion or political outlook or affiliation. Pat Haran from County Fermanagh was eventually recruited from the ESB in Dublin. Haran, who had a doctorate in engineering and considerable experience at home and abroad, was a Catholic. The initial disquiet at this appointment soon fizzled out as the force of Haran's personality and his obvious ability soon forged even the begrudgers into a tight team. He turned a smug and complacent public utility into a taut privatised concern that was able to compete aggressively in a global market.

In her work with NIE, Mary was regularly reminded of the old days of the Ulster Workers' Council strike, when loyalists gained access to the grid, stopped the generation of electricity in Northern Ireland and forced the British government to bring an end to the power-sharing government in Stormont. Under the new dispensation, the grid was no longer vulnerable to such a takeover because electricity generation was taken out of the hands of NIE. Private companies now operated the power stations, and NIE was responsible only for the transmission, distribution and supply of electricity—a part of the process that was still regulated. There was still another way to ensure a supply of electricity in case of emergency.

At the start of the Troubles, the electricity interconnector between the South and the North of Ireland was destroyed by an IRA bomb, and despite a lot of talk about reconnection, the political will never seemed to exist to recommission it. Pat Haran and Mary McAleese decided to do something about it. The interconnector is situated almost on the border, near Crossmaglen, in County Armagh, near Martin McAleese's place of work and where he was very well known. Mary asked Martin to find out if the workers would be safe if work commenced to repair the interconnector. Martin contacted Paddy Short, a publican in Crossmaglen who is related to Claire Short, the former British government minister, and also to Dermot Ahern, the future Irish government minister. Short referred Martin to Jim McAllister and both set about their inquiries. Both were able to pass on assurances that there would be no interference with the workforce. NIE commenced work, and soon the interconnector was up and running again. Mary also supported the board's plans to set up another interconnector with the Scottish electricity system, and through them to the various European systems, in order to make absolutely certain that Northern Ireland could never again be held to ransom as it was in the 1970s, and so that it would become attractive again to inward investors.

Her attitude to working on boards was typical of that of a barrister: get a brief, read yourself into it, learn it and work with commitment within its confines. It was an effective method, and it soon earned her a place on yet another board. Paul McWilliams, chairman of the Royal Hospitals' Trust, invited her on to the board, yet again as a non-executive director. Among her fellow board members this time was the former unionist Lord Mayor of Belfast John Carson, and he and Mary worked together as part of a tight team. She was not long on the board when she was asked to take on two important jobs: to chair the Complaints Committee and to be a member of the team which was advocating the placement of a new maternity unit in the Royal Victoria Hospital.

Dr James McKenna had issued a report on the state of the health service in Northern Ireland, a report which recommended rationalising all acute hospital services. In the cases of the Royal Victoria Hospital and the City Hospital in Belfast, both huge rambling hospitals, it made sense for each to become a centre of excellence in one or more areas of acute care. Both hospitals had an existing maternity unit, but one of them was to go and the other was to be totally upgraded. The "political" battle for the site of the new maternity hospital was well and truly joined. The fact that the City Hospital is located near the loyalist Sandy Row and the Royal Hospital is on the nationalist Falls Road only served to intensify the feelings on all sides of the argument.

Mary, along with Paul McWilliams and William McKee, the chief executive and some members of staff, formed the team that brought the case of the Royal Hospitals' Trust to the Northern Ireland minister for health Malcolm Moss. The team had done their homework, and their case was so strong that Moss felt obliged to decide in favour of the Royal Hospital. His decision caused an uproar, and the case was brought to the attention of the secretary of state for Northern Ireland Patrick Mayhew, who reversed the decision of Malcolm Moss. The decision was never acted on, and both hospitals continued to operate with their existing facilities until Bairbre de Brún of Sinn Féin was appointed minister for health. She decided that the unit should go to the Royal Hospital, but her decision was also appealed. . .

Apart from her full-time employment in Queen's University and the Institute of Professional Legal Studies, her membership of the various boards, and her work in promoting peace and reconciliation, Mary was active on many other committees. She maintains she is not the sort of person who is unable to say "No" and says she only took on work in which she was interested and which she thought she could do well. This is confirmed by letters of refusal from her to various organisations. In July 1995, for example, she refused a request from Michael Ancram, the Northern Ireland minister for education, to become a trustee of the Ulster Museum. Her interests were certainly widespread, as witness the numerous organisations of which she was a member.

She succeeded Lord Billy Blease as honorary president of the Northern Ireland Housing Rights Association, a voluntary body concerned with the rights of those who were homeless or in very poor accommodation, those who were vulnerable or had no security of tenure. It was an advisory and lobbying body, totally non-sectarian, and it attracted the services of several good young lawyers. She agreed to become a member of the Strategy for Sport steering group for a couple of reasons. One motive was to promote sport among women. Another arose when she heard one senior university administrator tell an audience that sailing was the sport with the greatest following in Northern Ireland. "He had obviously never heard of Gaelic games," she says. "And if he hadn't, how many others were like him? I intended to set them straight."

Mary had been a long-standing supporter and board member of the Flax Trust, a cross-community initiative in Ardoyne which was founded by her old friend Fr Myles Kavanagh, CP. Fr Myles was born and reared in Dublin, "around the corner from the Kimmage Inn", as he says himself. He was ordained a priest of the Order of the Cross and Passion in 1959 and was sent to Ardoyne in 1961. He is a priest who likes to spend time chatting to the men in the snooker halls and on street corners. His regular, challenging greeting to the young men of Ardoyne who were on the dole was, "Are you still living off your ma?" He knew his jibe was working the first time he got the response, "Hey, Fr Myles, I got a job!" His life's ambition for Ardoyne was that every young man and woman who was able would have a job. In the 1970s, when he was rector of the monastery in Ardoyne, he wrote:

> Unemployment—the degradation of not having the capacity to feed, clothe and house oneself, the indignity of a breadwinner living on handouts for himself and his children. This degraded state causes great anger. The anger expresses itself in violence or hides itself behind the terrifying apathy of a communal mental home or is all too easily focused into inter-community strife. The symptoms are the pastoral problems which the care of souls services. The question arises: Do I go on servicing problems or do I attack root causes?[‡]

This was the sort of talk, the sort of Christianity and the sort of priest that appealed to Mary, and she gave her full support to him and his work in her native parish.

In 1977 the Passionist Order was financially compensated for the damage done by a huge bomb which exploded beside the chapel in July 1972. The explosion, in which no one was injured, broke all the stained glass windows in the church and caused a lot of damage. It would take years to commission, make and install the new windows. In the meantime, Myles got permission from the authorities of the order to use some of the money as collateral for a loan to buy and restore the old Brookfield Linen Mill, initially as a safe place for a youth club and later, hopefully, as an industrial development centre.

Myles contacted priests such as Enda McDonagh and Austin Flannery, people to whom the Flax Trust was in line with their own ideas of reconciliation through economic development. He also needed expertise in setting up a business park for small companies. With help from the IDA in Dublin, he sent a proposal to the Northern Ireland Department of Commerce. No reply ever came.

His next contact was with a well-known anarchist, Geoff Jeffers, a Belfast man who had been living in London for years and who was an expert in founding small business parks in old factories and mills. He refused to help the priest. Jeffers was related to a loyalist leader from the Shankill Road, Sammy McCracken, who was in prison at that time. Criminal activity was getting out of control in the Shankill, and a delegation from the area asked Myles to use his good offices to persuade

---

‡   Myles Kavanagh, CP, private memo.

the Secretary of State Humphrey Atkins to release McCracken and so exert some control over the criminal elements. They explained that if the hoodlums were brought under control, there would be fewer confrontations between Catholic and Protestant youths on the peace line between Ardoyne and the Shankill Road.

Myles put the proposal to Humphrey Atkins, and McCracken was released. When Jeffers heard this story, he agreed to come to Belfast and start work on the plans for the shell of the old mill. Needing all the support he could get to raise money for building, Myles contacted Ardoyne people living in Dublin, people such as Eugene McEldowney in *The Irish Times,* Vincent McBrierty in Trinity College and Mary McAleese of RTÉ.

They succeeded in putting the money together, and by the time Mary went on the board of the Flax Trust in 1987, when she returned to live in the North, the trust had incubated hundreds of small industries and sent them out into the world of commerce. The businesses were 60 per cent Protestant and the workers were 60 per cent Catholic. The people of Ardoyne were reaping the harvest of their abilities and perseverance. However, they still had many difficulties, and foremost among them was the question of policing.

When the ceasefire of 1994 was called, Myles Kavanagh held a brainstorming session with five or six parishioners to see what could be done about this burning issue. Members of the group included Sr Mary Turley of the Flax Trust, Anne Tanney, principal of Holy Cross Girls' School, and Paul Shevlin. This man, who had a masters degree in personal development from Trinity College Dublin, was the prime mover in organising the Policing Conference. People would have an opportunity to express their views and speak of their experiences to anyone who would listen, including representatives of the RUC, and workshops would be organised on various aspects of policing. The committee decided to ask Mary McAleese to chair the conference.

When Mary arrived at the Flax Centre on Saturday, 1 October 1994, she found the Golden Thread Theatre full to overflowing. There were representatives there from every organisation in the district. She explained that there was only one rule governing the proceedings: "Respect the speaker!" The conference got underway with three local people, one after the other, speaking of their personal experience of policing. The evidence was damning and upsetting. Next to speak was David Cook, chairman of the Police Authority, and he was visibly moved. He admitted that he was shocked and dismayed by what the previous speakers had to say. After Cook came Alex Atwood of the SDLP and Joe Austin of Sinn Féin. Jimmy Grew, chairman of the Independent Police Complaints Commission, was the last guest to speak. The conference was then open to the floor, and that was the toughest part of all. Tensions were high and people were upset. They spoke across each other and tried to shout each other down in their efforts to be heard, and the job of the chair was not an easy one.

When Mary called an end to the plenary session, she announced that the conference would continue later in the day and on Sunday as a series of workshops at which everyone would get an opportunity to speak and to try to work on proposals for better policing. Ironically, although all the speakers from the floor were nationalists, those working in the kitchen preparing their refreshments were all unionists from the Shankill Road.

Six groups were formed to work on different aspects of policing over a period of time. Mary McAleese, Paul Shevlin and Professor Mike Brogden were appointed as facilitators, and the recommendations were published in the form of a booklet, "A Neighbourhood Police Service— Ardoyne". The last paragraph in the report is reminiscent of the strong feelings that were expressed in other nationalist areas around that time:

> We believe the 28 murders of members of our community by the British Security Forces, and the 79 murders by Loyalist death squads over the past 25 years, are legitimate reasons why we as a community have no faith or trust in the RUC. The "Conspiracy of Silence" among their ranks does not inspire us to have confidence in their ability to look after our everyday needs. Our community needs, wants, and demands a complete new Police Service which has our interest and well-being at heart—events have proven the RUC cannot fit this bill.[‡]

One of the most remarkable things about the recommendations of that Policing Conference in Ardoyne is that they are very akin to the recommendations made by Chris Patten in his famous report on policing in Northern Ireland a few years later.

If Myles Kavanagh were not a priest of a religious order with a vow of poverty, he would doubtless be a millionaire several times over. But he is apparently happy with his lot, and the people of Ardoyne may be thankful that his business acumen is working for them rather than for

---

‡   Ardoyne Association, p. 38.

290

himself. He is fulsome in his praise of Mary McAleese and honest in his assessment of the condition of religious orders:

> Mary's greatest quality is her openness to life, her intuitive understanding of life sources. This understanding is in the guts. It is an understanding that institutions and organisations try desperately to identify. Religious orders are dying because they don't have the capacity to identify the sources of life that drove their founders. There is a great honesty about her, and she stays straight and genuine. It is very difficult to be hypocritical with her, and that is a tendency in some Church people.‡

---

‡ Interview with author.

Chapter Twenty-Three

A Contemplative Commentator

> The monk told his story
> Of how he thought that he
> Could make reality
> Of the romance of the books
> That told of Popes,
> Men of genius who drew
> Wild colours on the flat page.
> (Patrick Kavanagh: "Lough Derg")

John Main was born into an Irish family in London in 1926 and had a brief career as a soldier before joining the canons regular. He gained a degree in law at Trinity College Dublin, later learned Chinese and was sent to work in Malaya, where he was introduced to a simple form of meditation by a Hindu monk, Swami Satyananda. The meditation, which became the contemplative foundation of his Christian life, challenged the mental prayer that was almost exclusively the practice in religious communities. Having taught international law for a time, he entered the Benedictine Order and was ordained in 1963. In his studies he discovered a connection between the *oratio pura*, the pure prayer of the Irish and European monastic tradition, and the "meditation" he had first practised in the East. The bridge was the calm, continuous repetition of a single word or phrase during the time of meditation. Main spent the rest of his life teaching meditation in the Christian tradition, and in 1975 he founded the Christian Meditation Centre in London. He died in Montreal in 1982.

Mary McAleese maintains that she never made a conscious decision to start practising Christian meditation in the John Main tradition, but that she "slipped into it". It was a natural progression, she says, from the shared prayer of the group to which she belonged. Undoubtedly she was also attracted by the silence and serenity which are intrinsic parts of the routine. She describes Christian meditation as bringing a distracted mind to stillness, silence and concentration, and opening it to the presence and influence of God. A mantra, the rhythmic repetition of a word or phrase—the "bridge" referred to by John Main—is used as a means of drawing the attention away from everyday thoughts and concerns. Any word or phrase can be used for this purpose. Mary's personal mantra is the Aramaic word *maranatha*, which means "Come, Lord".[‡]

She was very young when she had her first experience of Christian meditation, as she sat in childish wonder beside her grandmother in the flickering candlelight before first mass in the small church in Roscommon long ago. Brigid McDrury knew nothing of mantras or Irish monks or Hindu swamis, but Mary feels that her Christian meditation was completely instinctive, and somehow perhaps even purer for that.

On one occasion when Mary was attempting to simplify the mysteries of meditation to a five-year-old Emma McAleese, she explained that silence was a necessary prerequisite.

"Sit up straight now and be very quiet," she told her daughter. "Say the word '*maranatha*' again and again in your mind. Soon God will talk to you."

Five minutes later, when Mary was deep in meditation, Emma spoke again.

"Mammy, is God talking to you now?"

"Yes!" answered her mother, distractedly.

"Well, will you tell him that when he's finished with you, I'm still waiting!"

Apart from the obvious spiritual dimension of meditation, Mary finds it a very useful tool in everyday life. It has a "centring" effect, in that it helps to filter out all distractions and allows the practitioner to concentrate the mind on a single subject, a very helpful device indeed for someone with such a busy lifestyle.

Dom Laurence Freeman, the Benedictine monk who founded the World Community for Christian Meditation and has edited many of John Main's writings, is a good friend of Mary's and, over the years, has been something of a spiritual director for her in her meditation. Two years after Main died, in 1982, the first John Main Seminar was convened. Isabelle Glover addressed the gathering on the subject of "Indian Scriptures as Christian Reading". Since then, the annual three-day seminar has been addressed by such people as Dom Bede Griffiths

---

[‡] *Maranatha*: regarded as the first Christian prayer. The Evangelist John uses it at the end of the Book of Revelations.

and Jean Vanier. In 1994 the guest speaker was the Dali Lama, and a year later Laurence Freeman himself was the main speaker.

In 1997 Mary was invited to be the keynote speaker when the John Main Seminar was held in St Patrick's College in Drumcondra, in Dublin, the first time it had been held in Ireland. Her book, *Reconciled Being—Love in Chaos*, is based on her talks to the assembly that year. A second edition, entitled *Love in Chaos*, was published in 1999.

In her book she makes several references to Brian Keenan, the Belfast academic who was kidnapped in Lebanon, and to his book, *An Evil Cradling*, in which he recounts his experiences. Keenan subsequently launched Mary's book shortly after she became president in 1997. *Love in Chaos* is full of anecdotes. In it she draws widely on her life experience, on her own childhood and youth, on the experiences of her children and on the lessons she has learned during a lifetime of working for peace and reconciliation. Her love of poetry shines through, and pride of place is given to the Ulster poets: Seamus Heaney, John Hewitt, Tom Paulin and particularly the former Presbyterian minister W.R. Rodgers. She gives some fresh insights into the reasons for the Troubles and into what is necessary to ensure that they never recur. The theme of hope is never far from the surface, and it is that which occupied the mind of Archbishop Desmond Tutu when he wrote the foreword to the second edition: "On reading Mary McAleese's book, I realised why there is so much hope in the midst of much that still fills many with a despair of ever seeing the end of the 'Troubles'."[‡]

She speaks with fondness and huge respect of one of her heroes, Gordon Wilson, the gentle, quiet-spoken man who was injured in the Remembrance Day bombing in Enniskillen, and whose daughter Marie died by his side that day: "It is a rare person who arrives at that state of perfect spiritual serenity. I suppose they are saints of sorts, not necessarily beatified or canonised saints but the kind of people in whose presence we intuit the nearness of God."[§]

Serenity and energy working together in a person, the silence in the midst of clamour—this is a *leitmotif* throughout the book. Meditation is so important to her, such an intrinsic part of her life, that she was considering leaving her job in Queen's University and going to Florence to spend some months each year in the World Meditation Centre at the time she decided to seek a presidential nomination.

[‡]   Mary McAleese, *Love in Chaos*, (New York: Continuum, 1999), p. 10.

[§]   *Ibid.*, p. 60.

Fr Dermod McCarthy may have been the first priest to recognise Mary's preaching ability when he invited her to speak from the pulpit in the Pro-Cathedral in Dublin, but he was not the last. She was invited to speak in Knock, in Clonard and in Holy Cross Church in Ardoyne. No one could say she was not "in with the clergy", but certain members of the Catholic hierarchy must have thought that it was better to have such a troublesome woman on the inside, where they could keep an eye on her, rather than on the outside.

Her manifest love for the Catholic Church, with all its failings, did not prevent her from criticising Church authorities wherever and whenever she felt it was necessary. It was this propensity for speaking her mind that led Nick Lowry, whose book she launched in 1986, to question publicly her devotion to the Church. In explanation of her regular broadsides across the bows of Mother Church, Mary quotes her favourite pope, John XXIII, who challenged the people of God to cultivate a garden rather than guard a museum, and says that all good gardeners must sometimes be ruthless. She says that her affection for "good Pope John", and the faith she had in his loving and broadminded spirit, gave her hope and confidence, even when the Church's attitude, which had been open and receptive during his pontificate, became once again reticent and wary after his death.

Bishop Brendan Comiskey wrote to her in January 1997: "What you are calling for is a new kind of Church: repentant, humble, modest. Something like Jesus Christ! . . . What the Church and society have no need of today are unloving critics or uncritical lovers. You are certainly neither."[‡]

The Bishop had good reason to say that about her. Three years previously, in January 1994, she had criticised him publicly in the magazine *Intercom:* "My heart sank when I read Bishop Comiskey's view on that hoariest of old chestnuts, the 'clip on the ear' or the 'boot in the backside' . . . Sorry, Bishop Comiskey, but I wasn't one of those who shook their heads sagely along with you."[§]

She was much more scathing in an article she wrote later that same year about the lack of any worthwhile system of appeal available to the ordinary lay person who feels unjustly treated by a bishop. In the article she describes a Confirmation Day scene. The child has been brought forward by the sponsor and the chosen Confirmation name has been read out, but the bishop considers the name inappropriate:

---

‡   Letter from Bishop Brendan Comiskey to Mary McAleese, 28 January 1997.

§   *Intercom,* January 1994.

The lovely down-to-earth bishop asks, "What kind of name is that?" He deems it unsuitable. At this late stage, in front of the entire parish, a helpless, hapless child dies a million deaths at the altar, as the name she chose in simple good faith is binned ungraciously by His Grace (or is it His Lordship—I get all these titles mixed up.) The remaining children almost disintegrate in terror as the paragon of earthiness wends his way towards them. And there is no redress for this fictitious child, at least not on this earth.[‡]

The language in the article is bitter and angry, and some people were surprised that it was allowed to be published in a magazine that describes itself as "A Pastoral and Liturgical Magazine Published by the Catholic Communications Institute of Ireland". Fr Kevin Hegarty was the editor of *Intercom* at that time, but within six months of the publication of the article he was transferred to the parish of Kilmore in County Mayo.[§] *The Irish Times* republished the article in full, and the ensuing controversy generated quite a few letters to the editor on the subject. The bishops came under pressure to re-appoint Fr Hegarty to his former position. Eventually they succumbed, but Fr Hegarty refused to take his old job back. Some of the bishops, including Brendan Comiskey, attacked Mary in various publications, saying that no bishop would ever act like the fictitious bishop in her article. When they accused her of having embarrassed the Church unnecessarily, she made it her business to speak personally to several bishops, including Brendan Comiskey, to tell them that the article was not fictitious, that the incident had in fact occurred, and that the only reason she wrote the piece as fiction was to protect the child involved.

Mary was one of the first journalists to write in Catholic publications on the issue of clerical sexual abuse of children. In October 1995, she wrote an article on the subject in *The Universe*. Seven years later the journalist David McKittrick had this to say about the article: "Seven years ago the state of the Church was denounced by an Irish academic as 'a shabby bleak procession of Pontius Pilate lookalikes, abusing priests, disinterested abbots, impotent cardinals and unempowered parents'. The critic, Professor Mary McAleese, is now the President of Ireland."[†] In that same year she spoke of the Church's ambivalence to

---

‡   *Intercom*, August 1994.

§   Publishing this article was not Kevin Hegarty's only transgression. He had also incurred the wrath of the hierarchy by publishing articles about sexual abuse of children by priests.

†   *The Independent*, 9 November 2002.

homosexual priests and urged the authorities to take their heads out of the sand and face the reality:

> The sexual orientation may not be generally known, particularly if they remain celibate as they are supposed to, but is it the case that being gay is an impediment to ordination or that it could annul an ordination in the same way that certain impediments can annul a marriage? No one seems willing to provide an answer, for this is another classic case where the Church prefers to fudge the problem by denying its existence rather than meeting it head on and in the open.[‡]

In 1996 the committee advising the Irish bishops on the drafting of their first ever guidelines on child sex abuse did not recommend mandatory reporting. On this question Mary McAleese was adamant: the reporting should be compulsory. Shortly before the publication of the hierarchy's report, Mary told Bishop Seamus Hegarty and a lawyer member of the committee, Ted Jones, that she would lead a campaign against the hierarchy if mandatory reporting was not included. Dominic Burke, a Derry-based expert in child care, confirms that Bishop Hegarty sought his advice on the subject and that he completely supported Mary's view. The bishops subsequently took the advice, and mandatory reporting was introduced.[§]

By the mid 1990s, Mary McAleese was recognised as one of the country's most influential lay commentators on Catholic Church affairs, and her obvious commitment to the Church was equalled only by her obvious divergence of opinion with some of the major authority figures in that same Church. In 1993, Fionnuala O'Connor wrote this about her in her book *In Search of a State—Catholics in Northern Ireland:* "Mary McAleese is the only Northern Catholic laywoman to have a significant public profile based at least in part on her religious beliefs. Her access to bishops and Church authorities generally—as a lawyer who has advised the hierarchy on abortion and divorce legislation—is fairly unusual for a lay person, and almost unique for a woman."[†]

Her biggest bone of contention was still the role of women in the Church. This difficulty came to the fore once again at the start of the 1990s when Cardinal Joseph Ratzinger issued a statement which effectively said that those people who sought ordination to the

‡   *The Universe*, April 1995.

§   Interview with author.

†   Fionnuala O'Connor, p. 30.

priesthood for women were putting themselves out of communion with the Church. Such was her upset at the statement that she wrote a letter to Pope John Paul II:

Dearest Holy Father,

I am grateful that you have spoken on the subject of women priests and that in so doing you have acknowledged the importance of this issue in the modern world. I accept completely the sincerity of the view you have so emphatically expressed but I am nonetheless disappointed and more than a little concerned. . .

This letter may anger you. I understand that Cardinal Ratzinger has warned that those who do not accept the teaching on women priests are out of communion with the Church. He may be right, but in the deepest recesses of my soul I hear the voice of the Lord whom I love so very much telling me that the disappointment I feel is righteous. It is justified. Once before I wrote to you and begged you to look again at this whole vexed issue. I know you did that and did so to the utmost of your great ability. I am grateful that you did but I remain, and will until the day I die, convinced beyond a shadow of a doubt that on this subject the Church is wrongheaded and is flying in the face of the will of God.

. . . I know how much good you have accomplished and yet I also know that around this issue your epitaph will be written. The danger is that it may also be the Church's epitaph.[‡]

Her reply from Rome was signed by Monsignor L. Sandri of the Secretariat of State: the pope had read her letter and understood her position; he hoped she understood his position and he would pray for her. This was the third letter Mary had written to the pope, and she was satisfied enough with the response. She could not, realistically, have hoped for much more. She referred to these letters in an address she gave to the first annual conference of BASIC, a Dublin-based group which was founded to lobby for the ordination of women to the Catholic priesthood. In the same address she said it was remarkable that Cardinal Cahal Daly found himself unable to respond to a petition signed by 20,000 people on the subject of women priests, whereas the pope was able to respond to her letters on the same subject.

BASIC is an acronym for Brothers and Sisters in Christ. One of the founders was Soline Vatinel, a Frenchwoman from Versailles who settled in Blackrock, County Dublin. She had come to Ireland for the first time,

‡   Mary McAleese, private papers.

298

on holiday, in 1969. She liked the country so much that she came to live in Dublin in 1973 and to obtain a degree in history from Trinity College. She says that during all her adult life she has been convinced that God is calling her to the Catholic priesthood. In 1993 she, along with her husband Colm Holmes and Fr Eamonn McCarthy, who was a curate in Baldoyle at the time, founded BASIC. In 1993 Soline Vatinel read an article in *Intercom* by Mary McAleese on the subject of the ordination of women. Vatinel wrote to her to let her know that there was now an organisation founded specifically to fight for the cause of women priests. She invited Mary to join BASIC and was delighted to receive a positive reply by return of post.

"I greatly admired Mary's courage. This was no jumping on a bandwagon. Our membership was quite small at the time and she was a prominent lay Catholic, yet she was prepared to stick her neck out and join us. For all she knew we could have been a bunch of cranks. She is a woman of great integrity who always follows her conscience."‡

At that first conference on 25 March 1995, traditionally the Feast of the Annunciation but in another dispensation the World Day of Prayer for the Ordination of Women in the Catholic Church, Mary spoke to three hundred people gathered in the Jesuit Conference Centre in Milltown Park, Dublin. The group consisted of women and men, clerics and laity and Irish and foreigners. The attendance might have been greater but for the statement of Cardinal Ratzinger. Among the speakers were Fr Enda McDonagh, professor of theology in NUI Maynooth; Fr Michael O'Sullivan, SJ; Fr Eamonn McCarthy; and the Revd Ginnie Kennerly, of the Church of Ireland. Three women who felt called to the Catholic priesthood also spoke: Soline Vatinel, Delma Sheridan and Jackie Hawkins.

Mary's address was entitled "Coping with a Christ Who Does Not Want Women Priests Almost as Much as He Wants Ulster to Remain British". She came out fighting: "They say the debate is closed. I think they had better turn up their hearing aids."§

She continued:

As the Franciscan theologian Leonardo Boff has said, "At critical moments it is always the women who show the most courage." Just as it seems the Church has not enough champions to man the

---

‡   Interview with author.

§   BASIC, *Women Sharing Fully in the Ministry of Christ?* (Dublin: Blackwater Press, 1995), p. 20.

barricades under the onslaught of secularism, righteous cynicism and retreat from priesthood, here are women saying "Let us help." And back comes that all too familiar voice which says "No" to change, a voice I am all too familiar with in Northern Ireland in a different context: No to change, No to dialogue, No to power sharing, No even to listening and to talking.[‡]

She made it very clear that the God she believed in was the God of Love and the God of the Open Mind, no matter what any priest, bishop, cardinal or even pope might say:

If I truly believed that Christ was the authority for the proposition that women are to be excluded from priesthood by virtue simply of their gender I would have to say emphatically that this is a Christ in whose divinity I do not and will not and cannot believe. That is not said lightly. That Christ is too small of mind, too mean of heart to be the Christ of the gospel whom I believe in and whom I know, I like to think, at least as well as the pope might know him. He is, after all, my Father and Mother too.[§]

Her address ended with an excerpt from 'Resurrection' by one of her favourite poets, the troubled former Presbyterian minister, W.R. Rodgers.

It describes Mary Magdalene lamenting for the loss of Christ just as we lament for the loss of the full gifts of women flowing through the blocked up veins of the Church bureaucrat. Let us pray for the by-pass which is soon to come:

"It is always the women who are the Watchers
And Wakeners . . .
Slowly his darkened voice, that seemed like doubt
Morninged into noon; the summering bees
Mounted and boiled over in the bell flowers.

"Come out of your jail, Mary," he said, "The doors are open."[†]

"Over the years the Catholic Church has spoken with authority and certainty on many issues, only to change its mind on them," says Mary. She often refers to "poor Galileo", and asks, "If the Church has been wrong so often on so many issues, how many more might she be wrong on?" As if on cue, before the end of 1995 Cardinal Joseph Ratzinger announced that the Church's teaching on the subject of women priests

---

‡   *Ibid.*, p. 14.

§   *Ibid.*, p. 19.

†   *Ibid.*, p. 21.

was infallible! Mary's response was, "They're wrong about infallibility as well!"

Soline Vatinel says about Mary's address and their campaign:

> It was an extraordinarily powerful talk. It was the first one of the day, in the morning, and it was a great wake-up call. People still talk about it, and I remember the details of it very well. She referred to my attempts to get a meeting with Cardinal Daly. I had been trying for almost a year to persuade the cardinal to see me, but the promised date for the meeting never came. Eventually he did agree to see me after I sent him a Valentine card. I'm afraid the romance didn't blossom. Despite two hours of talking, he still would not accept the petition which had more than 20,000 names on it. When Mary was elected president, we presented her with a painting of the Last Supper by the Polish artist Bohdan Tiasecki. This painting is nearer the truth than the famous painting of Leonardo de Vinci because the women and children are in it as well as Christ and the Apostles.[‡]

The proceeding of that first conference were published in the form of a book, which was launched by the Dominican historian Sr Margaret McCurtin, in Dublin. Mary McAleese and Soline Vatinel were members of a group which visited Áras an Uachtaráin to present a copy to President Mary Robinson. Little did Mary think, as she presented the book to the president that day, 30 October 1995, that on exactly the same date, two years later, she would be elected as the next occupant of Áras an Uachtaráin.

Chapter Twenty-Four

There's a Job Going in Dublin

So when in Dublin I arrived to try for a situation
I always heard them say it was the pride of all the nations
("Dublin Jack of All Trades"—Anonymous)

Who was the first to think seriously of Mary McAleese as President of Ireland? Many people claim this distinction, and many more say the thought ran through their minds on 12 March 1997 when Mary Robinson announced she would resign the presidency early to work for the United Nations. Dr Maria Moloney, a school friend of Mary's and sister of the influential Belfast solicitor Denis Moloney, rang her brother the following morning with the prophetic words:"I have no doubt that Mary McAleese will be the next President of Ireland. Ring Martin immediately." Martin maintains he thought of her as a possible candidate when the Labour Party originally proposed Mary Robinson back in 1990. Harry Casey says he thought the same thing on the same day: "There's a president in Mary McAleese."

Harry Casey is one of ten children born and reared seven miles west of the town of Longford. When he was still in national school, one of his teachers, Chris Farrell from County Mayo, awoke in him an abiding interest in "the national question", as it was known at the time: the whole issue of partition and the lack of political movement in Northern Ireland. In 1982, he went to work as a teacher of religion and English in St Patrick's Classical School, Navan. One evening he visited a family who had just settled in the town. The Nethercotts, whose sons Raymond and Andrew had recently enrolled in the school, were from Belfast, and Harry wanted to welcome them to Navan and offer his services to help them settle in. As he was talking to Elizabeth Nethercott, the boys' mother, the pictures on a muted television set caught his eye. Mary McAleese was speaking to camera on the programme.

"That's a woman I would love to meet," said Harry.

"Would you, really?" asked Elizabeth. "She's a friend of ours, and if you would like to meet her we'll introduce you to her. She lives just outside Dunshaughlin."

Ray Nethercott, the father, had worked in the ill-fated Ford factory in Belfast. When it closed he did not remain idle for long and got a job with Timoney's in Gibstown, County Meath. A few months before the family moved to Navan, Ray arrived to find a suitable family home and stayed for a while with the McAleeses in Mooretown, as he knew them through Mary's youngest aunt, Anne McManus, in Belfast. The Nethercotts were Evangelical Catholics, and they and Harry soon became very friendly and began to attend prayer meetings together.

Harry soon got the opportunity to meet Mary McAleese. Little did they realise, as they shook hands for the first time, the effect each would have on the life of the other. Harry was to become her close friend and one of the key people in securing for her the Fianna Fáil nomination for the presidency.

While the McAleeses lived in Mooretown, Harry was probably their most regular visitor. He was also a regular babysitter, and all the McAleeses, including Charlie, later claimed that Harry Casey had "adopted" them. He and Mary attended prayer meetings together over several years, and his work as her director of elections in the 1987 general election only served to cement their friendship even more.

Casey was a clerical student for a time before he became a teacher and writer of religion textbooks. At the end of the eighties, he was doing postgraduate work in theology, as a layman, in the Irish College in Rome. Although he had decided several years previously that the priesthood was not for him, being among clerical students and priests again made him begin to reconsider his decision. During that year, Mary and Martin went to Italy on a holiday, and Harry and a few clerical friends joined them for a week of travelling. When the time came for the McAleeses to return home, Harry was more undecided than ever. Shortly after Mary arrived back in Ireland, she wrote him a letter: "Come home, Harry. I'm sure there's a fine woman waiting for you here in Ireland, and I'm sure you will make each other very happy."

He accepted her advice, and shortly after he returned home he met Mary Hayes, a sister of Liam Hayes, the former Meath footballer and editor of *Ireland on Sunday*. When the couple married in August 1993, the liveliest topic of conversation among the 270 guests, according to Harry, was Mary McAleese's after-dinner speech. His former primary schoolteacher, Chris Farrell, was enchanted by her, and that was enough to convince Harry, if he needed convincing, of the power of Mary's eloquence.

On the evening of 12 March 1997, Mary had a headache and decided to go to bed early, just before the *Nine O'Clock News* on RTÉ One. At a quarter past nine, Martin answered the phone to an excited Harry Casey.

"Did you hear the news, Martin? Mary Robinson is not going for another term. Now, don't put down the phone until you've heard me out. I'm going to ask you to encourage Mary to stand as a candidate in the presidential election. Chew on it for a few days and then I'll meet you."

When Martin went in to check on Mary, he mentioned that Mary Robinson had announced her resignation. "Mary said nothing in response to what I told her, but there was something in her eyes. I knew she was thinking the same thing I was."

As to why he spoke to Martin before approaching Mary herself, Harry explains: "Mary is a woman of extraordinary vision and energy, but Martin is the powerhouse. He drives the engine. There was no point in me even talking to Mary unless Martin was 100 per cent sold on the idea. If he was fully on board, it might happen. Without his complete and utter backing, there was no chance."

The following Sunday, Harry travelled to Rostrevor, where he and Martin discussed the proposition. It was decided that Harry would ring Mary the following evening and raise the subject without any preamble. On Monday evening, as Mary was driving home from Belfast, Harry called her on her mobile phone.

"Mary, I'm going to say something to you now that might cause you to swerve. So slow down and listen and don't crash the car. I'm just going to say this, and then I'll hang up and come back to you later . . ."

When he rang her at home later that night, he told the first of the many "white lies", as he calls them, that he would tell her over the next few weeks: "Mary, I've been talking to Eoin Heaney, a local Fianna Fáil councillor here, and he says there is great interest in you as a candidate. Your name has been suggested by several senior people in Fianna Fáil."

When there was no response from Mary, he called on his considerable reserves of *plámás* and told her about all the support that was "out there" for her if only she would agree to let him float her name. He mentioned Fianna Fáil because he presumed that would be her party of choice. In that he was correct. Martin's original idea, before any other candidate was mooted, was that Mary would make the perfect agreed candidate for the major parties, and with that in mind the first messages were sent to all TDs and senators in some areas.

What did Mary think of the whole idea of trying for a nomination?

What did she think of these people who were making plans for her and around her and trying to seduce her with half-truths and untruths?

When Harry rang me that Monday evening while I was driving home I was stunned. I remember the impact more than the details. The idea, once it was articulated, hit me like a blow. My breath was taken away. When I came to myself again after several seconds, I was convinced that the whole thing was pure nonsense. The day after Mary Robinson announced her resignation, I got a letter from Joe Martin, an old friend of mine whose opinion I have always respected. In that letter he said straight out that I should seek a nomination. Joe was not trying to flatter me by saying that, but that was more or less what I took from what he had to say. I did not really consider the proposal seriously. John Hume was the only Ulster person I would have considered for the job of President of Ireland. I was very hard on poor Harry for a while, blocking him at every move, playing devil's advocate. But his persistence began to pay off. After a while I became used to people saying it was time to have the first Northerner in the Áras, and if John Hume was not interested, maybe Mary McAleese might be the person best suited to the job. I began to think to myself: is this really a risible idea, or could it perhaps be a runnable idea?‡

Mary, Harry and Martin sat down together the following weekend to have a long, hard look at their options. Harry says that Mary still believed that many Fianna Fáil people were mooting her as their candidate of choice, but Mary says she "never believed a word of that auld nonsense from the start". As Harry and Martin brought their considerable influence to bear on her that Sunday, she spent most of the time laughing at them. By the end of the evening, all were united on one thing: if John Hume declared an interest in the presidency, that was the end of any talk of Mary McAleese seeking a nomination. But as the spring days lengthened and Hume still failed to show any interest in the job, Mary starting giving the possibility of a nomination serious consideration.

Her deliberations were significantly influenced by the intervention of Denis Moloney. When he met Mary in Clonard shortly after St Patrick's Day, he told her out straight that he thought she was the person best suited to be the next President of Ireland, and that if she agreed to seek

‡ Joe Martin: director of the South-Western Education and Library Board in County Tyrone

305

a Fianna Fáil nomination he would give her his total and complete backing. She realised how influential he was and that his support would open many doors for her, North and South. The Moloneys and the McAleeses had been good friends for years and had often gone on holidays together. Denis and his only sister Maria, a former board member of the Harland and Wolff Shipyard, were well placed to gather such support which, if channelled correctly, could eventually translate into votes for Mary. Denis is a well-known solicitor in Northern Ireland, the senior partner in the law firm of Donnelly and Wall. His vast circle of friends includes judges and justices, members of the diplomatic corps and many senior civil servants on both sides of the border. He is an influential lay Catholic and acts as legal adviser to the Diocese of Down and Connor.

The Moloneys' father, Denis senior, was, unusually for a Catholic, a senior officer in the RUC. When he and his wife Pearl were killed in the Kegworth Air Disaster in 1989, Mary moved into Denis's house to comfort him and his sister and to organise things for them. Over a period of five horrific days, she was in regular contact with John Hermon, chief constable of the RUC, while the police were attempting to identify the bodies at the accident site. Michael McAtamney was assistant chief constable at the time. His wife and Mary were fondly referred to as "the kitchen girls" during that long sorrowful week, as they catered for the hundreds upon hundreds of visitors to the Moloney house. Mary and Martin sat beside Denis and Maria in the principal mourners' car on the day of the funeral. They were close. There was no question about the unreserved support of the Moloneys for Mary McAleese in her attempt to get a nomination. Anything they could do for her they would do.

Denis, Harry and Martin were prepared to use everyone they knew to promote the idea of Mary as a Fianna Fáil candidate, but no one suspected that the first person to mention her name to a top party functionary would be Fr Alex Reid. During a phone conversation with him, Mary mentioned that she was coming under a fair amount of pressure to let her name be floated. When she asked him what he thought of the idea, he replied that he thought it was a great idea. Mary then asked him if he would sound out Martin Mansergh on the possibility during one of his regular meetings with the taoiseach's adviser. During a meeting in the middle of April, the priest innocently asked Mansergh if Mary McAleese would have any realistic chance if she sought a Fianna Fáil nomination for the presidency. Mansergh was slightly taken aback by the seeming innocuousness of the priest's enquiry, but replied that such a question could not even be considered until after the general election. Whatever Martin Mansergh's answer might have been was purely academic. The important thing was that his conversation with Alex would be reported in the right circles. Mary's hat was now in the ring.

Casey was anxious that she should start immediately to show her face at as many events as possible. St Peter's College in Wexford was celebrating its centenary that spring, and Harry and Mary Casey had been invited to the celebrations. He contacted Fr Peter O'Connor, a friend of his who was organising the event, and invitations were arranged for "Professor Mary McAleese, the Pro-Vice-Chancellor of Queen's University Belfast, and her husband, Martin". Harry insisted that the trip would be worth her while. Bishop Brendan Comiskey would be there and the Papal Nuncio Luciano Storero, plenty of politicians, both local and national, and most importantly plenty of Fianna Fáil people.

The plan was that Mary and Martin were to drive from Roscommon, where they had spent the previous night, collect Harry and Mary Casey in Navan and drive on to Wexford. Mary had never shown much interest in fashion. Until the children were born she had made most of her own clothes, and although they were usually made from very good materials and beautifully finished, they were certainly not fashion statements. Martin, who regularly complained about Mary's lack of dress sense, took advantage of the Wexford occasion to stop at McElhinney's shop in Athboy on the way to Navan. Harry had suggested that the famous women's fashion shop would be a perfect place to get Mary a complete new outfit. Mary describes the visit to McElhinney's as "a pantomime", with discarded clothes scattered on every square inch of floor and Martin saying, "That's lovely, but don't bother wrapping it; she'll wear it."

With Mary looking very elegant in a new suit, blouse and shoes, the McAleeses arrived at the Casey's house earlier than expected. Mary Casey was cleaning the kitchen floor, and despite the new clothes, the other Mary got down on her knees and helped her. When the floor was gleaming and while Mary Casey was dressing for the journey to Wexford, the would-be presidential candidate dug out the necessary ingredients and proceeded to "run up a few wee buns for the baby-sitter". Martin and the Caseys were very happy to see her climb into the car with "no damage that you'd notice" done to the new outfit.

307

Throughout the months of April, May and June, neither Martin nor Denis Moloney nor Harry Casey approached any politician directly, but they contacted friends and acquaintances all over the country, asking them to write to Fianna Fáil elected representatives, national and local, suggesting Mary as a candidate. They hoped to build up a network of support that would reach into every constituency, and in that way to reach every Fianna Fáil politician. They were also assessing the potential strength of support for Mary, gauging reaction when her name was mentioned and adding to their list of influential supporters. People like Alistair McDonald of the SDLP decided to use their influence on her behalf when John Hume made it clear he had no presidential ambitions, but many other friends in the North gave her their support from the time they first heard the whisper.

Fr Alex Reid was already a supporter, and Mary's other colleague from the Clonard peace ministry, Jim Fitzpatrick of the *Irish News*. Mary and Martin were friendly with Kevin O'Neill, who with his brother Sean O'Neill won All-Ireland football medals in the 1960s. Kevin and his wife Mary had many friends in Fianna Fáil, and when Martin contacted them and sought their support, they were "delighted to be able to do something for her". Martin also contacted the former nationalist MP Frank McManus in Enniskillen, whose brother, Fr Sean McManus, was very influential among the Irish in America. Frank McManus subsequently put Martin in touch with Conal Gibbons, son of Hugh Gibbons who played on the Roscommon team which won the All-Ireland football final of 1944, and who later became a Fianna Fáil TD. Conal, who later became a district justice, was also a close friend of Pat Farrell, general secretary of Fianna Fáil, and was well-versed in Fianna Fáil strategy. He spent an evening with the McAleese's in their cottage in Roscommon advising them on their tactics.

The GAA connection stretched as far as Donegal. When Martin was training as a dentist, his partner in practical laboratory work was Sheena McEniff, niece of Brian McEniff of the McEniff Hotels family and manager of the Donegal team which won the All-Ireland football final in 1992. When Martin contacted him to seek his support for Mary, he promised to use all his influence. Not all Northern contacts were so easy to win over. When Martin phoned the influential former GAA president Peter Quinn, he was taken aback when the Fermanagh man told him straight out that he was committed to Albert Reynolds.

The first person in whom Martin confided Mary's presidential ambitions was a dentist friend from County Cork: Mike Cronin, from

Middleton, was perfectly willing to use his strong Fianna Fáil connections throughout the county in favour of Mary. Other dentist friends of Martin's who promised to use their influence were Paul Sullivan, who had worked in Bessbrook and Crossmaglen for four years before opening his own practice in Castleknock, and Dr Eamonn Murphy from Rathfarnham, who numbered among his patients the Fianna Fáil chief whip Seamus Brennan.

Denis Moloney had connections throughout the Irish communities in England, particularly in Manchester and London, where his influence spread from the palace of Cardinal Hume through convents and parochial houses to the Irish homeless and those who worked for them. He and Martin also called on all Mary's many Church contacts, both Catholic and Protestant, North and South, and friends in the legal profession were not neglected. Eugene Murphy, a solicitor with the firm of Eugene F. Collins, who had represented Mary in her action against the *Sunday Independent*, gave his support from an early stage. Another solicitor and supporter, Neil Faris, had a brother who was a Presbyterian minister in Cork, the Revd John Faris. Martin had no hesitation in ringing him and asking him to use his influence among the Presbyterian community there. At the other end of the legal spectrum, Mary's supporters in law enforcement were ably represented by her old friend and ally Michael Ringrose, who worked hard and long for her. Harry Casey went to visit Martin Naughton, the millionaire from County Louth who had contributed so generously to Queen's University, and he also came on board without hesitation.

By American Independence Day, 4 July 1997, the general election in the South was over, and President Mary Robinson had presented their seals of office to a Fianna Fáil/Progressive Democrat coalition government, with Bertie Ahern as taoiseach and Mary Harney as tánaiste. Still, Mary McAleese had not made any attempt to approach any politician. On that most American of days, however, she and Martin were attending a garden party at the residence of the American Consul to Northern Ireland. John Hume was there and Mary spent a while talking to him. Fr Alex Reid was also there, and a Jesuit priest who was a good friend of the McAleeses', Fr Paul McNelis, professor of economics in the University of Georgetown, in Washington DC. Both priests had considerable expertise in reading signs, subtle and otherwise, and both were of the same opinion: Mary should make every effort, as soon as possible, to get the Fianna Fáil nomination—in other words, they did not think Hume would run.

When she and Martin arrived home in Rostrevor that evening, Harry was waiting impatiently to find out what Hume had had to say, or how they read his body language. When Mary said she thought Hume would not seek the presidency, Harry was delighted. After a phone call to bring Denis Moloney up to date on the day's events, Mary sat down and drafted a letter to Bertie Ahern to let him know she was available as a candidate for a Fianna Fáil nomination. When all were happy with the letter, they printed three copies: one to go by registered post to the taoiseach's office in Government Buildings, and two to be delivered by hand by Harry Casey in Dublin that night: one to St Luke's, the taoiseach's constituency office in Drumcondra, and the other to Fianna Fáil headquarters, 13 Upper Mount Street. They were taking no chances.

She was committed, and now it was time to contact the politicians. Before any of them had an opportunity to speak to a Fianna Fáil elected representative, Mary got a chance to speak to the party guru himself, Martin Mansergh. The McAleeses were at a concert in the National Concert Hall when Mary spotted him during the interval. She had long since formed a deep respect for this Oxford-educated Protestant republican historian, a man whose understanding of and insights into Northern Ireland life had earned him the position of special adviser on Northern Ireland to the taoiseach of the day during three administrations.[‡] Mary made her way across the foyer and, having engaged him in conversation, told him exactly what she had in mind. Mansergh listened politely, and although he did not say that he thought the idea was a good one, neither did he disparage it. Mary was heartened by the fact that it seemed to give him food for thought.

"It must have been very clear to him that I, as a Fianna Fáil presidential candidate, would solve a lot of Fianna Fáil's problems in one fell swoop. I could be the compromise between the *realpolitik* and the common good."

The problems referred to by Mary were very real and very serious. Everyone knew that Albert Reynolds wanted to be President of Ireland. Some others in the party had been mentioned as possible candidates during the previous couple of years: Charles Haughey, David Andrews, Máire Geoghegan-Quinn and Mary O'Rourke. But as the mists cleared and the new government settled in, it became obvious that Reynolds was the strongest candidate from within the party. It was also clear that his

---

‡   Mansergh served as special adviser on Northern Ireland to Charles Haughey, Albert Reynolds and Bertie Ahern.

candidacy would create problems of its own. Albert Reynolds claims that Bertie Ahern asked him to stand for the presidency in 1996, a year before Mary Robinson announced she would not seek re-election. A year later, with the country ready to go to the polls in a general election, Ahern wanted Reynolds to stand for his old Dáil seat, to keep it safe at all costs. Then, if he were subsequently elected president, his seat could be more effectively defended by a member of the Reynolds family in a by-election. But by July 1997 the general election was over, and the new FF/PD coalition government was relying on the support of the independent deputies Mildred Fox, Jackie Healy-Rae, Harry Blaney and Tom Gildea. Some influential people in Fianna Fáil were no longer as convinced as they had been that Albert's seat in Longford-Roscommon could be easily defended if he were elected president.

Another problem facing Fianna Fáil was that the tánaiste Mary Harney had told Bertie Ahern that she could not support the candidacy of Albert Reynolds. The former taoiseach had embarrassed Harney's Progressive Democrat colleague and co-founder of the party Des O'Malley some years previously at the Beef Tribunal. Memories can be long in politics, particularly when a memory is embarrassing.

The PDs were not the only ones with bad memories of Albert Reynolds. When he succeeded Charles Haughey as taoiseach and leader of Fianna Fáil in February 1992, he fired eight government ministers and nine ministers of state. Weeding out potential subversion and rewarding faithful support may have seemed like a good idea at the time, but now the sacked ministers had an opportunity to settle a score. The campaign, which later became better known by the acronym ABBA— Anybody but Albert—was beginning to gain momentum.

Not only did the McAleeses, Denis Moloney and Harry Casey understand the implications of these scenarios, they also understood that the time had come to move their campaign up another gear. On a Saturday afternoon in mid-July, Casey visited Mary and Martin where they were holidaying with the children in the little cottage in Croghan, in Roscommon. All three were of the opinion that a full and accurate account of who Mary was and what she had done should be on the taoiseach's desk as soon as possible, and with that in mind Mary sat down to write her curriculum vitae. From the time she finished her dinner on Saturday until four o'clock on Sunday morning, she was in and out from the bedroom to the kitchen, from the computer to the critics by the fireside; all redrafting, refining, distilling, until all were happy that any more work on the document would be counterproductive.

The finished product was twenty-one pages long. It contained a list of forty-eight organisations, both national and international, professional, business and academic, of which she was a member. The document gave an account of her work and achievements in Queen's University and the Institute, described some aspects of her cross-community work and, in a personal narrative, gave a résumé of her experience in law, in broadcasting, in journalism and in administration. The years she spent working for the eradication of sectarianism merited all of four lines in the document, and there was no mention at all of her work with the Clonard peace and reconciliation ministry. "The Croghan Document", as it was dubbed that night, was handed to Cathal McGinty for editing. Sandra Garry, who prepared the manuscripts of Harry's religion textbooks, was charged with the layout and final typing. By the time the document was posted to the taoiseach, it had been cut down to eleven pages and was concise, polished and to the point.

During the McAleeses' holiday in Roscommon that July, they travelled to the Knock Shrine in County Mayo to visit their friend Monsignor Dominick Grealy. They had become friendly with him after Mary had preached in the basilica a couple of times during the national novena. When Monsignor Grealy brought them into the dining room, he called the staff in from the kitchen and introduced Mary with the words: "I'd like you all to meet Mary McAleese, the next President of Ireland." Martin says he found the introduction very moving, probably because it was the first time he heard the name and the title uttered aloud in the same sentence. The monsignor was in a position to be very influential on Mary's behalf. Many priests and bishops would sit at his table during the summer pilgrimage season, and he was not going to miss an opportunity to promote his friend Mary McAleese. Martin, who must have been delighted to be able to exert some Church influence at a remove, remained in regular contact with him all during the summer and describes him as "a crucial cog in the wheel", both for Mary's nomination and during her election campaign.

A few days after the visit to Knock, Mary phoned Patricia Casey, with whom she had become friendly after their appearance on *The Late Late Show* during the abortion referendum. Casey was prepared to give unqualified support to her new friend and to use her considerable influence on Mary's behalf. The Cork-born psychiatrist was well placed to exert some influence on the Fianna Fáil organisation as she was retained by them to advise on matters of ethics. Mary introduced Patricia Casey to Harry Casey, and when Patricia read the letter of introduction Harry had written, she decided that it should be sent to every member of the Fianna Fáil parliamentary party: TDs, senators and members of the European Parliament; everyone except the new senators who had not yet been officially appointed, and Albert Reynolds.

Patricia Casey contacted the Wicklow TD Dick Roche, for whom she had canvassed in the previous election. He promised that he would mention Mary's name and qualifications to his fellow TDs and also to the party leader, which he did. The network of friends of Mary McAleese was by now working as efficiently south of the border as it was in the North. Ciarán Taaffe, vice-president of the Dublin Institute of Technology, was a friend of the McAleeses through Eibhlís Farrell. Taaffe lived in Blackrock, outside Dundalk, where he was particularly friendly with one of his neighbours, Dermot Ahern, the minister for social, community and family affairs. It was Ciarán Taaffe who organised Mary's first meeting with a government minister. She and Martin visited Dermot Ahern in his office in Government Buildings in July. Martin says that he was becoming irritated by Ahern's wariness and the circumspect way he responded to what Mary had to say. They found out afterwards, however, that when the minister's private secretary returned to the office, having left Mary and Martin to the door, he greeted Ahern with the words, "You know who you've just met, Minister? You've just met the next president."

Mary Hanafin, a friend of Harry Casey's since they had been in college together in NUI Maynooth, was the first Fianna Fáil TD to be approached directly by him. She explained that she could not give unconditional support to McAleese because rumour had it that Michael O'Kennedy, the former European commissioner, was going to seek a nomination. O'Kennedy represented Tipperary North, the constituency of Mary Hanafin's father Des Hanafin, and she would be expected to support any move from that area. But in the meantime, she was prepared to help Harry Casey, and by extension Mary McAleese, in any way she could, on the basis of friendship. She advised Harry to visit Dáil Éireann a few times in order to get to know some of the backbenchers. When he went there for the first time, she introduced him to Brian Lenihan, who proudly proclaimed himself a former pupil and colleague of Mary McAleese, from the School of Law in Trinity College. The network was working far better than expected.

When Casey left Leinster House that day, he went into Power's Hotel at the corner of Kildare Street, where he phoned Mary and Martin, who were staying in the cottage in Croghan.

313

"Mary Hanafin says Albert is in with the strongest chance," he explained to the couple, who were both trying to listen to him on Martin's mobile phone, as the cottage had no land line. "She says there was a quiet straw poll done around the country within the party, and despite the whole notion of a by-election in Longford-Roscommon, he's proving very strong. She says your candidacy hasn't enough exposure. You need a strong lobby . . ."

"Who are you telling?" interrupted Martin. "We all know it's time for some serious lobbying. Any suggestions from Mary Hanafin?"

"I asked her what she would think of us approaching Mary O'Rourke," said Harry, "and she said, 'Try her!'"

Harry knew Mary O'Rourke from his home place. Her son Aengus O'Rourke was at school where Harry's brother Seamus was teaching, and Mary O'Rourke often arrived to collect her son from the Casey house on a Sunday evening after a game of tennis. Mary McAleese, of course, remembered the government minister very well from their days on the Fianna Fáil Women's Committee. Harry, as usual, made the initial phone call. It was an agreed procedure that Harry or Martin or Denis Moloney would make these calls, in order to give a politician room to manoeuvre, or even to ask them to call back some other time. Mary O'Rourke said she would love to meet Mary McAleese again and invited her to call to her house in Athlone the following Saturday evening at seven o'clock. Mary remembers the visit very well:

My abiding memory of the O'Rourke house is how easy it was to be comfortable in it. It was first and foremost a family home, cosy and welcoming. There was no fuss, no indication that we were entering the home of a senior government minister. Mary O'Rourke herself welcomed us at the door and brought us in. After a while her husband Enda came home from mass. He made the cup of tea and brought it in to us, and then the four of us discussed the situation from top to bottom and from all angles: the possibilities, the probabilities, the difficulties. We chatted for a couple of hours, and Martin and I found the insights we got that night, both from Mary and from Enda, very useful later on. Mary O'Rourke made no promises, but by the time we were leaving, I knew in my heart and soul that I had a friend in court.

Mary O'Rourke was a worthwhile friend to have in court. She was deputy leader of Fianna Fáil, minister for public enterprise, and the most senior of the ministers sacked by Albert Reynolds. Her parting words to Mary McAleese were reminiscent of the advice given by Mary

Hanafin: "Make sure your name and your business are made known to as many deputies as possible, as soon as possible."

Thanks to the efforts of the Northern network, especially Mary O'Neill, the next member of Fianna Fáil to be approached was Rory O'Hanlon, a relation of hers. He, along with Gerry Collins, Noel Davern, Vincent Brady and Ray Burke, was among the ministers fired by Reynolds. Patricia Casey, the psychiatrist, also knew O'Hanlon as a former minister for health. O'Hanlon was leas-cheann comhairle of the Dáil at that time and, more importantly from Mary McAleese's perspective, chairman of the Fianna Fáil party: the person who would organise the election for a party nominee for the presidency, if an election were to be held. Mary and Martin met Rory O'Hanlon in the Fairways Hotel, outside Dundalk, and he turned out to be as non-committal as the others. He listened politely to the would-be president and promised exactly the same thing as the others: "I will mention your name."

Siubhán Uí Dhubháin, a sister of Mary's close friend Eibhlís Farrell from Rostrevor, was married to Tomás Ó Dubháin from Corca Dhuibhne, the Gaeltacht area of west Kerry. Tomás, who was a good friend of the Fianna Fáil Minister of State for the Gaeltacht Éamon Ó Cuív, arranged for Mary to meet him in the Burlington Hotel in Dublin. She did not get to meet Ó Cuív's cousin, Síle de Valera, the minister for arts, heritage, Gaeltacht and the islands, but she had a phone conversation with her. It was important to Mary, both symbolically and practically, to have these two ministers on board. They were grandchildren of Eamon de Valera, former taoiseach, former president, and the founder of Fianna Fáil. But were they on her side? How could she be sure? One after another, the TDs and the ministers were saying the same thing: that they could not promise support; that there were candidates from within the parliamentary party; that they would mention her name to colleagues and to the taoiseach. Dick Roche was the only TD who told her, unequivocally, that he would support her.

Mary had received a letter from the taoiseach, a brief, formal acknowledgement of her letter to him. It was short on information, almost as deficient in language as the reply Harry Casey received from Noel Dempsey, his local TD and minister for environment and local government: "Dear Harry, I have passed on the name of that person to the party leader." It is not surprising that Dempsey gave a cold welcome to the idea of McAleese entering the nomination race. He had been Albert's man since the day the then taoiseach took him off the backbenches and gave him his first taste of ministerial office. He had a fierce personal loyalty to the former taoiseach, but felt that his candidacy for the presidency might not be the best thing for Albert himself. He later said he imagined an Albert presidential campaign as "weeks of wall-to-wall Beef Tribunal re-runs".[‡] Other ministers who had Albert to thank for their first appointments were Charlie McCreevy, the minister for finance; David Andrews, the minister for foreign affairs; and Brian Cowen, the minister for health.

Dempsey's running mate in the Meath constituency, Mary Wallace, minister of state at the Department of Justice, Equality and Law Reform, was slightly more forthcoming than her neighbour when Mary and Martin met her in her office, but she still gave the line the campaigners had by then come to expect: "I will mention your name." The other minister of state at the same department, Frank Fahey, was very encouraging and supportive when Martin rang him. He was upbeat and cheerful, full of chat and good cheer, until he was asked, "Can we rely on your support?" His answer was the same as everyone else's. The senior minister in the same department, John O'Donoghue, was effectively unreadable and unreachable, as he never returned a single one of the many phone calls to his office. Martin McAleese, who maintains that O'Donoghue is well known for not returning calls, says he enjoyed many a chat with his secretary.

At the end of July, Martin phoned Pat Farrell to find out if Mary was being considered as a serious contender within the party. The general secretary of Fianna Fáil gave the husband of the would-be candidate no indication of how he or anyone else felt about Mary or her bid for the nomination. When Martin asked him straight out if they could rely on his support, he said he was on his way to the Galway Races. A few weeks later, at a different sporting venue, Farrell's espousal of the McAleese cause would be totally unambiguous. One man who was not pleased to have his name linked to that of the Belfast woman was the Cork MEP Brian Crowley. He rang Mary to assure her that he was Albert's man and to express his annoyance that some people might think differently. At least her name was being mentioned.

John Hume left for a short holiday in France at the beginning of August without giving any indication of his plans for the future. Everyone was waiting for some signal from the Derry man, but some were waiting with less patience than others. Albert Reynolds was

---

‡   Interview with author.

reasonably certain of the Fianna Fáil parliamentary party's support for his candidacy, and he had good reason to presume on that support: a reported £10,000 worth of survey suggested strongly that he was the party's choice for the job. He had retained the services of Communiqué International, the public relations firm headed by Peter Finnegan, a former member of the Fianna Fáil National Executive. Albert's son Philip was a member of this team, as were Mary McGuire and Brian Crowley, the indignant MEP.

In fairness to Communiqué International, the survey was conducted before Mary McAleese's campaign became public, at a time when the presumption was that the only Fianna Fáil backed opposition to Reynolds, if any, would come from within the ranks of the parliamentary party. Furthermore, it was carried out before Michael O'Kennedy announced his intention to seek the party nomination, on 16 August, a declaration which further eroded Reynold's support base. The former taoiseach lost even more backing when the minister for foreign affairs David Andrews entered the race.

Dana Rosemary Scallon, the Derry-born singer who won the Eurovision Song Contest for Ireland for the first time in 1970, had returned from the United States to express her intention of standing in the presidential election. She sought a meeting with Bertie Ahern to discuss the possibility of a Fianna Fáil nomination. The most amazing aspect of this particular stage of the race is that the media were seemingly oblivious to what was happening inside Fianna Fáil. Even by the end of the first week of August, journalists speculating in the national papers on prospective presidential candidates were making no mention at all of Mary McAleese. The usual "informed sources within Fianna Fáil" were obviously not being kept very well informed.

Then on Monday, 8 August, the *Irish News* carried a story on its front page under the headline "Professor Mary McAleese Now Set to Seek Nomination". Like a piece of Jungian synchronicity, John and Pat Hume arrived back in Ireland later that same day, and John announced that he would not be seeking the presidency as he had too much still to do in the North to consolidate the work for peace already done: "It's my duty to stay here and use all our energies to achieve the lasting peace and lasting settlement all sections of our people want."[‡]

Harry Casey was at home in Navan when he heard the announcement on the five o'clock news on RTÉ. Fifteen minutes later his phone rang.

‡   *The Irish Times*, 10 August 1997.

The caller was a private secretary in the Department of the Taoiseach: "The taoiseach will meet Professor McAleese in his office in Government Buildings at 2 p.m. tomorrow," she said.

"Thanks very much," was all a flabbergasted Harry Casey could think of saying. This was the meeting without which no other meeting was of any significance.

Martin Mansergh met Mary and Martin in the foyer of Government Buildings the next day, Tuesday, 9 August. It had been reported on the one o'clock news that Sinn Féin had accepted the Principles of Senator George Mitchell and would be entering talks with the other political parties in Stormont. By the time Mansergh and the McAleeses had discussed this latest development, they had arrived at the door of the taoiseach's office. Inside, Bertie Ahern and Seamus Brennan, the Fianna Fáil chief whip, were waiting for them. Mary had a letter in her hand.

"I hope that's not another letter for me," quipped the taoiseach.

"Actually it is," said Mary. "Is there a problem?"

"We could wallpaper Government Buildings with all the letters that have come in here telling us what a wonderful candidate you'd make," he explained.

Martin McAleese, Harry Casey, Patricia Casey and Denis Moloney had been working on the theory that most people know more than a hundred other people reasonably well. They had written to everyone they knew, asking them to write letters of support for Mary McAleese to the taoiseach, and asking them to ask their friends, relations and colleagues to write also. The evidence of the success of the campaign was piled about a foot deep on the taoiseach's desk.

When Bertie Ahern invited her to make her case, she knew it was the opportunity she had been hoping for. Fifteen minutes face to face was all she needed to persuade two strangers, two hardbitten sceptical politicians, two of the most influential people in the country, that she was the person best qualified for the job of President of Ireland. She gave a potted history of her life and her work for peace and reconciliation. She spoke of her vision for the presidency and said she was the person best placed to put flesh on the vision, to be a bridge builder between the two traditions on the island. When she finished speaking, the questions came thick and fast, but she was comfortable all through the interrogation, thanks, she says, to her meticulous preparation. Austin Currie's disastrous presidential campaign was resurrected, as she knew it would be. She fielded this, and questions on her Catholicism and her nationalism, effortlessly enough, and Bertie

318

Ahern and Seamus Brennan, two men not easily impressed, seemed to be enthusiastic about her answers. She has a clear recollection of the meeting:

Whatever the taoiseach had in mind that day, he was not prepared to share it with me. Throughout the meeting he remained inscrutable. He neither encouraged me nor disheartened me. He explained at the outset that there were good people within the ranks of the party who wanted the nomination; but he saw no reason why my status as a former member of Fianna Fáil should be a hindrance to me in my efforts. He explained that the nomination of a candidate was a question for the parliamentary party and not for himself. He could, however, have dismissed me out of hand if he wanted, as my position was unprecedented. Although Cearbhall Ó Dálaigh was not a member of Fianna Fáil when he was nominated, there was nobody within the parliamentary party to oppose him at the time. I understood the implications of all that was happening as the meeting progressed, and I appreciated the fact that a door was being left open for me. When the meeting ended the Taoiseach asked me to stay in contact through the Chief Whip Seamus Brennan or through the chairman of the party Rory O'Hanlon. He also advised me not to rest on my oars, but to conduct an aggressive canvass of the members of the parliamentary party. As Martin and I left Government Buildings that day, I realised that I actually had a realistic and viable chance of becoming the Fianna Fáil presidential candidate.

Martin McAleese says he had two very strong reasons for accompanying his wife to the meeting:

Firstly, I was determined to dispel rumours that I would never give up my work in the North and provide the support that would be so necessary to Mary if she was elected president. Secondly, I was anxious to study the taoiseach's reactions while Mary was making her case. By being physically present I succeeded in my first aim. My second aim was not so easily achieved. A professional poker player would have been envious of Bertie's ability to maintain an impenetrable demeanour.

As Seamus Brennan said goodbye to them, he reminded them that they had only one week left to work on the remaining members of the parliamentary party before the selection meeting on the morning of Wednesday, 17 September. As Martin Mansergh left them at the door of Government Buildings, he told Mary that she had put a stronger, clearer and more persuasive case than any of them thought she possibly could. He left her with kind and encouraging words: "Your position is much stronger now as you leave here than it was when you were coming in."‡

‡   Martin McAleese, from memory.

Chapter Twenty-Five

There's No Such Thing as a Sure Thing

> The dangers round our days are like the rain
> that falls on good and evil equally.
> Only the fool, the privately insane,
> wears the assurance of his victory.
>
> (John Hewitt: "Breastplate")

The friends of Mary McAleese were hindered in their canvassing because they had no phone numbers for the newly elected TDs. To add to their troubles, there were eleven newly appointed senators for whom they had neither home addresses nor telephone numbers. Two days before Mary met Bertie Ahern in Government Buildings, Harry Casey rang Olive Melvin, private secretary to the taoiseach, to explain the importance of getting the telephone lists. He gave the secretary the fax number of Sandra Garry in Navan and impressed on her that getting the list was not only important but urgent. Harry was teaching a class in St Patrick's Classical School on the day of the meeting, but during the morning break he drove to Sandra's office to see if a fax had come. It was there: a full list of all the members of the Fianna Fáil parliamentary party, complete with home addresses and telephone numbers. Harry says that as soon as he saw the list, he knew that Mary "was in with a fighting chance of getting the Fianna Fáil nomination".

That evening he wrote a letter to 113 of the 114 people on the list. In it he claimed that Mary McAleese would be the choice of the people of Ireland as their president, if only they had the opportunity to vote for her:

> . . . At 46, Mary, a gifted listener and communicator and a successful academic, public broadcaster, journalist and administrator, has the qualities of ambassadorship and leadership which the Presidency calls for. She also brings the added unique dimension which springs from profound experience of life both North and South of the border. As we stand at the dawn of the third Millennium, I can think of no better or more imaginative

choice for the Presidency in these days that are heavily scented with the promise of peace. In conclusion may I suggest that you nominate Mary McAleese for the Office of president. I unreservedly recommend her for the position of "First Citizen" and will be very happy to discuss the matter further with you, should your busy schedule allow it.[‡]

They had seven days in which to secure the support of more than 50 per cent of the parliamentary party; in which to find out how effective their network was in getting the better of three stalwarts of the Fianna Fáil establishment. They thought they were about to discover how loyal or capricious some of these particular voters might be, but who was to say where loyalty lay: to friendship? To party? To the good of the country?

On Wednesday, 10 September, Mary Hanafin welcomed Mary and Martin McAleese to Leinster House. She then handed them over to Dick Roche, who brought them for a cup of tea and showed them around. Although the TDs and senators were in the middle of their summer break, the Dáil had been recalled for two days to debate the report of the McCracken Tribunal, and the McAleeses now had the fortuitous opportunity to visit some of the politicians in their offices. They had already decided whom to approach and whom to avoid. There was not much point in visiting Charlie McCreevy, for example, who would be proposing Albert Reynolds; or Marian McGennis, who would be seconding him. But wasn't Mary Hanafin seconding Michael O'Kennedy, and wasn't she helping Mary McAleese? Could they equate helping with support, or support with a vote?

In a comment on this dichotomy, Noel Dempsey, with his tongue planted firmly in his cheek, later characterised Mary Hanafin's willingness to help the McAleeses as "typical Fianna Fáil friendliness and an innate reluctance to refuse help to someone who needed it"[§]. At least the McAleeses knew where they stood with the first Fianna Fáil TD they approached that day. This call was to the office of John Ellis of Sligo-Letrim. Martin knocked on the door—no answer. He walked in and knocked on an inner door—still no answer. When he opened this door he found John Ellis sitting working at his desk.

"Excuse me. I'm Martin McAleese and this is my wife Mary. She is . . ."

---

‡   Harry Casey; private papers.

§   Interview with author.

"Hold on there," said Ellis. "I wouldn't like you to be wasting your time with me. I'm voting for Albert Reynolds."

"OK. Thanks," said Martin. At least he didn't tell them he would mention Mary's name.

Mary and Martin say that over that two-day period they actually found some truth in Noel Dempsey's flippant remark. Several politicians who said they could not support Mary went out of their way to introduce her to others who would possibly give her a vote! They agree that all the politicians they spoke to, with one nameless exception, were pleasant and well-mannered. They knew they must be breaking a rule of some sort as they walked around the corridors of Leinster House knocking on TDs' doors. They were in Rory O'Hanlon's office when the inevitable call came from the superintendent of the Dáil. Superintendent Éamon O'Donohoe said he had received several complaints about a man and woman who were walking around the corridors without permission. He wanted to see them in his office immediately. Off they went down the stairs, feeling like a couple of bold children on their way to the principal's office.

The superintendent explained the rules governing the movement of visitors and then said: "I hope you get this nomination. If you do, you can certainly count on my vote. Here's the phone number of my office. If you have any problems getting signed in or moving around the building, just ring me." And off they went.

Some newspaper reports had mentioned a group of Munster TDs, including Brian Crowley, Batt O'Keeffe and Denis Foley, as being completely loyal to Reynolds. The McAleeses did not have time to waste on trying to change people's loyalties. They needed to concentrate their efforts on those who were either anti-Albert or open to suggestion, particularly ministers and ministers of state. With this in mind, they approached James McDaid, the Donegal man who was minister for tourism, sport and recreation. They also visited a politician from the opposite end of the country: the Cork man who was minister for education and science, Micheál Martin. By Friday afternoon they had met everyone they wanted to meet, and their network was working with people they did not know, in places they had only heard of. Martin later learned that Pat Farrell, the general secretary of Fianna Fáil from Carrick-on-Shannon, who had said he had to rush off to the Galway Races when asked if he supported Mary a couple of weeks previously, had spent another weekend canvassing for her. Some of those phone calls were made on his mobile phone from the sanctuary of Old

Trafford, the home of Manchester United, where Farrell spent a Saturday afternoon in the company of Seamus Brennan.

Mary and Martin were joined by Harry Casey and Patricia Casey, and by Denis Moloney via phone, that Friday evening to review the week's work and plan the campaign for the remaining four days. They all agreed that if the Sunday papers did not carry the story of Mary McAleese's candidacy, they were in trouble. Harry set out to help their publicity campaign. In his house in Navan he had forty envelopes ready to be delivered to the news editors of the Sunday papers and the news desks of RTÉ radio and television, plus several other radio stations. In each envelope was an introductory letter about Mary and a much abbreviated form of her CV. To ensure the maximum possible coverage, they needed to deliver the envelopes that night. Harry decided to enlist the help of Elaine White, whose mother, Carmel White, was the regular babysitter in the Casey home. Elaine, who was a law student in NUI Galway, agreed to drive to Dublin and deliver the letters by hand. Harry searched his pockets and gave her all the cash he had—£75— and off she went in her mother's eleven-year-old Ford Fiesta. Elaine had no experience of driving in Dublin. She drove as far as the North Quays, where she spoke to a taxi driver who was parked there.

"I've forty letters here to deliver by hand, and I've £75 for you if we can do it," she said. He looked at the addresses and told her she had a deal.

"They must be very urgent when you can't wait for the post," said the taxi man. "What's in the envelopes?"

"Information about the next President of Ireland," said Elaine.

"And who might that be?" asked the taxi man.

"Mary McAleese," she answered.

"Never heard of her. Tell me about her," he said.

"You do the driving and I'll do the talking. Mark my words, when this election's over, and Mary McAleese is the next president. . ."

All the expenditure was reimbursed by Martin and all costs were borne by the McAleeses, of course, and as they perused the newspapers that Sunday evening, all agreed that it was money well spent. Every newspaper carried stories about her; the main evening news on RTÉ ran an item on her campaign. Every member of the Fianna Fáil parliamentary party knew who she was, what she stood for and what she wanted.

On Monday morning, the friends of Mary McAleese started ringing the radio chat shows, and the switchboards of *The Gay Byrne Show* and *The Pat Kenny Show* were jammed. When Harry Casey rang Donal

O'Neill, Marian Finnucane's producer on *Liveline*, he told Harry that an unusually high volume of calls had come in about Mary.

"Well, then, do something about it," said Casey.

By Monday morning the country's gamblers had also heard about her. Some people had got odds as high as 20/1 on Mary McAleese a week before the Fianna Fáil selection meeting, but by Monday morning she was being quoted at 5/1.

The weekend before the parliamentary party meeting saw some other developments that would influence the course of the presidential election campaign. Rumour was confirmed on Sunday when the Labour Party announced that their candidate would be Adi Roche, the charismatic founder of the Chernobyl Children's Project. Martin McAleese was delighted. He felt that the choice of the young, good-looking, popular and highly respected Roche only served to strengthen Mary's bid. "How would Albert have fared against her on a level playing field?" he asks.

A presidential candidate must be nominated by at least twenty members of the Oireachtas or four local authorities. Dana Rosemary Scallon announced that she would be an independent candidate and would seek to be the first contender ever nominated by county councils. Mary Banotti looked set to be the Fine Gael candidate. Whoever was chosen as the Fianna Fáil candidate would have a tough fight for the presidency.

During the first two weeks of September, a lot was happening outside the impenetrable world of Fianna Fáil internal manoeuvres. Diana, the popular Princess of Wales, was killed in a car crash in Paris, and the saintly Albanian nun Mother Teresa of Calcutta died in India. Archbishop Sean Brady and the minister for foreign affairs David Andrews represented the people of Ireland at Mother Teresa's funeral. Even before he arrived home from the funeral in India, Andrews announced that he was pulling out of the nomination race. Perhaps, even on the other side of the world, David Andrews had heard the rumour that was upsetting Michael O'Kennedy: that the ABBA people were now quietly canvassing on behalf of Mary McAleese. O'Kennedy was annoyed, and with good reason. People who had never shown any concern about the safety of his Dáil seat were now letting him know how worried they were about his Tipperary seat. Would Fianna Fáil be able to hold it if he were elected president? O'Kennedy was long enough in politics to be able to read the signs. He did not withdraw, but his heart was no longer in the contest.

On the night of Tuesday, 16 September, the night before the meeting of the parliamentary party, Martin McAleese was trying politely to evict the friends and well-wishers who had gathered in their apartment in Ballsbridge. The main reason for his anxiety was that Mary had not yet begun to write her speech for the next morning. Michael and Oonagh Ringrose, Deirdre and Michael Delaney and Ciarán Taaffe left around eleven o'clock, and Harry Casey was the last to leave, throwing final words of advice over his shoulder even as he walked towards his car. Eventually only Mary, Martin and Eibhlís Farrell, who was staying overnight, remained. Mary spoke briefly on the phone to her mother and father and then to Charlie McAleese and Christine Cole, the housekeeper, in their own house, Kairos. The children were all asleep because, despite the fact that their mother might well be writing herself into history with the speech she was about to compose, they were expected to write their usual lessons in school the next day. Mary had spoken to every Fianna Fáil TD and senator she had intended to speak to, either in person or by telephone. She was satisfied that she was as well prepared as she could be. All that remained was the speech.

During a meeting of ministers and ministers of state that was going on in the Fianna Fáil headquarters in Lower Mount Street that evening, only two references were made to the selection of a candidate the following morning. The first was when Bertie Ahern said it would be nice to be in a position to decline the offer of a prospective candidate from outside the party, but when circumstances demanded. . . He later exhorted everyone to vote for the best candidate. Albert Reynolds was with Peter Finnegan and the rest of his team in the headquarters of Communiqué International, and was therefore privy to neither Bertie's exhortation nor his regretful remarks. According to their figures, Albert's team were confident that the former taoiseach would win the nomination comfortably on the first count.

The following morning, the bookies reflected the confidence of the Communiqué International meeting in 26 Herbert Place by quoting Albert Reynolds as the clear favourite at 2/7. Mary was quoted at 6/1, but if the bookies knew that she still had no proposer and seconder their odds might have been more generous. Paddy Power was offering 14/1 on the dispirited Michael O'Kennedy. When Dustin the turkey announced on *Den 2* that he would run on the Fianna Fowl ticket, Paddy Power quoted odds of 1000/1 on the turkey.

At last Mary put down the phone. Her final call had been to Patricia Casey. Now the talking was all done and it was time to start writing.

Martin and Eibhlís went to bed around 12.30, and Mary was left with that most intimidating of all writer's instruments, the *tabula rasa*, the blank page, or in her case the blank document in Microsoft Word. Although she considered it the most important document she had ever written, and although she intended to use all the care and skill at her disposal to craft the best speech she could possibly create, she was not sure she would get a chance to read it. Rory O'Hanlon, acting as chairman of the party, had obtained permission from members of the parliamentary party for the three contestants to address the selection meeting, but so far Mary had found neither a proposer nor a seconder. In spite of all the plotting and scheming of the ABBA contingent, in spite of all the fears of a by-election in Longford or Tipperary, in spite of the fact that most of the TDs and senators thought that Mary McAleese was the best person for the job, none of them would show their hand before the vote.

She had been told she would have five minutes to speak to the members of the parliamentary party, but she would not be happy until she had a speech that would say all she wanted to say in less than four minutes. By half past three that morning, she had a speech that was succinct, strong, clear and focused. It would last less than three minutes. In the small study at the head of the stairs, she had spent three hours preparing a three minute speech. Now she knew it off by heart. She was up again at half past six. Special attention was paid to the make-up before they sat down to breakfast. When Eibhlís went off to work, Mary tried out the speech on Martin. During the next hour or so she made a few tiny changes, and then it was time to print the finished, polished product. But the printer would not work. They checked the connections, turned it off and turned it on, pushed buttons, pleaded and cajoled and threatened, but all to no avail. Eventually Mary sat down with a pen and a piece of paper. They wanted to be in Leinster House in plenty of time, so they did not bother writing out a second copy.

They left the car in the Setanta car park, walked along Molesworth Street to the Kildare Street entrance and by 10.30 were sitting in the Dáil restaurant—alone. They watched dozens of members of the Fianna Fáil parliamentary party coming and going, passing them by, but not one of them stopped to speak to them or wish them good morning. Mary Wallace showed them the way to the lift, and they stepped out on the fifth floor of Leinster House at 10.45, with three-quarters of an hour to go before the start of the meeting. The doors of both lifts on the fifth floor are side by side, ten yards from the door of the parliamentary party meeting room. Mary and Martin took up position opposite the lifts, with their backs to the wall. No one could go into the room without seeing them and passing them.

In the house in Rostrevor there was a large map of Ireland on the wall of the kitchen. Every constituency in the state was clearly marked on that map, with a picture of every member of the parliamentary party. They were able to put a name to every face that passed them, able to address each person by name. Martin was very uncomfortable.

"I was ready to drop the whole idea. I wanted to be anywhere else other than that corridor. We felt like a pair of beggars, greeting people by name and getting nothing in return but grunts and mutters and averted eyes. Nobody wanted to admit they knew who we were."

Mary was more pragmatic: "It needed to be done."

Although they both understood the political game that was being played out in front of their eyes on that corridor, they also felt totally shut out from this party that Mary wanted to stand for. They felt isolated, vulnerable and let down. Where were all the people who had hinted so strongly that they would support her? Where were all the others who said they would "mention her name"? There was no one to call her by name this morning. More importantly, who was going to propose or second her at this meeting that would be starting in a short while? Protocol dictated that a person who was not proposed and seconded could not address the meeting. Fifteen minutes left and still no proposer. Martin was not prepared to wait any longer. As Dick Roche emerged from the lift, Martin grabbed him by the arm.

"Dick! Aren't you proposing Mary?"

"No. I thought Mary O'Rourke was proposing her," said Roche.

The meeting room was almost full at this stage, but Mary O'Rourke had still not arrived. Martin doubted that any arrangement had been made for O'Rourke to propose his wife. He had been talking to her on the phone the previous evening, and she had not mentioned even the possibility of proposing her. She had, however, mentioned another possibility: that there might be no need of a proposer and seconder. Roche said he had never heard of such a thing and went off to find Rory O'Hanlon. It was after 11.25 when O'Hanlon came out of the room and approached Mary.

"Who's proposing you?" he asked.

"I don't know," she replied. "At this point I don't know if anyone is proposing me."

328

O'Hanlon disappeared back into the meeting room and closed the door behind him. Within two minutes he was back out.

"There'll be no proposers and no seconders. The other candidates and their proposers have agreed to that. Each candidate will be invited to speak for three minutes," he said. "You will speak first because your name comes first alphabetically."

And that's how it happened!

"Either of the other candidates could have got rid of me, there and then. They would have been perfectly within their rights to insist that we follow the rules. That would have been the end of me, and I would not have been a threat to whichever one of them was elected. I was very grateful for their generosity," Mary says.

Martin says what Mary probably thought but didn't like to say: "When Rory O'Hanlon told us about the new procedure, I couldn't believe that Albert had left the door open for her like that. I can only put it down to overconfidence on his part. If I was in his shoes, I'm afraid I would have insisted on party rules being obeyed."

At half past eleven the door of the meeting room was closed and Rory O'Hanlon started the meeting, leaving Mary and Martin standing in the corridor outside. The fact that there was no chair in the corridor was lost on them, as neither of them would have been able to sit still. Eventually Pat Farrell, the general secretary of Fianna Fáil, came out and invited Mary to step inside. Both the meeting room and the anteroom were packed, and several people were standing around the walls beneath the portraits of the former leaders of Fianna Fáil, as there were not enough chairs for everyone. There was a chair left vacant for Mary at the top table, but she had no sooner sat when she was asked to address the gathering. She stood and assessed the layout of the room, and then walked to a place where she would have the best view of everyone. Dermot Ahern was seated immediately in front of her.

When she had their full attention she began to speak: "*A chairde*, the Constitution sets a clear agenda for the Presidency, but ultimately the role wraps itself around the person and signs of the times. The president must be seen as a figurehead for a dynamic Ireland growing more complex by the day, an Ireland in which the prospect of lasting peace based on consensus looks tantalisingly close. . ."‡

Although she had the piece of paper in her hand, she never once looked at it. She watched the faces all around her. She says that as she

---

‡   Mary McAleese, personal papers.

spoke she saw smiles appear on several of those faces, saw people looking at each other and nodding their heads. It was obvious to all that not only was the speech itself very well crafted, but that this woman was a gifted speaker. Those who understood such things realised that she was telling the Fianna Fáil faithful exactly what they wanted to hear, and doing it superbly.

Michael O'Kennedy was the next to address the meeting and he spoke without notes. Indeed no notes were necessary for what he had to say. It was a strange speech. He asked his party colleagues not to vote for him for his own sake, or for the party's sake, or even for the sake of the government, but only for the good of the people of Ireland. The applause this time was neither as loud nor as long.

Then it was time for Albert Reynolds to address the meeting, and he also spoke without notes. He spoke of the many roles of the president, but spoke mainly, as an industrialist, of the president's function in promoting Irish industry. He spoke considerably longer than the other two candidates and got a long and enthusiastic round of applause.

The chairman then stood to explain the voting procedure: each member of the parliamentary party could write the name of one candidate on the piece of paper supplied for that purpose. The winner would be the first person to gain half the total votes plus one. Among those who were absent from the meeting were Mark Killilea and Jim Fitzsimons, who voted by post and fax, and Ray Burke, who had left his sealed vote with the party chairman before going abroad. The minister for environment and local government Noel Dempsey was in Canada on government business. His explanation for not making a voting arrangement is, "I did not know I could vote by proxy. It's as simple as that. But if I had voted, I would have voted for Albert."[‡]

The "shafting of Albert" filled many column inches in newspapers in the coming days and weeks, and many speculative articles have since been written about plots, intrigues and conspiracies masterminded by friends and former friends of Reynolds. It is said that the taoiseach showed his ballot paper to the former taoiseach just before he cast his vote, so that Reynolds could see his name clearly written on it. Reynolds read this gesture as a kiss of death: that Bertie Ahern was so certain of Albert's defeat that he could afford to waste his own vote.

When the result of the first vote was announced there was no winner. Albert Reynolds had 49 votes, Mary McAleese 42 and Michael

‡   Interview with author.

O'Kennedy 21. The chairman announced that O'Kennedy was elimated and that a further round of voting should take place between Reynolds and McAleese. A ten minute break was called and the smokers headed for the corridor. That was when Martin heard the news.

"As soon as I heard the result of the first ballot, I knew Mary would win the second vote. My confidence was strengthened a lot when several of the new TDs came over to me to check the spelling of 'McAleese'."

It had all come down to single combat between the Longford man and the Belfast woman. Reynolds was already at a disadvantage because one of his most fervent supporters, Senator Paddy McGowan, had left the meeting for a medical appointment. It was probably the least of his disadvantages. As the delegates began to file back into the room for the second vote, those people who had been so reluctant to show their hands previously were now losing their shyness by the minute. Whispers were becoming distinctly audible and conversations noisy. People were slapping each other on the back and laughing aloud before the result was even announced. Eventually Rory O'Hanlon declared the final tally: Reynolds 48 votes; McAleese 62 votes—a clear victory on the second count. Albert had one vote less than his first round total, presumably that of Paddy McGowan. Mary received all Michael O'Kennedy's votes, bar one. It was the end of an era and the beginning of an era.

Chapter Twenty-Six

Leaks and Rumours of Leaks

Here, often, a man provoked has had his say,
stung by opinion or unjust event,
and found his angry words, to his dismay,
prop up his adversary's argument.

(John Hewitt: "The Iron Circle")

Martin McAleese was the first person outside the Fianna Fáil parliamentary party to hear the news of Mary's win. From where he stood on the corridor he could hear the applause, but he did not know who was being applauded until Pat Farrell came out to bring him in to congratulate his wife. Thanks to mobile phone technology, the press knew the result of the vote by the time Mary and the senior party members came down the stairs.

In the St Louis Convent in Kilkeel, County Down, the McAleese children were anxiously waiting to hear the news from Dublin. The principal, Dr Celestine Devlin, had promised to let them know as soon as he heard, and Kathleen Collins, Mary's friend from Ardoyne who taught in the school, had promised the same. From the time the Angelus rang at noon, the whole school was in a limbo of waiting. Now it was almost one and all radios were tuned to RTÉ. The choice of the Fianna Fáil parliamentary party was the first item on the *News at One*, and the school building shook as both pupils and teachers erupted in a cacophony of cheering, clapping of hands and stamping of feet. Emma, Saramai and Justin were bewildered as they were swamped by congratulating friends and teachers. It would take a while for it to sink in: their mammy was going to be a candidate in the presidential election; in a few weeks time their mammy could very well be the President of Ireland.

Seven mile east, in Rostrevor, Claire and Paddy Leneghan were also listening to the *News at One*. Both admit to shedding a few tears as they heard the news. Paddy says, "I felt a great pride that she got the nomination, that she was considered good enough to be the candidate of the Fianna Fáil party, a party that was in government and had such a choice of its own candidates."

Claire says, "Of course I was very proud of Mary. But I was also sick with worry for her. It was an awful upsurge of emotions."

In Belfast, Denis Moloney was so nervous that he could not go to work that day. The quiet man in the McAleese campaign sat with his sister Maria in her house waiting for word from Martin in Dublin. Shortly after midday the phone rang, and despite his anxiety, he slowly and carefully lifted the receiver. Through a cacophony of voices he heard his old friend clearly: "Denis, Mary has it! Can you hear me? She just got the nomination!"

It was lunchtime in St Patrick's Classical School in Navan, County Meath, but Harry Casey was sitting in front of the television in the house of his friends Kevin and Patsy Reilly, where he had come, as he says, "to watch history being made live on TV". When the result of the first count was announced, he rang Martin on the mobile.

"The second vote has just been counted," said Martin. "They're about to announce the result. I'll ring you back in a minute."

That call, of course, was never made, as Martin had other things on his mind and other duties to perform. Harry did not care whether he heard the result from Martin McAleese or from Charlie Bird, as long as the result was the right one for him.

Back in Dublin there was pandemonium in Leinster House and in Buswell's Hotel across the road, where Fianna Fáil workers had been marshalling reporters and explaining to the news photographers just where Albert would walk, who would be with him and where he would stand while giving his victorious press conference. All attention was now focused on Mary McAleese; every microphone and camera was aimed at the woman whose face would not have been known to many people in Dublin an hour beforehand.

The next morning in *The Irish Times*, Matt Kavanagh's photograph, taken in the meeting room shortly after the announcement of the result, showed a compassionate, sympathetic Mary McAleese with her hand on Albert's back. He was looking every bit the crushed and dejected man, admitting publicly that he was "very disappointed". Some people of a less than charitable disposition voiced the opinion that Mary might have been shoving the former taoiseach out of her way. She has this to say about the victory:

> As the voting was going on I was very much at my ease. I knew I had given it my best, and if that was not good enough, then so be it. When the result was announced, my immediate thoughts were of those two men who had spent their lives working for the party

and for the country. Of course, I was delighted for myself, but I was careful. I did not want to do or say anything that would deepen their disappointment or intensify the hurt they must have been feeling. However, when we reached Buswell's Hotel, I found it difficult not to laugh when I saw the confusion and commotion I had caused among the members of the press. I hope the satisfaction I took in their obvious fluster was not sinful.

Many people will remember the cartoon in *The Sunday Tribune* the following Sunday: Albert Reynolds as Julius Caesar, Bertie Ahern as Brutus and Mary McAleese as the new Empress; the laurel wreath that had graced Albert's head now sitting on Mary's. Bertie has one hand firmly around Mary's waist, while with the other he is stabbing Albert. The dying Albert is groaning with his last breath: *"Et tu, Bertie!"* The members of the Fianna Fáil parliamentary party took a very unified public stance on all aspects of the selection, and all agreed that Bertie Ahern's behaviour before and during the election was beyond reproach. However, many deputies said afterwards that they could not help remembering Charles Haughey's description of their party leader: "the most devious, the most cunning, the most ruthless of them all".

But it was Mary's day, and it was Albert Reynolds who reminded everyone of that fact: "This is her day. I'll be with her all the way."[‡] Mary had some nice things to say about Albert also: "Albert Reynolds very often gave me hope to waken in the morning and face a new day."[§]

As Mary walked from Leinster House across Kildare Street to meet the members of the media in Buswell's Hotel, she was flanked by the taoiseach Bertie Ahern and the Party Chairman Rory O'Hanlon. As outriders, and to complete the scene of total party unity, she had the Deputy Leader of Fianna Fáil Mary O'Rourke and the Chief Whip Seamus Brennan.

Certain journalists later said that Mary's selection was a done deal, a *fait accompli* long before the meeting, and the only effective way of keeping Albert Reynolds out and of avoiding a by-election. It was said that when Ray MacSharry refused to seek a nomination, an outsider was the only logical choice. Some deputies, however, spoke of the power of Mary's eloquence at the selection meeting and of how her speech affected them. It is clear, with the passing of time and the settling of the political dust, that there is an amount of truth in both versions. It is also

---

‡ *The Irish Times*, 18 September 1997.
§ *Ibid.*

clear that Mary McAleese, who was unsure of her eligibility as a candidate until a few minutes before the meeting started, can hardly be counted among those who "shafted" Albert Reynolds.

At one o'clock that day, 17 September 1997, and without any inkling of it on her part, Mary McAleese's private life came to an end. It was as though she stepped through the looking glass. From that moment on, until she was elected President of Ireland, she belonged to Fianna Fáil. After her election she would become the property of the people of Ireland. It would take her a while to realise that she might never again drive her own car, might never again have the luxury of being totally, utterly alone.

When the press conference was over, Micheál Martin invited Mary and Martin to lunch, and along with them went some senior officers of Fianna Fáil: Pat Farrell, Wally Young and Martin Mackin. After the tension of the morning, a reasonable person might look forward to a leisurely lunch. But already the Fianna Fáil machine was in operation, and the lunch consisted of large dollops of plans, strategies, approaches and tactics, with a smidgen of chicken salad thrown in.

Mary said afterwards, "The Fianna Fáil engine was ticking over, ready for a campaign. If the face on the posters was not the one that was expected, what real difference did that make to the operation?"

Once the party officers had extracted the promise of an early meeting the following morning, Mary and Martin were free to head for Rostrevor for an evening of celebration with their family and friends. Harry and Mary Casey were there, but Denis and Maria Moloney did not join them that evening. They phoned Mary from Belfast to congratulate her. At long last, as Denis voiced the words "Well done, Mary" the emotional strain of the whole campaign seemed to dissipate and he wept for pure joy.

On that same day, 17 September, Brian Mullooly of Fianna Fáil was elected cathaoirleach of Seanad Éireann, and Des Geraghty was elected vice-president of SIPTU by more than 51,000 votes. The First National Building Society announced that, with the quoting of the company on the stockmarket, 250,000 of its shareholders would earn themselves a Christmas present of a couple of thousand pounds. On any other day any one of these stories would make the headlines, but it is not every day that Fianna Fáil rejects a former leader and taoiseach, nor selects a woman from a Belfast ghetto to be its candidate for the highest office in the country.

Bright and early the following morning, Mary kept her second appointment with the taoiseach. The ABBA people, of course, were delighted with Mary's selection, but now Bertie had to assuage the resentment of Albert's loyal supporters. In what was widely seen as an ameliorating move, he offered Mary a choice of either Brian Cowen or Noel Dempsey as her campaign director. Mary says it was obvious which one Bertie Ahern wanted her to choose, and as she had no strong feelings in the matter, she went with the man from County Meath, the ambitious young Minister for Environment and Local Government Noel Dempsey.

Dempsey confirms that he was the original choice and says that he himself mooted Brian Cowen:

> I was approached by Pat Farrell on the cabinet corridor and asked would I be Mary McAleese's director of elections. Pat went on to say that both he and the boss wanted to pull the Albert Reynolds faction on board, and that I was the man best suited for that job. I said I would have no problem doing whatever they thought best for the party, but if they wanted to bring the Albert faction on board they might think of asking Brian Cowen to take the job, as he would be more closely identified with Albert than me. I also suggested that they ask Mary McAleese herself.[‡]

The following Saturday, the Progressive Democrats met to decide which candidate they would back in the upcoming election. The choice was between Mary McAleese and Dana Rosemary Scallon. Mary had met the PD leader Mary Harney shortly after her first meeting with Bertie Ahern and had impressed the newly appointed tánaiste. That meeting had been organised by Councillor Mae Sexton, a friend of Mai Casey, Harry's sister. Mary Harney had told her that her job at the selection meeting was "to sell McAleese". Twenty minutes later she had sold her well, and the Progressive Democrats had endorsed Mary McAleese as their candidate also. She now had the support of both government parties, and her prospects were better than ever.

Four women were now declared as candidates in the presidential election. The others were Mary Banotti, who had defeated Avril Doyle to gain the Fine Gael nomination; Adi Roche, who was the chosen candidate of the Labour Party, Democratic Left and the Greens; and Dana Rosemary Scallon, the first person in the history of the country to gain a nomination without the backing of one of the main political parties.

The fourth woman was now beginning to have serious reservations about her choice for director of elections. Candidate and director were having lunch in the Commons, the prestigious restaurant on St

‡ Interview with author.

336

Stephen's Green. Dempsey decided to begin as he intended to continue and took what he later called "a firm line". It was what Mary later called "a very inflexible line" and what a member of the campaign team later called "pure bloody thick".

"There will come a time when you and I will have totally different views on a matter. At that time you will have to trust my instincts and judgment. If you're not prepared to do that, you should maybe look for a different campaign director."[‡]

It was a long time since anyone had spoken to Mary McAleese like that. This was not the sort of talk that sat easily with a woman who was not used to seeking the advice of others. She now says: "I accepted what he had to say even though it bothered me a lot to relinquish my own judgment. During the campaign I frequently disagreed with him, but I yielded to his political skills and experience. I must now admit that, more often than not, he was right—either right or exceptionally lucky!"

It was like being at confession. Dempsey invited her to tell him anything that he should know, anything that he should be prepared to handle at some future time. She was completely open with her director about her work with Fr Alex and the Redemptorist peace mission. Dempsey was delighted with the information and saw it as a trump card to be held in reserve and played with great effect when necessary. But this time it was Mary who was inflexible: she was adamant that she would not allow him to breathe a word about her involvement. The work of the peace mission was ongoing, secret and highly sensitive. Any breach of confidentiality, not to mention any attempt to capitalise on her work, could have tragic and very far-reaching consequences. In this matter it was the minister's turn to yield graciously, however reluctantly.

On Thursday, 25 September, the campaign of the Fianna Fáil presidential candidate was officially launched in the Shelbourne Hotel. The Mary McAleese who went on show to the party faithful that night bore little resemblance to the woman who had addressed the parliamentary party meeting. Gone were the long hair and the conservative suit. Even the make-up she had been using for years was now no more. Helen Cody had been charged with re-inventing Mary McAleese, giving her a total makeover, creating what the stylist later described as "a friendly image—chic, but definitely not austere". Mary Bruton was appointed as her hairdresser, and Mary's new wardrobe was drawn from the creations of several Irish dress designers, including Deborah Vale, Miriam Mone and

‡ Interview with author.

Mary Gregory. Vivienne Walsh was given the job of coordinating her jewellery. Not even the smallest detail was left to chance.

The campaign team had something much more fundamental than her wardrobe or her hairstyle to create before Mary's candidacy was launched: they needed a campaign slogan. Mary herself had been speaking of "bridge-building" and "embracing the nation" during the time she had been seeking the nomination. Now Fianna Fáil was employing not one, but two public relations companies, Arks and the Larkin Partnership, to see what they could come up with for her publicity campaign. Back in June of that year, during the general election campaign, Gerry Nagle of Arks had been in charge of Fianna Fáil publicity. However, halfway through the campaign, P.J. Mara had appointed Martin Larkin of the Larkin Partnership to "share the responsibility", as he said, a decision that was not much to the liking of Arks. With both factions once again employed on the same job, the resultant tensions ensured a delay in creative output. Pat Farrell, Jackie Gallagher and Des Richardson maintained that all work on the McAleese publicity campaign was collaborative, but it is generally accepted that Martin Larkin was responsible for redevising Mary's own phrase and incorporating it in a poster: "Mary McAleese . . . Building Bridges".

The launch of the campaign was the occasion of her second meeting with her director of elections Noel Dempsey, who describes the effect her speech had on him that evening:

> It was my first time to hear her speak in public. Initially I thought she was coming from miles behind, and that the only thing she had going for her was that, against all the odds, she managed to get the Fianna Fáil nomination. I had heard some of my colleagues describing her speech to the parliamentary party as electric, but until that day in the Shelbourne I had no real idea of what that meant. As I listened to her the hairs on the back of my neck began to stand up. She was something else. Then I heard her deal with the press in the questions and answers session. She not only answered each question, but anticipated the second and third questions and answered them before they were asked. The press didn't like it. In retrospect I learned two very important things about Mary McAleese that night: number one was that she was a superb public speaker and number two was that there would be no love lost between her and the press.[‡]

---

‡ Interview with author.

The campaign was to last six weeks, an unusually long time. In the Fianna Fáil headquarters in Lower Mount Street, it was being planned like a military operation. In a situation reminiscent of the McAleese kitchen in Rostrevor, there was a large map of Ireland on one wall; but here, in place of constituencies, there were towns and cities, villages, islands and local radio stations all marked with pins and flags. The RTÉ studios in Donnybrook were marked with a red flag bearing the number 5, representing the number of pre-arranged interviews on various shows. Martin, Noel Dempsey, Brian Lenihan, Liam Murphy and Caroline Callaghan gathered at eight o'clock most mornings. The team was augmented by Martin Mackin, the press officer, and Eileen Gleeson, the public relations consultant, Pat Farrell and P.J. Mara. Maurice O'Donoghue and Noel Whelan looked after accommodation and travel arrangements, and Wally Young was in charge of special events. As Eileen Gleeson relates: "I had been asked to be part of Albert Reynold's campaign if he had succeeded in his nomination attempt, and I had declined on the basis that I had just worked on the June general election and could not afford any more time away from by business. I was then asked by Pat Farrell to give a hand in setting up Mary's campaign. After spending only one day with her, I knew I wanted to be involved with her campaign. I knew it would be special."[‡]

South of the border Mary did not enjoy the same celebrity status as the other women candidates. Her team, recognising this as her most immediate problem, ensured that within two weeks she had been a guest on every local radio station in the state. They also made sure that her photograph was in every newspaper in the country. Among those who came aboard during those first few weeks was a friend and former student of Mary's, Liz O'Donnell, the PD government minister. She was joined by Garvan McGinley, the national organiser of the Progressive Democrats, Caitríona Meehan from the Fianna Fáil Press Office, and John Murray, director of the Government Information Service.

The campaign had a very insipid start. The four women were friendly and polite, too friendly and too polite, perhaps, for the taste of an Irish public that was reared on more piquant political fare. Almost from the start the campaign was styled as a contest between the heart and the head—the heart of Adi Roche and the head of Mary McAleese—a generalisation that was unfair to both women. Mary's reputation as an intellectual was safe enough, but during the second week of the

‡   Interview with author.

campaign, Adi Roche's perceived loving nature took a beating. Anonymous allegations of bullying were made against her by people who had worked with her in the Chernobyl Children's Project. This story was quickly followed by references to her brother, Dónal de Róiste, and to the controversial circumstances in which he had left the army twenty-eight years previously. As an attempt to vilify the candidate and to damage her campaign, the stories were successful. Adi Roche was personally hurt by the groundless allegations, and her election campaign was critically damaged.

Mary McAleese sympathised with her at a reception for Boutros Boutros-Ghali in the College of Surgeons. "I empathised with her and told her that I was disgusted with the way she was treated. I had brothers and sisters of my own—eight of them altogether, not to mention sixty first cousins. If we, as candidates, did not stand together against allegations like this, we would all be vulnerable. I felt very sorry for Adi Roche and for her parents."

Prior to the publication of the allegations, Adi Roche was enjoying a comfortable lead. According to the opinion polls she had 38 per cent support compared to Mary's 35 per cent. Mary Banotti was in third place with 18 per cent, and Dana brought up the rear with 9 per cent. Although many people saw the word "conspiracy" written all over the attacks on Roche, they opened up the first chink in her armour. A week after the first allegation was published, her rating had dropped to 22 per cent, and by the end of the campaign it was at 13 per cent.

Historically, no more than three candidates could contest a presidential election because only the main political parties, Fianna Fáil, Fine Gael and Labour, could nominate candidates. When Dana sought and got the support of the county councils, she opened a door to anyone else who wished to follow her. Although, as the campaign progressed, it became clear that she did not have a realistic chance of winning the election, she was always going to be a formidable runner. She had honed her speaking skills and refined her lines of argument in the Bible Belt of the United States, where she had been a well-known Catholic evangelist before announcing her intention to seek the presidency. Nevertheless, the friends of Mary McAleese, for two good reasons, were delighted to see her entering the fray. Firstly, McAleese would get most of her transfers; and secondly, Dana would attract most of the flak from the anti-Catholics and the anti-clerics. Noel Dempsey had this latter fact in mind when he refused to contact party organisers on the county councils; refused, in fact, to organise a sanction on Dana's nomination.

Mary Banotti was the only professional politician among the contenders. Although Dana Rosemary Scallon would acquit herself very well as a member of the European Parliament in the years to come, she was slow to blossom during the presidential election. Mary McAleese, however, was shaping up as a candidate whose political savvy owed more to her own nous than to her brief fling with politics in 1987. She was a natural on a platform or in front of a camera and had a way of working a crowd that left everyone feeling that they knew her well, and more importantly, that she knew them.

Noel Dempsey says "I was absolutely delighted by her natural political talent: the way she could work a room and make everyone feel included. She was a joy to work with. Early on I thought to myself that we had some slight chance of winning, but as time passed I became more and more convinced that the campaign was very winnable."

All her political ability would soon be needed, as would that of her director of elections, because the campaign that was insipid would soon become turbulent and the politeness that marked the interaction between candidates would soon be replaced by anger and passion.

As a member of An Garda Síochána, Derek Nally had first-hand knowledge of the lasting trauma suffered by victims of crime. His hatred of violent crime led him to found the Irish Association for Victim Support at the start of the 1980s. Shortly after its foundation, he invited Mary McAleese to join him on the steering committee of the new organisation. He knew of her background in penology, her involvement with the Commission of Inquiry into the Penal System, and her obvious interest in the conditions of prisoners. However, as he explained to her at the time, he understood that she shared his concern for the welfare of the victims of crime. In 1997 Derek Nally, following Dana's example, was nominated through the county council route and became the token man in the race for the presidency.

John Caden was probably the best-known of Nally's supporters. He had been the producer of *The Gay Byrne Show* on RTÉ Radio One, and afterwards director of programmes for Radio Ireland.‡ Caden asked his friend Eoghan Harris to help devise a campaign strategy. The most obvious approach was to promote Nally as the paradigm of good, traditional, old-fashioned values, morals and manners, and that was how he came across.

On Monday, 13 October, Nally was to appear as a panellist on John

‡   Radio Ireland later became Today FM.

Bowman's *Questions and Answers* on RTÉ One television. Seven years previously, the same programme had been the venue for the shattering of Brian Lenihan's presidential hopes when a ghost from his past life came to haunt him live on air. Now the current Fianna Fáil contender, Mary McAleese, was to join Nally on the panel, along with Seán Dublin Bay Rockall Loftus. The fourth guest was to be the political journalist and future editor of *The Irish Times* Geraldine Kennedy, to whom Nally had revealed, in the 1980s, that her phone was being tapped.

The previous day, Emily O'Reilly had written an article about Mary McAleese in the *Sunday Business Post*. The article contained excerpts from secret Department of Foreign Affairs internal memoranda which had been written by Dympna Hayes after meetings with Mary McAleese in January and May of that year. Hayes, first secretary in the Anglo-Irish Section of the Department of Foreign Affairs, wrote the memos to Seán Ó hUiginn, her head of section. The substance of the article was that Mary McAleese was "soft on Sinn Féin", if not totally supportive of them, at a time when the IRA was not on ceasefire.

Although the Monday morning newspapers did not have much to say about the revelations in the *Sunday Business Post*, Eoghan Harris decided that the concurrence of the allegations with Nally's appearance with McAleese on *Questions and Answers* was too good an opportunity to pass up. The friends of Derek Nally decided to release a press statement at five o'clock that day, just in time for the evening news programmes.

It took the form of a personal statement from Nally, and it attacked McAleese, based on the allegations in Emily O'Reilly's article: "Like me, most Irish people would never vote for Sinn Féin, peace process or no peace process, because they have been carrying on a murder campaign for 25 years. One of their victims was Garda Gerry McCabe."[‡]

The connection between the presidential candidate and the murderers of Garda Gerry McCabe was widely seen as an outrageous and shameful thing. Even if the tie was unintentional, some subsequent sentences in his press release showed what he thought of his former colleague. The statements were based on the premise that the reported contents of the leaked memoranda were true: "that she worked to a different moral agenda than most people in the Republic" and that the memoranda caused him to have "prima facie suspicion that she was not a proper person to be President of the Irish Republic" (*sic*).

---

‡   Derek Nally's press statement, 13 October 1997.

Mary and Martin's initial reaction was fear for their children, who were still in the North. They immediately rang Charlie McAleese and Paddy and Claire Leneghan, explained the thrust of the press statement, and asked them not to let the McAleese children out of their sight. Later that evening an RUC patrol car blocked the entrance of the McAleeses' avenue in Rostrevor as a protective measure for the family.

By the time Mary arrived in the RTÉ studios for *Questions and Answers*, the initial shock had worn off, but she was coldly angry at what she considered the "dangerous stupidity" of Nally's statement. As the panellists took their places behind the desk, the tension was palpable. Halfway through the programme, Derek Nally, with a dramatic flourish, took a piece of paper from the inside pocket of his jacket and waved it at Mary McAleese, asking her at the same time what connection she had with Sinn Féin. When Mary responded, "I have never had any association with Sinn Féin . . . I have always been strongly opposed to violence," he went on the offensive, reading from the piece of paper and repeating the allegations from the *Sunday Business Post* of the previous day.

When she was asked directly if she ever had talks with Sinn Féin, she was in trouble. She was not in a position to disclose much about her work in the peace ministry while that work was still at a very sensitive stage; yet she could not tell an outright lie. She also had to balance her obligations to the ministry with her responsibility for the safety of her own family. She knew that there were plenty of people of violence in the North for whom these allegations would be justification enough to harm, or even to kill, members of Mary's immediate family. The first of several calls had come from the children that morning. They were concerned about the radio reports of the *Sunday Business Post* article, accounts that suggested that their mother was supportive of the Provisional IRA. They felt that they were now targets. Mary and Martin agreed with their children's analysis of the situation and shared their concern. They considered moving them out of Rostrevor altogether for a while. Mary describes that time as the only phase of the campaign during which she became "furiously, protectively angry". The word most commonly used by her friends and family to describe her during those few days is "seething".

Noel Dempsey was not seething. He was not remotely concerned by the allegations against his candidate. He still thought that Mary's objections to any mention of her involvement in the Clonard peace ministry was a wrong call. He wanted to use it . . . but not just yet. In fact he did not want Mary speaking to any reporter, just yet. On the Tuesday he was unable to contact her, but he says he left a message on her mobile phone: "I don't want you to speak to any reporters about the *Sunday Business Post* article or about what was said on *Questions and Answers* last night. Not a word to any journalist!" Mary says she never received the message.

On that Tuesday, 14 October, Derek Nally was canvassing in Dublin, telling the press at every opportunity, "The issue has to be cleared up immediately" and "I am extremely worried." Among his other issues of concern that day was the welfare of those living south of the border: "This is a very, very serious thing for the people of the Republic of Ireland." Regarding the rest of the country he said, "If that's where Mary McAleese is happiest that's grand." He afterwards explained that he intended no lack of respect to Northerners.[‡]

That evening the candidates were attending a debate in Trinity College, where the motion for deliberation was "Is the next president going to be a clone of Mary Robinson?" Shortly before the debate started, Mary discovered that Sean Flynn of *The Irish Times* had invited John Caden to write an article on the leaked documents for Wednesday's edition. No great political astuteness was necessary to guess what the thrust of the article would be.

When Derek Nally got the opportunity to speak at the debate, he once again attacked Mary, but she denied the charges so vehemently that the audience was soon convinced that there was no basis for the allegations. One of the students inquired of Nally, "Do you want a sworn statement from her?" Eventually Derek Nally said he accepted Mary's word on the matter: "I don't need any such definitive proof. She said it and that is good enough for me."

But Caden's article was still due to appear in *The Irish Times* the following morning. Before she left the hall, Mary asked Caden to withdraw it, especially in light of Nally's acknowledgement that there was no basis for the allegations. He refused. She then approached Nally.

"You know me and you know where I stand. You have used those words mischievously just as you yourself are being used. Most of all, you have put my children's lives at risk. You are deliberately whipping up hysteria which you know to be unfounded. I don't like what this election has done to a decent man."

The following morning John Caden's article appeared in *The Irish*

‡ *Irish Independent*, 15 October 1997.

Times. In it he gave his own analysis of the leaked reports: ". . . In short, this comes across as a conversation between good acquaintances, reported to Mr Ó hUiginn, a man in sympathy with Ms McAleese, and who values her opinions highly. Against that background, given a reputable civil servant reporting to a reputable head of section in a memo that was leaked to a reputable journalist, to any sensible reader it all rings true."‡

Whatever damage that section of the article did to the McAleese cause, the final part only damaged Nally's campaign. "Derek Nally does not accept the McAleese denial," wrote Caden, in spite of the fact that all those who were at the debate the previous night heard him accept her denial. More amazingly, at one o'clock that day, Nally released the following statement to the press: "I accept the analysis of John Caden's article published in today's *Irish Times.*" Not surprisingly, the same *Irish Times* described Derek Nally as a person who was "in the grip of his advisers". The Nally camp suffered its first major split the following day when John Caden left them, and Nally himself delivered the *coup de grace* on *The Late Late Show* when he stated publicly that it was a mistake to let Eoghan Harris on board his campaign team.

The editorials on Wednesday's *Irish Times* and *Irish Independent* said very uncomplimentary things about Nally's attack on McAleese, and both agreed that she alone came out of the affray undamaged. *The Irish Times* opined: "The most charitable interpretation of Mr Nally's attack is that his tongue ran away with him . . . It may be that he was ill-advised. He was certainly ill-informed."§

Mary has this to say of Derek Nally:

> He was a person for whom I had the height of respect when we worked together, and I always thought him a decent, highly principled man. He brought fine values with him into the presidential election campaign, but unfortunately he allowed others to trash them. He came into the contest late and was low in the polls. In a moment of weakness he allowed others to lead him down a road that on his own he would never have travelled. As soon as he realised his mistake he drew back and did the decent thing.

Thursday morning's *Pat Kenny Show* brought some good news and some bad news for the McAleese camp. Gerry Adams, the Sinn Féin leader, was a guest on the show. When Kenny asked him who he would

‡   *The Irish Times,* 15 October 1997.

§   *Ibid.*

vote for if he had a vote in the presidential election, Adams replied that he would give his number one to Mary McAleese, number two to Adi Roche, number three to Mary Banotti and number four to Dana. He said he would not give any vote to Derek Nally. This straight answer to a straight question caused John Bruton, the Fine Gael leader, to issue a statement in which he questioned the qualifications of the government's presidential candidate "who was endorsed by Sinn Féin".

By way of answering that question, Noel Dempsey responded with a question of his own: were the secret Department of Foreign Affairs memos leaked by Fine Gael people? Veiled references were made to a lunch in Longfield's Restaurant in Dublin at which John Bruton and his adviser Roy Dooney were joined by Eoghan Harris, a couple of days before the documents were leaked. Bruton vehemently denied that either he or any senior member of Fine Gael had any part in the leaking of the documents.

By early afternoon, the see-saw of public opinion was back on a horizontal plane after Eoghan Harris gave a classic performance on *News at One*. He admitted that his main motivation in helping Derek Nally was to inflict as much damage as he could on the McAleese campaign.

"I would vote for Donald Duck if he opposed Mary McAleese . . . She's an arrogant and self-sufficient candidate who's using the Southern election to advance her career. She not a Sinn Féiner of course. Let me say she's not a Sinn Féiner. She's a Mé Féiner."

The verbal assault continued and the insults flew thick and fast. Then came the unforgettable metaphor: "She's a tribal timebomb! She's an unreconstructed Northern nationalist who will drag all kinds of tribal baggage with her if elected." It was all music to Noel Dempsey's ears, too bitter and too melodramatic by far to inflict any damage on the candidate. It could only do her good in the long run. Even in the short term, she was to benefit from Harris's studied outburst, as was obvious on the following night's *Late Late Show*.

The five candidates were invited to join Gay Byrne live in the studio. If Byrne and his audience were hoping for verbal fireworks they were sadly disappointed. The programme was remarkable for its tameness. Before they went on air, the political parties, especially Fianna Fáil and Fine Gael, were practically eviscerating each other over the conduct of the campaign, but the conduct of the candidates reflected none of this tension. They were the personification of friendliness and affability. At one stage, in total frustration at his inability to instigate any controversy among them, Gay Byrne said, "You're so kind and embracing and so loving to each other"—just what he didn't need on *The Late Late Show*.

Even when he tackled Derek Nally about the performance of Eoghan Harris on *News at One* the previous day, all he got was an attempt by the former garda to distance himself: "Harris wasn't on my campaign. He was one of those backroom cloaked people who was pulling the strings. What's important was I got rid of them early."

Even Banotti's attempt to call McAleese's Irishness into question with her reference to Fianna Fáil "having to look outside the jurisdiction" for a candidate rebounded on her. The following morning all the newspapers agreed: things were looking good for Mary McAleese.

Chapter Twenty-Seven

'Twas a Sunday Night in Galway

There was half a million people there of all denominations
The Catholic, the Protestant, the Jew and Presbyterian
Yet there was no animosity no matter what persuasion
But "fáilte" hospitality inducing fresh acquaintance.

("The Galway Races"—traditional)

By the end of the week, Mary McAleese was still comfortably ahead in the polls, and Fianna Fáil and the gardaí were doing their utmost to find the source of the leak of the secret documents. Mary's campaign team were confident that whatever damage they had initially caused was now well contained. But their self-congratulation was premature. More leaks were on the way. The *Sunday Business Post* and *Sunday Tribune* had the full texts of three separate memos from Dympna Hayes ready to print. Mary got sight of them for the first time late on Saturday night. Ironically she had attended the twenty-fifth anniversary dinner of the SDLP in the Burlington Hotel in Dublin that night, where she had spend a lot of time with her old friend Eddie McGrady, her local SDLP representative of many years and a man for whom she had worked on occasion. She also had the opportunity to spend some time talking to her other friend of many years, Seamus Mallon, the deputy leader of the party. The following morning the newspapers carried pictures of a cheerful Mary McAleese in animated conversation with John Hume and his wife Pat. Little did she realise, as she left the company of so many SDLP friends that evening, how aggrieved she would feel in the coming days at the lack of support from senior members of that same party, at their vacillation in the face of a concentrated attack on someone who had supported them since their foundation.

Staff members of the Department of Foreign Affairs regularly write confidential reports which percolate through the system and end up in DFA headquarters in Dublin. There they are colour designated, depending on their source; for example, memos from Northern Ireland form what is known as "the Green Book". Since the foundation of the

Anglo-Irish Conference and the Maryfield Secretariat, officers of the Department of Foreign Affairs have been in the habit of meeting prominent nationalists in the North for informal discussions on a wide range of subjects. One area of concern has been the establishment and maintenance of a nationalist balance on public bodies, and people like Mary McAleese were sometimes asked to suggest names of suitable candidates for various committees. They were also asked their opinions on many areas of public life in Northern Ireland. The whole thing was an informal consultation process, built on trust on both sides.

In January 1997, Dympna Hayes rang Mary McAleese in Queen's University Belfast and invited her to lunch. She said she wanted her impressions on third-level education in Northern Ireland and the peace process. The two women enjoyed each other's company and met several times over the next couple of months. Mary was happy to share her experiences and her insights with the woman she knew to be a senior civil servant. She had no idea, however, that after each meeting Hayes was writing an account of what was said and sending it back to Dublin. Mary says that when she saw the account in the *Sunday Business Post* on 19 October she was shocked.

"I was appalled by the spin that was put on those meetings. I did not recognise the accounts in the newspaper as reports of any conversation I ever had with anyone."

According to the report in the newspaper, Dympna Hayes wrote this account of her impression of Mary McAleese's ideas on the political situation in the North on 28 January 1997: "On a personal level McAleese has no interest in participating in the upcoming elections in 'any shape or form' in the absence of an SDLP-Sinn Féin election platform."[‡]

This was akin to saying that Mary supported Sinn Féin, as the establishment of a common election platform with the SDLP was one of the aims of that party. The second memo was written in the month of May, shortly after the general election in Britain and Northern Ireland. Mary McAleese and Dympna Hayes met for dinner, after which Hayes reportedly wrote, "She was very pleased with Sinn Féin's performance in the general election and confident that they will perform even better in the local elections; she expects Mick Murphy, the Sinn Féin candidate in Rostrevor, her own constituency, to pick up a seat this time."[§]

---

‡   *Sunday Business Post*, 19 October 1997.
‡   *Ibid.*

The report then gave McAleese's alleged reasons for the SDLP's lack of success in Mid-Ulster. "McAleese feels that a lot of the 'new' Sinn Féin support has come from the young middle-aged and upwardly mobile Nationalists rather than the first-time voters, and that they see Sinn Féin as far more likely to deliver on the political front than the SDLP. She attributed the SDLP's failure to pick up either of the Mid-Ulster or West Tyrone constituencies in part to their poor PR."[‡]

This second report also mentioned a chance meeting between Mary McAleese and the leader and deputy leader of Sinn Féin.

"She returned from London last Monday evening on the same flight as Adams and McGuinness. Both of them were in great form and had thoroughly enjoyed their visit to Westminster. (A well-known and highly successful consultant from Touche Ross, whom McAleese has known for many years, was seated beside her on the plane and proceeded to ignore her for the rest of the journey after hearing her exchange with the Sinn Féin leaders.)"[§]

Even if Eileen Gleeson, her press officer, could limit the damage to Mary from the "spin" that she claims was put on her political views, the report of a third memo, from the same source, had the potential to damage Mary's electoral hopes beyond repair. This third memo was a report of a meeting between Dympna Hayes and Bríd Rodgers, later to become deputy leader of the SDLP. Rodgers was born and reared in Gweedore, in the Donegal Gaeltacht, and later settled in Lurgan, County Armagh, where she became the local SDLP representative. In 1983, Garret FitzGerald nominated her to the Senate in Dublin. In 1987, 1992 and again in 1997, she was an unsuccessful candidate in the Westminster elections for the Upper Bann constituency.

On 3 April 1997, just before the elections in the North, Dympna Hayes visited Bríd Rodgers in her home in Lurgan. According to the report, Rodgers' complaints focused solely on the nationalist side:

> Ms Rodgers is concerned with the poor coverage available to the SDLP in the *Irish News* of late. She puts this down to the fact that the editor-in-chief of the *Irish News*, Mr Jim Fitzpatrick, has recently formed an unofficial alliance with Father Alex Reid (a Redemptorist priest in Clonard Monastery) and Mary McAleese of QUB. Referring to the group as the "triumvirate", Ms Rodgers described their main object as promoting a new Nationalist

‡   *Ibid.*

‡   *Ibid.*

consensus which owes more to Sinn Féin than the SDLP. All three are in regular touch with the Sinn Féin leadership and are in reality pushing the Sinn Féin agenda.[‡]

The government presidential candidate was being accused of owing allegiance to Sinn Féin, of being in league with the Sinn Féin leadership, at a time when the IRA was not on ceasefire; but her election director was muzzling her, insisting that she would not counter the charges. Neither Mary nor Martin could understand his position. She wanted to face the media and contradict the reports at the earliest opportunity, and Martin agreed with her in this. Dempsey, however, was adamant: "No contact with the press. Not a word. Let this run." On this Sunday, of all days, the director of elections and the candidate were to be in each other's company from morning to night; there would be no opportunity for Mary to say that she never received his phone message.

Once a year the Fianna Fáil faithful pay their respects to the father of republicanism at the grave of Wolfe Tone in Bodenstown Cemetry in County Kildare. This was Bodenstown Sunday. Mary and her party joined the official retinue in the graveyard that morning, after which they avoided, with a lot of difficulty, all questions from the news media. Still in County Kildare, they regrouped, relatively unscathed, in Michael Smurfit's lavishly appointed K Club, outside Straffan, before sitting down to lunch in the Yeats Room. Along with Mary and Martin were Noel Dempsey, Eileen Gleeson, Caroline Callaghan and Martin Mackin. The publication of the leaked secret memos and how to deal with the allegations contained in them were the only topics of conversation during the meal. Mary was anxious to speak out, not only to clear her own name, but also to protect Alex Reid and Jim Fitzpatrick. The more she thought about the allegations the angrier she became. Since Fr Alex had started his work for peace in Belfast thirty years previously, no one, neither a unionist nor even a loyalist, had ever accused him of "pushing the Sinn Féin agenda".

"It's time to speak out!" declared Mary, and everyone at the table agreed with her; everyone except Noel Dempsey.

There was an added complication that day: the candidate was expected to face the news media in the Skeffington Arms Hotel on Eyre Square in Galway at 7.30 that evening, before attending a FF/PD rally in the Great Southern Hotel, a couple of hundred yards away across the square, at 8.30. How could she face the media and say nothing about the

---

‡   *Ibid.*

351

leaked documents and the allegations? The only feasible solution was to cancel the press conference. The team knew that this alternative would seriously antagonise an already irritated press corps, but Dempsey was not for turning:

> I knew that any denial of the allegations would be much stronger coming from somebody other than Mary. It was only a question of time before somebody would speak up for her, and I needed to make space to allow that to happen. We didn't know what else would be released in the papers, and we couldn't spend the campaign answering allegations and commenting on other people's opinions of her. It was a gamble, but all my political instincts told me it was a gamble that would pay off. Everyone knew how eloquent Mary was and how well she could explain her position, but any third party from the North speaking on her behalf was going to be far more effective.[‡]

It was decided that Mary McAleese would arrive in Galway too late for the press conference, but just in time for the rally in the Great Southern Hotel. Wally Young was selected to post notices for the media in the Skeffington Arms at the appropriate time, and Pat Farrell was appointed to phone individual journalists about the cancellation of the press conference. No clear reason was to be given for Mary's delay in advance of her arrival in Galway. She did not like the situation. From her broadcasting days, she knew how eagerly the journalists would be waiting to question her about the revelations and how frustrated they would be at this denial of the opportunity. She also realised that, thanks to her, the perspective of some of the evening news programmes would have to be redesigned. She was not looking forward to her eventual meeting with the media.

She and Martin had a long afternoon ahead of them. They read every newspaper in the place from cover to cover before Denis Lawlor, their driver, took them for a long leisurely drive through the centre of Ireland. The Fianna Fáil press office issued a report that Mary and Martin were delayed due to personal business. The story was embellished when Noel Dempsey announced that he arrived in Galway at 6.15 rather than 5.15 because of heavy traffic congestion on the Dublin–Galway road. He explained that because of their late start from Kildare and the state of the traffic the McAleeses would be at least an hour late arriving in Galway and, regretfully, the press conference would have to be cancelled.

---

‡   Interview with author.

352

By 8.30 that night the local Fianna Fáil and Progressive Democrat dignitaries were ready and waiting on the steps of the Great Southern to welcome the government candidate. They were joined in the doorway by national figures such as Bobby Molloy, Éamon Ó Cuív, Noel Tracy and Margaret Cox. In the hotel ballroom, more than six hundred members of both parties waited to give Mary McAleese a welcome she would never forget. Noel Dempsey, as choreographer and orchestrator in chief, was everywhere at once. When Denis Lawlor rang to let him know that they were in Galway and ready to drive into Eyre Square, Dempsey directed all the dignitaries to the exact spot the car would stop. He also formed forty or fifty supporters into a double line between the car and the door of the hotel like a guard of honour on either side of the candidate, or a human shield between her and the members of the news media.

The plan was for Mary to be met inside the hotel by a piper, but the arrangement was quickly changed. The piper was repositioned at the spot where Mary would emerge from the car. He was told to accompany her inside and to play "very loudly". As soon as Mary and Martin arrived, the "human shield" formed a tunnel between the car and the door of the hotel. There was a lot of pushing and shoving, and people quickly got very intense as reporters reached towards her with microphones and shouted questions through the phalanx of supporters and the skirl of the pipes. Neither the reporters nor the minders were prepared to give an inch, and the keen of the pipes only added to the pandemonium. Having gained the hotel lobby, Mary's next objective was to negotiate the stairs as far as the first floor, where a room was reserved for her use.

Memories of the events of that evening are many and varied. Jim Fahy, RTÉ's western correspondent, remembers somebody pulling him back as he was trying to follow Mary upstairs. He was told afterwards that the person responsible was none other than Noel Dempsey.

Catherine Cleary confirmed this story in the following day's *Irish Times*: "Mr Dempsey got carried away with the bluster of it all. Launching himself across the lobby of the Great Southern in Galway he grabbed RTÉ's Jim Fahy and tried to drag him away from the Fianna Fáil and Progressive Democrat presidential candidate, Prof. Mary McAleese."[‡]

According to Emily O'Reilly: "What was meant to be an orderly walk suddenly became a mêlée. Reporters lunged towards the candidate,

---

‡   *The Irish Times*, 20 October 1997.

shouting questions about the Rodgers memo. McAleese kept walking, shielded by handlers who attempted to keep the media away."‡

Noel Dempsey makes a certain admission in his account of events: "As soon as Mary arrived she was mobbed by journalists, led by Jim Fahy. Eileen Gleeson had advised her to smile and be pleasant and keep walking, which she did to perfection. As Mary was making her way up the stairs to the room we had set aside, the media scrum took off after her. I grabbed the tail of Jim Fahy's coat and slowed him down enough to let Pat Farrell get ahead of him and bring Mary into the room."§

Mary has very vivid memories of the occasion. "No sooner had we left the car than we were surrounded by people shouting at us. The whole place was in uproar. Microphones and tape recorders were being pushed into my face and cameras were flashing continuously. People were pushing so much that I was afraid I would be knocked down. I must say it was a most undignified occasion."

The incident, as seen on the nine o'clock news on RTÉ television that night, looked more like a fracas at a football match than a rally for a presidential candidate. The cameras concentrated on the pulling and shoving and the shouting of blame and insults, and the general impression was of an unruly mob. When Mary emerged from the ballroom at the end of the rally, she was still annoyed at her earlier treatment. Many reporters were still there, waiting for an explanation of her silence in the face of the claims in the newspapers, but she had nothing to say to them except: "I explained my position on *The Late Late Show*." By bedtime that night, Mary McAleese and the members of the news media were equally infuriated with each other.

In Navan, Harry Casey was having what he later described as "a not-so-quiet little nervous breakdown" as he watched the television news. He could reach neither Mary nor Noel Dempsey, but he eventually succeeded in contacting Liam Murphy, his former principal teacher in St Patrick's Classical School who was now a member of Mary's campaign team. Murphy explained that Dempsey had Mary under what amounted to a vow of silence. Harry, who could see no sense in the strategy, was beside himself with frustration. He rang RTÉ and complained about the standard of journalism on the *Nine O'Clock News*. Around 10.30 he contacted Fr Brendan Callanan, provincial of the Redemptorists in Ireland, in Ligouri House on Orwell Road. Fr Callanan was Fr Alex

---

‡   *The Irish Times*, 20 October 1997.

§   *Sunday Business Post*, 26 October 1997.

Reid's superior, the man who had invited Mary into the peace mission in Belfast. Harry introduced himself and explained his concern.

"I am amazed that someone like yourself has not issued a statement by now defending Mary," seethed Harry.

"We certainly have issued a statement," retorted the priest. "We faxed a press statement to RTÉ early this evening."

"Are you telling me for a fact that the RTÉ news desk got your fax before the *Nine O'Clock News*?" asked Harry.

"They did," responded the priest. "We checked after sending it."

Fr Callanan's press statement was in the newspapers the following morning:

> . . . The Redemptorist Peace Ministry team is non-political, i.e. it does not purport to support, not does it in fact support, the position of any political party . . . The benchmark of the Redemptorist Peace and Reconciliation team is the call of the Gospel to seek out ways and means of developing and promoting a more peaceful, a more reconciled and a more just society. This ministry team abhors violence in all its forms. Mr Jim Fitzpatrick and Ms Mary McAleese were invited to join the Peace Ministry Team precisely because they share these convictions. Their contribution to the Peace Ministry in association with us has been a valuable one. It is deplorable that because of this ministry they would be in any way slighted.‡

Jim Fitzpatrick issued his own statement in which he said, "This was a genuine and sincere initiative and it is both hurtful and malicious to suggest any subversive motivation by any of the individuals involved. Professor McAleese is an honourable and trusting individual who is totally committed to peace."§

The release of these statements was certainly welcomed by Mary and her team, but what was really needed was a similar testimonial from a heavyweight Northern political figure. A declaration from a senior SDLP figure that Mary had always supported them and had never backed Sinn Féin would have done nicely, but the silence from the North was deafening. SDLP politicians were taking seriously their stated policy of non-interference in political affairs south of the border. On that Monday, the only Northern politician to make any comment on the published allegations was Lord John Alderdice, leader of the Alliance

---

‡ *The Irish Times*, 10 October 1997.

§ *Ibid.*

Party, who stated emphatically that Mary should withdraw her candidacy.

On that same day, Monday, 20 October, Mary was still in the west of Ireland, canvassing on the Aran Islands. She started on the easternmost of the Gaeltacht islands, Inis Oírr, and then went on to Inis Meáin before arriving on the main island of Inis Mór. The full-strength support team of the previous night had dispersed: Dempsey back to his government department and the various local representatives to Dáil, Seanad and Council. Although she was accompanied by only two senior politicians, Éamon Ó Cuív and Bobby Molloy, a host of journalists were recording every event and every word. They were becoming more and more frustrated and annoyed at Mary who, still under interdict from Dempsey, was holding firm to the "no comment" party line on the matter of the leaked documents.

Despite the windy and showery weather, Mary and Ó Cuív toured Inis Oírr on the flat bed of a trailer pulled by a tractor. On Inis Meáin she was greeted by Dara Beag Ó Flatharta, the island poet, who had written a poem of praise in her honour. She did not understand the Irish words *"gnúis nach bhfaca mé claon ná cam inti"*, but Éamon Ó Cuív explained that the poet was speaking of her "face in which was seen no inkling of deceit". When Dara Beag tore the page from his notebook of lined blue paper and diffidently presented her with the paean of praise, she was moved—not so the throng of journalists whose increasing frustration at the candidate's silence was heightened by the isolation of the islands and the proximity of the parties. Reports to Noel Dempsey in Dublin of the increasing tension on the islands seemed to fall on deaf ears at first, but that was soon to change.

He was coming under a lot of pressure to let her speak. All the phone calls to Fianna Fáil headquarters carried the same message: Mary McAleese's continued silence was being read as arrogance, and what was Dempsey going to do about this? At midday he phoned Wally Young on Inis Mór and told him to organise a press conference. The only place available at short notice was a room in a heritage centre, and it was soon packed with reporters, locals and Mary's campaign team. The candidate sat at the top of the room, flanked by Éamon Ó Cuív and Bobby Molloy. The fact that it was not the most comfortable place for a press conference and that most of the journalists had to sit on children's school chairs or stand around the walls only added to the tension of the occasion.

It became immediately obvious to all present that neither the candidate nor the members of the media were at their ease. Some journalists described Mary's performance as terse and abrupt. Catherine Cleary later wrote this description of Mary: "She twisted the rings on her fingers with slightly shaking hands and her neck was flushed. It was the first and last time she looked uncomfortable and it was difficult to read whether it was a sign of nerves or barely suppressed rage."‡

Mary was undoubtedly still annoyed by what she considered "the appalling behaviour of some members of the media" the previous night, but she was even more upset by what she called "the inaccuracy of their reporting and their lack of research". In speaking of the newspaper coverage at the time, she points out the lack of any significant reporting of her work for peace and reconciliation. There was no mention of her numerous anti-violence articles in magazines and newspapers, nor of the many radio pieces in which she condemned those who espoused violence. There was no serious attempt by any journalist to balance the claims in the DFA documents with her work on the Sectarianism document, nor with the years she and John Lampen spent attending meetings from one end of the country to the other, nor with her many contributions to the Inter-Church Dialogue. The amount of cross-community groups, peace initiatives and reconciliation bodies she was involved in was legion, but the only one mentioned in the press during those days was the Redemptorist peace ministry—and references to that body were often tinged with suspicion of Mary's role in it.

She later wrote in her diary, "All the work that was Mary McAleese for the last twenty years completely ignored in favour of a vague person's third-hand comment in an internal memo."§

Having weathered her trip to the Aran Islands, Mary's next major engagement was still in the west of Ireland. All the candidates had been invited to attend a debate in NUI Galway that evening, under the chairmanship of Harry Whelehan, the former attorney general. Mary Banotti, who arrived late due to travel difficulties, missed the highlight of the evening. Many of the seven hundred people who thronged the hall in the university were hoping that Mary McAleese would address the controversial allegations: her supporters in expectation of a comprehensive burying of the accusations; others in anticipation of a chance to bury the government candidate. All were hoping for a good evening's entertainment.

---

‡   *The Irish Times*, 1 November 1997.

§   Mary McAleese, private papers.

The debate began at 8.30. At a few minutes after nine, just before Mary rose to speak, she was handed a slip of paper containing a transcription of the first item on the *Nine O'Clock News*. She describes the moment as the lifting of a great weight from her shoulders. The silence from the North had at last been broken. Dempsey's bet had paid off. As she stood to address the audience, Mary knew that she did not have to defend herself. That job had now been done admirably by John Hume, Seamus Mallon, Dr Joe Hendron and even by Bríd Rodgers herself. The top ranks of the SDLP had joined forces to rubbish the idea of Mary McAleese as a Sinn Féin supporter. As the Galway audience gave her a standing ovation, she let the statements of the heavyweights of Northern nationalism speak for themselves.

John Hume said that as a person who had worked very closely with Fr Alex Reid over the years "that suggestions that he and his two colleagues, Jim Fitzpatrick and Professor Mary McAleese, were engaged in anything other than work for peace and a total end to violence, is not only false but is an absolute outrage".[‡]

Seamus Mallon agreed with all that Hume had to say and added that there was no sense to John Alderdice's demand that Mary should stand down. Joe Hendron did not put a tooth in it: "This woman is no Provo!" he stated.[§]

Although Bríd Rodgers had previously criticised the leaking of the memoranda, she had refused to speak on the substance of the reports: "My only response is, and will remain, 'no comment'." But on that evening she spoke out with her colleagues: "I wish to refute the unworthy implications from some quarters in relation to Professor McAleese, Mr Fitzpatrick and Fr Alex Reid."[†]

She later wrote to Mary, explaining that her delay in speaking out was in keeping with the SDLP's policy of non-interference in the politics of the Republic. Many people now claim credit for pressurising John Hume to break that policy. Some members of the party who were not prepared to wait for the nod from Hume before they supported their old friend and colleague subsequently found themselves in trouble with the party leadership. One of these was Brian Mulligan, chairman of the Rostrevor Branch of the SDLP.

It was rumoured that Mary McAleese had refused to support the

---

‡   *The Irish Times*, 20 October 1997.

§   *Irish Independent*, 21 October 1997.

†   *The Irish Times*, 20 October 1997.

SDLP's Eddie McGrady during the Westminster general election in May of that year and had thrown her weight behind Sinn Féin. Mulligan issued a clarifying statement on behalf of his branch, noting that Mary had not only made her house available for SDLP meetings during the general election campaign, but had made the facilities of her own private office available for secretarial work. She had explained at a McGrady campaign meeting in April that, because of her dual roles as director of the Institute and pro-vice-chancellor of QUB, she would not be able to play a public role in support of McGrady. She added that she would certainly do her best for him in a private capacity. She was thanked at the meeting by such senior local figures as Rory McShane and Brian Mulligan himself.

She was asked to conduct a telephone canvass among her many local acquaintances with a view to persuading some of them to become active in McGrady's campaign. After making several calls, Mary realised that the SDLP support base had shrunk greatly in the area. Many of the people she spoke to told her they intended to vote for Sinn Féin. She rang McGrady's office and appraised Margaret Richie, his constituency secretary, of her concerns and of her conviction that a lot of work needed to be done to regain lost ground.

All was now clear, and it seemed perfectly obvious to everyone that the candidate's politics owed nothing to Sinn Féin. The SDLP had opened the floodgates and messages of support were flooding in, but the director of Mary's campaign was still not happy. Realising the power of her eloquence, the man who had successfully silenced her for so long now wanted an opportunity for her to tell her own story. He wanted her to do a major television interview.

On Tuesday morning she was in Limerick, where she was finding it difficult to get a copy of the Belfast nationalist morning newspaper the *Irish News*. She had heard about Tom Kelly's article of support for her in that morning's paper and was anxious to read it. Eventually she rang her father who read the article to her over the phone.

"Never has Mary McAleese espoused violence . . . In fact all her on-the-record comments stated very clearly her opposition to all forms of violence."[‡]

Noel Dempsey now cared little about who supported her, about who said she was a peace activist or a mediator or an uncanonised saint. It mattered little that Martin McGuinness stated that in his mind she had always been an SDLP supporter. Noel Dempsey wanted the interview,

---

‡   *Irish News*, 21 October 1997.

the major television one-on-one which would give her the chance to shine in front of the whole country. RTÉ had been putting pressure on him to get Mary to do an interview with Éamon Lawlor on *Prime Time*, and Lawlor was ready and waiting in a Limerick hotel to ask her the questions. Dempsey was convinced that his candidate would get an easy ride.

He had already challenged RTÉ on the discrepancy between *Prime Time's* coverage of Mary McAleese and their treatment of Mary Banotti. Just ten days previously, at a meeting with the Director General of RTÉ Bob Collins and several other senior executives, including Kevin Healy, Ed Mulhall and David Blake-Knox, he had criticised the national television station for their comparatively tough treatment of his candidate. He told them that he had watched with increasing disbelief the previous evening a profile of Mary Banotti that he considered "more of a party political broadcast on behalf of Fine Gael, than a profile of a presidential candidate". As a result of that meeting, he was now convinced that Mary would get every opportunity to put her case in a *Prime Time* interview.

Mary was tense and under pressure from the outset and was unable to conceal her annoyance at the style and the intensity of the interview. She does not have happy memories of it:

> It didn't feel like a TV interview as much as a savage grilling. I felt like a suspect, like a person who could not be trusted. The questions came like machine-gun bullets. My work with the peace ministry was outrageously characterised as being almost subversive, and there was not a word, not a mention, nor even a question, about my years of work for peace and reconciliation, about my work against violence on radio and in newspapers and magazines. I was under pressure, but by the time it was over I felt I had told the story as it needed to be told. It was a tough, gruelling interview. Noel Dempsey told me he was happy with my performance, and I put my trust in his assessment.

It did not help that Mary had to leave a rally to do the interview and to return to the stage afterwards, but it was worth the trouble. Dempsey was not the only one to think she had performed well. The general impression was that, despite being under pressure, her sincerity shone through. This was reflected in an *Irish Times*/MRBI poll taken two days later, on Friday, 24 October, which put McAleese still ahead and found that Banotti had not succeeded in taking any advantage of the government candidate's troubles.

Her status as a "bridge-builder" was enhanced by a statement from Eddie McGrady, who broke one of the SDLP's golden rules and actually endorsed a candidate in a Southern election: "Mary McAleese can make a real and meaningful contribution to the resolution of conflict in Ireland . . . she had a unique insight into the Nationalist and Unionist traditions North and South."‡

At the end of that week support and endorsements started to come from the other side of the political and religious divide in the North. The Revds Sam Burch, Ken Newall and Tim Kinahan issued a joint statement: "As ministers from within the mainline protestant denominations and from the unionist community, we wish to bear witness that, in all of these contacts, we have never detected in our Redemptorist colleagues (including Professor McAleese) a desire to promote any political agenda. We would have strenuously challenged any attempt to do so."§

Dr David Stevens, the general secretary of the Council of Churches in Ireland, called her ". . . a person who is open to other people's religious and political views. I don't see her as being involved in any Sinn Féin or violence agenda."†

Statements of support from nationalist politicians and unionist clergy were to be expected, possibly, but Mary claimed to have received messages of support from unionist politicians. By the end of that week, the only one to be made public was from Harvey Bicker, a UUP councillor on Down District Council, who said, "Mary McAleese is clearly the best person for the job, the best person to lead Ireland and represent Ireland abroad into the next century."¶

A week before Fianna Fáil chose Mary as their candidate, Harvey Bicker rang her at home in Rostrevor to offer his assistance with her nomination attempt and her subsequent election campaign. The pair had never met, but Bicker—whose solicitor was Nick Fenton, Anne Fenton's husband—had followed her career with interest and explained why he wanted to help her.

Having been raised among Catholic neighbours in Poyntzpass, County Armagh, his childhood was as atypically free from sectarian tensions as Mary's own:

---

‡　*The Irish Times*, 25 October 1997.

§　*The Examiner*, 23 October 1997.

†　*The Irish Times*, 27 October 1997.

¶　*The Examiner*, 23 October 1997.

When Mary Robinson became president my community tried hard to find a point of contact with her. The fact that Nicholas Robinson's father was an officer in the British army was enough. If Albert Reynolds was elected, this time my community would have looked on him as just another foreigner. But if Mary McAleese became president, my community would look on her as a fellow Northener and one of their own. The "Building Bridges" campaign slogan struck a chord with me. Only a Northern president would have been in the position to build the bridges that she later did. I wanted to be on that journey with her and I didn't mind being a lonely figure at the time. I knew I would not be lonely for long.[‡]

Those who were questioning Mary's claim of support from unionist political quarters were silenced by a statement from a most unexpected source: from a man who had tabled questions about her in the Westminster parliament. On Sunday, 26 October, John Taylor MP, deputy leader of the UUP, said on RTÉ radio's *This Week* programme, "I never considered Professor McAleese to be a supporter of Sinn Féin."[§]

Speaking of any members of the SDLP who might possibly consider Mary McAleese a Sinn Féin supporter, he continued:

> But I do not believe that those members of the SDLP are representative of the SDLP throughout Northern Ireland. I think they are a minority. She is an out and out Nationalist, a very, very green Nationalist, and promotes her Catholicism too much. She overdoes it. But, having said that, and pointing out how different she is from me, as a Protestant and a British citizen here in Northern Ireland, she is a most able person. She steered the new campus in Armagh in an excellent and efficient way, and although we disagree in politics and religion, I found her quite easy to work with.[†]

If Mary had been able to dictate Taylor's script, she could hardly have been more satisfied with it. Even his criticism of her would be seen as a badge of honour to many voters in the Republic.

The daily deluge of statements of support gave Mary great encouragement, but nothing gave her as much comfort as a package she received from a sister of her old *anamchara* Fr Justin Coyne when she was at her lowest ebb. Sr Gemma Coyne was a nun in England. Having

‡   Interview with author.

§   *The Irish Times*, 27 October 1997.

†   *Ibid*.

read of Mary's troubles, she decided to send her a present. It was Fr Justin's cross, the one he had worn since his days as a novice. Mary says that when she opened the package and realised what was in it, a great weight lifted off her. She remembered her old friend speaking to her about courage and confidence. "I was ready to tackle, with confidence, whatever difficulties lay ahead," she says, "but more importantly, having done my best, I was ready to accept whatever was in store for me."

Chapter Twenty-Eight

Come to the Edge

"Come to the edge."
"It's too high."
"Come to the edge."
"We might fall."
"Come to the edge."
And they came.
And he pushed them.
And they flew.

(Christopher Logue: *Come to the Edge*)

According to Tuesday's *Irish Independent*, Mary was almost home and dry. Their IMS poll published that morning put her support at 49 per cent, Banotti's at 32 per cent and none of the rest at any more than 7 per cent. The previous evening, while the other candidates were doing some last minute canvassing, the Belfast woman was in Manchester, speaking at the Irish World Heritage Centre. The chairman of the centre Michael Forde had invited all the candidates, but Mary was the only one to accept the invitation to a function that could hardly be considered part of the campaign as very few of those attending it would be voting in the presidential election.

On Tuesday morning, gardaí arrested a man in connection with the leaking of the internal Department of Foreign Affairs memos. The man, an advisor to a former Fine Gael government minister, was brought to Lucan Garda Station, where he was held all day for questioning before being released without charge. Around the time he was being released, the five candidates were preparing for their final television appearance. RTÉ's traditional moratorium on election campaign coverage on the day before polling meant that Tuesday night was the last opportunity viewers had to hear what the candidates had to say. *Prime Time* was the programme in question, and Miriam O'Callaghan was the presenter.

Mary McAleese had such a bad flu that she was finding it difficult to speak. As the five candidates arranged themselves around the panel desk, Mary made sure she got an outside position, and just as the programme was about to go live, she moved her seat even further from the rest of the panel. The programme was not long on the air when it became obvious that the other four candidates were prepared to do most of the talking and most of the attacking. Mary was able to avoid speaking too much and at the same time was able to isolate herself visually from much of the conflict. A month later a friend told her, "Your best television performance was that night on *Prime Time* when you said nothing."

By Wednesday morning, the day before polling, no bookmaker in Ireland was giving better odds than 1/12 on Mary McAleese, and many of them were not prepared to accept any bet on her at all. Martin McAleese had long since put his money on her—an amount, he says, that will remain undisclosed. Every newspaper, North and South, had her as hot favourite. A visitor would have been forgiven for thinking that the people of Rostrevor were able to vote in the election. Mary's posters decorated every lamp-post, and two huge photographs of her hung at each end of Mary Street. Her family and friends were taking nothing for granted and spent the day making calls to those who had a vote. But what about the woman herself? She says she was unruffled.

"I was very calm in the midst of all the *ruaille buaille* that was going on around me. I was by no means overconfident. In fact, the opposite was true. But I knew I had done my absolute best during the campaign. I knew I could have done no more and was therefore prepared to accept whatever the next day would bring."

It is undoubtedly true that the prospect of John Hume's declaring an interest in the presidency helped Mary's cause greatly by opening people's minds to the possibility of a Northerner in the Áras. But what would Mary do if her grand endeavour ended in failure? Bertie Ahern raised the prospect with her in private.

"What will happen if you don't win? Will you go back to Queen's?"

The same question was asked, and answered, in public by Steven King, advisor to David Trimble and a member of the Queen's University Graduates' Unionist Club: "Professor McAleese has nailed her colours to the Republican mast . . . has shown her true colours having obtained the nomination of Fianna Fáil, the Republican Party . . . I trust that win or lose the Presidency she will play no further part in academic life in Queen's University."

King and some other unionist commentators erroneously claimed that by seeking the presidential nomination she had broken her contract with Queen's and would be unable to return as pro-vice-chancellor. Others raised the question of security if she were to return to a high profile job in the North. Very few people knew that, even if she had not sought the nomination, Mary had not intended to spend much longer in Queen's University. Only the previous summer she had said as much to Sir Anthony Campbell, chair of the Council for Legal Education, and the person to whom she, as director of the Institute of Professional Legal Studies, was accountable.

Her contract as director was due to expire in 1997, and although the members of the Council for Legal Education were pressing her to renew it, she was not prepared to remain more than a further year in the position. The end of that extra year would coincide with the expiry of her term as pro-vice-chancellor. Mary had an offer to spend part of each year in Florence training teachers of meditation. She was also anxious to become involved in training qualified lawyers in mediation and dispute resolution, having undergone training both in the UK and the US in both disciplines. She had also devised and taught courses in them for trainee lawyers and had found the exercise so worthwhile that she now wanted to promote the practice. She also looked forward to having time for some serious reading and a little writing. Apart from Sir Anthony Campbell, she had disclosed her plans only to a small number of Institute colleagues whose promotional prospects might be influenced by her departure.

By the morning of polling day, Thursday, 30 October 1997, it seemed as if all thoughts of Florence and the teaching of dispute resolution would be put on the back burner for at least another seven years. All the analysts were of one voice: that McAleese would win on the second count. Martin McAleese agreed with the general consensus, and although the candidate refused to acknowledge any confidence in the outcome, she was also quietly buoyant. Voters were presented with two ballot papers that day. As well as voting for a new President of Ireland, they were invited to vote on the proposed seventeenth amendment to the Constitution: that proceedings of the Cabinet would remain confidential under the law.

Neither Mary nor Martin had a vote in the election. Although they had an address within the jurisdiction—the apartment in Dublin—they say they felt it would be unfair to claim the right to vote, as the apartment was not their family home. In fact, the apartment was not even their residence during much of the election campaign. Fianna Fáil had installed them in a suite of rooms in the Portmarnock Hotel and

Golf Links, in a beautiful location on the coast north of the city, for the last three weeks of the campaign. On the morning of election day, with all the hard work done, Martin and Noel Dempsey relaxed with a quiet game of golf. Mary and Eileen Gleeson headed for the shops of Grafton Street for some retail therapy. It was the first break any of them had for six long, gruelling weeks.

The McAleese children, who were enjoying their Halloween mid-term break, joined their parents in the hotel, while all the Leneghans packed into the apartment in Dublin. In the afternoon, Emma, Saramai and Justin went to the cinema with their uncle Clement Leneghan. On their way back to Portmarnock on the bus, Justin was seated beside a woman who was reading that day's *Evening Herald*, which had a picture of the McAleese family on the front page. The woman looked at Justin, then back at the paper. She then looked around at the girls, and then back at the paper again. She later told them she needed to convince herself before asking, "Are you the young McAleeses?" Justin introduced himself and his sisters and the four of them had a good chat. "I'm on my way home," she informed them. "I wasn't going to bother voting. But you can tell your mother from me that she has three lovely children, and as soon as I've had my dinner I'm going to go and vote for her."

On Friday morning the children gathered in their parents' room to follow the count on television. The tallymen had already noted a couple of interesting facts about this particular election: firstly, the turnout was the lowest ever in a presidential election; and secondly, it looked as if the new president would win by the biggest margin ever. By lunchtime the phone was ringing non-stop and the visitors were queuing in the corridors. Everyone agreed that she had it, but still it was not certain. By the time Mary Bruton came to fix her make-up and do her hair, there was still no definite news from the count centre. Eventually, at half past four, Eileen Gleeson walked in. She crossed the room in a couple of strides and threw her arms around Mary. "We've done it!" she said. The victorious roar that went up from her supporters all around the hotel masked the few sobs in the bedroom.

It was time for the McAleeses to join the rest of the family in the apartment. Even as Mary was emerging from the car in Ballsbridge, she could hear the party going full blast in "Independent House". Then, above the clamour and the commotion, she recognised the voice of her deaf brother John. He was standing at the open window trying to get her attention. "Mary! Mary! You've won! You've won!" It was a poignant family reunion, the swing and sweep of emotions, from euphoria to the staggering humbling reality of it all, catching the Leneghan family just as they started to come to terms with their eldest daughter and big sister being elected President of Ireland. As Mary embraced her parents in the doorway, Paddy's gratification at her elevation was tempered by Claire's distress at what she later called the "loss of her daughter". They all wiped their away their tears for the first full family photograph in years.

All too soon, Mary and Martin were ushered back into the car and whisked off to the Parliament Hotel in Dame Street, opposite the gates of Dublin Castle, where the large room over the entrance had been reserved as a dressing room for them. Mary, having heard nothing of this, thought it was a secret arrangement until she met a crowd of her Trinity College friends waiting for her at the hotel door.

Safely ensconced in the upstairs room, she changed into the dress Martin had bought in confident anticipation of this occasion. Half an hour before the official announcement of the result of the election, Mary and Martin, with the taoiseach and the tánaiste, walked across Dame Street and through the gates of Dublin Castle. Mary took her place with the other candidates on the dais in St Patrick's Hall for the announcement of the official result and the details: 58.67 per cent for Mary McAleese, 41.33 per cent for Mary Banotti in the second count. In the first count there was a total of 13.82 per cent for Dana Rosemary Scallon, 6.96 per cent for Adi Roche and 4.69 per cent for Derek Nally. The tallymen had it right that morning. When they left the Castle for the Fianna Fáil/Progressive Democrat celebrations in the Herbert Park Hotel, they found themselves in a strange car with a strange driver. For the foreseeable future she would travel nowhere without an armed garda escort and a garda driver in a state car.

Denis Moloney, who had travelled from Belfast with his sister Maria that morning to be in Dublin for the count, had spent the day between the apartment and the RDS count centre. Having gone to Dublin Castle to witness his friend taking her place in the history of Ireland, the unassuming solicitor, who had done so much to make it all happen, now faded quietly once again into the background, as he sat into his car to drive home to Belfast.

At noon the next day, Mary was back in St Patrick's Hall in Dublin Castle—this time to receive the official parchment of her appointment as president elect of Ireland. As the Angelus bells began to peal throughout the city, Lieutenant Colonel Des Johnston snapped to attention in front of his soon-to-be commander-in-chief. After standing stock still for several seconds, he took one measured pace forward, clicked his heels together, saluted, and placing the parchment in her outstretched hands, he solemnly intoned, *"Cuirim in iúl duit, leis an gcáipéis seo, go bhfuil tú tofa mar Uachtarán na hÉireann."* ("With this document, I hereby inform you that you have been duly elected eighth President of Ireland.")

"Go raibh maith agat," she replied. ("Thank you.")

The ceremony lasted no more than thirty seconds, and one of the photographers missed it.

"Can you do it again?" he asked.

"You can't recreate history," he was told.

She had eleven days before her inauguration. She knew that every waking minute of those days would be busy, but she wanted to spend her first night as president elect at home in Rostrevor with her family and friends. The following morning, as she, Martin and the children left the house to go to mass, they were met at the gate by the Longstone Pipe Band and several thousand well wishers who accompanied them to the chapel. The band played several verses and choruses of "A Nation Once Again" before being persuaded to play something slightly less partisan. Coincidentally, the Church of Ireland Bishop Brian Hannon, who knew nothing of Mary's homecoming, was on his first pastoral visit to Rostrevor to preach in the Protestant church. As he emerged from his car and saw an ecstatic crowd of several thousand surging towards him, led by a band playing "The Star of the County Down", the poor man was convinced that no other bishop in the history of Ireland had ever been given such a welcome for a simple pastoral visit. When he found out the truth, he enjoyed the fun of the situation so much that he often told the joke against himself afterwards.

Every street in the village was thronged by the time mass was over in the Star of the Sea Chapel. As she and the family emerged from the building, she was surrounded by a mixed escort of RUC and Garda detectives, who made no attempt to keep at bay the hundreds of relatives, friends and acquaintances who swarmed around her to congratulate her and wish her well as the procession slowly made its way back to the house; and her old friend Tommy Sands sang his song "Mary on the Misty Mourne Shore", now rededicated to a different Mary.

She spent the afternoon in the kitchen of Kairos making sandwiches, scones and endless pots of tea for the gardaí, the RUC and the incessant stream of visitors to the house. Others offered to do the work, and they pleaded with her to sit down and relax, but it was important to her to be hostess in her own home. The kitchen, dining room and sitting room upstairs were packed, and the people downstairs were spilling out into the garden. The police at the gate were fighting a losing battle trying to keep strangers away. Seemingly there were no strangers. It was a busy, tiring, hectic, happy, wonderful day.

On Monday the children went back to school, and Mary and Martin had a meeting with senior RUC personnel to discuss security matters. After the meeting, Martin went back to work in Crossmaglen and Mary returned to the Portmarnock Hotel and Golf Links in Dublin. By that time she considered it her home away from home: "They took very good care of me. They did everything with such a good grace that when I arrived back that day it was like going home again."

There was a lot Mary needed to find out about staffing in the Áras. Would she be able to appoint her own personal assistant? Christine Cole had been their housekeeper for years in Rostrevor; would she be able to bring her to the Áras? What about a special advisor? The gardaí, the army, the civil service and the Office of Public Works all had their areas of responsibility in the Áras, and it would take Mary some time to find the lines of demarcation. She made it very clear before she moved in that she did not want to upset any system that was already in place. Peter Ryan, who had been secretary general under President Mary Robinson, was about to retire, to be replaced by Brian McCarthy. He was of immense help to Mary in preparing for the inauguration.

When she and Martin visited the Áras for the first time, they were told that their private quarters would be on the second floor, where the Robinsons had lived before them, but that the arrangement would be only temporary. Asbestos removal was due to begin in the building, and it would be a major operation. The McAleeses discovered that the de Valeras and the Hillerys had lived in the West Wing, a part of the Áras that had been specially built as a dormitory block for a visit by King Edward VII of England. When they investigated it, they found it to be eminently suitable as a family wing. It had its own back entrance through a private yard, and the family could come and go without trailing through the public rooms. They could have their own kitchen and sitting room, just like home. There was even a ground floor bedroom for Granda Charlie who was getting less and less mobile. The arrangement seemed perfect.

On the Friday morning before the inauguration, Martin worked in his surgery in Crossmaglen before travelling to Kilkeel to collect the children from school in the Louis Convent. It was a job he did not relish. It was the children's last day in the school, and they were going to be devastated. Mary had wanted to be there to collect them, to say goodbye to all in the school and to thank them for making her children's time there so happy, but she was unable to get away from her duties in Dublin. She sent a faxed note to Martin and asked him to read it out if he got an opportunity. When Martin arrived at the school, the principal, Dr Celestine Devlin, and the vice-principal, Seán Rodgers, welcomed him and brought him into the school hall and on to the stage. From the assembled pupils in the body of the hall, the young McAleeses were invited to join their father on the stage, and each of them was presented with a gift.

When the words of farewell and thanks had all been spoken and the parting gifts had been presented, Martin was asked to say a "few words". After speaking on his own behalf, he explained that Mary was very disappointed that she was unable to be there herself. He suddenly remembered the faxed note in his pocket. Taking it out, he had a quick glance at it before starting to read it aloud. He found the task difficult:

> I had only glanced at the note previously. It wasn't very long, but it said all the right things exactly as they should be said—a masterpiece as only Mary could write it. It was one of the most moving letters I have ever read, so emotionally charged that I had to deliver it very slowly in order to keep my own emotions in check. Afterwards, when I sat down beside Seán Rodgers, he asked me how, in the name of God, I had managed to finish the letter.
>
> Suddenly it was time to go. There was hardly a dry eye in the place, and our children were inconsolable. As I was driving to Dublin, the children cried non-stop. I was broken-hearted for them and felt totally powerless as they talked, between sobs, about leaving their friends and relations to go to strange schools in a strange city and begin a totally strange new life. We were heading for a new reality, but that terrible sadness and loss was another reality. I could only hope and pray that they would prove to be resilient and not end up as three casualties of the presidency.
>
> We stopped in Drogheda for burgers and chips to try to relieve the mood. My most vivid memory of that stop is of Justin complaining that, to add to his complete misery, Sara had just killed his Tamagotchi.

That night Mary and Martin were guests on *The Late Late Show*, and Gay Byrne asked Martin how he had spent the day. He told the story of the Tamagotchi, a little electronic gadget containing a "virtual" pet. The following day, he and Justin were shopping in Dublin when a couple of women recognised Martin from the previous night's show. One woman addressed him: "Is this the young fellow whose Tamagotchi got killed?" Then turning to Justin, she offered her condolences: "We're sorry for your trouble, son."

The death of the virtual pet was soon forgotten in the flurry of activity as the children prepared for the big day. Helen Cody helped them choose the clothes for the occasion. Mary, Martin, Peter Ryan and Eileen Gleeson were busy with the guest list for the inauguration. As the occasion was hosted by the government, only a limited number of places were reserved in St Patrick's Hall for guests of the president. Every ounce of diplomatic skill was required as Mary and Martin sorted and sifted through the numerous relations and friends.

Mary McGonnell, a librarian in Ballynahinch, was an old friend of Mary's from Belfast, and the pair corresponded regularly. As the librarian shared the future president's love of poetry, she sometimes sent her poems or recommended books to her. So it was that during the dark days of the campaign she sent her a poem by the English poet Christopher Logue, "Come to the Edge", a poem he had written in 1968 in honour of the French poet Guillaume Appolinaire. At the time Mary was being unfairly attacked by the media, Mary McGonnell had thought that Mary could use it in a speech to urge people to trust her and believe in her. Although she did not use it at the time, she now wanted to make it an important part of her inauguration address. When she contacted Logue by phone and asked his permission, he said he would be delighted and honoured.

The morning of 11 November was bright and cold. In room number 307 in the Portmarnock Hotel, the president elect was dressed in a caramel coloured velvet suit and cashmere coat by Miriam Mone. She had learned her address almost by heart, especially the poem which would be a *leitmotif* during her presidency:

> "Come to the edge".
> "It's too high."
> "Come to the edge."
> "We might fall.'
> "Come to the edge.'
> And they came.
> And he pushed them.
> And they flew.

Martin looked out the window at the cavalcade of military outriders, at the ranks of gardaí, at the convoy of cars, at the presidential Rolls Royce with the national flag flying on its fender. In just a short while another flag would also fly on the car: the gold harp on the blue background—the standard of the President of Ireland.

The aide-de-camp and the bodyguards were waiting in the corridor as Martin looked around the room for the last time, his attention caught by the flashing of the radio-alarm clock on the bedside locker: 11.11 a.m. on the 11th day of the 11th month—a providential time, he hoped, to leave for a meeting with destiny. He looked at the woman he had loved since the first time he saw her, nearly thirty years previously; the woman from the ghetto of Ardoyne with whom he had walked every step of this journey. As she looked up and their eyes locked, he reached out and took her hand, as he had done so often over the years. Not a word was spoken—none was needed—as they turned for the door, hand in hand.

Appendix

Supplementary Career Information

Mary McAleese's membership of professional associations included:
Northern Ireland Bar
Republic of Ireland Bar
European Bar Association
International Bar Association (N.I. Rapporteur)
Institute of Advanced Legal Studies
Irish Association of Law Teachers
Society of Public Teachers of Law
British and Irish Legal Technology Association
Irish Centre for European Law
Faculty of the National Institute of Trial Advocacy (UK) (NI)
Through the Glass Ceiling

She was also a member of the following bodies:
UK University Parliamentary Group
Business in the Community
Belfast Strategy Group
Association for Victim Support
Council for Social Welfare
Executive Committee of Focus Point
Board of Flax Trust
Commission for Justice and Peace
BBC Broadcasting Council for Northern Ireland
Strategy for Sport Steering Group
Joint Inter-Jurisdictional Legal Education Sub-Committee

She was also a member of various delegations, commissions and
    working parties dealing with issues ranging from ecumenism to
    anti-sectarianism and from social inclusion to community policing:
Roman Catholic Episcopal Delegation to the New Ireland Forum
"Ballymascanlon" Ecumenical Talks for twenty years
Commission of Inquiry into the Irish Penal System
Irish Bishops' Commission of Inquiry into the Irish Penal System
    (under the auspices of Council for Social Welfare)

Roman Catholic Church delegation to the Commission on
    Contentious Parades in Northern Ireland
Co-Chair of Inter-Church Working Party on Sectarianism
Co-Author of Discussion Document on Sectarianism
Guest Speaker and Tutor at Corrymeela on understanding and
    eradicating sectarianism
Facilitator, Community Conference on Policing in Ardoyne
Guest Lecturer at John Main Seminar, Dublin 1997

Bibliography

Ardoyne Association. *A Neighbourhood Police Service–Ardoyne.* Belfast: Ardoyne Association, 1994.

Ardoyne Association. *Policing in Ardoyne.* Belfast: Ardoyne Association, 1994.

Bardon, Jonathan. *Belfast: An Illustrated History.* Belfast: Blackstaff Press, 1982.

BASIC. *Women Sharing Fully in the Ministry of Christ?* Dublin: Blackwater Press, 1995.

Beckett, J.C. *The Making of Modern Ireland 1603–1923.* London: Faber and Faber, 1966.

Behan, Dominic. *Ireland Sings.* London: Essex Music, 1965.

Bew, Paul and Gillespie, Gordon. *A Chronology of the Troubles 1968–1993.* Dublin: Gill & Macmillan, 1993.

Bew, Paul and Gillespie, Gordon. *The Northern Ireland Peace Process 1993–1996: A Chronology.* London: Serif, 1996.

Bleakley, David. *Peace in Ireland.* London: Mowbray, 1995.

Connolly, Paul et al. *Too Young to Notice.* Coleraine: University of Ulster.

Council For Social Welfare, The. *The Prison System.* Dublin: The Council For Social Welfare, 1983.

Craig, Maurice James. *Some Way for Reason.* London: W. Heinemann, 1948.

Craig, Patricia, ed. *The Belfast Anthology.* Belfast: Blackstaff Press, 1999.

Darby, John. *Conflict in Northern Ireland.* Dublin: Gill & Macmillan, 1976.

De Blaghd, Earnán. *Briseadh na Teorann.* Baile Átha Cliath: Sairséal agus Dill, 1955.

Devlin, Paddy. *Straight Left.* Belfast: Blackstaff, 1993.

Duncan, William, ed. "Law and Social Policy", *Dublin University Law Journal,* 1987.

Dunn, Séamus, ed. *Facets of the Conflict in Northern Ireland.* Basingstoke: Macmillan, 1995.

Farrell, Michael. *20 Years, A Concise Chronology of Events in Northern Ireland 1969–1988.* Newtonabbey: Island, 1988.

Ford, Brian J. *Cult of the Expert.* London: Hamish Hamilton, 1982.

Gallagher, Michael. *Political Parties in the Republic of Ireland.* Manchester: Manchester University Press, 1985.

377

Healy, T.M. *The Great Fraud of Ulster*. Tralee: Anvil, 1971.

Heaney, Seamus. *Preoccupations*. London: Faber and Faber, 1980.

Heaney, Seamus. *New Selected Poems 1966–1987*. London: Faber and Faber, 1990.

Hewitt, John; Ormsby, Frank, ed. *The Collected Poems of John Hewitt*. Belfast: Blackstaff, 1991.

http://www.rte.ie/new/2002/0625/north.html

Hynes, Sr Mary, ed. *Horizon*. Belfast: Brookfield Learning Centre, 1999.

Inter-Church Meeting. *Sectarianism: A Discussion Document*, Irish Inter-Church Meeting, 1993.

Jackson, Alvin. *Home Rule: An Irish History 1800–2000*. London: Weidenfeld & Nicolson, 2003.

Jones, Emrys. *A Social Geography of Belfast*. London and New York: Oxford University Press, 1960.

Kavanagh, Patrick; Quinn, Antoinette, ed. *Selected Poems*. London: Penguin, 1996.

Keenan, Brian. *An Evil Cradling*. London: Vintage, 1993.

Kenna, G.B. *The Belfast Pogroms 1920–1922*. Dublin: O'Connell Publishing, 1922.

Kiberd, Declan and Fitzmaurice, Gabriel. eds. *An Crann Faoi Bhláth: The Flowering Tree*. Dublin: Wolfhound, 1991.

Liechty, Joseph. "Christianity and Identity in Ireland". Paper for ECONI Conference, 1995.

Logue, Christopher; Reid, Christopher, ed. *Selected Poems*. London: Faber and Faber, 1996.

Lyttle, W.G. "Betsy Gray or Hearts of Down", *The Mourne Observer*, 1968.

McAleese, Mary. *Love in Chaos*. New York: Continuum, 1999.

McAleese, Mary. *Reconciled Being–Love in Chaos*. Berkhamsted: Arthur James, 1997.

McCarthy, Justine. *Mary McAleese: The Outsider*. Dublin: Blackwater Press, 1999.

Mac Gréil, Micheál, ed. Report of the Inquiry into the Irish Penal System, The Commission of Inquiry into the Irish Penal System, 1980.

McKitterick, David; Kelters, Seamus; Feeney, Brian; Thornton, Chris. *Lost Lives*. Edinburgh: Mainstream Publishing, 1999.

McKittrick, David. *Through the Minefield*. Belfast: Blackstaff, 1999.

MacLysaght, Edward. *Irish Families: Their Names, Arms and Origins*. Blackrock, Co. Dublin: Irish Academic Press, 1957.

MacMaoláin, Seán. *I mBéal Feirste Dom*. Baile Átha Cliath: Oifig an tSoláthair, 1942.

McNeice, Louis. *Collected Poems*. London: Faber and Faber, 1966.

MacRéamoinn, Seán, ed. *Authority in the Church*. Blackrock, Co. Dublin: Columba Press, 1995.

MacSwiney, Terence. *Principles of Freedom*. Dublin: The Talbot Press, 1921.

Maguire, Anne, with Gallagher, Jim. *Why Me?* London: HarperCollins, 1994.

Mallie, Eamonn and McKittrick, David. *The Fight for Peace*. London: Mandarin, 1996.

Mercer, Derrik et al. *Chronicle of the 20th Century*. France: JL International Publications, 1988.

Montague, John. *Collected Poems*. Oldcastle, Co. Meath: Gallery, 1995.

Ó Briain, Art. *Beyond the Black Pig's Dyke*. Cork: Mercier, 1995.

O'Brien, Conor Cruise. *States of Ireland*. Frogmore, St Albans, Herts.: Pantheon, 1972.

O'Byrne, Cathal. *As I Roved Out*. Dublin: Three Candles, 1946.

O'Connor, Fionnuala. *In Search of a State: Catholics in Northern Ireland*. Belfast: Blackstaff Press, 1993.

Ó Searcaigh, Cathal. *An Bealach 'na Bhaile/Homecoming*. Indreabhán: Cló Iar-Chonnachta, 1993.

Ó Siadhail, Micheál. *Hail! Madam Jazz: New and Selected Poems*. Newcastle upon Tyne: Bloodaxe, 1992.

O'Toole, Fintan. *The Irish Times Book of the Century*. Dublin: Gill & Macmillan, 1999.

Pizzey, Erin. "How the Women's Movement Taught Women to Hate Men". http://www.mensrights.com.au/page15fhtm.

Pizzey, Erin. *Scream Quietly or the Neighbours Will Hear*. London: Pelican, 1974.

Prison Study Group, The. *An Examination of the Irish Penal System*. Dublin: The Prison Study Group, 1973.

Redemptorist Community of Clonard Monastery. *The Clonard Monastery Centenary Booklet*. Belfast: Phoenix, 1996.

Rodgers, W.R.; Longley, Michael, ed. *Poems*. Oldcastle, Co. Meath: Gallery, 1993.

Rowley, Richard. *City Songs and Others*. Dublin and London: Maunsel, 1918.

Scarman, Leslie. *Report of Tribunal of Inquiry into Civil Disturbances in Northern Ireland in 1969*. London: HMSO, 1972.

Stewart, A.T.Q. *The Narrow Ground*. London: Faber and Faber, 1977.

Stewart, Gill and Tutt, Norman. *Children in Custody*. Aldershot: Avebury, 1987.

Sullivan, T.D. ed. *Speeches from the Dock*. Dublin and Waterford: M.H. Gill and Sons, 1909.

Thomson, David. *Woodbrook*. London: Barrie & Jenkins, 1974.

Walsh, Pat. *Irish Republicanism and Socialism*. Belfast: Athol Books, 1994.

Welch Robert. *Oxford Concise Companion to Irish Literature*. London and New York: Oxford University Press, 2000.

Williams, Glanville. *Learning the Law*. London: Stevens, 1963.

Wilson, Des. *Democracy Denied*. Cork: Mercier, 1977.

Acknowledgments

I am indebted to many people for their help and support in the preparation of this book. Initially, and above all, I wish to express my gratitude to Mary McAleese, President of Ireland. In allowing me to write her authorised biography, she demonstrated a confidence in me that I, in the months that followed, did not always share. She was always patient with me and generous with her time, setting aside many an evening, after a full day of engagements, to answer my endless questions and give me insights into her life and her thoughts. She also gave me unrestricted access to any and all documents I sought, including many personal papers, diaries and letters. For all this, and for her many other kindnesses, I am deeply grateful.

I also wish to express my gratitude to the president's husband, Doctor Martin McAleese, the man with the magic memory, and to Emma, Justin and Saramai. Thanks also to the president's secretary general, Brian McCarthy, and to Eileen Gleeson, special adviser to the president, for details relating to the election campaign in 1997. My labours would have been much more arduous were it not for the help of Grainne Mooney, the president's personal secretary. Thanks to Helen Carney in the President's Office and to the aides-de-camp who were at all times welcoming and friendly and a mine of information: to Colonels Bernard Howard, Brian O'Reilly and Traolach Young; to Commandants Dermot O'Connor and Tom Boyce; to Captains Sue Ramsbottom, Mick Treacy, Pauline O'Connell and Peter Devine; and to Corporals Valerie Colton and Alan Walsh. My special thanks to Rose McBride, Bernie Carroll and the household staff for the sustenance, both physical and psychological.

I remember with affection Charlie McAleese, Martin's father, who went to heaven during the preparation of this book. He was a gentle, convivial and gracious man, greatly loved by his family and missed by all who were lucky enough to know him. There is the fill of another book in the stories Charlie told me. May he rest in peace.

I am grateful to the president's family, particularly to her parents, Paddy and Claire Leneghan, for their cordiality and openness and for the many hours they spent answering my innumerable questions about the early days of their eldest daughter.

Tá mé buíoch d'Fhoras na Gaeilge a léirigh a muinín ionam an chéad lá riamh nuair a cheap siad mé mar oide pearsanta an Uachtaráin agus a thacaigh

381

liom ón tús le leagan Gaelige an tsaothair seo, go háirithe Mícheál Ó Gruagáin, iar-phríomhfheidhmeannach, Áine Seoighe, Liam Ó Cuinneagáin, Alan Titley agus Joe Mac Donnchadha a tháinig i gcomharbacht ar an Ghruagánach. Ní beag an chabhair a fuair mé ón Choiste Coimisiúnaithe: Deirdre Davitt, Aodán Mac Póilín agus Diarmuid Breathnach.

I wish to acknowledge the valuable assistance of the following people who spoke to me about aspects of the life of Mary McAleese or who provided me with information or documents: Damien Leneghan; Denis Moloney; Maria Moloney; Father Alex Reid; Minister Noel Dempsey; Harry Casey; Mary Casey; Father Dermod McCarthy in RTÉ; Soline Vatinel; Bridget Pickering; Balinameen Heritage Group; Seán Ó Cadhain in Raheny Library in Dublin; Harvey Bicker of Down District Council; Gay Byrne; Sean O'Rourke; Father Brendan Callanan; Corporal Dan O'Connell; Maurice O'Donoghue; Father Albert Cosgrove in Canada; Seán Mac Stiofáin; Anne Maguire in London; Des Casey; Éamon Casey from the Irish Consulate in Chicago; Máire Uí Mhuirthile; Father Myles Kavanagh in Holy Cross, Ardoyne; Dominic Burke; Bishop Patrick Walsh; Michael Ringrose; Oonagh Ringrose; Dolours Price; Máirtín Ó Muilleoir; Ralph MacDarby; Pádhraig Ó Giollagáin; Father Philip Smyth in Bristol; Barry Cowan; Father Greg McGivern; Cathleen McManus; Seán McManus; Professor Vincent McBrierty; Patricia Montgomery; Tomás Mac Giolla; Joe Mulholland; David Norris; Michael McCarthy: Nuala Kelly; Bernard Keogh; Bernie Ní Bheagáin; Fintan Cronin; Des Cryan; Monsignor Denis Faul; Tim O'Connor; Peter Feeney; Brian Keenan.

Thanks to Steve MacDonogh, Máire Ní Dhálaigh, Terry Fitzgerald and Siobhán Prendergast at Brandon for their guidance and assistance. A special thanks to those who gave me valuable advice, having read sections or full drafts of the book: Tomás Ó Ceallaigh, Séamus Ó Murchú, Professor Gearóid Ó Tuathaigh, Micheál Ó Conghaile, Róisín Ní Mhianáin, Joe Ó Dónaill, Father Dermod McCarthy, Jenny MacManus, Pádraig Ó Snodaigh and Mícheál Ó Ruairc.

To those whose encouragement has meant so much to me in the preparation of this book – to my own family, Jenny, Aoife and Colm; to Eddie and all my relations and friends; to my colleagues in Gaelscoil Míde – I want to say *Nár laga Dia sibh*. To all who helped me in any way, and whose names are not mentioned here, thank you also. Any error in this book is my own responsibility.

Index

Please note that names beginning with Mc are treated as if the same as Mac.

385

Fitzpatrick, Colm, 118
Fitzpatrick, Jim, 277, 278, 279, 308, 350, 351, 355, 358
Fitzpatrick, May, 74, 75
Fitzsimons, Jim, 330
Flags and Emblems Act, 59
Flanagan, Patrick Banahan, 22
Flannery, Fr Austin, 288
Flax Trust, 287–9
Flynn, Jim, 125
Flynn, Sean, 344
Flynn, Sheena, 118
Focus Point, 221
Foley, Denis, 323
Ford, Brian J., 218
Forde, Michael, 364
Forsythe, Clifford, 240
Four Weddings and a Funeral, 284
Fox, Mildred, 311
Franco, General Francisco, 53
Freeland, General Ian, 65
Freeman, Dom Laurence, 293–4
Free Welsh Army, 16
Friel, Brian
    Translations, 174
Froggat, Peter, 261
Frontline, 168–9, 172–3
Fruithill Park, 78, 80, 119, 125, 235
Fulton, Professor Seán, 256, 263

Gaelic Athletic Association (GAA), 39, 85, 101, 102
    Gaelic football, 84, 99, 100, 128
    O'Donovan Rossa Club, 85, 100, 101, 214
Gallagher, Jackie, 338
Galway, 101–2, 159–60, 201, 263, 351–3, 357–8
Gardner, Professor John, 255
Garry, Sandra, 312, 321
Gaughan, Michael, 121
Gaynor, Harry, 199
gay rights movement, 147–8
Geary, Paddy, 168
Geoghegan-Quinn, Máire, 310
George Washington University, 250
Geraghty, Des, 335
Gerry, Elbridge, 59n
gerrymandering, 59
Gibbons, Conal, 308
Gibbons, Hugh, 308
Gibson, Anne, 282
Gibson, Ian, 216
Gibson, Lord Justice Maurice, 247

Gibson, Justice Terry, 282
Gildea, Tom, 311
Gillespie, Anne, 219
Gillespie, Eileen, 219
Gilmartin, Eileen, 14, 36, 44
Gilmartin, Jack, 15
Gleeson, Eileen, 223, 339, 350, 351, 354, 367, 372
Glenbryn, 68
Glencairn, 35, 37
Glencree Reconciliation Centre, 151
Glens of Antrim, 50
Glen Villa, 235
Glover, Isabelle, 293
God Knows, 179
Golden Pheasant Inn, 42, 134, 135
    UVF killings, 138–9, 140
Good Friday Agreement, 225
Grade, Michael, 283
Graham, Edgar, 246
Grand Opera House, 214, 215
Gray, Betsy, 20
Gray, George, 20
Gray, John, 127
Grealy, Monsignor Dominick, 312
Great Famine, 8, 26
Great Southern Hotel, 101, 351, 352, 353
Green Party, 336
Greer, Professor Des, 114, 237–8
Gregory, Mary, 338
Gregory, Tony, 230
Grew, Jimmy, 290
Griffin, Dean Victor, 148
Griffith, Arthur, 143
Griffiths, Bede, 293
Guerin, Veronica, 223
Guildford, 218, 219
Guildford Four, 219
Gunning, Ellen, 224

Hamill, Aidan, 100
Hanafin, Des, 163, 313
Hanafin, Mary, 224, 313–15, 322
Hannon, Bishop Brian, 369
Hanvey, Seamus, 111
Haran, Pat, 285–6
Harney, Mary, 11, 223, 228, 309, 311, 336, 368
Harris, Eoghan, 176, 341, 342, 345, 346, 347
Harris, Noel, 61
Haughey, Charles J., 147, 170, 223, 224–5, 226, 227, 228, 230, 232, 233, 241, 242, 274, 310, 311, 334

388

391

392

Mansergh, Martin, 274, 306–7, 310, 318, 319
Mara, P.J., 224, 338, 339
marching season *see* Orange Order
Martin, Joe, 305
Martin, Dr John, 11, 71
Martin, Micheál, 323, 335
Maryfield Secretariat, 349
Mary Immaculate School, Stillorgan, 69
Mason, Revd Gary, 269
Mater Hospital, 33, 69, 98, 113, 162
Maxwell, Eileen, 38
Maxwell, Florence, 37–8
Maxwell, Jack, 38
May, Sir John, 219
Mayhew, Patrick, 276, 287
Maze Prison, 30, 34, 95, 177, 178, 179, 182,
     183, 185, 194, 195, 260
   "blanket" protest, 179, 183
   "dirty" protest, 180
   H-Blocks, 179, 180, 181, 182, 183, 185,
     189, 192–3, 246
Medawar, Sir Peter, 157
Meehan, Caitríona, 339
Melvin, Olive, 321
Merrigan, Matt, 151
Mhac an tSaoi, Máire, 143
Middlemass, Henry Stewart, 79, 364
Milne, Dr Kenneth, 269, 271
Mitchell, Des, 260
Mitchell, Senator George, 265, 318
Molloy, Bobby, 353, 356
Moloney, Denis, 11, 302, 305–6, 308, 309,
     310, 311, 314, 318, 324, 333, 335, 368
Moloney, Maria, 302, 306, 333, 335, 368
Moloney, Oliver, 169
Moloney, Patricia, 254
Molyneaux, Jim, 240
Monaghan bombing, 120–1
Mone, Miriam, 337, 372
Montague, John, 207, 216
Montgomery, Eric, 261
Montgomery, Martin, 82
Montgomery, Pat, 166
Moore, Ian, 259
Mooretown, 149, 157, 169, 197, 198, 207,
     210, 211, 234, 236, 303
Morgan, Dermot, 198
Morris, Fred, 245
Morrison, Colin, 282
Morrison, Van, 267
Moss, Malcolm, 286–7
Mother Teresa, 283–4, 325

Mulcahy, Michael, 224
Mulhall, Ed, 198, 360
Mulholland, Joe, 174–5, 178, 180–1, 187, 188,
     190, 220
Mullan, Seamus, 125, 208, 210, 236
Mullen, Chris, 221
Mulligan, Brian, 358–9
Mullooly, Brian, 335
Munro, Harry, 20
Munroe, Dr George, 255
Murnaghan, Sheelagh, 119
Murphy, Dr Eamonn, 309
Murphy, Eugene, 309
Murphy, Liam, 339, 354
Murphy, Mick, 349
Murphy, Canon Pádraig, 67
Murray, Catherine, 20
Murray, Denis, 82
Murray, John, 339
Murray, Fr Raymond, 177, 222
Myers, David, 106

Nagle, Gerry, 338
Nally, Derek, 221–2, 341–7, 368
National Council for Civil Liberties, 167
National Institute for the Deaf, Belfast, 69
National Institute of Advocacy, USA, 251
National Union of Journalists, 204–6
Nationwide, 197
Naughton, Carmel, 259
Naughton, Martin, 259, 309
Needham, Richard, 284
Neighbourhood Police Service—Ardoyne, 290
Nethercott, Andrew, 302
Nethercott, Elizabeth, 302–3
Nethercott, Ray, 303
Nethercott, Raymond, 302
Newall, Revd Ken, 361
New Ireland Forum, 200–3, 204, 205, 210,
     223, 242
Newman, Bishop Jeremiah, 200, 201
Newry Customs Office, 72
News at One, 332, 346, 347
Newsnight, 177
New Ulster Political Research Group, 188,
     189
Nice Treaty, 232
Ní Chonaill, Eibhlín Dhubh, 82
NICRA *see* Northern Ireland Civil Rights
     Association
Nine O'Clock News, 170, 304, 354–5, 358
Noonan, Joe, 231

Norris, David, 147–8, 155, 222
North, Dr Peter, 272
Northern Ireland Civil Rights Association (NICRA), 61, 62, 63, 127
Northern Ireland Electricity (NIE), 281, 284–6
Northern Ireland Executive, 120–1, 127
Northern Ireland Housing Executive, 146
Northern Ireland Housing Rights Association, 287
Northern Ireland (Temporary Provisions) Act, 72
Nugent, Kieran, 179

O'Boyle, Nora, 118
Ó Briain, Muireann, 151
O'Brien, Conor Cruise, 143, 172, 179
O'Brien, Kate, 119
O'Brien, Martin, 268, 269, 272
O'Brien, Fr Niall, 210
Ó Broin, Deiric, 266
O'Callaghan, Miriam, 364
O'Connell, John, 219
O'Connor, Fionnuala, 297
O'Connor, Fr Peter, 307
Ó Cuív, Éamon, 315, 353, 356
Ó Dálaigh, Cearbhall, 319
O'Donnell, Liz, 339
O'Donnell, Turlough, 238
O'Donoghue, John, 316
O'Donoghue, Maurice, 339
O'Donohoe, Éamon, 323
Ó Dubháin, Tomás, 315
O'Farrell, Creena, 216
Ó Fiaich, Cardinal Tomás, 180, 181, 185, 210, 211, 269
Ó Flatharta, Dara Beag, 356
Ó Floinn, Liam, 10
O'Friel, May, 49, 215
Ó Giollagáin, Pádhraig, 168
O'Hanlon, Charlie, 79
O'Hanlon, Paddy, 62
O'Hanlon, Rory, 167, 315, 319, 323, 327, 328–9, 331, 334
O'Hara, "Eileen" (née McDrury), 22
O'Hara, Jim, 56
O'Hara, Patsy, 183
O'Hara, Seamus, 269
O'Hara, Willie, 22
O'Hare, Brian, 235
O'Hare, Danny, 262
O'Hare, James, 112

O'Hare, Paschal, 227
Ó hEithir, Breandán, 198
Ó hEocha, Colm, 200, 202
O'Higgins, Kevin, 151
Ó hUiginn, Seán, 342, 345
O'Kane, Ellie, 112
O'Kane, Hugh, 112
O'Kane, James, 253
O'Keeffe, Batt, 323
O'Keeffe, Denis, 97
O'Keeffe, Peter, 84–9, 93, 96–7, 128
O'Keeffe, Sylvi, 97
O'Kelly, Kevin, 172–3
O'Kennedy, Darby, 166
O'Kennedy, Michael, 313, 317, 322, 325, 326, 330, 331
O'Leary, Cornelius, 162, 163
O'Leary, Michael, 127
O'Leary, Olivia, 188
Omagh bombing, 260–1
O'Mahony, Bishop Dermot, 201
O'Mahony, Michael, 244
O'Malley, Brian, 223
O'Malley, Des, 223, 228, 311
O'Malley, Peter, 163
O'Malley, Una O'Higgins, 151
Ó Muilleoir, Máirtín, 252
Ó Muirí, Éamonn, 174
O'Neill, Donal, 324–5
O'Neill, John, 148
O'Neill, Kevin, 308
O'Neill, Mary, 308, 315
O'Neill, Pat, 218
O'Neill, Sean, 308
"Operation Motorman", 72
Orange Order 8, 36 123, 125
    marches, 15, 35
O'Reilly, Emily, 161, 342, 353–4
O'Reilly, John, 163
O'Reilly, Myles, 41–2, 134–5, 137, 138–40
O'Reilly, Tony, 41–2, 134, 137, 138–40
Ó Ríordáin, Seán, 158–9
O'Rourke, Aengus, 314
O'Rourke, Enda, 314
O'Rourke, Mary, 223, 310, 314–15, 328, 334
O'Rourke, P.J., 60
Orr, Daphne, 239
Orr, Sir David, 256
Orr, William, 20
Ó Searcaigh, Cathal, 31
Ó Siadhail, Micheál, 217
Ó Snodaigh, Aengus, 229

397

ALSO PUBLISHED BY

BRANDON

GERRY ADAMS
Hope and History: Making Peace in Ireland

"A fascinating account of his journey through the peace process, from the first tentative discussions with a priest called Father Reid, to his present position sharing the pages of *Hello!* with The Corrs, the international stage with Nelson Mandela."
Daily Mirror

ISBN 0 86322 330 3

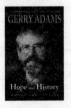

GERRY ADAMS
Before the Dawn: An Autobiography

"One thing about him is certain: Gerry Adams is a gifted writer who, if he were not at the center of the war-and-peace business, could easily make a living as an author, of fiction or fact." *New York Times*

ISBN 0 86322 289 7

ADRIAN HOAR
In Green and Red: The Lives of Frank Ryan

"Adrian Hoar's biography of Ryan is a well-written and cogent if exculpatory narrative of his life." *Village*

ISBN 0 86322 332 X

HENRY SINNERTON
David Ervine: Uncharted Waters

"Revealing . . . Ervine is an impressive advocate of modern unionism." *Irish Examiner*
"[A] valuable contribution to the understanding of the troubles." *Irish World*

ISBN 0 86322 301 X hb
ISBN 0 86322 312 5 pb